Theory in American Sociology

Major Sources and Applications

THEORY IN AMERICAN SOCIOLOGY

Major Sources and Applications

ALVIN BOSKOFF

EMORY UNIVERSITY

Thomas Y. Crowell Company

NEW YORK : Established 1834

To Priscilla

301
B743

Preface

Theory, methodology, and research collectively produce a mature discipline. Sociology can no longer favor any one of these, nor can it disregard the incessant interchanges among such specialized sociological enterprises. Consequently, it is gratifying to see not only recent sophisticated treatments of research design and analysis (methodology), and a staggering mass of completed sociological investigations, but also a growing interest (in books, articles, and courses) in organized attempts at identifying and resolving sociological problems—the realm of theory.

Because of the vast literature on sociological theorizing, a proper appreciation of theory (both its contributions and limitations) is clearly a difficult task. My provisional solution in this book is necessarily a compromise, but one that may be revised without major surgery. I have come to the conclusion that it is impossible to discuss sociological theories without dissecting the nature of theory itself and also giving some attention to variant forms and levels of theoretical statements in sociology. These are the aims of the introductory chapter, which, to my knowledge, have not yet been incorporated in any textbook on substantive sociological theory.

But the next decision concerns coverage. It seems necessary to introduce the student to representative "high points" in the classic period of theorizing, even though (*a*) some important countertrends or lost trails are thereby ignored and (*b*) the earlier proponents of distinctive concepts, problems, and viewpoints must receive little or no mention. Indeed, even the handful of theorists from the classic period (discussed in Chapters 1 and 2) are

v

treated—purposely but regretfully—with brevity. On the other hand, theories are constructed and refined by *men* who had careers, difficulties, intellectual developments, and some degree of consistency in their personal forays with sociological explanation. Therefore, I have tentatively selected eight theorists (in Chapters 3 through 9) who worked between World War I and the immediate present. My primary objective in each case was to organize the theorist's suppositions, problems, concepts, and theories in a sympathetic but critical fashion, with concern for his enduring contributions to the larger stream of sociological theory. Since these men wrote a great deal and generally avoided the hobgoblin of consistency, these interpretive summaries are themselves subject to further examination and perhaps revision. In most instances, I have dealt directly with primary sources (and translations), rather than summaries and interpretations by others. I realize with a little dismay that this book also consists of interpretive summaries and may be subject to the inherent limitations of secondary works. *Caveat emptor.*

While a detailed review of several important theorists is indispensable, it is uncomfortably evident that this alone does not promote an adequate appreciation of either the past or the potential of sociological theories. Students want and need to see the interplay between theoretical leads and innovative problem formulations on the one hand and specific, theoretically relevant investigations on the other hand. Part II was developed to explore the utility of the more general formulations of the masters and their successors in such substantive areas as the operation of simple and complex groups, social inequality and mobility, social deviation, the social sources of ideological and attitudinal differences, and the complex phenomena of social change.

Again, the heritage of sociological theory is too long and complex for any single work. This book was designed either for a semester course in sociological theory, or a one- or two-quarter arrangement. In the latter case, a one-quarter course may concentrate on Part I, with limited use of the discussions in Part II. However, a two-quarter sequence in sociological theory can profitably deal with both Parts in sufficient depth to provide a firm base in sociological theory. In either case, the availability of many primary writings in paperback editions provides an excellent opportunity to supplement assignments with direct access to the "stars" themselves.

In somewhat different form, the discussions in this book have been carried on with both undergraduate and graduate students. Their interest in theory has always been gratifying, and I have learned a great deal from their questions and their papers. My debt to contemporary sociologists—either as my mentors or as helpful critics—is beyond repayment. Specifically, I would like to acknowledge my long-time appreciation of Harry Alpert, Robert K. Merton, the late Howard W. Odum, Rupert B. Vance, the late Howard P. Becker, Talcott Parsons, and John T. Doby. Finally, I have been very fortunate in having the expert help and encouragement of Thomas Simpson and James Neyland of the Thomas Y. Crowell Company.

A. B.

Contents

CONTENTS

Introduction

Major Forms
of Theory and Focal
Sociological Problems

Theory is a much-abused term in popular speech, as well as among participants in intellectual discourse. It has been equated with vagueness and impracticality, with avoidance of reality, with dogmatism, and with philosophizing. But these indictments stem from a fundamental misunderstanding, which can be dispelled by considering a few crucial aspects of theorizing as a responsible enterprise of any discipline.

First, a remarkably prevalent use of theory among humans must be noted. When we attribute motives to friends, associates, public figures, etc., we are unwitting theorists. As we explain the intricacies of a football play or the complexities of a favorite recipe, we necessarily deal with theories. And as we seek to account for our difficulties, our mistakes, our achievements, our tastes or distastes, the threads of theory are gathered and interspersed through our thoughts and the expression of our thoughts in speech and writing.

In fact, much of what we call "culture" consists of prefabricated theories about the proper juxtaposition of resources (physical and human) in specified types of social situations. For example, proverbs, sayings, and adages offer witty or pithy connections between several components of social action: "honesty is the best policy—when others are honest too"; "birds of a feather flock together"; "a job well begun is a job half done"; "where ignorance is bliss, 'tis folly to be wise." Similarly, religious injunctions and doctrines, political philosophies, economic rules (the law of supply and demand, Gresham's Law), the verbalization of artistic styles (the sonata form, the sonnet form), and the omnipresent techniques of advertising rest on more or less implicit conclusions or theories. In other words, cultural norms and techniques usually constitute "solutions" to recurrent "problems" in social situations, based on the creative connection of selected means to crucial dimensions of experience.

Second, we must obviously define "theory" so that we may distinguish theoretical statement from other forms of verbal or symbolic expression. Perhaps we may begin by identifying the basic structure of any theory.

CONCEPTS

Every theoretical statement contains two or more independently defined variables, factors, dimensions, or types of events. In sociology and other social sciences, the facts or data are the phenomena of social behavior, which are either directly observed in process or recorded in such social products as official statistics, printed summaries of various kinds (books, magazines, diaries, letters, statutes, etc.), or in such objects as buildings, paintings, sculpture, furniture, clothing, machines, gadgets, toys, weapons. Since social phenomena are quite complex, as well as recurrent in varying degrees, concepts are necessary to distinguish different aspects of social behavior and also to provide a common "location" for closely similar instances. Thus, we may conceptualize behavior of persons that corresponds to the same rule as "conformity." Or we may describe (conceptualize) as "social control" the *means* by which persons influence the behavior of other persons to prevent them from straying from conformity. Concepts, therefore, are the chief ingredients of a theory, because they refer to experiences (or parts of experiences) in which we have some continuing interest.

ASSERTION OF A RELATIONSHIP

Idle or intermittent interest in phenomena may stop at conceptualization, classification, or definition (in the dictionary sense). But theory derives from a special and abiding interest in such phenomena. Essentially, this is expressed in the desire to account for some regularity or patterning in a set of phenomena. For example, why is age at the time of first marriage decreasing? Why do hourly wage workers vote Democratic in presidential elections? Why are the children of working mothers no more delinquent than those of non-working mothers? In short, a theory attempts to answer a generalized question that confronts us (or is raised by our zest for explanation) in a myriad of specific forms: how does knowledge of one (or more) phenomenon (phenomena)—called the independent variable(s)—enable us to account for the patterned aspects of phenomena—the dependent variables—that are the center of our interest?

In its simplest form, a theory is designed to deal with the situation that is summarized in the fourfold or contingency table. (See Table 1.) To generate the kind of interest that a theory satisfies, the facts or data must first be clustered in either pair of diagonal cells of this table. Obviously, each concentration of instances (1,4 or 2,3) presents a distinct pattern—and therefore a particular problem for solution. Assuming that a significant clustering is in fact found, a relevant theoretical statement may account for this pattern in one of several ways.

Causal relation

When the relationship is asserted to be causal, the independent variable is presumed to operate in such a manner that antecedent functioning of that variable is always (or almost always) followed

3

by a predictable state of the dependent variable. Conversely, instances in which the independent variable is absent are never (or almost never) followed by the appearance of the dependent variable.

INDEPENDENT VARIABLE

		High (present)	Low (absent)
DEPENDENT VARIABLE	High (present)	1	2
	Low (absent)	3	4

TABLE 1.   Patterned relationship for theory involving two variables or concepts.

Correlational relation

Unlike the causal assertion, correlational linkages between concepts ignore the question of time sequence and may also avoid the problem of the strength of the linkage (except in a superficial way). Thus, if we assert that people who are upwardly mobile tend to be politically conservative, the relationship between upward mobility and political conservatism is open to several explanations. Mobility may generate conservatism. But on the other hand, conservatism may be interpreted as a prerequisite for mobility. Another possibility is that both processes coexist. Furthermore, the relation between mobility and conservatism might be due solely to their respective relations to a third variable—e. g., nationality, early socialization, or community type. Finally, the correlation may be interpreted as an accidental or "chance" result, which has little probability of recurring in similar investigations or which defies the search for causal links or the mediation of other factors.

4

As Radcliffe-Brown pointed out thirty years ago, "The world is full of accidental correlations." [1]

Neutral functional relation

Theoretical statements may be called "neutral functional" if they assert that the "independent variable" in some way conditions, limits, or facilitates the operation of some other variable. For example, "federal financial policies of the forties and fifties contributed to the development and expansion of suburban areas." Note that this theory is not causal—except in a very attenuated sense—since it allows for other significant factors in suburban development. It is likewise not a correlational statement, since the asserted connection is clearly unidirectional (federal financing——>surburban development). Furthermore, this statement permits no inference about the relative desirability of the relationship. Hence the "neutral" term in our designation.

In practice, functional relations may be found in two forms. First, as the theory just mentioned illustrates, a functional statement may refer to two (or a limited number of) variables or concepts drawn from some conceptually "closed" social system (group, complex organization, community, society). But another type of functional statement connects a variable or set of variables with a relevant system as a "dependent variable." Thus, "a minimal amount of social mobility is practically necessary for the continuity of society." Or, "the romantic love complex serves as a device for sustaining the marital-kinship system in industrial societies."

This second type of functional assertion is clearly a preliminary, "trial balloon" sort of theory. Essentially, it focuses on a direction of connection without having an explicit concern for two kinds of significant problems. First, how can a theorist responsibly connect a component variable to an entire social system? What is the "handle" (core variable or component) to which the explanatory variable can be attached? In short, theoretical statements must seek to deal with factors on the same level of conceptual complexity (com-

[1] A. R. Radcliffe-Brown, *A Natural Science of Society* (New York: Free Press, 1957), p. 79.

ponent with component, system with system). Second, this kind of theoretical statement necessarily diverts attention from the mechanisms (or intermediate processes) by which the independent variable produces some pattern of effects. In practice, this would require additional theories of a causal or correlational type to bridge the logical and empirical gaps that seem to be inherent in functional statements.[2]

Normative relations

In contrast to all preceding types of conceptual relations, theoretical statements that employ normative–teleological relations are *extra-scientific* in intent. Instead of seeking relations between sets of data (already gathered or to be sought in terms of an objective design), this type of theory asserts a relationship of desirability or undesirability between variables. In the *retrospective normative* type, a vaguely stated relation between phenomena is accompanied by a value judgment about the relationship. An illustration of this is Hegel's theory of the progressive realization of reason, as ultimately recorded in the rise of the German state.[3] This may be interpreted as (*a*) asserting a relation between reason and forms of social organization (presumably a teleological relationship), and (*b*) evaluating the later phases of this relationship as more desirable (a normative theory). Similarly, normative theories may be *future-oriented*—that is, concerned with selecting a desirable combination of phenomena. Thus, Marx pointed to an eventual "classless" society, which would be superior to all preceding forms in its eradication of conflict, exploitation, and misery.[4]

Significantly, normative theories usually contain an objective component (causal or correlational), which is often implicit or suggested. Consequently, precipitate rejection of such theories may be premature. For instance, Gibbon's theory of the debilitating

[2] Harry C. Bredemeier, "The Methodology of Functionalism," *American Sociological Review*, XX (April, 1955), pp. 173–180; Carl G. Hempel, "The Logic of Functional Analysis," in Llewellyn Gross, ed., *Symposium on Sociological Theory* (New York: Harper & Row, 1959), pp. 271–307.

[3] G. W. F. Hegel, *The Philosophy of History*, many editions.

[4] Karl Marx and Friedrich Engels, *The Communist Manifesto*, many editions.

effect of Christianity on the Roman Empire was clearly an attempt to forge a connection between a personally favored set of phenomena (the Roman Empire) and the institutional villain in the piece (Christianity).[5] On the other hand, beneath his emotional bias, we may discover a potentially useful focus on the impact of new religious systems on the operation of formal political structures. Then we might reformulate Gibbon's problem in such a way as to determine and explain the conditions under which specific kinds of religious movements either compete with, supplement, or contribute in no definable way to different forms of political centralization.

APPLICABILITY

Universally valid theoretical statements, unless they are merely tentative formulations, tend to be looked upon as suspect by thoughtful people—both scientists and laymen. A theory that explains everything, on close analysis, turns out to explain nothing (e. g., "love makes the world go round"; "the history of all hitherto existing society is the history of class struggles"; etc.). Virtually no serious theoretical statement can encompass (*a*) all the significant empirical variations in a given field of interest and (*b*) alterations or changes in the presence, direction, and degree of relationships among relevant variables. Consequently, an important component of theory is a qualifying phrase that indicates some practical restriction on the scope of the asserted relationship. The simplest form is often found in the phrases "other things being equal" and "holding certain factors constant." More often in the social sciences, theoretical statements specify (or should specify) the time periods, types of societies, or the levels of social organization for which the theory is crucial.

Thus, for example, Albert Cohen's theory of delinquency was specifically designed to apply to lower-class boys in contemporary Western urban communities.[6] Or Burgess' concentric theory of

[5] Edward Gibbon, *Decline and Fall of the Roman Empire* (2 vols.; New York: Modern Library, n.d.), I, chs. 21, 28, 32; II, chs. 37, 47, 71.
[6] Albert K. Cohen, *Delinquent Boys* (New York: Free Press, 1955), ch. 5.

7

urban growth was clearly limited to economically advanced cities in modern capitalistic societies, without reference to the deviations that might be attributed to unique geographical and topographical features.[7]

In summary then, a theory is a statement that is formulated to provide a testable answer to one kind of problem in interpreting experience: what explains the non-accidental—or random—recurrence of patterns or regularities in human experience? To answer that basic question, every genuine theory (whether true or false) creatively translates experiences into asserted relationships between (or among) facets of those experiences (variables and concepts), with due regard for the possibility that other settings may present either different or more complex patterns.

LEVELS OF THEORIZING

Given the major features of components of a theory, we must recognize the existence of several levels of theorizing. Theorists may legitimately have different foci of interest in developing statements of relationship between and among variables. Three distinct levels of theory can be identified.

Empirical generalizations

This is the most specific variety of theoretical statement and yet, by itself, is the least satisfying to the theorist. An empirical generalization summarizes the relation between data on two (or a limited number of) variables at specific times and locations. For example, we might conclude that "middle-class families spend proportionately less of their incomes on food than do lower-class families in the United States during 1969." Obviously, this is a correlational statement. In sociology, many empirical generalizations seem to be correlational in nature, though there does not seem to be any logi-

---

[7] Ernest W. Burgess, "The Growth of the City," in Robert E. Park, Ernest W. Burgess, and R. D. McKenzie, eds., *The City* (Chicago: University of Chicago Press, 1925), pp. 47–62.

cal barrier to causal or functional statements at this level of specificity. But empirical generalizations are tantalizing in their combination of precision and uncertainty. If two variables are associated in some definite manner in one set of experiences, does the same association persist or change over time? Does the association remain when another dependent variable of similar type is substituted? And, in the generalization just mentioned, are class differences also found in voting, childrearing, being influenced by mass media, etc.?

Problem-area or nuclear generalizations

Theoretical statements on this level may be logically impeccable summaries of sets of empirical generalizations, or a problem-area theory may provide the logical basis for deriving an adequate number and range of empirical uniformities. Some years ago, this theoretical level was described by Merton (borrowing from T. H. Marshall) as "theories of the middle range." [8] However, this seems to be rather a negative label for an important type of theory. Essentially, such a theory deals with the most significant core relationships in a distinctive area of interest as generally recognized by practitioners of a discipline or of closely related disciplines. Thus, for example, it would be possible to have a limited number of theoretical statements on the sources and effects of stratification. To be more positive, it might be more appropriate to call this level "problem-area" or "nuclear" theories.

In the last forty years, sociologists have devoted major attention to nuclear theories, and to the relation between empirical generalizations and nuclear formulations. The advantages of this focus should be quite evident. First, it demands an accompanying recognition of central problems rather than an anarchic scattering of efforts wherever data come to hand. Second, it enables us to assess properly the trivial and the transitory aspects of empirical gen-

---

[8] Robert K. Merton, *Social Theory and Social Structure* (New York: Free Press, revised edition, 1957), p. 9; Robert K. Merton, "Discussion of Parsons' 'Position of Sociological Theory,'" *American Sociological Review*, XIII (April, 1948).

eralizations and the vague—rather than the general—aspects of all-encompassing theories or explanations. Third, it compels us to search for parsimonious explanations, the underlying regularities in numerous patterns, thus providing an evolving record of achievement, rather than to depend on the dubious rewards of circumscribed, though competent, labor. Finally, the construction of nuclear theories offers legitimated guidelines for subsequent investigations and empirical generalizations. Plainly, the deficiencies of a discipline become most evident when problem-centered theories are attempted. More specifically, the problem-centered theorist often discovers that the mechanisms by which empirical patterns are "produced" are either implicit or absent in a relevant set of empirical generalizations, so that his theoretical difficulties, if properly communicated or translated, become explicit clues to new investigations and possible reanalyses of existing studies.

General theories

The ultimate ideal of any discipline is a small number of principles or laws that succinctly summarize the most fundamental relationships for the range of phenomena identified with that discipline or field of knowledge. These general theories presuppose a massive and reticulated empirical base and an adequate number of nuclear theories to structure relevant empirical resources. The task of constructing meaningful general theories, then, is so great that the theorist must be extremely knowledgeable or incorrigibly courageous.

In practice, general theories in sociology have often *preceded* their factual bases and the more limited generalizations that undergird durable general theory. However, if general theories are sufficiently clear (that is, translatable into closely related, specific problems), they may be useful as stimulants to potentially valuable empirical generalizations and nuclear theories.

General theories may be classified in a few basic forms.

1. *Trend theories.* These theories assert a simplified direction in the development or change in social phenomena. Spencer's theory of

movement from homogeneity to heterogeneity is a classic instance. But Toennies' analysis of Western civilization as the replacement of *Gemeinschaft* by *Gesellschaft* is a perennially revived specification of Spencer's thesis. Durkheim, Simmel, Giddings, Odum, Redfield, Park, Sorokin, MacIver, and Becker have likewise worked with minor variations on this theme.

2. *Major cause theories*. Formerly known as *monistic determinisms*, these theories conclude that varied social phenomena stem from a seminal social condition. For Marx, this was "class position"; for Pareto, the distribution of residues; for Gumplowicz and others, the phenomena of conflict; for Freud (insofar as his work has sociological relevance), parent-child relations in their sexual ambiguities.

3. *Process–series theories*. The intent of this type of general theory is to order social phenomena by focusing on a limited number of key processes in a definite and recurring time sequence. As an early example, we have Tarde's theory of invention——→opposition——→imitation——→adaptation.[9] Another "process theory" is built around the basic sequence: contact, conflict, accommodation, assimilation.[10] More recently, Parsons and Bales have postulated a set of "phase movements" in social organization (see Chapter 9).[11]

It should be obvious that students of society cannot choose from these three levels, as they must in voting or in purchasing goods and services. All three levels of theory are necessary to cope with (*a*) the range of available data (as well as future accumulations of information and relevant social experience) and (*b*) the inevitable unevenness of explanatory achievements in the various problems to which sociologists are dedicated. Indeed, much of the criticism of theoretical attempts probably derives from the failure—either on the part of the critic or the theorist—to clarify the connections be-

[9] Gabriel Tarde, *The Laws of Imitation*, trans. Elsie C. Parsons (New York: Holt, 1903), pp. 141–166.

[10] Ludwig Gumplowicz, *Outlines of Sociology*, trans. F. W. Moore (Philadelphia: American Academy of Political and Social Science, 1889). This has been recently retranslated by Irving L. Horowitz (New York: Paine-Whitman, 1963); Albion W. Small, *General Sociology* (Chicago: University of Chicago Press, 1905); Robert E. Park, *Race and Culture* (New York: Free Press, 1950), chs. 14, 16.

[11] Talcott Parsons, Robert F. Bales, and Edward A. Shils, *Working Papers in the Theory of Action* (New York: Free Press, 1953), ch. 5.

tween some chosen level of theory and either or both of the remaining levels. When a theory is called "vague," for example, the probability is very great that it is a general theory and its relation to nuclear theories and empirical generalizations is ignored.

On the other hand, a common difficulty with theoretical statements—as expressed in criticisms of their apparent "irrelevance to reality" or "abstruseness"—is the failure to identify the focal problem or problems for which the theory provides an answer. This is often applicable to those empirical generalizations that emerge from studies that are not rigorously derived from an explicit conceptual scheme and from a central problem or question extracted from that scheme. For a staggering set of examples, one should consult Berelson and Steiner's *Human Behavior: An Inventory of Scientific Findings* (particularly Chapters 7–15). In this work, the authors tried to collect and order empirical generalizations around "major aspects of human behavior" or concepts rather than around problems. The resultant "inventory," despite the immense labor involved, is less than satisfactory, simply because this massive filing system cannot be used for any purpose but handy reference.

But general theories also assume, explicitly or implicitly, that more specific, nuclear problems can be taken for granted, that instead a single basic problem (normally undefined) is sufficient to constitute a rationale for general theory. Given this orientation, it is quite understandable that general theories are received with a certainty of uncertainty, with the disquieting inability to discover either (*a*) the single basic problem or (*b*) the several nuclear problems that provide the materials for an underlying and therefore more widely useful problem. All this, of course, presupposes some evolving agreement on a limited number of core problems in sociology.

From the varied writings and researches of the past seventy-five years, several recurring interests among sociologists can be identified. Since these interests are necessarily interrelated, and since the pursuit of any one of them may lead to a practical concern for one or more portions of a sociological network, any classification of sociological problems must be somewhat arbitrary and unequal to the normal quest for mutually exclusive items. Nevertheless, perhaps six nuclear problems provide continuing spurs to the sociologist in the unending search for explanations of social behavior in conceptually manageable social systems.

NUCLEAR PROBLEM AREAS

Formation of social groups

The ultimate origins of human association no longer tempt the sociological theorist. Instead, he is impressed with the continual creation of new groups or associations within the framework of a larger system (nation, community, or complex organization). Consequently, the basic problems in this area concern the conditions that (*a*) impede satisfactory association in existing contexts; (*b*) generate common appreciation of a value, norm, or technique; (*c*) recruit a properly qualified membership; and (*d*) create and sustain an identity that is distinct from other associations of their members.

Internal differentiation

Social groups function through the evolution and management of meaningfully different skills, responsibilities, rewards, and opportunities among their members. What factors account for the relative degree of differentiation and for the standards by which substantive differences are chosen? How are patterned differences sustained over considerable periods of time? What aspects of the operation of groups can be attributed to given forms or types of internal differentiation? In short, the theorist is deeply committed to explaining the impact of division of social labor (in its varied forms and detailed applications) on the participation of persons and on the career of groups as products and as stimulants to differentiated social participation. Familiar concepts in this area are role, status, position, rank, stratum, class, function, subgroup, and subculture.

Socialization

Differentiation and changes in differentiation present *potentialities* for social participation. Roles, statuses, etc., must be learned, unlearned, connected, and isolated from one another in the experience of many persons. Socialization as a theoretical problem, then, concerns the focal social conditions (and related psychological mechanisms) that help to explain acquiring awareness of differentiation; learning the approved motives, values, and behavior patterns of a role; experimenting with the "fit" between role requirements and other features of the person (inherent or acquired); learning appropriate expectations from those in similar and/or complementary roles; managing simultaneous roles; substituting roles or statuses in a socially approved sequence; and also failing in any of these aspects of socialization. In recent decades, these problems have been studied by means of such concepts as social self, peer groups, reference groups, relative deprivation, identification, and internalization.

Coordination and control

Social systems require some degree of specialization in skills and responsibilities. But this solution creates practical and theoretical problems that are at the core of sociology and other social sciences. Essentially, these problems concern the interrelation of specialized components through processes of coordination, timing, management of crucial conflicts, and interpretation of guiding values. Major theoretical problems in this area therefore include the factors in recruitment to coordinating positions; sources of conflict and strain; variations in the distribution of power and decision-making; and social processes in conversion of power into authority.

Deviation and innovation

Since role specifications are rarely perfectly clear and since controls on social behavior cannot be exercised universally or uniformly, the number of variations in behavior is quite large. However, sociologists are primarily interested in *socially evaluated variations*—that is, those variations that affect the operation of other persons in the same role or those in related roles. Deviation, or significant variation in behavior, is the focal process in the practical initiation of change in groups, communities, or societies. *Innovation* may be defined as desirable or potentially desirable deviation, whereas threatening forms of deviation have been conceptualized as crime and vice, maladjustment, alienation, rebellion, etc.

If it is assumed that the potential for deviation is quite high, then there are two fundamental problems concerning deviation that face the theorist. First, what aspects of given social organizations (power structure, degree of specialization, etc.) serve to *encourage* deviation in selected categories of participants? Second and equally important, what factors help to account for (*a*) incorporation of deviation into a legitimate role or (*b*) the development of deviant roles either within—or at the borders of—a specific social system (such as a school, family, corporation, or congregation)?

Social change

Deviation in any form is a *necessary* but not a *sufficient* condition in the phenomena of social change. As a distinctive area of interest, social change may be defined as the set of processes by which new components and/or revised relations among components of a social system are developed. This definition contains the premise that social change is most critically identified in the extent to which initial deviations (whatever their origin) produce adaptive revisions (derivative consequences) in other facets of behavior and social organization. Therefore, theories of social change must furnish answers to such questions as these: What social factors condition the transmission of material, ideological, and organizational innovations? What are the mechanisms by which pre-existing status systems and power structures receive re-evaluation and revised methods of recruitment and operation? How are varied sources of resistance to derivative consequences diverted, modified, or dissipated? Finally, what are the major factors in legitimizing or institutionalizing the complex of specific changes that form the texture of a given sequence of social change? Parenthetically, each of these theoretical questions is two-edged, since both "success" and "failure" of potential changes must stir the explanatory skills of the sociologist.

SOME GENERAL TENDENCIES IN THEORY

It would be very satisfying if we could review the past hundred years or so of sociological theorizing and conclude that one or two clear lines of development can be identified. Of course, theorists in any definable period used all three levels of theoretical formulation and, with many conceptual labels, have touched upon the major problem areas just noted. However, two general tendencies seem worthy of consideration as summaries of a rich and variegated heritage.

Sociological theorizing has largely shifted from ideological or normative forms (implicitly justifying some structure or criticizing patterns of social phenomena from the standpoint of some political or religious value system) to more objective theoretical statements. While no sociological theorist has ever been "value-free," there is an enormous difference between the works of such men as Sumner, Spencer, Ross, and Ward and those of Simmel and Durkheim.

To discuss the great number of theorists—from the classical Greeks to the present—would require a detailed and awesome treatment of the history of sociology, which is not at all the purpose of this book. Instead, we may refer to an earlier attempt at summarizing the "stages" in this general shift. First, we may identify an emphasis on *social philosophy*, which involved statements about desired kinds of society, proper forms of social interaction, and prescriptions for changes of government, economy, religion, and family. Some examples are the social philosophies of Plato, Rousseau, Hegel, Mill, Spengler, St. Simon, and Sorel. For the Western world, the heyday of social philosophy was the seventeenth through the mid-nineteenth century. Second, in reaction to social philosophy, was the development of *social theory* as an attempt to achieve objective, "scientific," or "positive" explanations of human phenomena. This developed in three forms.

1. *Reductionist social theory* tried to account for social phenomena by "reducing" these to non-social conditions or factors (e.g., biological forms, chemical processes, mechanical principles, geographic and climatic conditions). Sorokin's classic work, *Contemporary Sociological Theories*, contains excellent summaries and critiques of such theories.

2. *Imperialistic social theory* derived from the same objective as the reductionist form, but instead tried to explain social phenomena as consequents of *social* variables or processes. However, theorists of this type also assumed that one social process or form could explain a wide range of phenomena (normally the province of such other disciplines as economics, political science, history, or psychology). For example, such theorists as Tarde, Spencer, Gumplowicz, Giddings, and Marx tended to focus on the explanatory role of imitation, differentiation, conflict, consciousness of kind, or class position. In retrospect, the objectivity of these theories seems well below the claims of their proponents, who seemed to simplify their explanations in line with their personal preferences on public questions of the time.

3. *"Modern" sociological theory* continues the old scientific intent on the pursuit (not the choice) of sociological problems, but with some added elements of great importance. First chronologically, is the identification of a set of core theoretical problems—which is really a collective product of the work of such men as Simmel, Durkheim, Weber, Cooley, and Mead. Second, though the terms were not in use forty years ago, modern theorists began to combine the three levels of theorizing discussed above. By 1920 or so, sociological theorists were sketching broad frameworks, focusing on limited historical and/or current social patterns (e.g., suicide, labor–management conflicts, migration, family problems, and political behavior), and even gathering and analyzing empirical data as best they could with available tools. Finally, and most recently, modern sociological theorists are becoming more comfortable with "open" systems of theory—i.e., sets of explanations that are applicable to limited populations or time periods, and that are subject to alteration as situations change. While the ultimate aim is usually one of formulating explanations with the greatest generality (or applicability), it is recog-

nized that premature "systems" of theories (rather than concepts) may be fundamentally "unscientific." In short, modern theorists regard explanation as probabilistic and "correctable" through both empirical investigations and the interconnection of theoretical clues from other problem-areas.

As just suggested, the primary working level of theorists has also shifted, though somewhat unevenly, from general theories (1840–1920) to empirical generalizations (1920–1945), briefly back to general theory (1945–1955), and currently to nuclear theories. There is some difference of opinion now about the relative value of nuclear and general theories, but the former seem somewhat more acceptable. Years ago, "theory" was equated with general theory, but this narrow conception is probably not now common among theorists, methodologists, and specialized researchers.

SELECTION OF THEORISTS FOR ANALYSIS

Though the earlier phases of theorizing are highly interesting and instructive, this volume consciously emphasizes the "modern" phase, from about 1840 to the present, with greatest concern for the past forty years. Since modern theorists borrow from and re-work the contributions of their predecessors, the earlier periods are certainly not ignored. But I have not tried to trace the theoretical ancestry of each concept or each theorist, nor have I tried to spell out the immediate historical setting in which important theories were constructed.

Generally, two methods of selecting men as representative of developments in sociological theory can be used. First, one can approach this complex process *prospectively*—by locating past "crises" in explanation and then identifying the theories that gained acceptance as solutions to these crises. Or one can use a *retrospective* orientation, seeking out men whose work contributes most (or contains distinct possibilities of doing so) to our currently evolving appreciation of sociological theories. (See Figure 1.) The first method would necessarily focus on many temporary successes, which might have little relevance for contemporary theories. How-

18

ever, with the advantage of hindsight, the second method enables us to concentrate on those who have survived the vicissitudes of intellectual fashion and historically limited controversy. Therefore, the latter method has been chosen for selecting theorists to be represented in this book. Regretfully, such theorists as Tarde, Spencer, Sumner, Ross, Ward, Pareto, Ogburn, and Alfred Weber as well as other candidates had to be omitted.

More positively, the theorists were chosen to represent complementary contributions to general and nuclear theorizing in sociology—an evolving fund of sociological explanations to which

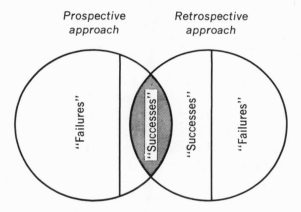

FIGURE 1.   Expected relation between two
means of selecting theorists for analysis.

contemporary sociologists continually return. Comte and Marx are first presented as seminal general theorists who form a bridge between the "imperialistic" theorizers and the "modern" thinkers. But Marx also is an early source of nuclear theories in stratification, coordination, and social change. Toennies is important as among the first to connect a general theory of social structure and change with a nuclear emphasis on different forms of socialization. Cooley represents and crystallizes the sociological approach to human behavior as socially learned in determinate settings. His analysis of personality provides a theoretical link between Toennies and the work of G. H. Mead and his followers of recent decades.

While each of these might have been "replaced" in this treatment by various men (e.g., St. Simon, Ross, Veblen, Tarde, deRoberty), this is scarcely possible in the cases of Durkheim, Simmel, and Weber. Durkheim combines all levels of theorizing; but more important, he provides the first major emphasis on several nuclear problems (coordination, socialization, innovation–deviation, and change). Simmel's work parallels that of Durkheim in many respects, but his orientation is somewhat less deterministic. However, Simmel is indispensable for his examination of the dynamics of group formation and the relations between conflict and coordination. Weber contributed to every nuclear problem in sociology, with the exception of the problem of socialization, by using historical materials as data for numerous limited generalizations.

In a sense, these seven theorists represent the initial capital of modern sociological theorizing. The "investment" of these assets may perhaps be adequately summarized by the eight theorists of Chapters 3–9. Thomas and Znaniecki represent attempts to "simplify" nuclear problems by analyzing the sources and consequences of subjective perceptions in social situations. Znaniecki in particular tried to develop role theories that would explain not socialization (relative conformity), but variation and innovation in social systems. Mead, their contemporary at the University of Chicago, supplemented emerging role theories by specifying the *process* of early socialization in enduring—though correctable—form. But while socialization theories were being embellished, complex structures were also receiving much attention in the twenties and thirties. Park symbolizes the attempt to explain differentiation (status, occupation, race) in urban settings as reflected in spatial patternings. MacIver and Sorokin are perhaps most important in time because they designed their concepts to focus on explanations of social change in highly complex societies—moving from nuclear to general theories.

Despite these achievements, the major substantive difficulty of sociological theories between the two world wars had been an inability to deal with the *mechanics* of continuity and change in nuclear social phenomena—or particularly, the processes for detailing asserted relationships. Though it remains a serious problem today,

Mannheim and Parsons are included primarily because they tried to devise potential answers—Mannheim, through theories of elites and influence processes, and Parsons, by means of theories concerning the functional bases and consequences of structured power. Both Parsons and Mannheim, incidentally, drew heavily on many of the preceding theorists (particularly Durkheim, Simmel, and Weber), and this suggests some genuine continuity in sociology despite heated controversies in the formative years and the competitive orientations of political–ideological, "applied," and empiricist sociologists during the forties and fifties.

SELECTED REFERENCES

Boskoff, Alvin, "From Social Thought to Sociological Theory," in Howard Becker and Alvin Boskoff, eds., *Modern Sociological Theory* (New York: Holt, Rinehart & Winston, 1957), pp. 3–32.

Durkheim, Emile, *The Rules of Sociological Method* (Chicago: University of Chicago Press, 1938).

Gross, Llewellyn, ed., *Sociological Theory: Inquiries and Paradigms* (New York: Harper & Row, 1967), pp. 220–253.

———, *Symposium on Sociological Theory* (New York: Harper & Row, 1959), chs. 4, 8, 9, 18, 19.

Kaplan, Abraham, *The Conduct of Inquiry* (San Francisco: Chandler, 1964), chs. 34–37, 42.

Mills, C. Wright, *The Sociological Imagination* (New York: Oxford University Press, 1959), chs. 2–4, Appendix on Intellectual Craftsmanship.

Parsons, Talcott, *The Structure of Social Action* (New York: McGraw-Hill, 1937; Free Press, 1949), pp. 33–39.

PART I

*Seminal Sources
of Sociological Theory*

1

The Old Masters

I

There is a strong tendency in modern American sociology that so exalts the value of modernity that any prolonged reference to the trail-blazers is received with impatience and the suspicion of intellectual vagrancy. Many younger sociologists remember with displeasure their forced exposure to courses in the over-crowded history of social thought. If sociology advances by empirical research, it is often argued, then it is useless to dally in the twisting alleys of the past when the broad highways of investigation beckon so insistently.

But this impatience is an impediment that American sociologists often circumvent—temporarily and sometimes unwittingly—in the search for fruitful insights into specific problems. Part I is devoted to a review of sociological currents that are contemporary in that they are implicitly or explicitly used today, regardless of whether their origins are in the past generation or over one hundred years ago.

Auguste Comte (1798–1857)

Let us first turn to the "old masters." As an arbitrary but workable beginning, there is Auguste Comte, whom many acknowledge as the traditional "father of sociology," but few have given this tradition much consideration. Yet Comte is surprisingly "modern." If we disregard his moralizing and the question of the relative originality of his formulations, the residue is remarkable for its identity at several points with the major orientation of American sociology. Though he failed to practice his principles, Comte provided the first cogent exposition of the necessity and the strategy of studying social phenomena scientifically. Indeed, it would be difficult to summarize the scientific approach more satisfactorily than did Comte in his triad of observation, experimentation, and comparison.[1]

But it is in a special attitude toward social data that Comte continually commends himself to contemporary sociology. Viewing society as a functional system based on the division of labor, Comte developed an orientation not far removed from the much-discussed and implicitly accepted "structural–functional" approach. Religion and marriage receive particular functional emphasis as institutional sectors in the societal system, but the main burden of Comte's system is the explication of the political institution as a compensatory organ. This analysis derives from the identification of two "ideal typical" social structures—the *domestic association* and the *political society*—which foreshadow similar concepts of Toennies, Durkheim, Cooley, and others. The latter type of society, Comte observes in a general theory, tends to develop an exaggerated division of labor with a consequent neglect of the interrelations of specialized skills. The state functions ideally, then, as a

[1] Auguste Comte, *The Positive Philosophy*, trans. and abr. Harriet Martineau (2 vols.; London: George Bell, 1896), II, pp. 241–257.

coordinator of human groups and activities, as a defense against the *anomie* that Durkheim later traced to the same sociological source.[2]

This functional analysis is part of *social statics* ("the general theory of the order of human societies"), which Comte analytically separated from *social dynamics*. Since he viewed dynamics or change as "progress," one may accept his logic, but not his premises.[3] For Comte's functional analysis—as all good functional analysis—implicitly concerned itself with dynamics of a non-teleogical nature. When he strayed from this functional approach, as in the "law of the three stages" of progress, his analyses of dynamics became interesting but forced, mechanical rather than dynamic, and metaphysical rather than scientific.

Comte's conception of social class is rarely cited, yet it reappears with variations in the work of Marx, Durkheim, Weber, Veblen, and others. Essentially, class is said to develop from the differentiation of functions in the economic sphere and from the control patterns that regulate the differential contributions of groups in society (a nuclear theory). Thus the phenomena of class become understandable for Comte as natural, functional groupings that are required to insure social control in complex societies. With the advent of industrialization, the source of control comes to reside in industry, in industrial needs and disciplines, and the problems of control reflect themselves in altered social alignments headed by industrial leaders.[4] Because of his concern for "progress," Comte never extended this analysis; yet it appears to be the conceptual starting-point for industrial sociology.

[2] *Ibid.*, pp. 272–295. A good summary is Harry E. Barnes, "The Social and Political Philosophy of Auguste Comte," in Harry E. Barnes, ed., *An Introduction to the History of Sociology* (Chicago: University of Chicago Press, 1948), pp. 81–109.

[3] Comte, *The Positive Philosophy*, I, pp. 218–219, 228; McQuilkin DeGrange, "The Method of Auguste Comte," in Stuart A. Rice, ed., *Methods in Social Science* (Chicago: University of Chicago Press, 1931), pp. 33–36.

[4] Comte, *System of Positive Polity* trans. Frederic Harrison (5 vols.; London: Longmans, Green & Co., Ltd., 1875), II, pp. 242–249.

Karl Marx (1818–1883)

Karl Marx has been the "bad penny" in the last century of social thought. Though he has been shown to be palpably wrong and biased on many points, his formulations continually reappear as the specter that cannot be dispelled. Particularly among German sociologists, whose influence on American sociology has been enormous, Marx is the *fons et origo* of sociological problems, and his solutions continue to be a negative guide to current thought. Spencer, his contemporary, has largely been forgotten after a period of astounding popularity. But Marx in his polemics, his satirical criticisms, his search for a scientific utopia, set the question that still animates modern sociology: what are the nature and dynamics of modern Western social systems?

As a would-be sociologist, Marx dealt with this issue most succinctly and with the most clarity in his *The German Ideology* (1846) and his *Critique of Political Economy* (1859). Society, he observed, is an organic ensemble of social relations among men, with "social" meaning "cooperative bonds between persons." Every level of cooperation (social stage) is related to a corresponding mode of production whose combination creates productive forces (a general theory). It is often forgotten that Marx included social relations under the concept "productive force," thereby giving brief recognition to the non-material factors in the economic structure. (Marx himself sometimes forgot this distinction.) These productive forces, which are taken to be basic in the social structure, are organized by a social division of labor expressed in the pattern of ownership of the instruments of production.[5] Marx never defined "class" consistently, but it appears to refer to the grouping of individuals with similar positions in the division of labor; therefore, it becomes the key unit of social structure in complex societies. Normally, there is a balance between productive

[5] Karl Marx, *A Contribution to the Critique of Political Economy* (Chicago: Charles H. Kerr, 1904), pp. 11–12.

techniques and the pattern of ownership; and consequently, the class structure is stable.

However, changes in productive techniques, which were left unexplained by Marx, come into conflict with the existing structure of social relations and the underlying property relations. Just how this "conflict" arises is a typical Marxian mystery, which Marx himself could explain only by impairing the utility of the formulation. Out of respect for facts, Marx was forced to admit a crucial distinction between *objective* changes in production and the *subjective* reactions of persons in the form of ideologies, thereby opening a field of investigation that historical materialism could not enter without ridiculous consequences. But the subjective factor and its psychosocial determinants have since remained distinctive problems in sociology.

Marx had to connect objective conditions and subjective reactions, yet his analysis remains the focus of continued controversy.[6] The solution (a general theory) that Marx contrived is, however, not as clearly stated as some believe. Marx insisted that property relations are the *basis* of legal and political organization and "social consciousness" and that material surroundings are *related* to philosophy, modes of criticism, etc. Yet Marx alters these essentially neutral statements by declaring that social existence *determines* the consciousness of men, diluting his subject (from property relations to social existence) precisely when he was invigorating the verb. The result is a very tenuous connection from which Marx noted bothersome empirical exceptions. If subjective reactions to objective changes in production derive from ideologies, and if the ideologies in turn are not reliably traceable to objective social distinctions, of what value is Marx's explanation of change and class conflict? Here Marx notes the phenomena of what he calls "false consciousness," a challenging concept in the fledgling sociology of knowledge (see Chapter 13). But what factors account for attachment to "objectively inappropriate" ideas? While Marx left this unanswered, we may note its recent investigation in the fields of public opinion and "reference-group" theory (see Chapter 13).

It is fashionable to view Marx and his uncritical interpreters with

[6] Karl Marx and Friedrich Engels, *The German Ideology* (New York: International Publishers, 1939), pp. 20–30.

professional disdain, though such great thinkers as Toennies, Durkheim, Simmel, and Weber could not develop their special contributions to sociology until they had critically analyzed and "tested" his theories against historical facts. In particular, Marx contributed the first important analysis of the economic institution as it is related to the total social structure of modern societies. As a result, he brought into the forefront of sociology four interrelated aspects of society that are now quite legitimate problems of research. Following Comte, Marx analyzed the *social division of labor* in terms of changing economic roles and their relation to non-economic role-clusters. This led to the unusual emphasis on *stratification* as a reflection of focal social institutions. Though Marx placed undue emphasis on the economic sector, his insights into class structure are beginning to bear fruit in the modern functional approach to class (a nuclear theory). In the same way, Marx came to touch on the problem of *social control* through the strains (conflicts) generated by economic changes and their effects on class relations. Finally, these processes of differentiation were seen to be related to a variety of *ideational systems* characteristic of subgroups in society, paving the way for a sociology of knowledge and a sociology of occupations.

Ferdinand Toennies (1855–1936)

In a sense, the work of Ferdinand Toennies constitutes a turning-point in the heritage of the "old masters." Neither Comte nor Marx had given sociology more than token independence as a distinctive social science. While Comte tended to be quite vague in depicting the structure of society and rather sweeping in his conclusions, Marx tried to reduce society to an analysis of economic structure. By recognizing the importance of *social relationships* and *social groups*, Toennies provided the first system of sociological concepts applicable to society as a whole or to any of its constituent parts.

All empirical social data, whether derived from history or contemporary events, could be classified and interpreted with the aid of the now famous ideal types of social relationship—*Gemeinschaft*, or primary groupal, and *Gesellschaft*, or associational. *Gemeinschaft* relations are based on sentimental attitudes (*Wesenwille*) among persons; these attitudes spring from consanguinity or prolonged social contact. Such relations characteristically involve valuation of the relations themselves, rather than specific interests pursued through these relations. Obligations are therefore generalized, and the solidarity of participants is expressed in unquestioned adherence to encompassing social values. By contrast, *Gesellschaft* relations are built on rational attitudes of self-interest (*Kurwille*) mobilized for specific ends and organized by formal or contractual relations. In this case, the continuity of the relationship is not guided by tradition; solidarity is limited to the period in which specific mutual benefits are exchanged.[7] Toennies employed these concepts in a supplementary rather than an antithetical manner, gauging their relative weight in concrete relations. Consequently, he was able to interpret Western society as a vast social process in which *Gemeinschaft* relations increasingly give way to those of the *Gesellschaft* type (a general "trend" theory).

However, social relations were viewed not only as effects, but as conditions. Toennies tried to show that each form of organization (either predominantly *Gemeinschaft* or *Gesellschaft*) stimulates distinctive kinds of motives, viewpoints, expectations, and dependencies among its members. In short, he asserted a socializing role for groups as determinants of social personalities (a nuclear theory).

Social relations not only are repeated but become intermingled with one another through the accumulation of interests and activities of the same participants. Toennies therefore classified social groupings on the basis of *organization*. The simplest type is the *social circle*, a complex of informal social relations among three or more persons. *Social collectivities* are loose groupings organized about some common cultural or physical traits (language, race, etc.), about which there is awareness and a feeling of unity. These

[7] Ferdinand Toennies, *Community and Society*, trans. and ed. Charles P. Loomis (East Lansing: Michigan State University Press, 1957), Pts. I and II.

become *social corporations* with the development of formal organization, division of labor, and bureaucracy.[8]

Beyond these influential formal concepts, Toennies has left surprisingly little impression on modern sociology. However, he is the author of a much-neglected work on public opinion that outlines the importance of public opinion in modern *gesellschaftlich* society (a nuclear theory) and demonstrates the influence of specific groupings in shaping public opinion as an instrument of social control comparable to religion in medieval society.[9] (Cf. Comte's theory of social control in political society.)

Emile Durkheim (1858–1917)

Apparently unaware of Toennies' work, Emile Durkheim employed concepts that were initially similar, but he extended his analysis and conceptual scheme to pursue three major sociological problems. In the course of his investigations, Durkheim evolved a consistent framework of problems, methodology, and theories that impressively solidified the status of sociology and guided its ultimate transformation into conspicuously modern channels.

Durkheim consistently analyzed society and specific social phenomena as reflecting the shared values, ideas, beliefs, and sentiments of associated individuals. Consequently, he defined sociology's major objectives as the study of the source, essential characteristics, and behavioral consequences of values.[10] In *The Division of Labor in Society*, it was assumed that population characteristics and intensity of interaction determine both the consistency of values and the relative impact of values on members of society (a general causal theory). Thus, for example, mechanical solidarity identifies societies where similarity of kinship and social skills is accompanied by

[8] Rudolph Heberle, "The Sociological System of Ferdinand Toennies: 'Community' and 'Society,'" in Barnes, *An Introduction to the History of Sociology*, pp. 234–236.

[9] *Ibid.*, pp. 238–240.

[10] Emile Durkheim, *Sociology and Philosophy*, trans. D. F. Pocock (New York: Free Press, 1953), p. 59.

strong values (*collective conscience*) and, by implication, strong motivation for conformity to such values. On the other hand, where specialization and division of labor become quite marked, central value systems are replaced by segmented interests and values. Solidarity derives from perceived interdependence between and among persons and social categories, rather than from direct dependence on clear, referential rules or injunctions (a nuclear correlational theory).[11]

But Durkheim was also concerned with the mechanisms by which persons respond to values and to other social instruments of determining (or influencing) social behavior. This led Durkheim to explore on several occasions what we would now call the problem of socialization—how persons acquire validated participation in groups. In three works—*Moral Education, Education and Sociology*, and *Sociology and Philosophy*—the components of a nuclear theory were presented. At this point, it is necessary only to restructure his various discussions with the advantage of retrospection, but in the spirit of Durkheim's apparent theoretical intentions. First, Durkheim focused on values that contained moral directives or appropriate ways of treating other persons.[12] Second, Durkheim analyzed the distinctive features of moral rules as (*a*) obligation, (*b*) desirability, (*c*) regularity, (*d*) understanding, and (*e*) relation with group affiliation. But third, Durkheim focused on moral obligation or respect as the key to values, thereby turning to the question of the social genesis of morality.[13] Durkheim seems to have formulated two answers. In societies characterized by mechanical solidarity, the most important and most effective source of morality is the religious institution. However, in complex societies (organic solidarity), neither religion nor the state can effectively sustain moral obligation. Durkheim suggested that institutionalized religion depends on non-rational symbols and on indoctrination, which are not applicable to practical situations in society.[14] Likewise, the state tends to rely on force and on fear, which interfere

[11] Emile Durkheim, *The Division of Labor in Society*, trans. George Simpson (New York: Free Press, 1947), Bk. I.

[12] Durkheim, *Sociology and Philosophy*, p. 36.

[13] Emile Durkheim, *Moral Education*, trans. Everett K. Wilson and Herman Schnurer (New York: Free Press, 1961), pp. 29–30, 64, 120.

[14] Durkheim, *Sociology and Philosophy*, p. 56; *Moral Education*, p. 11.

with essential attitudes of respect. Therefore, morality practically requires the operation of *intermediate socializing groups*, which can more easily explain and demonstrate the validity of moral rules as integral parts of social participation. Indeed, Durkheim clearly located the responsibility for "moral education" only in groups that are available and meaningful for persons. However, he also demonstrated that such intermediate groups as family, school, and occupational associations provide *specialized*—and by inference, *sequential*—effects on the internalization of morality (thereby anticipating Parsons' theory of socialization).[15] In effect, Durkheim suggests that, in organic solidarity or its approximation, morality serves as a functional alternative to an all-encompassing institutionalized religion (a general functional theory).

Durkheim was among the first theorists to treat deviant behavior sociologically, in terms of the availability and individual perception of value systems. In his classic work, *Suicide*, Durkheim brought the problem of deviation and social control to the crucial empirical level of individuals in specific social groups or categories. Crime was for Durkheim a critical index of solidarity; in *Suicide*, he focused on a particularly dramatic category of crime with amazingly significant implications for criminology and the entire discipline of sociology. After an extensive, empirically based critique of biological, climatic, and psychiatric explanations of suicide rates, Durkheim proceeded to test his fundamental methodological premise that social facts are explainable by other social facts. By a remarkably skillful comparison of suicide rates for such socially relevant categories as sex, marital status, occupation, and religious affiliation, Durkheim was able to discover group differences in suicide (empirical generalizations). But more important, he found varieties of suicide related to the social-control patterns of different groups and societies.

In groups that subordinate individual needs to the collective success of the group, suicides characteristically are of the *altruistic*

15 Durkheim, *The Division of Labor in Society*, Preface to the Second Edition, pp. 5–10, 17–18, 28; Emile Durkheim, *Suicide*, trans. John A. Spaulding and George Simpson (New York: Free Press, 1951), pp. 370–384. Cf. Talcott Parsons *et al.*, *Family, Socialization and Interaction Process* (New York: Free Press, 1955), pp. 296–306.

type and reflect a strong, almost mechanical solidarity or discipline —as in the cases of hari kari and military sacrifices. *Egoistic* suicide also derives from the guiding values of specific groups, but these values stress individuality and relative freedom from specific group guidance in periods of personal crisis. This is for Durkheim the explanation of higher suicide rates among single men (isolated from a solidary group) than among married men and among Protestants than among Catholics and Jews. Still a third type of suicide, the *anomic*,[16] occurs in groups that have lost a collective consciousness (*collective conscience*) of any kind and that are relatively devoid of discipline and norms. Thus Durkheim not only established a firm sociological basis for understanding crime, but clearly distinguished typical processes of social control and the cultural basis of social and personal disorganization in the phenomenon of *anomie* (all nuclear theories).

More generally, deviation of all types becomes more probable as societies develop greater specialization and indirect interdependence, while the content and the impact of the collective consciousness becomes more blurred and less accessible to individuals. In *The Division of Labor in Society*, Durkheim concludes that specialization tends to produce (or encourage) greater rationality (which threatens existing values), individualization, mobility (and a resultant comparison of values), constant instabilities and needs for readjustments, *anomie*, innovation, rebellion, and intergroup conflicts (a general causal theory). Yet Durkheim did not try to provide a sociological justification for conformity to established patterns, as some critics have declared.[17] Specifically, he asserted

---

[16] Durkheim, *Suicide*, Bk. II, ch. 5. See also the analysis of anomic suicide in Marvin E. Olsen, "Durkheim's Two Concepts of Anomie," *Sociological Quarterly*, VI (Winter, 1965), pp. 37–44, as well as an attempt to reduce the three types of suicide to one by Barclay D. Johnson, "Durkheim's One Cause of Suicide," *American Sociological Review*, XXX (December, 1965), pp. 875–886.

[17] Durkheim, *The Division of Labor in Society*, pp. 289–293, 333–335. On the other hand, see such discussions of Durkheim's alleged "conservatism" as Emile Benoit-Smullyan, "The Sociologism of Emile Durkheim and His School," in Barnes, *An Introduction to the History of Sociology*, pp. 511–514, 518–520; and Lewis A. Coser, "Durkheim's Conservatism and Its Implications for His Sociological Theory," in Kurt H. Wolff, ed., *Emile Durkheim* (Columbus: Ohio State University Press, 1960), pp. 211–232.

that both conformity and deviation (particularly rebellion) reflect the "true nature" (normal operation) of human society.[18] While moral rules must guide behavior—from a practical standpoint—such rules require respect and obligation. When rules become *sacred*—that is, are endowed with an immutable power—the element of obligation tends to diminish and the possibility of latent or open deviation increases (a general functional theory). One important form of such deviation is the creation of *ideals*, which may be defined as new goals for behavior that can enlist the respect of those who have lost a sense of personal obligation to existing values. "A society cannot be constituted without creating ideals." Indeed, says Durkheim, the function of ideals is to transfigure reality. This is accomplished by collective actions of similarly disenchanted persons in periods of "collective ferment," [19] but not by unstable or irresponsible persons. By implication, Durkheim makes the startling point that people with genuinely solid morality are thus not dependent on the specifics of current rules; instead, they possess a generalized obligation to social rules that allows them to accept (or even create) new ideals or new implementation of old values.[20] On the other hand, people with uncertain morality may subtly alter *obligation* till it becomes *obedience*, making conformity rather than values the primary consideration in behavior (a general causal theory). But the latter are not guardians of society, for "society is nature arrived at a higher point in its development, concentrating all its energies to surpass, as it were, itself." [21]

The final problem in Durkheim's evolving schema is his analysis of religion and its cultural consequences. In his *Elementary Forms of the Religious Life*, the basic analytical distinction between the *sacred* and the *profane* enabled Durkheim to locate religion or the religious sphere as distinct from religious aspects of other activities. Briefly, the realm of the sacred consists of objects and processes that have been attributed with extraordinary power and must not be touched; while the profane category encompasses the remainder of experience—which is treated as having distinctly lesser power,

18 Durkheim, *Sociology and Philosophy*, pp. 65, 70.   19 *Ibid.*, pp. 90–97.
20 Durkheim, *Moral Education*, pp. 137–138.
21 Durkheim, *Sociology and Philosophy*, p. 97.

and therefore can be manipulated without special care or concern for psychologically unusual consequences. Religion is defined as a socially structured consolidation of the sacred, composed of three collectively derived or created "parts." [22] First, *religious ideas* or beliefs involve two processes: (1) the definition of some unusual power or force; and (2) the symbolic transfer of this power to selected objects, animals, or men. Second, *religious rites* prescribe the special circumstances in which the sacred may be directly or indirectly experienced or, alternatively, must be scrupulously and symbolically avoided (the negative rites). Rites translate beliefs into visible form and thus lend continuity to the ineffable. Third, the *cult* is the regular or recurrent organization of believers who reinforce one another's beliefs through membership and participation in appropriate rites. Religion, then, in Durkheim's often quoted words, is "a unified system of beliefs and practices relative to sacred things . . . , beliefs and practices which unite into one single moral community called a church, all those who adhere to them." [23]

Durkheim's explanation of religion rests on two fundamental points. First, sacred objects possess attributed power that is morally rather than physically superior to the non-sacred realm. Second, religious systems implicitly derive the notion of moral power from the intimations of accomplishment and potential gained in regular association (a functional theory). In short, according to Durkheim, religion is a means by which members of a society represent their society to themselves (*collective representations*).[24] It follows—though Durkheim did not derive this implication—that (*a*) highly differentiated segments of a society would develop somewhat different religions; and (*b*) as the structure and capabilities of a society evolve (e.g., from mechanical to organic solidarity), the character of beliefs, rites, and cults would likewise be expected to change (general correlational theories).

If religion as an institutionalized system is a creative expression of specific social systems, then there is a religious dimension (vari-

[22] Emile Durkheim, *Elementary Forms of the Religious Life*, trans. Joseph W. Swain (New York: Free Press, 1947), pp. 37–40.

[23] *Ibid.*, p. 47.   [24] *Ibid.*, pp. 200–209, 225, 231.

ously defined as a set of attitudes of respect, awe, or moral obligation) that pervades human association. However, according to Durkheim, the sacred and religious aspects of society constitute one manifestation of the ideal (the domain of interpretations that is "added to" the "real" or "given" world of experience). The other manifestation of the ideal is the *conceptual*, by which men seek to describe and organize experience,[25] as distinct from the religious–sacred, which seeks to transmute or transfigure experience by means of values. Significantly, concepts—as in the case of religion—are said to reflect the major features of social systems (a functional theory). Such concepts or categories as class, time, space, force, causality, and totality are wrought out of perceptions of collective experiences—the awareness of association, the rhythm or pace of interactions, the ground or area used by the group or community, the achievements of cooperative effort.[26] Durkheim thus traces language and logic to social experience. Perspective, orientation, intellectual manipulation are social facts learned from social experience and conditioned by cues presented by salient characteristics of given human associations.

Clearly, Durkheim has formulated a sociology of knowledge that extends the more circumscribed version of orthodox Marxian theory (see pp. 29, 313). Associational patterns represent the *substructure*, while the *superstructure* consists of a changing relation between the religious–sacred and the conceptual. Durkheim suggests, further, that the religious component of the ideal predominates in periods of simple social organization and close association, when immediate experiences are overwhelming and when the desire to achieve comprehensive explanations is paramount (a correlational theory).[27] As religious ideas become banal or fail to command respect, they are not necessarily discarded, but may be perceived as contributing to other usages. Thus, it might be expected that there would be a growing emphasis on empirical description and manipulation, with a consequent emergence of the autonomous "disciplines" of art, philosophy, the law, science, and business from religion.

[25] Durkheim, *Sociology and Philosophy*, p. 95.
[26] Durkheim, *Elementary Forms*, pp. 434–443.   [27] *Ibid.*, pp. 421–430.

Durkheim is perennially useful for serious students of society because he clarified or pioneered intelligible discussion of crucial sociological problems. First, he furnished a comprehensive analysis of the varied social consequences of social differentiation and specialization. Second, he explored the collective basis of cultural creativity (values, ideals, concepts, religions) without reducing cultural products to the status of mechanical outputs of rigid associational structures. Third, the individual is conceptually and theoretically incorporated into analyses of society through the problem of moral obligation and its variants. Fourth, perhaps for the first time in the history of ideas, Durkheim conceptualized deviation as a response to socially defined opportunities and pressures on meaningful categories of persons. Finally, by inference, he suggested an orientation to social change [28] by illuminating the social conditions that promote conformity, as well as the processes that spawn ferment in the twin-engined vehicle of the ideal—the dynamic stages of the religious–sacred and the creative phases of conceptualization.

Charles H. Cooley (1864–1929)

The sociology of the old masters generally proceeded without benefit of a psychology or, more properly, a useful conception of personality as a vehicle of social phenomena. It had largely emphasized *structure* and assumed the operation of *process*—which is a legitimate viewpoint of preliminary study. Charles H. Cooley, however, developed a functional–organic view of social structure that was addressed to this very problem; in his quiet, almost unassuming manner, Cooley was able to guide the direction of American sociology so significantly that he is now perhaps the most cited American sociologist of his period.

Cooley's essential position is quite modern. Society and its various forms exhibit a differentiated unity in which influences are

[28] Robert N. Bellah, "Durkheim and History," *American Sociological Review,* XXIV (August, 1959), pp. 447–461.

mutually exchanged among constituent persons and groupings. Yet this is not a rigid, fully determinate structure; continued examination of social life reveals what Cooley calls a "tentative process" in which plan is mixed with drift, experimentation with unconscious motives, so that a continuous process of selection and redefinition is noted. In a clear foreshadowing of Thomas and Znaniecki's work, Cooley analyzed social process into dynamic social situations in which persons and their active tendencies (attitudes) respond to situational cues.[29]

Through a happy combination of the concepts of process, structure, and personality, Cooley demonstrated the social character of the self and proceeded to show the emergence and development of human personality in the *primary group*. This famous analysis seems to be a crucial supplementation of Durkheim's focus on moral obligation as the essence of social structure. For the primary group, with its intimacy and diffuseness of interests, is the originator and transmitter of moral obligations through its strategic role in personality development (a nuclear theory). In other words, moral obligations become internalized in individuals as invisible bonds of solidarity in the functioning of primary groups.[30] When voluntary associations arise to pursue more specialized interests, the fruits of primary social relations come into conflict with formalized structures and values, exposing the individual to situations in which moral obligations recede before impersonal, specialized, and fractional demands (a nuclear causal theory). Yet primary groups are inextinguishable because they are essential to personality and ultimately to the successful operation of society (a functional theory);[31] they seep into what we now call secondary groups with such consistency that contemporary sociology pursues their study in industrial sociology, sociometry, and "small groups."

Cooley's psychological sociology is a more considerable contribution than his analysis of institutions, yet the latter derive also from his organic approach. However, in what often seems to be a

[29] Charles H. Cooley, *Social Process* (New York: Charles Scribner's Sons, 1918), pp. 3–9.

[30] Charles H. Cooley, *Social Organization* (New York: Charles Scribner's Sons, 1909), pp. 23–32.

[31] *Ibid.*, pp. 32, 53–57.

violation of his fundamental orientation, Cooley tends to distinguish primary groups and institutions as separate rather than correlated processes. The institutions are conceptualized as organized systems (secondary groupings) that are concerned with basic needs of associated individuals and find expression in enduring sentiments, beliefs, customs, and appropriate symbols. Institutions are organically interrelated among themselves in any social organization, but the problem is their integration with persons.[32] Cooley's insights into these relations have been long neglected, though modern sociologists sometimes develop lines of thought and research that parallel his ideas. Essentially, Cooley observes, a complicated social structure, which necessarily fails to develop or sustain moral obligations, requires compensatory bonds. Where Durkheim found these bonds in the interdependence based on the division of labor, Cooley looked for more specific expressions of interdependence in *communication, public opinion,* and *social class* (a functional theory).[33]

Through improved media of communication, a substitute for consensus in the forms of specialized publics and a general political public make complex social organization feasible (a functional theory). But it must be remembered, says Cooley, that guiding values whose supervision and interpretation rest in a special social class are basic to the institutions of a complex society. Class-control of some kind or degree is therefore inherent in secondary social organization. The class system operates ideally as a means of assigning to individuals a more or less appropriate place in the social whole (a functional theory), ranging from positions of control and coordination to those of differently valued specialized skills. Caste and "open class" are alternative types of institutional control, the relative presence of which depends on homogeneity in the population, the rate of social change, and the extensiveness of communication among members of society (a correlational theory). Cooley used rough objective criteria of class—such as occupation, income, and culture or style of life. But his main contribution in this area was to connect stratification realistically with the institutional order, with-

[32] Cooley, *Social Process,* pp. 285–286, 292–301; *Social Organization,* chs. 28, 29.
[33] Cooley, *Social Organization,* chs. 6–10, 12.

out at the same time equating class exclusively with the economic system.[34]

[34] *Ibid.*, pp. 140–141, 209–249; *Social Process*, pp. 292–295, 302, 336.

SELECTED REFERENCES

Aron, Raymond, *Main Currents in Sociological Thought: I* (New York: Basic Books, 1965).

——, *Main Currents in Sociological Thought: II* (New York: Basic Books, 1967).

Cohen, David, "Comte's Changing Sociology," *American Journal of Sociology,* LXXI (September, 1965), 168–177.

Cooley, Charles H., *Sociological Theory and Social Research,* Robert Cooley Angell, ed. (New York: Holt, 1930).

DeGrange, McQuilkin, *The Curve of Societal Movement* (Hanover, N.H.: The Sociological Press, 1930).

Jandy, Edward C., *Charles Horton Cooley: His Life and His Social Theory* (New York: Dryden Press, 1942).

Nisbet, Robert A., ed., *Emile Durkheim* (Englewood Cliffs, N.J.: Prentice-Hall, 1965), Pt. I.

——, *The Sociological Tradition* (New York: Basic Books, 1966).

Parsons, Talcott, *The Structure of Social Action* (New York: McGraw-Hill, 1937), chs. 8–11.

Wolff, Kurt H., ed., *Emile Durkheim* (Columbia: Ohio State University Press, 1960).

2

The Old Masters

II

Georg Simmel (1858–1918)

Despite the brilliant contributions of the men we have already considered, sociology remained essentially a personal rather than a collective discipline at the beginning of the twentieth century. Its subject matter was still vague and its choice of problems was interesting though not conspicuously rational. It is therefore ironic that Simmel, a philosopher who made a relatively brief excursion into sociology, should have provided the touch of organization that was required. As a matter of fact, Simmel never constructed a coherent theoretical system for sociology and never performed a single piece of empirical social research. His sociological writings are predominantly a series of essays that contain numerous restricted analyses of exceptional brilliance. What, then, is his significance for modern sociology?

Georg Simmel's orientation to sociology is quite similar to that of Toennies, Cooley, and Durkheim, but he translated the amorphous vision of sociology into an approach that is marked by distinctive units of observation. Viewing society as a process, a "becoming," he identified its operation not in individuals, but in concrete interactions or social relationships between and among individuals. The field of sociology thereby became the study of the *forms* of association (i.e., relationships), and any sociological problem became analyzable as a complex of social relationships.[1]

Scattered through his writings are discussions of the major forms of interaction—competition, cooperation, superordination–subordination, compromise, and accommodation. Yet Simmel seems to have devoted the most thought and analytical skill in delineating some of the minor processes of sociation—sociability, tact, coquetry, loyalty, gratitude, jealousy, secrecy, etc.[2] In this manner, Simmel really pioneered in demonstrating the importance of noncoercive relations that appear in the interstices of social structuring. These more subtle relations supplement the institutional bonds and contribute to the characteristic unity of the larger organization (a functional theory).

Perhaps the most important theoretical problems raised by Simmel as crucial to sociology were:

1. What dimensions of interaction account for the continuity (but not necessarily the stability) of groups?
2. Given the existence of conflict in human interaction, what are the major conditions and social consequences of conflict?
3. How is personality development affected by sequence and complexity of socialization agents in modern societies?

Group organization and differentiation

For the first problem, Simmel explored the role of the number of group participants; the quantitative specialization of social roles; the significance of often-neglected reciprocal aspects of authority, power, and domination; the subtle contributions of secrecy and information control; the practiced use of conventional social mechanisms, such as tact, diplomacy, sociability, and superficiality or

[1] Georg Simmel, *The Sociology of Georg Simmel*, trans. Kurt H. Wolff (New York: Free Press, 1950), pp. 8–11, 21–23.
[2] *Ibid.*, Pt. I, ch. 3; Pt. IV, chs. 2, 3; Pt. V.

sophistication; and the formation of "intermediate" or "sub" groups by which individuals are effectively but indirectly enmeshed in some larger social constellation (e.g., a university, a metropolitan community, a business firm, or a religious organization).[3]

The core theoretical formulation, however, may be found in Simmel's analysis of the *triad*. Essentially, the simplest social relation—between two persons or two roles—is marked by its fragility, immediacy, and dependence on the emotional consonance of the pair or dyad. In short, when differences arise, the relationship is endangered because no mechanism for resolution or settlement is available. Relative permanence of social relations requires an impersonal (or impartial) addition—a third person or role—as the basis for all types of genuine social groups (a functional theory). In other words, Simmel asserts that the operation of groups (as distinct from tenuous relations) requires a minimal structure of social specialization—the triadic form. Only with the triad is (*a*) authority (as compared with personal influence or coercion) possible and (*b*) conflict manageable. Indeed, the "third element" adds objectivity, reason, and the means of canalizing deviant or creative contributions from the other roles.[4]

But, realistically, the triad offers opportunities for exploitation. If two persons or subgroups in a system are of roughly similar power, their unilateral attempts to influence the third element, or their direct interference with one another, present advantages to the third party in acquiring rewards, and in allocating rewards to the members (a nuclear functional theory). Alternatively, the third party may actively seek to obtain these advantages by forming coalitions with the stronger of two subgroups. This further weakens the isolated subgroup and allows the third party to dominate the subsequently isolated former ally.[5] Simmel seems to regard freedom for exploitation as a consequence of vague or ambiguous social structures (a functional theory). By implication, the

[3] *Ibid.*, Pt. I, ch. 2; Pts. III and IV.

[4] *Ibid.*, pp. 123–127, 145–153; Theodore Mills, "Some Hypotheses on Small Groups from Simmel," *American Journal of Sociology*, LXIII (May, 1958), pp. 642–650.

[5] Simmel, *op. cit.*, pp. 154–169.

techniques of coalition formation and "divide and rule" are incompatible with a well articulated hierarchical structure, in which subordination to rules or authoritative roles reduces the possibilities of manipulation.

Conflict

Conflict, for Simmel, is a persistent phenomenon of social structure and social interaction, rather than a deficiency of social order. Consequently, while he attributes conflict to inborn drives (a causal reductionist theory), his major theoretical statements are concerned with the social circumstances of hostility, conflict, and opposition.[6] One fundamental theory, expressed in various forms and illustrations, asserts that both the severity of conflict and the social mechanisms for its control are largely determined by the type of social structure in which conflict occurs (a nuclear causal theory). In small, intimate relations, conflict develops with great intensity of emotion, because the emotional response serves to blot out or deny the previous unity of the persons involved (a functional theory).[7] Thus, converts, renegades, etc., develop a magnified hatred for (and in) their erstwhile mates, comrades, or close associates. Likewise, in small, primary-like groups, as compared with more formalized and specialized groups, conflicts are apt to get out of hand, to cumulate adhesions to the initial source of difficulty. This phenomenon, Simmel suggests, results from the inability to segregate activities and issues, and from a characteristic dependence on solidarity feelings or morale (a functional theory). Conflicts in complex groups tend to be localized or isolated; and, with the mechanism of formal controls, conflicts can receive special attention for containment, if not resolution.[8]

The positive social effects of conflict form another key theoretical segment in Simmel's writings.[9] In addition to the actual and potential difficulties produced by conflict, there are latent or barely

[6] Georg Simmel, *Conflict and the Web of Group-Affiliations,* trans. Kurt H. Wolff and Reinhard Bendix (New York: Free Press, 1955), pp. 28–38.

[7] *Ibid.,* pp. 45–48.   [8] *Ibid.,* pp. 65–67.

[9] *Ibid.,* pp. 91–108; Lewis A. Coser, *The Functions of Social Conflict* (New York: Free Press, 1956), pp. 121–137.

recognized social advantages that can be traced to conflict (functional theories). First, the process of conflict serves to unify—or de-emphasize differences in—contending groups, since successful opposition requires greater subordination to group goals than routine activities would require. One means of obtaining solidarity, however, is a purge of dissident or vacillating members. Therefore, tolerance and creativity are sociologically incompatible with extended periods of conflict. Second (and closely related), conflicts tend to accentuate or clarify the values and purposes of a group or category, thus reinforcing the sense of participation among group members. Third, hostility and antagonism likewise clarify the respective positions of opposing persons or subgroups in a social system. Ambiguities in opportunity for manipulation, exploitation, mobility, etc., are necessarily erased by processes of contention; a greater sense of realism may then be expressed in subsequent interaction between opposing parties. Fourth, in highly complex systems (such as metropolitan communities), antagonism and opposition provide protection against the impact of multiple (and conflicting) stimuli (demands, values, specific issues). Finally, borrowing from the work of Gumplowicz and Spencer, Simmel attributes to processes of conflict between unequals the development of rules, norms, morality, and custom.[10]

Socialization

Aspects of a theory of socialization are quite scattered—characteristically—throughout Simmel's essays. Perhaps the most fundamental part of his approach is the notion of personality development as a continuing process, conditioned and/or reinforced by the number and character of groups to which the individual is meaningfully exposed. Several specific ramifications of this orientation are particularly fruitful. First, in a much-neglected passage, Simmel explains the typical gregariousness of adolescents with age-mates as a consequence of lack of educational and intellectual development. Age-groups thus compensate for "immaturity" and also impede further development of individuality (a nuclear functional

[10] Simmel, *Conflict*, p. 95; *The Sociology of Georg Simmel*, pp. 409–416.

theory).[11] Second, Simmel noted the obvious correlation of personality development and the sequence of key group affiliations (parental family, school, family of procreation, occupational group, etc.). But less obvious is Simmel's conclusion that the individuality of a person stems from more diversified participation in groups (a nuclear causal theory). Under these circumstances, the individual yields less of his resources to any one group, thereby reserving for himself alternatives of thought and action that total immersion in any one group would exclude.[12] However, socially derived individuality also permits ambiguities and uncertainties as to "proper" behavior. But, as conflict between persons and groups clarifies and integrates values, so intrapersonal conflicts tend to impel persons to develop adjustments toward greater self-awareness and accommodation of differences (perhaps personal maturity).[13] By implication then, the primary group is only an *early* agent of socialization; dependence on the primary group can well explain deviations from expected personality development.

Third, the more developed the personality, the greater the willingness to expand group affiliations, particularly in the choice of different and complementary groups (a nuclear correlational theory). Simmel suggests that the search for contrasting groups seems to alternate *socializing* and *competitive* forms (a functional theory).[14] Thus, the harried businessman will seek membership in social clubs—an association that would be intensely criticized by the urbane scholar ensconced in his professional community. Indeed, the scholar would be expected to have great interest in such "unscholarly" activities as football, ice hockey, prize-fighting, and "dirty" politics.

Fourth, personality is significantly affected by the general character of one's occupation. The more specialized and narrowly defined an occupation, the less the emotional investment, and consequently the greater the opportunity to pursue varied interests (a nuclear functional theory).[15] People in emotionally absorbing oc-

11 Simmel, *Conflict*, pp. 134–135.   12 *Ibid.*, pp. 141–142, 150.
13 *Ibid.*, p. 163. Cf. Talcott Parsons *et al.*, *Family, Socialization and Interaction Process* (New York: Free Press, 1955), pp. 199–224.
14 Simmel, *Conflict*, pp. 155–156, 166–167.   15 *Ibid.*, pp. 185–189.

cupations (e.g., some physicians, commercial or industrial entre-
preneurs, artists), on the other hand, tend to view other activities
not as intrinsically valuable, but as extensions or derivations of
their central occupational passion. It would therefore be misleading
to conclude that specific occupations determine the perspectives
and behavior of their members. Rather, the way persons immerse
themselves in their work—not work requirements *per se*—affects
the level of interest and energy available for participation in and
appreciation of varied social experiences.

Max Weber (1864–1920)

For the present, the line of the "old masters" may be said to come
to an end with Max Weber, who is perhaps the single greatest
source of guidance and inspiration among contemporary American
sociologists. His erudition, tremendous industry, and remarkable
sense of proportion were combined in a series of fertile critical ex-
aminations of sociology, out of which have emerged a formidable
battery of positive contributions—most of which have been properly recognized only in the last twenty years. Weber appeared at a
time of crisis in sociology, when its promise was enormous but
clouded by lagging or tangential achievements. After his death, it
was gradually discovered that he had sharpened the focus of sociology, solidified some of the most valuable trends, developed fledgling insights into significant problems and hypotheses, and, most
enduringly, contributed a sorely needed methodological clarity.
These have been fully and capably analyzed elsewhere, and it is
perhaps necessary only to select a few of the more pertinent contributions for this discussion.

Using Toennies and Simmel as initial guides, Weber defined the
method of sociology as the analysis of the meaningful element in
social phenomena, thus giving significant weight to subjective factors as data in sociology. The method of *Verstehen* (interpretive
understanding) consequently aims to discover the subjective na-

ture of an event, object, or persons for a specific actor or group; and the meaning of such data resides in their relation to a given actor as means or ends of action. Thus, a collection of bricks and lumber is irrelevant to the sociologist; but it assumes meaning if, for example, it helps to understand the sacrifices of an individual motivated by the desire for a ten-room home on a fashionable street.

In most of Weber's writings, the quest for meaning in human behavior is reflected in a basic set of theoretical problems. Essentially, Weber focused on the relative importance of *rationality* versus *particularistic ends* or motives in members of social systems.[16] Though he used rationality in several senses, the most frequent usage refers to such qualities as the efficient adaptation of means to ends, the generalization of experience, and the emphasis on impersonality in social processes. On the other hand, the contrast with rationality is a complex but residual dimension; it includes behavior and values that reflect (*a*) concern for the specific and immediate, (*b*) interests of limited groups or social categories, (*c*) resistance to innovation, and (*d*) superiority of ends over means.

In retrospect, Weber appears to have been fundamentally absorbed by two questions: (1) What social circumstances help to account for the predominance of either rationality or its obverse? (2) What social and cultural consequences can be attributed to the ascendance of rationality or particularism?

To handle these questions in a manageable form for a range of specific historical settings, Weber developed his famous sets of *ideal types*—concepts that focus on relatively "pure" socially relevant intentions, motives, or assumptions. At the most primitive level are types of *social action*—[17] behavior directed toward influencing the behavior of other persons. Weber divided this type into the following:

1. *Rational–purposeful,* which is designed to achieve a specific, realizable goal in the most efficient manner.

16 Max Weber, *The Theory of Social and Economic Organization,* trans. A. M. Henderson and Talcott Parsons (New York: Oxford University Press, 1947), pp. 115–118, 158–171.

17 *Ibid.,* pp. 115–118.

2. *Value–rational*, which is the attempt to pursue with some efficiency an emotionally held or undemonstrable goal.
3. *Affectual*, which is based on the immediate impact of some feeling, unregulated by prospects of success or failure in producing a desired social response.
4. *Traditional*, which follows accepted practices simply because they have been repeatedly performed.

As a complement to types of social action, Weber distinguishes modes of *orientation*,[18] or motivations for the repetition of social actions. His three types of orientation are the following:

1. *Usage* (including custom, fashion, convention), which is based on conformity to prevailing models.
2. *Interest*, which derives from the anticipated reward to the actor.
3. *Belief in a legitimate order*, which is simply the moral obligation to behave in a given manner.

Next in order is Weber's typology of *social relationships*,[19] which refers to the patterns of reciprocal social actions that can be attributed to a set of persons. These may be seen as the following:

1. *Conflict relations*, in which social action is intentionally designed to overcome the resistance of others. Power, then, is the relative ability to overcome such resistance. Conflict always entails power relationships, but it does not follow that power always develops conflict.
2. *Communal or primary relations*, in which social actions of members are based on feelings of essential similarity or identity, whether affectual or traditional in motivation.
3. *Associational relations*, in which social actions derive from rational, utilitarian agreements about the common interests of members.
4. *Corporate relations*, which constitute a special development in either the communal or associational types. Briefly, the corporate relation insures the regularity of appropriate social actions by the "rational" use of a specific, legitimate agent of enforcement.

Since important social relationships necessarily entail the dimension of continuity and order, Weber locates the cardinal aspect of social order in the factors that create or sustain willingness to uphold a given order. In other words, order reflects obligation to

18 *Ibid.*, pp. 120–123.   19 *Ibid.*, pp. 132–139.

referential rules—the *legitimacy* of a pattern of expected social actions. A typology of *ascription* of legitimacy to an order is again basically motivational—traditional, affectual, value–rational, and legal (or related to previous formal agreements). Similarly, motives for *upholding* the legitimacy of an order are distinguished as affectual, value–rational, rational–purposeful, and ethical–traditional.[20]

Institutional analysis

By implication, an institution is a complex structure composed of a unique configuration of interrelated social action types, social relationships, and some dominant type of legitimate order. Thus, for example, any economic institution is a composite of rational social actions, an "interest" mode of orientation (toward the provision of utilities for some group or category), and a rational–purposeful legitimate order. Any political institution involves a legitimate order (authority) backed by physical coercion and encompassing a variable collection of social action and relationship types. In the same way, any religious institution is primarily composed of value–rational and traditional action types, variable proportions of communal, associational, and corporate relationships, and an order based on ethical–traditional elements. Weber seemed to direct his analysis of institutions to the legitimate order and its dynamic properties. On this level, he sought to investigate the interrelation of rational and particularistic processes in five substantive areas of social structure—religion; bureaucracy; law; stratification; and social change.

This general orientation can be discerned in Weber's famous analysis of modern Western capitalism, in which, in an unfinished comparative approach, he tried to demonstrate the value–rational (Protestant) basis of the legitimate order in an apparently rational–purposeful institution (economic organization). However, with something of Durkheim's interest in the religious institution,

[20] *Ibid.*, pp. 126–127.

Weber also employed this approach (bolstered by vast empirical resources) in clarifying the process of religious development. Briefly, Weber discovered that the religious interest is pursued through a series of religious ideas whose systematization is inhibited by traditionalism. When social crises occur (involving weakening of traditional values, emergence of group conflicts, and the sharpening of class differences), the traditional order is challenged by the emergence of a *charismatic* authority—the prophet—who seeks to give a more coherent structure to religious ideas (a nuclear causal theory). This process of religious rationalization may take one of two ideal typical forms—*ethical prophecy*, in which the prophet is himself the embodiment of a divine will (e.g., Mohammed, Jesus), or *exemplary prophecy*, in which the prophet provides a personal example guiding others to religious salvation. If the prophet is at all successful, he helps create a charismatic order that employs either asceticism or mysticism as religious means. The former involves rejection of current worldly values, while the latter is characterized by indifference to worldly events. Generally, a mystical religious development is difficult to sustain without reversion to traditionalism; but ascetic prophecy, which aims to reshape the world in the image of given religious ideas (worldly aceticism), ultimately signifies a genuine change in the religious structure. However, charismatic authority is transformed into more stable forms (traditional, rational, or mixed types) as a necessary practical consequence of insuring the status of followers and disciples, and of some orderly process of succession—until another crisis stimulates new prophets (a functional theory).[21]

Bureaucracy

Sociologically, bureaucratic organization is the product of typical developments in the corporate form, which stem from an initial emphasis on efficiency. Historically, bureaucracy was invented

[21] Hans H. Gerth and C. Wright Mills, trans. and eds., *From Max Weber: Essays in Sociology* (New York: Oxford University Press, 1946), pp. 287–293.

under a limited set of conditions—practical needs created by maintenance of a standing army, complexities of managing public finances, specialization of tasks and resultant "administrative" problems. However, bureaucracy presupposes certain favorable conditions—technical knowledge, a money economy, and a rising proportion of resources for consumption and for a variety of consumer demands (causal–functional theories).[22] Weber gives some attention to traditional forms of bureaucracy, but the more frequently encountered type is organized on rational–legal themes. In short, bureaucracy tends to reflect the dominance of rational over particularistic principles, at least in the formative and mature stages of bureaucracy.

While Weber viewed the operation of bureaucratic structures as applications of impersonal, technical-efficiency principles and of specialized dedication, he likewise theorized about the varied consequences of apparently rational intentions. One such consequence is concentration of power—through control of matériel, equipment, and finances—in key roles (a functional theory).[23] It is not always clear whether this is interpreted as a rational or non-rational effect. However, Weber further asserts that bureaucracies tend to become invulnerable to external assault, which thus develops dependence on rules as "traditions" rather than "instruments." In addition, in pursuing maximum efficiency, bureaucratic functionaries often restrict the flow of information (cf. Simmel's discussion of secrecy).[24] "The concept of the 'official secret' is the specific invention of bureaucracy, and nothing is so fanatically defended by the bureaucracy as this attitude, which cannot be substantially justified beyond these specifically qualified areas." But, given the general success of bureaucratic forms in any institutional sphere, one of the most significant consequences is the increasing rationalization of education—to prepare persons for specialized roles in various bureaucracies. In this way, too, bureaucracy tends to reduce prevailing social-class differences, since recruitment to training comes to be based more on ability than on family background (functional theories).[25]

22 *Ibid.*, pp. 204, 209–212.   23 *Ibid.*, pp. 221–224, 228.
24 *Ibid.*, pp. 233–239.   25 *Ibid.*, pp. 240–243.

Legitimacy and law

Weber's analysis of law contains another illustration of the crucial position of legitimacy and its dynamics in social phenomena.[26] In a broad sense, law reflects dominant motives for ascribing legitimacy to the behavior of group participants. Weber initially assumes two aspects of legitimacy as focal to the sociologist: (1) generality of application (formal vs. substantive law), and (2) relative dependence on intellectual or logical means as against emotional or *ad hoc* arguments in support of rules (rational vs. irrational law). Of the four combinations, Weber was principally concerned with formal–rational and substantive–irrational types, and especially with the effects of other institutional areas on the development of formal–rational legal systems.

Law or the legal order is conceived as an adaptive mechanism that is both responsive to special social processes and to the developing skills of a legal profession (a functional theory). Weber tended to explain innovations in legal rationalization as a consequence of a specialized group of legal experts whose primary aim is systematization of legal rules.[27] On the other hand, professionally created innovations are evaluated according to the experience and interests of different subgroups in society (a correlational theory). Specifically, commercial interests tend to encourage formal rationalization of law (empirical generalizations). Likewise, military groups with developed techniques favor legal formalization. In addition, both the requirements of an extensive market economy and the evolution of bureaucratic forms (in government, economy, voluntary associations of various kinds) directly or indirectly support existing tendencies toward more rational legal systems.[28]

In a brilliant but not adequately appreciated use of the "sociology of knowledge," Weber analyzed the divergent "ideological" orientations to legal formalization among social categories. For ex-

[26] Max Weber, *Max Weber on Law in Economy and Society*, Max Rheinstein, ed., trans. Edward Shils and Max Rheinstein (Cambridge: Harvard University Press, 1954), pp. 60–64.

[27] *Ibid.*, pp. 96–97, 199–223.   [28] *Ibid.*, pp. 91, 96, 131, 145, 260–267.

ample, *formal justice* in a legal system is typically repudiated by any authoritarian group (political, religious, etc.) because such laws serve to reduce the power of group leaders over group members (a functional theory). But formal justice is equally unacceptable to "democratic" groups, whose concern for substantive justice (i.e., difference and variety of individual and group needs) is thereby threatened. Those groups that desire predictability in legal systems—especially those in economic power positions—tend to favor formal, abstract justice. But competition among economic groups and the development of occupational specialization result in disillusion with formalism and in a tendency to favor legal rules that implicitly encourage expediency and flexible interpretations adapted to individual or subgroup needs.[29] Finally, Weber recognized the role of coalitions in promoting legal rationalization. For example, the complementary needs of the monarchy and the bourgeois groups in their fight against the nobility were well expressed in formal legal changes, particularly in urban areas and with respect to taxation policy (empirical generalizations). Legal systematization may also arise from compromises between and among status groups, which thereby resolve antecedent conflicts in some workable manner.[30]

Stratification

Weber's approach to stratification rests on his basic concern with the complexities of power relationships in society. The distribution or ordering of power (and authority) constitutes a continuing practical problem for the legitimate order. Essentially, Weber distinguishes three ways in which power is allocated—or how persons and social units are "stratified." One such mechanism is rational; it concerns distribution of power in terms of position in the economic sphere, in the market (*class differentiation*). A sec-

[29] *Ibid.*, pp. 228–229, 266–268, 303, 321–324.

[30] *Ibid.*, pp. 266–269, 321. Parenthetically, Weber did not try to explain rationalization of law as a necessary fruit of capitalism. England's capitalist development was accompanied by substantive, semi-irrational legal forms (equity, the jury system, the justice of the peace system). There is a strong tendency in Weber's work to explain legal rationalization by reference to political processes.

ond aspect or source of power is nonrational (traditional); it concerns the attributed or arrogated degree of "social honor" attached to different social categories (*status differentiation*). Finally, power may be distributed according to relative ability in influencing communal or societal decisions, thereby mixing rational–purposeful and value–rational types of social action (*power or party differentiation*).[31]

Conceptually, Weber made a very important observation about strata or ranked categories in terms of these three criteria. Class strata, for example, are inherently flexible; it is therefore normally difficult to classify persons who are identical (or very similar) in class status—except those who are completely unskilled.[32] Similarly, a party stratum involves considerable fluidity in membership. Therefore, the unity or self-awareness of a given stratum (cf. Marx's "class consciousness") is "highly relative and variable." By contrast, status categories reduce the variability of stratum consensus by developing characteristic value clusters (styles of life) that limit opportunities for contact with other status levels and with some class and party categories (a functional theory)—e.g., social distance mechanisms, such as endogamous marriage, and monopoly of certain formal educational channels. Consequently, study and explanation of stratification are more difficult and complex in systems dominated by class and party criteria.[33]

Weber is perhaps the man most responsible for emphasizing the meaningful interactions among the three dimensions of stratification, in contrast to the prevailing economic or political simplification of stratification phenomena. First, Weber explained the differential opportunities of economic categories (classes) as a reflection of a biased legal order (a functional theory), which presumably is developed through political bargaining processes. Second, status differences tend to develop from preceding differentials in the accumulation or control of property and other economic resources (a causal theory). Third, status offers special opportunities for subsequent access to economic resources. Fourth, party strata

[31] Weber, *Essays in Sociology*, pp. 180–195.
[32] Weber, *Theory of Social and Economic Organization*, p. 425.
[33] Weber, *Essays in Sociology*, pp. 187–191.

may represent either specific status groups or class groups, or both, or neither—though Weber does not specify the conditions under which these alternatives appear.[34] Thus, Weber seems to suggest that the distribution of power is a dynamic consequence of changing "opportunity-chains" among the three orders.

The relations between and among strata are likewise for Weber more complex than deterministic theories have asserted. In general, periods of limited or very gradual change in economic and political affairs encourage stratum distinctions that are based primarily on status or honor (a functional theory). When significant economic and political changes are accepted or are imposed, class distinctions assume greater prominence, with a resultant conflict between status and class strata—and with adjustments in the organization and operation of party strata.[35]

Social change

By implication, Weber sketched the rudiments of a theory of social change as by-products of his analyses of legitimacy and stratification. We may infer that Weber viewed social change as the process by which the legitimacy of social relationships—particularly the distribution of power—is altered. The proximate origins of social change can be found in the responses of a minority to the limitations of a traditional legitimate order in some institutional sphere. In such orders, dissatisfactions and conflicts between social categories normally arise. But when these crises encourage innovative ideals that are dramatically clothed in charisma, the first substantial basis for change appears. Essentially, Weber does not explain the phenomenon of the charismatic innovator, but instead assumes that his success alters the legitimate order by destroying allegiance to its rules (a causal–functional theory).[36] Change proceeds by the routinization of charisma—the development of a rational organization of followers of the new, and the translation of broad principles into specific directives. However, successful innovation and subsequent rationalization create (or aid in revaluing)

---

[34] *Ibid.*, pp. 185, 187, 190, 194–195.   [35] *Ibid.*, pp. 192–194.
[36] Weber, *Theory of Social and Economic Organization*, pp. 361–372.

new classes or status categories that try to extend their legitimated achievements to other spheres. Thus, change generates competition between traditional and newly formed status groups (a causal theory). The institutional expansion of innovation, then, becomes the stimulus for "politics" and the varied rational and particularistic adjustments that accompany revision in the focal legitimate order (government).

It would be false to suggest that this résumé of the "old masters" reveals a straight-line development in sociology. Yet these famous strands of sociological thought have a certain consistency

Nuclear problem	Major contributors
Group formation	Simmel
Internal differentiation	Comte, Marx, Simmel, Cooley, Weber
Coordination and control	Marx, Toennies, Simmel, Weber
Innovation – deviation	Durkheim, Simmel, Weber
Socialization	Toennies, Durkheim, Simmel, Cooley
Social change	Marx, Toennies, Durkheim, Weber

TABLE 2. "The Old Masters" and nuclear theoretical problems: relative contributions in retrospect.

that enables us to view them collectively from our current perspective as a repository of past sociological savings, from which we continually draw working capital for modern sociological enterprises. Like the British Constitution, they constitute a group of guiding ideas and conceptions that we alter by continual reinterpretation and emendations. In essence, these writings have sketched the major outlines of sociology by defining its subject matter, by formulating a set of generalized concepts, and by clarifying the basic methodological problems that beset a young discipline. (See Table 2.) Indeed, these contributions are as much a part of modern American sociology as the latest textbooks; but they are being re-analyzed, tested, and partially transformed by a handful of contemporary theorists who may well be the "old masters" of succeeding generations. In the remaining chapters of Part I, we shall try to analyze the contributions of these contemporary theorists to American sociology.

SELECTED REFERENCES

Bendix, Reinhard, *Max Weber: An Intellectual Portrait* (Garden City: Doubleday, 1960).

Coser, Lewis A., *The Functions of Social Conflict* (New York: Free Press, 1956).

———, ed., *Georg Simmel* (Englewood Cliffs, N.J.: Prentice-Hall, 1965).

Gerth, Hans H. and C. Wright Mills, trans. and eds., *From Max Weber: Essays in Sociology* (New York: Oxford University Press, 1946).

Parsons, Talcott, *The Structure of Social Action* (New York: McGraw-Hill, 1937), chs. 14–17.

Weber, Max, *The Theory of Social and Economic Organization*, trans. A. M. Henderson and Talcott Parsons (New York: Oxford University Press, 1947).

Wolff, Kurt H., ed., *Georg Simmel 1858–1918* (Columbus: Ohio State University Press, 1959).

Thomas and Znaniecki: Subjective Elements in Social Action

With the publication of the five-volume classic, *The Polish Peasant in Europe and America*, sociology in the United States entered a new and complex era in which two emphases have come to predominate. Especially stressed is an insistence on active research in contemporaneous social phenomena, which is regarded by many as the essential departure from traditional European sociology. But we have sometimes neglected the second and perhaps the more significant emphasis: concern for objective analysis of crucial subjective factors in social behavior. The apparent paradox of subjective materials and objective techniques has of course stimulated currents of extreme behaviorism and logical positivism, but sociologists of every persuasion have been compelled in one way or another to take account of such phenomena as motivations, feelings, sentiments, attitudes, etc.

Undoubtedly, this problem had received a good deal of prior at-

SEMINAL SOURCES OF SOCIOLOGICAL THEORY

tention in a variety of forms in the work of Cooley, Baldwin, Dewey, Ward, Small, Ross, Simmel, and Max Weber, among others. Much of this was, however, vague and unsystematic, without communicable techniques and quite immune to verification. Thomas and Znaniecki, in their individual and joint sociological careers, have combined awareness with research in a lengthy division of labor. While Thomas is usually accorded a unique and somewhat exclusive role in modern American sociology, it seems that a distinctly charismatic element is involved. For Thomas primarily contributed important concepts and a helpful methodological viewpoint, while Znaniecki, after collaborating on *The Polish Peasant*, proceeded to (*a*) refine their basic methodology, (*b*) participate in empirical research, and (*c*) develop a number of theoretical formulations in social psychology and sociology.

William I. Thomas (1863–1947)

The wide-ranging interests of W. I. Thomas make it difficult to classify him in the narrow manner most people employ in characterizing other individuals. He was in fact a walking illustration of one of his famous "four wishes"—the one for new experience. In a career that covered more than half a century, Thomas immersed himself in such diverse problem areas as comparative ethnology, immigration, personality, and delinquency. Yet these special excursions constituted varying attempts to investigate what Thomas took to be the central problem in human behavior—the relation of the individual to the social group.

Since social behavior is dynamic, and since practical social technique involves questions of directing change, Thomas regarded social theory as the "analysis of the totality of social becoming into . . . causal processes . . . ." [1] But according to his underlying formulation of the problem, both the individual and the group

[1] W. I. Thomas and Florian Znaniecki, *The Polish Peasant in Europe and America* (5 vols., Boston: Richard Badger, 1918), I, p. 36.

were viewed as processes in social becoming. Therefore, it was necessary to abstract factors or characteristics from both in order to study social behavior—through their interrelations. As his thinking developed in the collaborative project, *The Polish Peasant*, the "attitude" became the index of the individual, while the "value" was chosen as the primary symbol of the social group. Sociology was therefore approached as a special science devoted to the relationship between attitudes and a special category of values— those that regulate the relations between individual members of a group and between each member and the group as a whole, namely *social rules*.

These values or rules and the behavior associated with them constitute the *social institutions* of a society or community; the pattern of institutions is often referred to as the social organization of a society or community. But Thomas insisted that social values and social institutions can be fully understood only by analyzing the way they are reflected in the personal experiences of individuals. Thus, an early focus was on attitudes, which Thomas defined as the individual's orientation to action with respect to the use of some social value. As Znaniecki phrased it some years afterward, an attitude toward a value is its bearing on the individual, while the meaning of a value lies in its bearing on other values.[2]

At first, Thomas approached attitudes as reflections of organic impulses and formulated his famous set of "four wishes" or "forces which impel to action." In 1917 and again in the first two volumes of *The Polish Peasant*, the wishes were classified into desires for new experience, for security, for mastery or power, and for recognition or appreciation by others.[3] However, in his study of female delinquents (published in 1923), Thomas discarded the "desire for security" and substituted the "wish for response," which differs from the desire for recognition in that the former refers to primary group situations, while the latter applies primarily to position and

[2] *Ibid.*, pp. 22, 32–33; III, p. 7; Florian Znaniecki, "Discussion," in Herbert Blumer, *An Appraisal of Thomas and Znaniecki's The Polish Peasant in Europe and America*. Critiques of Research in the Social Sciences: I (New York: Social Science Research Council, 1939), Bulletin 44, p. 93.

[3] Thomas and Znaniecki, *op. cit.*, I, p. 73; III, pp. 33, 56–57.

63

status in the larger group.[4] The wishes were conceived as universal, persistent needs in the socialization of individuals—what we would now call "functional prerequisites." But in any given individual, Thomas asserted, temperament and the glandular system determine the relative strength of the wishes, though the expression of these basic desires was said to be influenced by the social group.

Thomas thus appears to have experienced in his early thinking a conflict between biological and social explanations of human behavior. It is interesting to note that in the third volume of *The Polish Peasant*, the four wishes are no longer interpreted as innate forces, but only as tendencies in attitudes as they become integral parts of character in the process of socialization.[5] As a matter of fact, Thomas at one time reduced the number of basic tendencies to two (desire for new experience and for stability) in the formation of personality, while the desires for response and recognition were clearly analyzed as acquired tendencies. However, by 1923, the study of values and attitudes was extended by the explicit concern for contextual relations known as the *situational approach*.

The germ of this approach may be found in the introduction to his *Source Book for Social Origins;* and, with a revised terminology, it briefly recurs in the methodological note of *The Polish Peasant*. In the former work, situations were primarily conceived as problem periods in the life of groups or societies, periods in which established habits and routines are disturbed by change. The objective conditions of change create *crises* that stimulate what Thomas called "attention"—or the mental attitude that takes note of the objective world and tries to manipulate it. These reactions to crisis, he found, were conditioned by the mental ability of individuals, by attitudes toward crisis (acceptance of or resistance to change), and by the cultural base of the group.[6] A decade later, Thomas regarded all social life as composed of situations, and he distinguished three situational components applicable to the analysis of any social phenomenon.

4 W. I. Thomas, *The Unadjusted Girl* (Boston: Little, Brown, 1923), pp. 4, 38–40, 249.

5 Thomas and Znaniecki, *op. cit.*, III, p. 33.

6 W. I. Thomas, *Source Book for Social Origins* (Chicago: University of Chicago Press, 1909), pp. 16–21.

First, each situation contains objective conditions in the form of the complex of values (economic, religious, etc.), which are presented to individuals and to which they must adjust. Second, Thomas noted the pre-existing attitudes of individuals relevant to immediate objective conditions. Finally and most significantly, situations were found to include individual and group interpretations (the definition of the situation) that necessarily precede definite activity.[7]

With the concept "definition of the situation" Thomas created a dynamic synthesis of subjective and objective factors that avoids the dangers of monistic determinism and the all too convenient rationalism that assumes men to be hedonistic calculators. Both social codes and individual attitudes were seen to offer guides for behavior, but the definition of the situation refers to the process whereby individuals select from relevant but competing guides a single course of action. The consequences of each selection then become part of succeeding situations.[8] Thomas therefore viewed cultural diversity—which has been variously explained by references to race, climate, diffusion, etc.—as the result of cumulative differential interpretation of experience by different peoples. However, the definition of the situation is a descriptive concept, the phenomena of which require some systematic explanation. Yet as early as 1918, Thomas laid down a "fundamental methodological principle" that is particularly relevant at this juncture. Values, attitudes, and—by extension—definitions of situations involve combinations of attitudes and values and must therefore be studied from that standpoint.[9] Since these combinations underlying behavior were taken to be part of the process of social becoming, Thomas selected a focus for their investigation in the strategic area of the

[7] W. I. Thomas and Dorothy S. Thomas, *The Child in America* (New York: Alfred A. Knopf, 1928), ch. 13; Edmund H. Volkart, *Social Behavior and Personality* (New York: Social Science Research Council, 1951), pp. 59–65. Cf. Thomas and Znaniecki, *op. cit.*, I, p. 68.

[8] Thomas, *The Unadjusted Girl*, pp. 42–43; Thomas, *Source Book*, pp. 14–17; W. I. Thomas, *Primitive Behavior* (New York: McGraw-Hill, 1937), p. 7. See also W. I. Thomas, *On Social Organization and Social Personality*, Morris Janowitz, ed. (Chicago: University of Chicago Press, Phoenix Books, 1966), especially Pt. III.

[9] Thomas and Znaniecki, *op. cit.*, I, p. 44.

social personality, which was perhaps the major recurring interest in his professional career.

Using different terms for his analysis, Thomas approached the study of personality with essentially the same viewpoint and conclusions as had Cooley and George Mead. The social personality is a process of continuously changing adjustment to social influences that present themselves in the form of practical situations. In this process, the individual reacts to what he finds in these situations; on the one hand, he injects his needs into the situation; on the other hand, he must reckon with the implied or expressed attitudes and values of other persons in specific situations. Thomas therefore sought to discover "lines of genesis" by which the personality develops and incorporates patterned responses to experience, i.e., how attitudes and values are developed.[10]

Personality was consequently viewed as a situational variable composed of such subvariables as behavior, attitudes, and "schemes." Every new situation, particularly those in early life, presents itself as initially indeterminate; the individual's behavior derives either from imposed social definitions or spontaneous definitions—or an unequal rivalry between the two. In any case, the individual must in practice "analyze" the situation to determine appropriate attitudes, though these become distinct only by manifesting themselves in behavior. With greater exposure to situations, the individual organizes definitions into generalized schemes of situations, which provide referential rules by which the individual seeks to control social reality for his needs. However, each individual is confronted by certain unique and critical experiences that provoke one or more particularized definitions. These deviations from general experience cause modification of existent schemes or construction of more or less divergent schemes whose manifestation in behavior reveals the essential uniqueness of each personality.

In view of the rich variety of specific personality developments, Thomas sought typical lines of genesis so that the personality variable in situations might be reasonably simplified and made amenable to some kind of economical investigation. As a result, we have his classic formulation of the Bohemian, the Philistine, and the Cre-

10 *Ibid.*, III, 11–13.

66

ative Personality.[11] The true Philistine is characterized by stable, conformist definitions of situations; his attitudes and behavior patterns merely reproduce prevailing social values. If the Philistine is over-socialized, the Bohemian reveals a personality development marked by mutually contradictory or inconsistent attitudes that sharply diverge from prevailing social definitions. Quite different from either of these types is the Creative Personality, which results from a reciprocal interplay between attitudes and social values, and which somehow includes attitudes receptive to change in the direction of some definite aim. Thus, the creative individual is capable of redefining recurring situations in accordance with his own development. Here again, of course, Thomas returns to the descriptive level in tracing types of personality development. But it is clear that he was also concerned with sociological explanations of alternative developments; one of his suggested programs for research specifically points to the role of unique experiences and the character of referential social groups (e.g., the family) as possible leads.[12]

The import of the situational approach for the analysis of social change was not disregarded by Thomas, for that problem is obviously a crucial part of such an orientation. However, he did not pursue the problem systematically, so that we are unable to find in his writings any explicit theory of social change. Yet there are some useful clues. Thomas identified two sources of change—the difficulty of transmitting social codes within the group and the introduction of new techniques, values, etc., either by conscious means or by chance.[13] Both factors present alterations in the objective conditions of situations (i.e., cultural change), but social change as Thomas appears to have viewed it depends upon attitudinal changes that express acceptance of such redefinitions of situations and translation of these attitudes into behavior. When these occur, the diminished influence of existing social rules on individuals symbolizes a period of relative *social disorganization*. This valuational chaos is removed only when new schemes of behavior

---

[11] *Ibid.*, III, 26–31, 52–53.   [12] Volkart, *op. cit.*, pp. 91, 298.
[13] *Ibid.*, p. 315; Thomas, *Primitive Behavior*, pp. 611–612. Cf. Gisela Hinkle, "The 'Four Wishes' in Thomas' Theory of Social Change," *Social Research*, XIX (December, 1952), pp. 464–484.

and new social rules, better adapted to the changed demands (attitudes) of group members, are produced in the process of *social reconstruction*.[14]

As Thomas pursued these problems and surveyed the available data, the outlines of a sociological methodology were progressively developed to form his most enduring contribution to modern sociology. Somewhat before functionalism had invaded modern anthropology and considerably before its formal introduction and systematic use in contemporary sociology, Thomas had criticized the uncritical comparative method and had underscored the contextual significance of specific social facts. The situational approach, with its focus on the individual in concrete situations, is a particularly clear application of two important functional principles—namely, the delimitation of a "closed" system of behavior, and analysis of the bearing of each variable to others and to the system as a whole. As he became more satisfied with situationalism, he also came to abandon traditional notions of causation for the more cautious method of *functional interrelation*. Instead of regarding values as causes of attitudes and *vice versa*—a position set forth in the first volume of *The Polish Peasant*—Thomas finally phrased the problem of relations between variables in the question: "What antecedents have what consequences?" More specifically, "Individuals differentiated in what ways and placed in what situations react in what pattern of behavior, and what behavioral changes follow what changes in situations?"[15]

Obviously, investigations of a snapshot nature are unsuited to this revised orientation. Therefore, Thomas repeatedly placed emphasis on a careful genetic method designed to reveal the sequence of significant data. Hence his trail-blazing in the field of sociology by insisting on full case records, life histories, and other "human documents," because these provide crucial information about the individual's attitudes, about the significance of specific social groups and values for the individual, about the role of critical situations and altered elements in situations, and about the specific reactions to trains of experience. But the culmination of these tech-

14 Thomas and Znaniecki, *op. cit.*, IV, pp. 2–5.
15 *Ibid.*, I, pp. 11, 18; Volkart, *op. cit.*, pp. 44, 296.

niques, as Thomas revised his reflections in his last decade of professional work, was the translation of these data into adequately verifiable relationships between relevant variables, with the aid of control groups and properly subordinated statistical analysis. Thus a clear insistence on techniques as subsidiary to the demands of significant sociological problems boldly made its way into American sociology.

Florian Znaniecki (1882–1958)

There is some reason to believe that, had Simmel continued his brief but rewarding interest in sociology, his thought and investigations would have developed in the direction taken by Florian Znaniecki. Both men were philosophers before they encountered the problems of the cultural sciences and therefore were inherently concerned not only with the theoretical significance of data, but with basic methodological problems that scientists often ignore or resolve uncritically by hasty reflection. Both men were repelled by conflicting currents of extreme naturalism and mystical idealism, of organismic and atomistic conceptions of society, and by the false dichotomy of stability and change. Both devoted much thought to the articulation of sociology as a distinctive science, with appropriate concepts, techniques, and problems. Finally, both recognized with considerable clarity that human behavior fundamentally involves the organization and objectification of subjective reactions to situations. (Simmel died just when Znaniecki, through his collaboration with Thomas, began to launch an empirical assault on these problems.)

Znaniecki first viewed human behavior through the prism of *culturalism*, a philosophical stance that asserts the relativity of values within an evolving empirical world. This empirical world—actuality—provides objective conditions for individuals who, in the process of experience, convert conditions into data, invest data with meaning, and thereby construct a realm of "cultural reality," or that part of actuality significant for active thought and for experience with empirical objects.[16] The essence, then, of social phenomena is, for Znaniecki, the creation and application of meaning, or *values*. Thus sociology cannot commit the error of unqualified behaviorism with impunity. As a special cultural science, sociology possesses a unique subject matter in meaningful human behavior and its organization, the study of which is fundamental to the understanding of the other, older cultural sciences. Nevertheless, while social values are of central theoretical importance, they are not primary data; they are hidden in the multiform manifestations of behavior and must be inferred from such behavior by careful interpretation. Yet values in themselves constitute a part of an all too speculative philosophy; but they must be viewed in their functional aspect—in their use by definable individuals—before they can furnish the basis for empirical generalizations about human beings. Briefly then, the task of sociology is the scientific investigation of the origin, organization, and dynamics of valuational systems in relation to inter-individual behavior.

These broad sociological problems may be phrased on four different but related levels, each of which entails different complexes of sociological data. The most elementary level, on which Znaniecki places great stress, is concerned with *social actions*—concrete and generalized behavior patterns directed toward other persons as their object. A second level of sociological focus is the area of *social relations*, which signifies the system of reciprocal duties and expectations that guides the mutual social actions of two or more persons. A third level emerges from the preceding two in the form of *social persons*, the social roles acquired by the individual in the course of his social experience. Finally, the most complex level encompasses the organization of interacting social persons as a unit, possessing referential value and functioning to achieve specifically meaningful ends—in short, the *social group*.[17]

These four levels provide what Znaniecki calls the basic "social

16 Florian Znaniecki, *Cultural Reality* (Chicago: University of Chicago Press, 1919), pp. 21, 50, 62.
17 Florian Znaniecki, *The Method of Sociology* (New York: Rinehart, 1934), pp. 107–121.

objects," elementary units of social phenomena abstracted from the otherwise bewildering mass of individual acts. For scientific purposes, however, these social objects are best conceived as dynamic, functional *systems*, theoretically immune from influences that are regarded as external to such units of investigation. In other words, these are logically closed systems whose organization is taken to be relatively autonomous and based on a limited number of interrelated variables. For many years, however, Znaniecki had insisted that the study of social actions is a primary task of sociology, since this most elementary social system is a unit in more complex social systems and logically precedes the examination of such abstract social processes as accommodation, conflict, dissociation, etc.

A dynamic use of the cultural approach is apparent in Znaniecki's orientation to social actions as empirical data. Social actions are explicitly defined first as conscious human actions directed toward other humans as their object. As social systems, however, they are viewed as dynamic patterns of values that exist only as they evolve. Their evolution is manifested in continuous selection, incorporation, and coordination of values by the actor with respect to some segment of experience, a conception that thereby rejects the common but misleading dualism of subjective and objective variables in social phenomena. Or as Znaniecki has phrased it, "an action in its total course manifests a gradual formation of a purpose which becomes gradually realized as it is being formed." [18]

Though social actions are understandably dynamic, they reveal a general pattern that Znaniecki now asserts is too changeful to be called a "structure." In *The Polish Peasant*, as we have already noted, Thomas and Znaniecki sketched the nature of social actions in terms of attitudes and values, but Znaniecki developed his analysis considerably beyond that point as early as 1925, again in 1936, and most recently in his *Cultural Sciences*. Basically, every social action contains for the sociologist an "active tendency," a set of attitudes, and a series of differentiated values relevant to five empirical aspects of the situation.

[18] Florian Znaniecki, *Social Actions* (New York: Farrar and Rinehart, 1936), p. 75; Florian Znaniecki, *Cultural Sciences* (Urbana: University of Illinois Press, 1952), p. 198.

The active tendency,[19] originally called the social tendency and somewhat differently conceptualized from the earlier term, is Znaniecki's substitute for such terms as "wish," "desire," and "urge," which erroneously posit a distinctive precursor of action separate from objective reality. Instead, the tendency is an inferred element in action that operates, in Znaniecki's words, "to realize the purpose of an action." But he is careful to describe the tendency as an emergent property, inherent in the action (not in the organism or the environment), and as revealed in changes in the situation initiated by the actor. Thus, the active tendency corresponds to a "force" progressively redefined during action and guiding individual behavior toward completion of an act. While this is not yet clearly definable on the conceptual level, it is important in analysis of actions containing obstacles to achievement of purpose. Attempts to remove or bypass impediments to completed action indicate to Znaniecki "persistency of tendencies," since recognition of and contention with obstacles clearly imply both some developed purpose (or tendency) and its continuation as an active element. Znaniecki even suggests an operational criterion of persistency in the comparative time periods spent in reacting to "normal" and "impeded" situations of similar purpose.[20]

If active tendencies derive from the course of social actions and social actions are conceived as functional systems of variables, then such tendencies must be related to these variables. Znaniecki has consistently refused to search for specific causes of active tendencies; in view of the difficulties presented by "instinct" theories and extreme cultural determinisms, he merely accepts the tendency as a datum. But the tendency provides an initial contact with some empirical complex, thereby requiring a series of decisions that, on the reflective level, become attitudes. Diverging from an earlier use of the term (which was shared with Thomas), Znaniecki defines attitudes as definitions of situations by the agent, by which two important types of decisions are reached: (1) the selection of significant facts from the empirical complex and relevant values bearing on

---

[19] Florian Znaniecki, *Laws of Social Psychology* (Chicago: University of Chicago Press, 1925), pp. 67–70, 127; *Cultural Sciences*, pp. 217–223, 259.

[20] *Cultural Sciences*, p. 223.

these facts, and (2) whether or not the situation thus defined can be adequately expressed in active behavior.[21] The evolution of attitudes is therefore a psychocultural phenomenon, conditioned by shared values and the judgments of the agent.

Since situations are consecutive and involve varying degrees of repetition, attitudes may develop and be applied in current situations, or they may be abstracted by potential agents as guides not to behavior but to thinking about behavior in other situations. In the former category are what Znaniecki calls *realistic* attitudes, while the latter type are called *ideational* attitudes, ideas about behavior that might be termed "objectified attitudes" or, more familiarly, "standards" and "norms."[22] The importance of ideational attitudes is their wide applicability by an agent. Znaniecki distinguishes in this category *retrospective* attitudes (referring to past situations of the agent), *prospective* attitudes (believed to confront the agent in the future), and *vicarious* attitudes (which refer to past, present, or future situations of other agents).[23] Such a classification, by the way, pointedly re-emphasizes that attitudes are meaningless apart from specific social actions and provides an explanatory tool for some of the inconsistent data of opinion and attitude research.

The definition of the situation in any social action reflects not only the social tendency but the objective aspects of the situation as evaluated by the agent. The empirical world is experienced by the agent not as things, but as values more or less relevant to a given situation. Znaniecki has identified five interrelated sets of values that, when selected and incorporated, comprise social attitudes, or the definition of the situation.[24] There is first the value attributed to the human object(s) of action—friendly or hostile, good or bad, superior or inferior, etc. This is called the *primary social value* in social action and is classified by Znaniecki into values of "accommodation" or "opposition." The instrumental process— the method of social action—likewise reveals the application of values, but of two types. It involves selection of an evaluated *social instrument* (material and/or ideational) for the purpose of produc-

21 *Ibid.*, pp. 242–248.   22 *Ibid.*, pp. 241–243.   23 *Ibid.*, pp. 251–258.
24 *Social Actions*, pp. 72–74.

ing a desired effect on the object (e.g., the speeches of Abraham Lincoln, atomic energy, the results of public opinion polls, a sum of money). But the significant aspect of the instrumental process is not the social instrument itself; it is rather the way the instrument is used—the *social method*. Thus, a given sum of money may be conceived by the defining agent as a bribe, a present, a bonus, compensation for legal services rendered, etc. Obviously, the primary social value conditions the choice of both instruments and their use.

A fourth significant value in social action is the expected reaction of the object to be affected—the *social reaction*. This is of course evaluated in terms of its bearing on the agent's purpose. However, the agent himself comes within the process of evaluation in modifying the social reaction and also as the reaction in turn affects self-feelings. As a result, the "reflected self," the socially evaluated traits of the agent, becomes an important element in the definition of the situation. If the reflected self is especially emphasized by the agent, an inevitable consequence is a certain devaluation of the primary social object and a re-evaluation of social instruments, which together produce an egocentric flavor. (Znaniecki calls this process "social subjectivation.") Yet when the reflected self is excluded from action, the significance of the resultant definition lies in its emphasis on objectivity, on extra-personal standards of evaluation of that action. Such "social objectivation" symbolizes recognition by the agent of shared values, and their acceptance by the agent is based on the fact that they are shared rather than that acceptance brings social approval to the agent.[25] In other words, cultural norms are valued for their own sake, not for their results.

Znaniecki's detailed analysis of social actions as dynamic systems viewed from the standpoint of the actor extends and considerably refines the pioneer work of Thomas. With the exception of the more recent approach by Parsons (see Chapter 9), it has no peer in contemporary sociological thought. Yet it has somehow lacked wide acceptance and is still rarely cited by researchers. But Znaniecki's treatment gives us a keen, comprehensive view of neglected fundamentals in social phenomena, and by his carefully thought out implications, contributes a highly useful orientation to the crucial problems of dynamism and change.

[25] *Laws of Social Psychology*, pp. 272–286; *Social Actions*, pp. 52–57.

While social actions are scientifically approached as closed systems of data, Znaniecki has repeatedly denied that they are either static or mechanical. The process of defining situations preparatory to action constitutes an inner dynamic that is not mystical, but is simply the empirical possibility of organizing the variables of social action in numerous ways. There is neither chaos nor mechanical order in social phenomena, for these conceptions are foreign to the peculiar order of social facts, which is essentially one of changing stability. In the light of this orientation, Znaniecki therefore classifies social-action systems in terms of their potentiality of producing change.[26] The lowest potentiality is found in *habitual* or repetitive actions, a polar type involving relatively little reflection by the agent and therefore permitting the formation of purpose at the very moment when the action begins. An intermediate type is *imitative* or reproductive action, in which initial definitions of the situation (i.e., the reproduction of some desired model) are revised during the early phases of action as the agent discovers situational obstacles to the desired goal. Once revised, however, the purpose becomes stabilized somewhat early in the course of the social action and remains unchanged.

For Znaniecki, the type of social action most distinctly human is the *creative* action, in which new values are produced by the agent. Characteristically, such actions manifest continuing alteration and evaluation of purpose throughout the duration of action; in effect, this expresses an attempt to reorganize the system of action in the light of a definition of the situation that interprets certain essential values as logically or practically incompatible. The solution is an innovation in that the basic elements of the situation are so revalued and re-combined that the completed action presents consequences that are not derivable either from the objective conditions of the situation or from previous reactions to a similar configuration of objective conditions. A remarkable but unmeasurable proportion of human actions are in this sense more or less creative, but they are often forgotten because the innovator is not aware of their significance or they fail to receive social acceptance and thus eventual conversion into habitual and imitative actions.

Once the nature of social actions is illuminated, it is possible to

[26] *Cultural Sciences*, pp. 200–212; Znaniecki in Blumer, *op. cit.*, p. 98.

understand more complex social systems. The *social relation*, for example, is a useful abstraction from repetitive social actions; it is simply the elementary bond between interacting individuals that is manifested in recognized values (duties and responsibilities) and that determines their reciprocal behavior in some defined situation. From the standpoint of a given actor, a related cluster of social relations constitutes a *social role*, a concept enabling sociologists to focus on the social aspects of human personalities rather than on the total personality of individuals. The approach of Thomas exemplifies the latter tendency, with the result that his analysis has been more nearly social psychological than sociological. Znaniecki, on the other hand, has been a keen advocate of studying social persons only in terms of single social roles conceptually isolated from the individual organism and combined with similarly isolated social roles of others to form *social groups*.

The social role is conceptualized by Znaniecki as a particularly significant complex that provides a crucial link between social persons and social groups. And like other social entities, the social role exhibits a dynamic organization of interdependent features.[27] Obviously, there is the actor or social person, but since no individual can assume a social role in isolation, a necessary condition is the existence of a *social circle*—several individuals involved in the performance of the role and bound to the actor by some common interest or complex of values. The normal functioning of the social circle is an indication that an actor is considered specially capable of performing some *social function*, which can be analyzed into a number of specifically valued actions (social, economic, technical, etc.) designed to satisfy the expressed needs of the circle. In connection with his function, moreover, the actor is granted a definite *social status* by his circle, consisting of rights, privileges, rewards, and the special recognition associated with the performance of his social function, from which he develops a relevant "self-image" or *social self*.

[27] *Cultural Sciences*, p. 397; Florian Znaniecki, "Social Groups as Products of Cooperating Individuals," *American Journal of Sociology*, XLIV (May, 1939), pp. 805–806; Florian Znaniecki, *The Social Role of the Man of Knowledge* (New York: Columbia University Press, 1940), pp. 13–14.

An excellent illustration of this type of analysis may be found in Znaniecki's work on the "man of knowledge,"[28] a class of roles that is empirically distinguishable into a number of familiar social roles—the technologist, the inventor, the sage, the scholar, etc. The technological leader, for example, operates in an occupational circle (military, religious, political, etc.) primarily as a definer of problematic situations and as the distributor of research problems for the technological expert. The latter role consists of summarizing relevant knowledge without regard for its practical application; and, in some cases, it may also require some experimentation or attempts to discover new knowledge and techniques for presentation to the technological leader.

Znaniecki theorized that role performance depends upon the relative emphasis given these components by the actor, since each component is a variable. Thus, should the actor emphasize: (*a*) *function*, the result would be highly dedicated performance of relevant skills, regardless of reward; (*b*) *status*, the result would be behavior designed to maintain one's reputation in the circle or group, regardless of compromises with function; (*c*) *social self*, the result would be actions calculated to raise self-esteem, regardless of the ill effects on other participants; (*d*) *social circle*, the result would be actions that protect, or defer to the welfare of, associates, despite the defection from duties called for by the social role.

By extension, as one continues in a role, one may change relative interest in these components. It is assumed that experience is necessarily accompanied by re-interpretations that cannot easily be predicted. While Znaniecki does not attempt explanations of such changes, he does indicate contributing conditions—such as the range of permissible variation in a role, changes in the personal and interest level of the social circle, changes in the evaluation of the actor (whether or not these are "justified"), and the impact of one's other roles in related or competing social groups.

In addition to this dynamic element, social roles normally appear in conjunction with complementary social roles in such a way that each reveals a definable bearing and influence on the other social roles. Under these conditions, the social circle, which is an incipient

[28] *Social Role of the Man of Knowledge*, pp. 33–55, 72–79, 100–138.

social group, becomes transformed into that more complex social system. Znaniecki's genetic approach to social groups (as an evolutionary process) leads to the conclusion that social groups always begin with specific functions performed in more or less definite circles of "followers." When the social persons involved recognize a collective purpose or function, the common values thus created (or extended) form the bases for a selective bond that generates a feeling of unity and separate identity. An important part of this development is the objectification and standardization of those roles considered essential to the collective operation of the group; each of these roles becomes the permanent property of the group and is assigned on a temporary basis to a succession of specifically qualified individuals. In short, the actions, relations, and social roles of a set of individuals have become "institutionalized." [29]

Essentially, then, a vital theoretical connection between "institution" and "social group" has been suggested, and even persuasively substantiated. As generally used by sociologists, "institution" appears to be a philosophic rather than an inductive concept, referring to specially sanctioned value systems that reflect a battery of "needs" or "interests." Thus, "institution" seems to summarize broad cultural categories, such as political, economic, religious, kinship, etc. But the empirical reference of these categories is either vague or vagrant; in some usages, institutions are connected with individual needs; in others, with "society"; and in a third, with a venerable social heritage. Znaniecki, on the other hand, has rejected both the conception of institution as a mere biopsychological product and the notion that institutions are basically external in source to social persons. Instead, institutions are shown to be inseparable from the development and functioning of specific social groups; every organized social group has, in fact, an institutional aspect, and similarly organized social groups contain the empirical foundation for some generalized "social institution."

In this manner, according to Znaniecki, "institution" is accorded a strictly sociological status, rather than a synthetic position acquired by invasion of other, specialized cultural disciplines. The so-

[29] Znaniecki, "Social Groups . . . ," *op. cit.*, pp. 799–811; Florian Znaniecki, *Social Relations and Social Roles* (San Francisco: Chandler, 1965), ch. 10.

called "economic institution," for example, is the proper province of economics with respect to easily recognized economic activities and associated values; but these become data for the sociologist's study of institutions to the extent that they reflect the structure of organized social groups, some of which may not be exclusively organized for economic functions.

The institutional aspect of organized social groups, which reveals itself in "impersonally patterned functions and statuses of [its] members" is conceptualized by Znaniecki as the *group institution*.[30] This term apparently coincides with the more familiar "system of institutional roles." However, some social groups are partly institutionalized by other groups; i.e., the former derive some of their functions, rights, and privileges from the latter, as in the case of a state university founded and supported by a state legislature. In such an event the "dependent" group is called an *institutionalized group*.[31]

Znaniecki at this point suggests the nature of the connection between institution, group, and society. For society is, sociologically speaking, the "total complex of social groups which are institutionalized by a large, united and relatively independent social group." From this definition, societies may be classified according to the sources of institutionalization: the political society (the state), the religious society (the church), the national culture society (a nationality),[32] and the class society (some organized social class). Though this classification is helpful, many would perhaps hesitate to accept an orientation to society that seems to exclude the more ephemeral social relations and groupings, so brilliantly analyzed by Simmel. But Znaniecki sees no genuine ground for opposition, since these less patterned social phenomena are often precursors of organized groupings. A genetic rather than a cross-sectional approach is thus indispensable in distinguishing significant data from the interesting curiosities that detain the theoretic function of sociology.

[30] Florian Znaniecki, "Social Organization and Institutions," in Georges Gurvitch and Wilbert E. Moore, eds., *Twentieth Century Sociology* (New York: Philosophical Library, 1945), pp. 207–212.

[31] *Ibid.*, pp. 212–215.

[32] *Ibid.*, pp. 215–216; Florian Znaniecki, *Modern Nationalities* (Urbana: University of Illinois Press, 1952), pp. 15–21.

SELECTED REFERENCES

Thomas, W. I., *On Social Organization and Social Personality*, Morris Janowitz, ed. (Chicago: University of Chicago Press, 1966).
Volkart, Edmund H., *Social Behavior and Personality* (New York: Social Science Research Council, 1951).

4

George H. Mead:
Interactional Theory

Though Simmel and Cooley had analyzed the subtle but important processes of social interaction, their conceptions were tentative, and they failed to ruffle the intellectual apparatus of their contemporaries. During the first two decades of this century, the dominant explanations of interpersonal behavior were based rather on some catalog of instincts or drives—or they drew sustenance from the newly dogmatic formulations of Freud and his variegated followers. Perhaps the leading opponents of biologized and metaphoric theories were John Dewey and J. Mark Baldwin, who provided a temporary reference point—as outsiders—for American sociologists concerned with social psychology. But it was G. H. Mead, a philosopher who called himself a "social behaviorist," who transformed theoretical clues into a focused set of theories on socialization and the functioning of groups.

Mead's basic theory of social interaction rests on the concepts of *adaptation* or *adjustment* and "the social," which he defines in a special way. Adaptation (and re-adaptation) is not the passive fitting of organism to environment, but an active process in which the organism affects (and partially controls) aspects of the environment. Consequently, adaptation is an evolving process that typically produces *emergents* as links between organismic and environmental properties.[1] Unlike deterministic theories of many hues, this conception emphasizes the interaction of components—what Mead called "the conditions of passage"—rather than the causal imprint of selected components. But the emergent—the adaptive or adjustive response—is said to be derived from the "conditioning character of the present," and not merely the first five years of life.

However, adaptation in humans is a phenomenon of sociality or *the social*. Mead described the social as an aspect of experience in which interactions simultaneously partake of the old and the new, the components and the product. "Sociality is the capacity of being several things at once." [2] Indeed, for Mead, the social dimension is intermediate conceptually (and perhaps temporally) between the properties of individuals and cultural products. The social, in short, corresponds to the process of readjustment among persons. From this perspective, the social represents inherent possibilities of change, not as an accidental or idiosyncratic process, but in patterned and therefore comprehensible ways.

Sociology, then, is distinctively the study of fundamental social processes as manifestations of the social or the adaptational aspect. Mead in fact argued that sociology's proper task is to clarify the "physiology" of social processes, to establish the actual functioning of persons in interaction, rather than to present an "anatomy" of social institutions or structures drained of the essence of sociality (as just defined).[3] Thus Mead refused to honor the dichotomy of order and change, viewing behavior as the empirical manifestation of the individual's experience in following or diverging from cues supplied by his environment.[4]

[1] Anselm Strauss, ed., *George Herbert Mead on Social Psychology* (Chicago: University of Chicago Press, 1964), p. 31; George H. Mead, *The Philosophy of the Present* (Chicago: Open Court Pub. Co., 1932), p. 64.

[2] Strauss, *op. cit.*, p. 339; Mead, *Philosophy of the Present*, p. 49.

[3] George H. Mead, *Philosophy of the Act* (Chicago: University of Chicago Press, 1938), p. 498.

[4] George H. Mead, *Mind, Self, and Society* (Chicago: University of Chicago Press, 1934), pp. 2–7.

DEVELOPMENT OF SOCIAL PERSONALITY

The first theoretical problem for Mead is the dynamics of social interaction itself. Simply stated, social interaction necessarily involves the presentation of cues (invitations to reaction) in the form of gestures, symbols, and language. These cues require responses, but Mead assumes that others perceive meaning in these cues, which Mead defines as the agreed upon response(s) appropriate to specific cues.[5] Consequently, social interaction is communication of meanings through initiating and responsive behavior. But meanings are complex emergents that arise from the vicissitudes of interaction and then become objectified in either gesture or language. Likewise, meanings (through language) stimulate further interaction (adjustive responses) by selective evocation of responses.

From the standpoint of new participants in social interaction (infants, children), meaning is first external and irrelevant to behavior. However, social process intrudes meaning on behavior and thereby changes behavior. The course of this process constitutes a second theoretical problem, which Mead called the development of "mind," but which we can appropriately label the emergence of "social personality." As conceptualized by Mead, the behavior of human organisms becomes significant when it can be shown to respond to cues communicated by other organisms in a socially adaptive manner. In social adaptation, the responsive organism interprets the behavioral cue as requiring a complementary or similar act (the "completion" of the initial act).[6] What explains the development of this interpretation and of the patterned responses that implement such interpretations?

Mead adopts (or adapts) Cooley's theory of the "looking-glass self" at this point. Essentially, he attributes the conversion of the organism into a social personality to processes of exchange and communication between individuals. The major mechanisms are not clearly described by Mead, but they seem to involve (*a*) gestures, signs, and language that experimentally evoke gestures from

[5] *Ibid.*, pp. 45–76, 145.   [6] *Ibid.*, pp. 76–82.

others; (*b*) responsive gestures to the latter, which in turn motivate others to alter their intended response in line with the previous reply; and (*c*) in each participant, an internal "conversation" in which the intended response is compared with the recalled effect of previous responses on others.[7] Though Mead did not make explicit reference to learning theory, it seems in retrospect that his analysis is based on processes of reward and punishment and on reinforcement in the development of response patterns.

In the earliest phases of the social personality, these mechanisms produce a practical distinction between organism and others, the cardinal aspect of which is the organism's conception of itself as both subject and object.[8] Self (organism as object) is in modern terms a set of attitudes and values that reflect the interpreted responses of others toward the organism and its behavior. It follows that "the self" (or self-conception) refers to continuous processes of social interaction, during which the "structure" and "functioning" of the self are conditioned by the special character and consistency of responses by others and by the individual's ability to select and interpret such responses at successive points in minimally organized social interaction. Obviously, Mead assumes (*a*) that the interacting persons possess normal physiological abilities, (*b*) that some persons in social-interaction processes already possess developed selves and experience in such interaction, and (*c*) that these interaction processes are not disrupted by the departure of the participants.

Mead pursues the developmental character of the self by specifying the changes in the individual's organization of his experiences with others.[9] In the earlier phases of the process of self-emergence, the individual comes to adapt his actions to his perceptions of the attitudes of specific persons toward him. The self under these circumstances is therefore dependent on the more direct, personal forms of social interaction with an "empirical" organization that seems capricious and erratic to the observer. With greater experience in social interaction, a more developed self arises, based on the individual's generalization and abstraction of attitudes and values from the recurrent interchange of symbols with

---

[7] *Ibid.*, pp. 134, 139-144.   [8] *Ibid.*, p. 138.   [9] *Ibid.*, pp. 158-171.

some set of persons. This higher-level generalization, which in effect "structures" social experience, is called the "generalized other," though Mead does not explain how the more empirical organization of interactions is transformed into the conceptualization of a crystallized set of social cues. In any case, the individual's conception of the generalized other may be taken as the mark of his verified participation in a group or social system.[10] Of course, the pre-existence of a functioning group also implies the pre-existence of a generalized other for its established membership. Indeed, it may well be assumed that the successful acquisition of a generalized other for a given individual normally depends on prior consensus on a generalized other among his "circle of interactors." Parenthetically, from this analysis, we may define a social group or definite social system in researchable form as a set of persons with demonstrably common conceptions of a generalized other, with respect to some limited task, objective, or recurrent activity.

The generalized other, then, is specific to limited social settings (groups, circles, cliques, etc.). Consequently, the self develops by acquiring (and organizing, accommodating, or insulating) different generalized others. "There are all sorts of different selves answering to all sorts of different social reactions." [11] It appears that the normal complement of "selves" that make up "the self" (or social personality) is closely related to the set of social roles that can be identified with given individuals. Each self (the elementary self, in Mead's usage) is conceptually linked to an appropriate role. More accurately, each self refers to socially mediated evaluations of individual response patterns, while "role" identifies the content and structure of these response patterns.

In Mead's framework, self, role, and generalized other form a minimal triad in which the major emphasis is given to the relation between self and generalized other. Thus, while Mead clearly derives roles and selves from the generalized other, the role (or role-playing) tends to recede in importance in favor of *role-taking* (the practice of anticipating the typical responses of others in a recurrent interaction system). Through role-taking, in which the individual evaluates his intended action as others would (based on past

10 *Ibid.*, pp. 90–91.   11 *Ibid.*, pp. 142–144.

85

responses), others indirectly control the pattern of behavior of the individual.[12] Thus, by inference, role-playing normally involves both role-taking (concern for the appropriate generalized other) and the intrusion of a prior self-conception that is confirmed or diminished by one's conception of the generalized others.

The rash judgment that Mead posits an "oversocialized conception of man," however, is belied by Mead's attention to the essential two-way nature of adaptation,[13] and more directly, the much-noted distinction between the "I" and the "me." Because of the easy reification of these two "components," the "I" and the "me" may be misinterpreted if we follow Mead's discussion too literally. The "me" may be described as the set of attitudes one cognitively accepts as a reflection of the generalized other. Note that the "me" can be traced to perception and evaluation of available (or previously available) responses of significant others. The "I," on the other hand, is for Mead the uncertain, unpredictable reaction of the individual to the practical implications of the "me" component. There is considerable ambiguity and vagueness about Mead's conception of the "I." [14] It seems to be a "residual" category, rather than a positive one. However, the "I" appears to represent the individual's experimental or exploratory approach to role specifications. Indeed, Mead suggests that the responses identified with the "I" are unpremeditated and receive attention only after they are made. "The 'I' appears in our experience in memory. It is only after we have acted that we know what we have done; it is only after we have spoken that we know what we have said." [15]

Clearly, social personality defined solely in terms of the "I" and the "me," as Mead suggests in the latter portion of Part III (The Self) of *Mind, Self, and Society*, is not only incomplete but contradicts his earlier discussion of the genesis of the self in the very same part. On several occasions, Mead refers to the "I" as the ego, a very inaccurate equation of two different concepts. Yet Mead's analysis

[12] *Ibid.*, pp. 90, 138, 155–156.

[13] *Ibid.*, p. 215. See also Gerald Chasin, "George Herbert Mead: Social Psychologist of the Moral Society," *Berkeley Journal of Sociology*, IX (1964), pp. 95–117.

[14] *Mind, Self, and Society*, pp. 175–178, 196–199.   [15] *Ibid.*, p. 196.

of the self implies a third component—a socially derived but somewhat autonomous set of personally held attitudes toward oneself as social object. Freud's concept of the ego is obviously appropriate at this point—but it is not necessary to transfer Freudian theories of ego-functioning. Mead in effect intimates the operation of this third component when he suggests that people tend to see themselves as others see them, and especially in the phenomena of self-respect and superiority or inferiority feelings.[16]

The relation of the "I" and the "me," however, depends on the nature of the situation in which the person functions.[17] Mead develops a brief but highly significant analysis of this issue in an unwitting confirmation of Simmel and Durkheim. The "me" is emphasized when acceptance in a social system or the benefit of its values and services is dominant for the individual. It is assumed here that the radius of personal concern and the appropriate circle of significant others are virtually identical. On the other hand, when doubts, "issues," and the need to transcend a limited social context through thought processes are dominant in given individuals, the "I" is released by shifting to another and wider circle of persons or values. If Mead at this point ignores the problem of motivational differences, he does suggest that the "I" constitutes a link between the person and new group experiences. The novelty of the "I" may be expressed in deviant behavior within a group or, more significantly, in the selection of another source of a generalized other.[18]

"One appeals from fixed conventions which no longer have any meaning to a community in which the rights shall be publicly recognized, and one appeals to others on the assumption that there is a group of organized others that answer to one's appeal—even if the appeal be made to posterity."

In short, the "I" (and the ego component) serves as a mechanism for evaluating the worth of a prevailing generalized other and for

[16] *Ibid.,* pp. 68, 204.

[17] *Ibid.,* p. 199. Cf. Georg Simmel, *Conflict and the Web of Group-Affiliation,* trans. Kurt H. Wolff and Reinhard Bendix (New York: Free Press, 1955), pp. 140–154.

[18] *Mind, Self, and Society,* p. 199; Robert K. Merton, *Social Theory and Social Structure* (New York: Free Press, 1957), pp. 239–242, 357–368.

87

selecting an alternative source of actual or anticipatory self-evaluation. Here is a rather explicit (and yet largely ignored) identification of the phenomena of "reference-group behavior," which Merton has analyzed and codified in recent years. The implication in Mead's writings is that personality develops through differentially patterned combinations of behavior derived from "I" and "me" components.[19] Indeed, it may be inferred that the social personality develops by substituting new or expansive reference groups for earlier ones. Surprisingly, Mead assumes "normal" processes of adaptation and socialization, ignoring the widespread phenomena of disturbed or maladjusted persons and malfunctioning groups or social systems.

LEADERSHIP

Employing this basic conceptual framework of "self" and "generalized other," Mead tried to account for the social derivation of leadership behavior (and roles) in social systems. Leaders tend to be persons who more or less accurately identify the values of a generalized other and also respond to these value implications by experimental assertions of the "I" (and ego) component.[20] Mead does not deal with the process by which preliminary "leadership" behavior is evaluated by others. However, by inference, the conversion of "I" attitudes into social behavior must in practice be positively evaluated by others in order to justify continuation of such behavior. Likewise by inference, the leader "candidate" feels —and tries to communicate this to others—that his "novel" responses are genuinely consonant with the generalized other. Consequently, the leadership role is, sociologically, a validated interpretation of the generalized other. Extending Mead's formulation somewhat, then, the "politics" of groups is essentially a process of competition between "I"-dominant persons who—whatever their ulterior motivations—seek to implement their personal conception of the generalized other. It follows that, over an extended period, leadership behavior must either represent or effectively alter the

19 *Mind, Self, and Society*, pp. 214–215.   20 *Ibid.*, pp. 214–216, 256–257.

generalized other.[21] Mead seems to favor the hypothesis that the leader, in interpreting the generalized other, eventually produces changes in the responses of interacting individuals, and therefore in the generalized other itself.

Another facet of leadership roles, according to Mead, is the ability to relate two or more generalized others.[22] This is of course possible only in individuals whose social personality is "I"- (and ego-) dominant and who have been exposed to members of other groups or social categories. Mead assigns great importance to mass communication and literature (novels, drama, etc.) as social mechanisms that make accessible a greater diversification of roles and generalized others. He does not attempt the theoretical leap from exposure to influence, however; the differential response to the existence of other groups, and thus the assumption or denial of potential leadership roles, are simply not identified as problems. Thus, "I"-dominant personality may be taken as a necessary but not a sufficient condition for leadership. In any case, Mead contends that only through leadership roles are groups (rather than individuals) capable of interacting with one another.

INSTITUTIONS AND SOCIAL CHANGE

Mead approached social organization from the standpoint of interpersonal interaction and evaluation, perhaps because he largely ignored the complex phenomena of bureaucratic organization over considerable time periods. In fact, Mead viewed institutions in very simple terms, assuming that institutions are equivalent to sets of "common responses" and shared "generalized others." [23] While the practical necessity of social control—processes that insure conformity to values of the generalized other—is often noted, Mead assigned primary responsibility for effective control to the "me" component and to the related processes of personal confrontation with representatives of the generalized other. Impersonal and indi-

21 Cf. Gaetano Mosca, *The Ruling Class*, trans. Hannah D. Kahn (New York: McGraw-Hill, 1939), pp. 244, 415–438.
22 *Mind, Self, and Society*, pp. 256–257.   23 *Ibid.*, pp. 167, 262–263.

rect methods of control, and even coercion, are largely excluded from consideration. Indeed, the underlying model with which Mead worked was apparently that of a small, relatively static community in which status differences are either non-existent or blurred.

Despite its limitations, Mead's approach to institutions provides clues to an analysis of social change—or of early phases in social change. Defining an institutional pattern as a narrowed range of responses by others to a given individual in specific circumstances (e.g., a war hero, a bereaved parent, a lovesick adolescent), Mead suggested that these responses (or anticipated responses) control the behavior of individuals by presenting more or less general prescriptions for behavior.[24] Mead contended that institutional patterns often (and characteristically) permit variation, flexibility, and originality in attitude and behavior. In fact, the operation of institutions through responses of significant others normally creates tendencies toward both "conformist" and "variant" behavior. Parenthetically, Mead recognized the existence of institutions that severely limit behavioral choice (the medieval church, the military); but he did not specify the conditions under which "oppressive" vs. "permissive" institutions develop.

But Mead assumed that institutional forms implicitly encourage individual innovations by transmitting values or ideals that are implied but not "adequately expressed." [25] In other words, Mead claimed that effective socialization tends to stimulate in some persons (a) an attachment for socially derived goals and (b) a dissatisfaction with aspects of available behavioral means. Innovation of some social significance, then, is a latent derivation of social interaction processes and of individual attempts to clarify and extend the pattern of institutional cues in relatively simple social systems.

In highly developed societies, however, Mead finds either inadequate perception of a generalized other or competition between two or more generalized others and institutional forms. In these circumstances, the individual is essentially "marginal" or isolated from significant responses. Mead not only asserts that the expected form of response is hostility (and resultant conflict) and emergent

24 *Ibid.*, pp. 167, 210, 262–263.   25 *Ibid.*, pp. 164, 217.

or re-emergent feelings of self-superiority over others, but he hypothesizes that such conflicts or oppositions are ultimately resolved by innovations ("reconstructions of the particular social situations and modifications of the given framework of social relationships . . . , these reconstructions and modifications being performed, as we have said, by the minds of the individuals in whose experience or between whose selves these conflicts take place").[26]

By implication, Mead translated the phenomena of social change into processes of innovation and processes of evaluating and accepting innovations. Innovations that eventuate in change ("social reconstruction" is Mead's term) depend upon sufficient common interest (a shared generalized other) among members of a social system to insure consideration of the innovation. Furthermore, acceptance of social innovations involves the resolution of differences between competing particularized generalized others by means of a new and more comprehensive generalized other.[27] For Mead, only individuals who have developed complex personalities (composed of different "me's" derived from several generalized others and an "I," presumably with its derivative ego) are competent to conceive a more universal generalized other and to create innovative behavioral responses in accord with that conception.[28]

The dissemination of the innovation therefore presupposes transmission of a revised generalized other, which in turn means alterations in the selves of the persons to be affected. Social change and personality change are therefore reciprocally connected. However, Mead does not present the mechanism or linkage processes by which a pre-existent self—constructed and validated by past responses of significant others—reconstructs itself.

Though Mead failed to construct a comprehensive theory of social change, this was apparently not his intention—nor was his conceptual framework adequate for such a task. Yet Mead, following the implications of his concept of adaptation, maintained a fairly explicit evolutionary approach to change and progress. His pragmatic-rationalist premises (derived primarily from Dewey and Peirce) led him to assume not only greater complexity of social processes, but greater and more efficient levels of adaptation by means of

[26] *Ibid.*, pp. 307–308.　　[27] *Ibid.*, pp. 308–309.　　[28] *Ibid.*, pp. 90, 275.

this complexity.[29] In this respect, it seems, the utility of his "social behaviorism" (personal interaction processes) becomes quite questionable. On the one hand, social complexity entails extensive specialization of groups and roles, which Mead explains as consequences of prior conflicts and oppositions. But these processes likewise involve practical difficulties in effective identification and reflection of generalized others.

Mead's "solution" to this theoretical discrepancy takes two forms. An implicit "solution" may be found in Mead's interpretation of the basic structure of society. In his view, society is a "systematic order of individuals in which each has a more or less differentiated activity."[30] In time, the individual is constrained to shift his role-taking activities in some socially ordered succession. From this experience, the individual comes to fashion for himself a progressively more adaptive generalized other, which reflects his perception of common features in specific generalized others. In short, Mead suggests that immersion in a structured variety of social demands and responses produces increasing capacity to coordinate this complexity in a meaningful manner. This of course now raises two crucial questions for students of society: (1) What social (and social psychological) variables hinder or encourage "movement" in exposure to some succession of roles? (2) What factors account for differences in personality among those with similar careers in role succession?

The second theoretical clue may be found in Mead's brief analysis of religion. The distinctive feature of religion for Mead is the expansion of a limited generalized other to "the larger world," "to the universe at large." Religious attitudes signify feelings of identification of self with a generalized other without concern for a definite goal.[31] Consequently, the function of religious ideas and religious organization is either to superimpose an expanded generalized other, or to create ideological linkages between social contexts, to which the individual can respond. In effect, Mead distinguishes a religious *function* from religious *forms*; and he regards the latter as a variable that in practice is adapted to social and personal require-

---

[29] *Ibid.*, pp. 310ff.   [30] *Philosophy of the Present*, p. 87.
[31] *Mind, Self, and Society*, pp. 275–276, 293–298.

ments for more indirect and impersonal control. Religious ideas thus may serve as components of social change, either as innovations themselves, or as a means of integrating innovations with the social interaction processes of a given population.[32]

SELECTED REFERENCES

Blumer, Herbert, "Sociological Implications of the Thought of George Herbert Mead," *American Journal of Sociology*, LXXI (March, 1966), 535–544.

McCall, George J., and J. L. Simmons, *Identities and Interactions* (New York: Free Press, 1966).

Mead, George H., *Selected Writings* (Indianapolis: Bobbs-Merrill, 1964).

Natanson, Maurice, *The Social Dynamics of George H. Mead* (Washington: Public Affairs Press, 1956).

Strauss, Anselm, ed., *George Herbert Mead on Social Psychology* (Chicago: University of Chicago Press, 1964).

[32] Cf. Hans H. Gerth and C. Wright Mills, trans. and eds., *From Max Weber: Essays in Sociology* (New York: Oxford University Press, 1946), ch. 13.

Robert Park:

Processes in the Community

Perhaps the single most influential person in American sociology is
Robert E. Park, whose approach to sociology is still widely accepted after more than forty years of persistent application. Unlike
other leading sociologists, Park was a journalist in experience and
temperament, and his writings often reflect the incorrigible curiosity and the disciplined superficiality of the reporter rather than the
usual approach of the theorizer. Indeed, Park's series of provocative essays that combine the flavor of the Sunday supplement with
the discipline of a sociologically oriented city editor have been
unique until now. This strong element of immediacy may explain the essentially unsystematic nature of his work and the numerous inconsistencies of definition and emphasis that Milla Alihan
clearly traced in Park's ecological writings. Yet there is a latent
pattern that has been somewhat obscured by the immense popularity of Park's teachings.

The core of Park's work is a curious amalgam of influences.
Through firsthand contacts he absorbed some of the ideas of John
Dewey (then at the University of Michigan) and of William James

and, most significantly, the formal concepts of Georg Simmel. At Chicago, Small and Thomas undoubtedly made some impression on his nascent thoughts about sociological problems. Rather early in Park's career, Booker T. Washington introduced him to the social investigation of the Negro. There is also evidence that Spencer, Darwin, and perhaps Marx retained a pervasive attraction for Park, but neither Durkheim nor Weber can be shown to have been theoretically useful in his formulations. However, his respect for Spencer and Darwin probably made Park receptive to the approach and theory of the plant and animal ecologists, for the latter came to be a predominant influence.

By 1921, as these strands of thought mixed, Park, in collaboration with Ernest W. Burgess, worked out a tentative synthesis, presented in *An Introduction to the Science of Sociology*. Thereafter, the "super-reporter," [1] as he called himself, proceeded to make several quasi-sociological studies in the field of immigration and Americanization. By the end of the twenties he had begun to publish a stream of exploratory essays in urban sociology, race relations, selected problems of social deviation, and human ecology. Most important, however, was his stimulating teaching and encouragement of sociological research at the University of Chicago from 1916 to 1939, when he "retired" to Fisk University.

BASIC STRUCTURES OF SOCIETY

Despite the varied sources of his ideas, if we can disregard some of the discrepancies in definition that reflect his failure to review his previous formulations, Park actually constructed a rather neat conceptual system. It is essentially a simple, straightforward, apparently neutral orientation to social phenomena, without much embroidery or highly sophisticated overtones, and with little of the muddy theorizing usually attributed to German idealism. Consequently, it has appealed to many American sociologists as a down-to-earth, realistic approach that could accompany empirical re-

[1] Howard W. Odum, *American Sociology* (New York: Longmans, Green & Co., Ltd., 1951), pp. 132–133.

search. And it was fortunately timed, for it can fairly be said that it faced no genuine competition from any other sociological system in the United States. *An Introduction to the Science of Sociology* therefore became the first handy American textbook of general sociology; in fact, the viewpoint and many of the concepts of this Chicago "bible" have been consistently echoed in virtually every introductory text published during the last thirty years.

Though Park himself did not describe it in these terms, his approach to sociology was primarily in terms of two interdependent "ideal types," which he conceived to encompass the basic conditions of human behavior. But he was convinced that sociology could not fruitfully study conditions as such, that, following Simmel, social phenomena were best conceived as processes of becoming, of changes in the life of a group or grouping. However, the fundamental social process is that of "interaction of elements and forces," by which Park means the social participation of persons in groups. This viewpoint inevitably led to emphasis on social relations [2]—a concept that Park never defined clearly—with secondary focus on social groups and institutions.

It was in the attempt to define the context of social relations that Park distinguished the ideal types of "society"—or the moral order —and "community"—or the ecological order.[3] This unfortunate choice of terms (not concepts) has led to considerable misunderstanding, since their use by Park contradicted their widely accepted meaning, and since Park often varied in his own usage. Yet, a little "rationalization" of this apparent confusion reveals the essential ideas to be relatively valid. The "moral order," as conceptualized by Park, corresponds to the familiar concept of "culture" or the "cultural order"—"the social heritage of habits and sentiment, folkways and mores, technique and culture." Park therefore identified "society" with consensus (moral uniformity), which is based on communication or meaningful interaction between persons.

[2] Robert E. Park and Ernest W. Burgess, *Introduction to the Science of Sociology* (Chicago: University of Chicago Press, 1921), pp. 11, 51, 163, 211, 280–284, 339–340.

[3] *Ibid.*, pp. 507–511, 574–575; Robert E. Park, *Human Communities* (New York Free Press, 1952), p. 157.

The social order (society) is composed of values and norms, but the most elementary parts or social forces are the attitudes, abstracted from the behavior of persons in interaction. Park conceived these "tendencies to act" to be of decisive importance and even proclaimed the attitude as the "distinctively social aspect" of human behavior.[4] Yet Park was somehow unwilling to lodge the attitudes consistently within the social order; as early as 1921, his approach to attitudes was centered on their presumed spatial dimension,[5] which Park unmistakably included under the ideal type of "community." Indeed, in a manner that is strikingly similar to von Wiese's classification of the basic social processes, Park divided all attitudes into those involving (*a*) the tendency to approach or (*b*) the tendency to withdraw. Park even translated three of Thomas' "four wishes" into spatial terms: the wish for security represents "mere immobility"; the wish for new experience signifies "freedom of movement and constant change of position"; and the wish for response translates to "the number and closeness of points of contact." [6]

This ambivalence with respect to the "social" also appears in two other concepts that would ordinarily be considered exclusively as related to the social order—*social status* and *social distance*.[7] Park defines social status as the level of recognition, the position awarded to persons by other persons upholding group standards. But, he asserts, status is a significant condition of social interaction that defines the degree of intimacy or aloofness permitted or prescribed in given relationships. This aspect of interaction—social distance—is variably described by Park in terms of sentiment and space, without sufficiently clear recognition of the disparity between physical and social space. Occasionally the distinction is observed; more often Park conceived of physical space and distance as an index of social relations. As we shall see later, he demonstrated in his ecological writings a tendency to reduce social space to physical space. "Social status" and "social distance" therefore re-

---

[4] Park and Burgess, *op. cit.*, p. 439; *Human Communities*, p. 174.
[5] *Human Communities*, pp. 164–166.   [6] Park and Burgess, *op. cit.*, p. 439.
[7] *Ibid.*, pp. 163, 282–285; *Human Communities*, pp. 164, 176–177; Robert E. Park, *Race and Culture* (New York: Free Press, 1951), p. 257.

tain dubious conceptual positions and further blur the essential features of the social element and the social order.

The ecological order—the community—was constructed as an ideal type by Park to describe the more visible, material context of human behavior, which is only analytically separate from the moral order among human beings. To Park, the ecological or biotic order refers to the territorial (spatial) distribution of persons whose interaction with one another is decidedly non-social and based on a persistent struggle for usable space.[8] On this level, culture, consensus, and communication are either lacking or are undeveloped; relations between individuals are mediated only by the resources of the physical environment.

In an undated paper, which could not have been written before 1933, Park reverts to an analogous set of ideal types that he had briefly sketched in 1925. The moral order is identified with what he designates as "culture," while the ecological order seems to be quite comparable to "civilization." "Culture" emphasizes *mores*, while "civilization" refers to the *techniques* of trade and commerce by which a territorial group is organized.[9] This usage of the terms is similar to MacIver's interpretation and apparently is drawn from Alfred Weber's "culture sociology." [10] But it should be noted that an important shift in analysis is involved in the use of these concepts. Both "culture" and "civilization" are products of social interaction and social organization, so that Park appears to have substituted a culturally saturated order dominated by rational and quasi-rational techniques of adjustment to the physical environment for a natural, non-social order. But this was only a conceptual interlude, for the prominence of the ecological order remained the keynote of Park's sociological theory.

In a way, Park reflected the tenacity of monistic determinisms in sociology, and particularly those that offered materialistic interpretations of social phenomena. Following the basic viewpoints of

8 Park and Burgess, *op. cit.*, pp. 508–511; *Human Communities*, pp. 157–160.
9 *Race and Culture*, pp. 12–16, 29–33.
10 Alfred Weber, *Fundamentals of Culture-Sociology*, trans. G. H. Weltner and C. F. Hirshman (New York: Dept. of Social Science, Columbia University, 1939), mimeographed. The original appeared in *Archiv für Sozialwissenschaft und Sozialpolitik*, XLVII (1920–1921), pp. 1–49.

Sumner, Marx, and others, he seems always to trace human behavior to an ecological substratum created by the struggle for existence. The ecological order, based on natural, free competition,
somehow contributes to an economic order that is part of a developing culture but is, however, unaffected by other norms. Out of
this preliminary but fundamental adaptation, and under the compulsion of controlling the ecological order in the interest of a
group, emerges a political order. Finally, at the top of this conceptual pyramid, with its broad ecological base, Park identifies the
moral order, which regulates the orders from which it derives.[11]
Thus "society" is viewed as a subtle, sublimated reflection of the
"community," superimposed upon a biotic balance that is rooted in
physical and physiological interaction.

The dynamic element for Park is then the conversion of "community" into "society" and, to a limited extent, the repercussions
of cultural changes on the ecological order. Consequently, "process" is not only a useful conception, but an extremely important
link in Park's theoretical system. Both ideal typical orders are approached through a series of characteristic processes, each of which
possesses a counterpart in the correlative order.

FROM ECOLOGY TO SOCIETY

The ecological processes have temporal and conceptual priority
in Park's schema. Significantly, cardinal importance is assigned to
competition,[12] which in its pure state involves interaction without
social (meaningful) contact. In the ecological sense, competition is
a process of unconscious contest between morally free human organisms for the life-giving resources of an area. However, competition is invariably modified by other processes in concrete human
aggregations. For as it proceeds, unplanned forms of unconscious
cooperation develop among human organisms; these forms are attributed by Park to the efficiency of competition in the framework
of simultaneously developing "social contacts." Thus competitive

11 *Human Communities*, pp. 157–159.
12 Park and Burgess, *op. cit.*, pp. 163, 507–511, 513, 574–577.

cooperation or *symbiosis* is a more advanced ecological process in that its operation contributes an elementary order in the community.

In the course of competitive and symbiotic relations, a natural division of labor emerges in which certain human organisms achieve a specially favored position in the struggle for existence. This position, which derives from successful competition, is important in the process of *dominance*,[13] by which a still more complex level of organization is attained. Dominance is likewise in its ideal sense a non-social complex of relations whereby the dominant organisms control the spatial distribution of organisms within the community and the distribution of resources and functions in the community.

Assuming an ideal typical purity, Park must take account of distinctively ecological *changes* in the community. At this point the processes of *invasion* and *succession* [14] register the basic dynamics of the ecological order. According to Park, the human ecological order comprises a spatial distribution of individuals characterized by freedom of locomotion or mobility, though mobility is in practice limited by dominance and the cultural order. Invasion refers to the initial alterations in spatial organization through the movement of alien organisms into a given community or, as the urban ecological studies demonstrate, movement of a group of organisms from one area to a distinguishably different one within a given community. Thus invasion precipitates changes in organization that eventuate in revised ecological relations. Park, in what is probably his most unsatisfactory piece of conceptualization, assumed an irreversible progression or cycle of changes in spatial and temporal relations and named this process "succession." As he used the term, however, it came to mean all processes of change—populational, economic, technological, political, ideational, etc.—that disturb and eventually transform some natural division of labor and the spatial distribution of populations. A more careful analysis of inva-

13 *Human Communities*, pp. 161–164.

14 Robert E. Park, "Succession, An Ecological Concept," *American Sociological Review*, I (April, 1936), pp. 171–179.

sion and succession as distinctively ecological processes can be found in the writings of R. D. McKenzie,[15] one of Park's most articulate disciples.

The magic of social contact and communication elevates human beings from the ecological to the social order and thus converts the ecological processes into social processes, which Park regarded as ultimately dependent on the ecological order. Social contact, the initial stage of social interaction, arises in the community from spatial propinquity and mutual sense perceptions; in time, physical contacts entail the communication of ideas and sentiments of various kinds, but this communication assumes one of two forms: primary or secondary contacts.[16] As Park developed these concepts, contacts based on intimacy and sympathy (cf. Cooley, Toennies, and N. Shaler) seem to be clearly "social," while the secondary or categoric contacts (which lack the features of consensus) tend to be marginal to society and occasionally are considered in ecological terms.

Park, however, regarded social relations as variously modified "competitive" relations, though he admits the essential priority of non-competitive relations in such groups as the family, and friendship circles, which he traces to a "craving for response." Competition, for example, becomes a social process of rivalry or conflict when human beings in the community consciously contend with one another for scarce resources of the environment. As the process proceeds from the ecological to the social level, rules are developed to control the conditions of contention and thus a political order is born. Dominance is transformed through social interaction into superordination–subordination relations, which are a kind of *accommodation* or resolution of conflicts between individuals. Secondary groups are then products of attenuated conflict whose resolution is recorded in custom and the mores, apart from the political order and laws. Accommodation also distributes and fixes the social

[15] R. D. McKenzie, "Ecology, Human," *Encyclopedia of the Social Sciences* (15 vols.; New York: Macmillan, 1931), V, pp. 314–315; R. D. McKenzie, "The Scope of Human Ecology," *Publications of the American Sociological Society*, XX (1926), pp. 141–154.

[16] Park and Burgess, *op. cit.*, pp. 282–286; *Human Communities*, pp. 243–244.

statuses of members of society in such a way as to limit competition and conflict.[17]

Finally, the most advanced social process, the farthest removed from ecological processes, is *assimilation*.[18] Unlike accommodation, assimilation is a gradual process by which individuals come to share values, interests, and attitudes on a relatively permanent basis through primary contacts with one another. Thus intimate groups like the family (traditional type) are marked by assimilation rather than accommodation. Park rightly connects personality development with assimilation, but his insistence on the unconscious nature of the process may be questioned. Since Park reserves unconscious interaction for the ecological order, it might be more accurate to view the products of assimilation as unconscious (i.e., the individual is often unaware of the gradual alteration in his values in given phases of the process), while the process of assimilation must involve meaningful relations with other individuals.

"Society" and "community" are therefore important dimensions of human behavior whose interrelationship is often a useful but unverifiable premise. Hollingshead refers to these concepts as "antithetical correlatives" and that paradoxical designation perhaps defines their character in the most accurate manner. "Community" is basically a moving equilibrium between environment and competing human organisms, while "society" through its system of values regulates and stabilizes that equilibrium as best it can.[19] In a limited sense then, "society" is analogous to *Gemeinschaft*, with its dominance of primary relations, cultural and biological homogeneity, religion, and limited mobility—what Park and Becker have called the "sacred society." The "community," on the other hand, is characterized by extreme mobility and heterogeneity, little direct contact between its members (and that of a non-social nature, similar to but not identical with secondary group contacts), so that it may be thought of as analogous to the "secular society." Of course, both the sacred and secular orders are sociocultural, but it is im-

---

[17] Park and Burgess, *op. cit.*, pp. 509–511.   [18] *Ibid.*, p. 736.

[19] A. B. Hollingshead, "Human Ecology," in Robert E. Park, ed., *An Outline of the Principles of Sociology* (New York: Barnes and Noble, 1940), p. 127.

possible to detach the sociocultural element from the human ecological order.

ORIENTATION TO SOCIAL CHANGE

The ecological and social orders, through their respective processes, produce dynamic emergents that Park believed to be major objects of sociological study. In the ecological order, these are primarily the community, the natural area, and the region. In the social order, on the other hand, there develops a series of social groups or groupings that Park seemed to distinguish into three types— primary groups; secondary groups; and quasi-social groups.[20] This classification is logically inconsistent; and although Park soon discarded it, he neglected to devise an alternative one. Not only do the primary groups include the family and traditional language groups, but they also include such ecological groups as neighborhoods, rural communities, and urban communities. Moreover, the secondary groups are arbitrarily divided into "conflict" and "accommodation" types, which are certainly not exclusively confined to secondary groups. As a matter of fact, according to Park, the secondary group category includes the gang, and a number of collectivities that do not strictly involve social interaction—e.g., classes, castes, nationalities, and denominations.

It seems probable that Park was not primarily concerned with "completed" social groups, but devoted his attention rather to the quasi-social groupings connected with the process of social becoming. These latter groupings, referred to as "forms of collective behavior," [21] therefore are focal to a theory of social and institutional change. But as we shall see, Park developed two distinct variations on this theme that are related to differing emphasis on the moral and ecological orders.

The process of change is analyzed by Park in a cyclical fashion: conditions, groupings responsive to conditions, cultural productions, acceptance and social control (institutionalization), and sub-

[20] Park and Burgess, *op. cit.*, pp. 50, 722.   [21] *Ibid.*, p. 924.

sequent difficulties, which become the conditions of succeeding cycles. Generally, Park attributed change to conditions of social unrest that destroy established group attachments and evoke new, fluid interrelationships between persons in society.[22] The first resultant reformations are crowds of various types, which are characterized by physical concentration and by movement of socially disturbed persons, a high degree of emotion, and a temporary form of solidarity. Concurrent forms of response to the conditions of change may involve physical dispersion, some rational discussion by the participants, and the development of more or less organized ideas or opinions on one or more specific issues of interest. These are the *publics*, which may become sufficiently attached to some course of definite action as to form social movements through the organization of what we now call *pressure groups*. Park was particularly interested in the public as a potential social group, though he gave most attention to the publics created by the modern newspaper. Incidentally, this interest in the spatial aspect of publics provides another indication of his persistent correlation of the social and ecological orders.[23]

Since Park gave only token consideration to the institutionalization phase of change, and since we shall examine his analysis of the problem aspect of change below, we may now turn to his explanation of the causes of social change. It is at this point that two basically contradictory interpretations appear for which no satisfactory resolution can be found in Park's writings—or in those of his immediate disciples. According to one version, the origins of social change may be found in social unrest, by which Park means widespread dissatisfaction with the way urgent needs are satisfied in some existing social order. The causes of social unrest, however, are not clearly traced by Park: at one point, it seems to be explained by continual social conflicts; at another point, it is attributed to vague disturbances in the "existing economic and social order"; at still another point, it seems to derive from technological changes that are imperfectly incorporated in a traditional social order.[24]

22 *Ibid.*, p. 54; *Race and Culture*, pp. 350–351.
23 Robert E. Park, *Society* (New York: Free Press, 1955), Pt. II.
24 Park and Burgess, *op. cit.*, p. 54; *Race and Culture*, p. 10.

But common to all these formulations is a basically *sociocultural* explanation of change.

The other approach to social change is from the ecological standpoint. Social unrest remains a significant condition of change, but unrest is said to be a product of new social contacts, which in turn are created by physical relocation of persons and groups. Thus, it is asserted, when migration and mobility reach a sufficiently accelerated tempo, the resultant opportunities for new interchange of ideas and techniques complicate the pattern of existing social relationships, and by so doing, release individuals from established social bonds. In emancipating individuals, mobility attenuates formerly unquestioned values and thereby originates a disorganizing process in which sacred relations are secularized and behavioral alternatives become not only possible but actual.[25] Social change is thereby reduced to position, movement, and physical distribution, and to the ecological processes of invasion and succession. But by what process does migration emerge, assuming that migration constitutes the crucial element in social change?

RACE RELATIONS AND INTERGROUP CONFLICT

It is perhaps significant that this general framework of concepts and theoretical insights, with its essential dualism, was applied by Park in originating two distinct specialisms in American sociology —race relations and urban sociology. In both areas, Park provided an outline for study and research, a viewpoint of basic though occasionally dubious objectivity, a set of guiding concepts, and a contagious curiosity that made active research one of the keynotes of American sociology. However, Park himself did little research of an extended nature in sociology; and despite his vast influence, he did remarkably little in the areas for which he is now best known. Park was an architect of research, concerned with the simplest of outlines, but these were apparently furnished in the form of suggestive comments characterized by a minimum of formality and a good number of valuable intuitive hypotheses.

[25] *Race and Culture*, pp. 13, 350–354; *Human Communities*, pp. 169–170.

In the field of race relations, Park was primarily concerned with a special problem in the social or moral order, though occasionally his approach involved use of the ecological order as well. Fundamentally, Park conceived of race relations as a transitional phenomenon in the social process of a society, a somewhat temporary disturbance in the development of consensus among groups in social contact with one another.[26] To bring order out of the numerous facts of racial difficulties, Park interpreted them as instances of social interaction that could be classified in terms of the basic social processes—contact, competition, conflict, accommodation, and assimilation. However, these processes were conceived to form an irreversible cycle in race relations, though no time specifications for each phase were asserted.

Park observed that contacts between racially distinct groups originate in mass migrations, which bring about accidental associations between "strangers" and settled populations. The "invaders" are not merely "out-groups," but predominantly folk groups with local, kinship-based cultures unaccustomed to the complexities of the "host" society. Contact therefore is followed by the efforts of one race to gain a foothold in a strange economic and ecological organization; first through competition, then, as communication develops, through rivalry and conflict.[27] Conflict develops in part from antipathies, but more often from attempts on the part of new racial groups to improve their status. Out of these conflicts, a *modus vivendi* or process of accommodation is devised by the "host." From mere territorial relations, there usually is created one of superordination–subordination (caste, slavery, etc.) in which some set of mutual (if unequal) obligations is involved. Under these circumstances, conflicts are reduced, but are not necessarily eradicated.

Accommodation prescribes a pattern of social distance between social groups that is expressed in such phenomena as segregation, restriction of opportunities, barriers to miscegenation, and the etiquette of face-to-face contacts. As Park viewed race relations, these processes occur primarily in an urban context, in which sec-

[26] *Race and Culture*, p. 116.
[27] *Ibid.*, pp. 116, 233; Park and Burgess, *op. cit.*, pp. 286, 319, 508.

ondary groups with their impersonal relations hinder the possibilities for assimilation. Yet accommodation ordinarily expands opportunities for cultural interchange and the reduction of cultural differences. The difficulty of assimilation seems to be explained by (*a*) whatever cultural differences remain; (*b*) the "racial uniform" of the subordinate group; (*c*) prejudice, which reflects resistance to change in the social order; and (*d*) a "racial will," which Park in 1918 believed was impervious to some cultural forms and receptive to others.[28]

Whatever the explanation, Park found that this situation inevitably produces individuals and groups of marginal status whose problems can be reduced to a moral hiatus—rejection of folk culture but lack of acceptance by the agents of urban culture. But if migrations continue to bring additional "strangers," the forms of accommodation may be strained and assimilation may thereby become more remote. However, Park believed that race relations would eventually, through intermarriage and acculturation, result in assimilation and that race conflict would come to be superseded by the conflicts of classes.[29] Thus, the sociologist is encouraged to approach race problems by establishing the contemporary level of interaction or association between specific racial groups and by evaluating the conditions that hinder or facilitate the transformation of race relations to more socially advanced processes.

URBAN STRUCTURE AND CHANGE

If race relations were conceived of as falling primarily within the moral order, Park approached his urban sociology from the ecological standpoint as a means of clarifying the social problems of complex social systems. Convinced of the priority of the ecological order, Park reasoned that social research could properly begin at the level of "community," particularly since the community offers a visible and often measurable object for study.[30] The city was chosen as a focus because it best exemplified the processes of be-

[28] *Human Communities*, pp. 167–170; *Race and Culture*, pp. 233, 257.
[29] *Race and Culture*, p. 116.   [30] *Human Communities*, pp. 14–24, 75–84.

coming, movement, and change, in what Park knew to be a continuous social laboratory for the sociologist. It was also the milieu that Park as a reporter most intimately knew and loved, the counterpart in exotic flavor to the isolated cultures of the anthropologist.

Park therefore made urban sociology a theoretical outpost of *human ecology*, in which he encouraged the study of "typical [spatial] constellations of persons and institutions" in the urban community. In his first outline of urban ecology ("The City: Suggestions for the Investigation of Human Behavior in the Urban Environment," 1916), the ecological pattern of cities was traced to the population base and to its concentration and distribution within a specific area—just as Durkheim had traced the organic solidarity of complex societies to population density and a resultant division of labor. Park likewise translated the pattern of population to a division of labor that could be analyzed dynamically in terms of developments in geographic location and in vocational types underlying social groupings. Thus, he sent his students "on the town" to obtain firsthand descriptions of urban life in its ecological setting, though many students reported their investigations primarily on the social rather than the ecological level.

With subject matter so rich and close at hand, methodology became increasingly important. Participant observation replaced academic aloofness as sociologists lived and worked in most parts of Chicago—among hoboes, adolescent gangs, transient boarders and roomers, racial and cultural minorities, restaurant workers, salesladies, etc. To supplement direct observation, personal documents, life histories, and social case records were secured to help indicate attitudes toward some aspect of urban structure, in the direction pointed by Thomas and Znaniecki's *The Polish Peasant in Europe and America.* Understandably, the data were transferred to city maps for graphic representation and comparison until the picture of the urban community could be grasped by patient location of dots on base maps, indicating the distribution of crime, delinquency, divorce, prostitution, dance halls, dwelling types, suicides, dependency, gangs, etc.

The urban division of labor was regarded by Park as an unplanned process with both cultural and geographical aspects. Consequently, he conceived of the city, ecologically speaking, as a mosaic of "natural areas," in each of which persons of similar culture congregate as end-products of ecological processes. The natural area became the unit of investigation for such statistical information as sex and age distributions, marriage and divorce rates, and crime and delinquency rates—in short, as a frame of reference for correlating urban facts and attacking urban problems.

With the help of such associates as Burgess and McKenzie, Park led the way toward depicting urban changes in terms of basic ecological processes intermeshed with secondary cultural factors. The city came to be thought of as a developing, unstable social order constantly reflecting the shifting equilibrium of ecological processes. It functioned through competition for location of myriad groups and services, and Park assumed that such competition inevitably resulted in the dominance of economic principles in distributing urban units. But Park presented contradictory accounts of urban ecological distributions. He was inclined to nominate migration and movement as the causal elements, but on occasion he recognized that migration was only an index of occupational and broad cultural developments.[31]

Competition, modified in part by culture, therefore was taken to be the basis for the process of segregation among linguistic, cultural, and racial groupings in relatively distinct natural areas that attract individuals and groups in terms of their respective interests and ability to compete for physical and social position. The city, then, was primarily a complex symbiotic process in which spatial and cultural functional units, rather than individuals, engaged in competitive cooperation with one another for mutual social survival. Since each natural area selects, and is selected by, individuals on impersonal grounds, the natural area was itself a process in which contacts are initially competitive, accommodative, and of a secondary-group nature. With maturity, some areas attain variable degrees of consensus, while other areas retain their impersonal character by continued mobility. Thus the casual, fractional, super-

[31] *Race and Culture*, pp. 10–11, 169.

ficial contacts of urban life are traced to the process of segregation and to the lack of consensus found in extensive cultural and spatial specialization.

Park left the elaboration of urban processes—such as zonal and sector theories, the determination of gradients, and careful empirical studies of migration and succession—to others.

During his stay at the University of Chicago, Park sprinkled so many ideas over the sociological landscape that it is difficult to consider them all and evaluate them properly. But there is little question that, through his scattered writings and inspiring teaching, American sociology was provided with a certain order and distinction that made competent research possible. His specific contributions, however, might be grouped into four areas:

1. Studies of communities from a definite conceptual standpoint of a sociological nature can fairly be derived from Park's influence. In particular, the urban community became a crucial part of sociological research and a new focus for the problems of social organization, social differentiation, deviation, and change. And analysis of urban communities has probably done more to remove sociology from the lecture platform than any other single development.
2. Park's continual emphasis on process and specific social processes (e.g., accommodation and assimilation), which was primarily borrowed from Simmel, supplemented the work of Thomas and Znaniecki and contributed a useful objective approach to social dynamics that could be applied to many sociological problems. Unfortunately, Park did not adequately test his hypotheses of social change and collective behavior, nor have his students attempted to establish more tenable generalizations in what is admittedly one of the most difficult areas of sociology.
3. Race relations as a special sociological study in the United States owes much to Park, despite the fact that he was not a specialist in race relations. His most lasting contribution in this area is the clarifying notion that race relations are basically similar to less spectacular social processes and therefore can be analyzed through a paradigmatic cycle of specific social processes.
4. Borrowing freely from the viewpoint and concepts of plant and

animal ecologists, Park established human ecology (as a means of studying internal differentiation) within American sociology. As a result, sociological research has acquired an explicit spatial dimension and a strong emphasis on empirical investigation, particularly in the analyses of community structure and community problems. Park's writings in ecology, however, have been found to contain basic assumptions and generalizations that conflict with the fundamental viewpoint of contemporary sociology and with recent empirical findings.[32] Yet the new "revisionist" ecology is unquestionably indebted to Park's "orthodox" ecological framework and to his followers of the Chicago school who have formulated significant research problems, developed a familiar battery of research techniques, and contributed a number of verifiable (if not always verified) hypotheses about the spatial division of social labor.

SELECTED REFERENCES

Faris, Robert E. L., *Chicago Sociology 1920–1932* (San Francisco: Chandler, 1967), chs. 3–5.
Park, Robert E., *Human Communities* (New York: Free Press, 1952).
———, *Race and Culture* (New York: Free Press, 1951).
Theodorson, George A., ed., *Studies in Human Ecology* (New York: Harper & Row, 1961), Pt. I.

[32] Milla A. Alihan, *Social Ecology: A Critical Analysis* (New York: Columbia University Press, 1938).

6

Robert MacIver:
A Meaningful Sociology

Often, a living pioneer receives little recognition unless he is also embroiled in controversy or sedulously prepares a public reputation. With few exceptions, Robert MacIver has been ignored or only faintly approved by a busy generation of American sociologists. In a thirty-year period (1917–1947), MacIver, who had been nurtured in a liberal British philosophical tradition, worked quietly, wrote in sociology and related fields, and helped transfer European insights to the American sociological scene. Work in the areas of philosophy, history, and economics preceded his enduring dual application to the fields of sociology and political philosophy, and these earlier interests have undoubtedly facilitated his role as critic of the dubious theories of Marx, Veblen, Ogburn, Pareto, and Spengler.

However, it is not primarily as an appraiser of contemporary theories that MacIver merits our attention. When he came to Columbia University in the late twenties, American sociology was feverishly disowning its speculative past and searching for new foundations. Park, Thomas, Znaniecki, Giddings, among others, were experimenting with new sociological conceptions and boundary-lines, with new techniques and new data.[1] System, organization, and consistency were as absent in American sociology during the twenties as in American society itself. MacIver, sympathetic to the social philosophy and investigation of Hobhouse and Graham Wallas, slowly constructed a systematic substructure for sociology, one that would suitably describe and analyze the peculiar nature of human association and its complex forms.

Perhaps the key contribution of MacIver, and of the tradition he both reflects and extends, is the distinctively sociological conception of the nature of social phenomena. The history of sociology is uncomfortably punctuated with mechanical, biological, and chemical approaches to human behavior. But MacIver recognized its complex, emergent nature, which he analyzed into three simultaneous but separable aspects. Most obviously, there is an *objective* dimension—composed of the physical and biological facts of organisms and their immediate environment. Secondly, we can distinguish the *subjective* aspect, the attitudes and sentiments of human actors toward one another and the physical environment—the psychological dimension. And finally, MacIver abstracts an *institutional* aspect, which corresponds to the persistence of shared values and a consequent order or regularity in behavior (the sociocultural aspect).[2]

Social phenomena, which MacIver variously identifies as "society," "community," and "social relationships," principally interest the sociologist in their subjective and institutional aspects. Indeed, the definition of society as "the maintenance of willed relations" is a fundamental union of these aspects.[3] The inclusion of a psycho-

---

[1] Robert E. Park and Ernest W. Burgess, *Introduction to the Science of Sociology* (Chicago: University of Chicago Press, 1921); Robert E. Park *et al.*, *The City* (Chicago: University of Chicago Press, 1925); W. I. Thomas and Florian Znaniecki, *The Polish Peasant in Europe and America* (5 vols.; Boston: Richard Badger, 1918); Florian Znaniecki, *The Laws of Social Psychology* (Chicago: University of Chicago Press, 1925); Franklin H. Giddings, *The Scientific Study of Human Society* (Chapel Hill: University of North Carolina Press, 1924).

[2] Robert M. MacIver, *The Modern State* (Oxford: Oxford University Press, 1926), p. 33.

[3] Robert M. MacIver, *Community* (London: Macmillan, 1924; 1st ed., 1917), p. 5.

logical dimension was of course significant in the earlier work of Toennies, Tarde, Cooley, Giddings, and Max Weber. But Mac-Iver, with Znaniecki, Thomas, and others, helped to establish the subjective aspect as a necessary component of social facts.[4]

Although any social fact inherently possesses analytically separable aspects, a useful classification of social facts must be based on the subjective and institutional aspects. Consequently, as early as 1917, MacIver made an important distinction between social relations as primary social facts and social institutions (which are their consequences) as secondary social facts.[5]

More recently, a further refinement in classification has been suggested; and, though quite consistent with the character of modern sociological investigation, it has been largely and inexplicably ignored.[6] Essentially, social relations—the interdependent activities of two or more persons—have been divided into two types. On the one hand, there are the similar but relatively independent activities of persons that produce familiar statistical facts—such as crime rates, birth rates, marriage rates, opinion poll results, and the like. While these facts issue from individual behavior, that behavior is "responsive to group or community conditions" and "dependent on suggestion, . . . leadership, and other social interactions." These are therefore called *distributive social phenomena*. But, on the other hand, many social relations reflect consciously willed, purposive agreements among persons expressed in concerted action —*collective social phenomena*, such as social movements, mobs, legislative processes, etc. A third type of social fact corresponds somewhat to MacIver's earlier designation of social institutions as resultants of social relations. These *conjunctural phenomena* are unplanned structures or aspects of larger, institutional systems— for example, the business cycle, the unemployment rate, the overall social division of labor, urban blight, internal migration patterns, etc.

[4] Thomas and Znaniecki, *op. cit.*; Florian Znaniecki, *The Method of Sociology* (New York: Rinehart, 1934); Florian Znaniecki, *Social Actions* (New York: Farrar and Rinehart, 1936).

[5] MacIver, *Community*, pp. 5–7.

[6] Robert M. MacIver, "Social Causation and Change," in Georges Gurvitch and Wilbert E. Moore, eds., *Twentieth Century Sociology* (New York: Philosophical Library, 1945), pp. 122–125.

114

There are of course many ways of classifying social phenomena. However, the significance of MacIver's classification rests on both its simplicity and its codification of graded orders of fact in sociological investigation. By implication, the core of sociology and the type of social phenomena most accessible to understanding and direct investigation is collective phenomena. From the standpoint of explanatory or causative objectives, these are the most central of primary social facts. Distributive phenomena, on the other hand, present little difficulty in data collection, but confront the sociologist with the necessity of explaining apparently accidental patterns of behavior by reference to other social facts. This was of course brilliantly accomplished by Durkheim in his justly famous analysis of suicide statistics more than seventy years ago.[7]

The essential nature of social facts, as viewed and classified by MacIver, is further encompassed in such terms as "process," "functional entity," and "changing equilibrium." Not only are social facts inherently expressive of interests, motives, evaluations (the subjective aspect), but they emerge and come to our attention as dynamic clusters of enshrouded meaning. Consequently, the principal objectives of sociological investigation are (*a*) to extract and correlate presumably relevant masses of social fact and (*b*) to discern the binding threads of meaning, as experienced by implicated actors, in the production and modification of social facts. MacIver has often acknowledged that the search for meaning—the operation called *Verstehen*—is a difficult and often a frustrating process, but the only one that is faithful to the character of social fact.[8] The statistical approach, so widely and confidently used, is consequently appraised as a preliminary tool, since statistics are not social facts but echoes of social facts that must be properly interpreted to yield social facts. Nothing short of sympathetic reconstruction of social situations, as assessed and responded to by social beings, can reveal the functional–subjective reality of social facts.[9] And since change is omnipresent in human behavior, the ul-

[7] Emile Durkheim, *Suicide*, trans. John A. Spaulding and George Simpson (New York: Free Press, 1951).

[8] MacIver, *Community*, pp. 9, 69, 218; Robert M. MacIver, *Social Causation* (Boston: Ginn and Company, 1942), pp. 262, 390–392; Robert M. MacIver, *Society* (New York: Farrar and Rinehart, 1937), pp. 474–478.

[9] *Social Causation*, pp. 388–392.

timate aim of sociology is neither description nor correlation, but the explanation of determinate variations in social facts—the quest for "social causation." [10]

SOCIAL STRUCTURE

Guided by this specifically sociological conception of social phenomena, MacIver has over the years constructed a coherent conceptual scheme for the study and analysis of society and of its various constituent parts as a "web of social relationships." During his period of progressive reformulation (1920–1947), it should be recalled, only one developed conceptual system had achieved extensive acceptance by American sociologists—the social process approach, principally applied in terms of ecological and demographic aspects of social phenomena. In 1922, Park and Burgess' *Introduction to the Science of Sociology* furnished a kind of agenda for research along these lines, yet it soon became evident that the "meaning component" was often ignored in the development of concepts and research. Critical sociologists—Znaniecki, Sorokin, Becker, Parsons, and of course MacIver, among others [11]—began in the late twenties and thirties to re-assess and revise the focus of sociological concern. While several critics made substantial suggestions for improvement, MacIver was probably the first to provide an acceptable alternative by interpreting and creatively synthesizing European and American concepts to form a "meaningful sociology" stripped of implicit value premises and philosophical cul-de-sacs.

The "sociological system" of MacIver seems to be implicitly built on two principles that are now widely accepted in one form or another under varying labels. First, there is the conception of

[10] *Ibid.*, pp. 65, 123, 176.

[11] Znaniecki, *The Method of Sociology;* Pitirim A. Sorokin, *Social Mobility* (New York: Harper, 1927); Pitirim A. Sorokin, *Contemporary Sociological Theories* (New York: Harper, 1928); Pitirim A. Sorokin, *Social and Cultural Dynamics* (4 vols.; New York: American Book Co., 1937–1941); Howard Becker, *Systematic Sociology* (New York: Wiley, 1932); Talcott Parsons, *The Structure of Social Action* (New York: McGraw-Hill, 1937).

social relations and social facts in general as functional systems embedded in determinate situations. The appropriate task of a conceptual scheme then is the analytic distinction of significant elements in the social situation and in the totality of related social situations called first "community" and more recently "society" by MacIver. But equally important to MacIver is the coordinate principle of social behavior as meaningful, which appears to be reflected in classifications of systems in terms of means and ends. Consequently, we find in MacIver's work a strong inclination toward pairs of concepts, though it should be clearly recognized that he rarely thought in terms of dichotomous or opposed pairs—as did Toennies, Durkheim, Gumplowicz, and Marx.[12] On the contrary, he paired these concepts to abstract complementary aspects of the same or similar social systems.

According to MacIver, society is analytically composed of three interconnected parts—interests, institutions, and associations. For the sociologist, interests are the source of all social activity and constitute the ultimate ends of all social organization. Institutions are special "reflections" of interests, forming an intermediate link between the latter and the immediate set of social means—the associations.[13] Thus, institutions possess a dual capacity in this conceptual scheme; they are considered as means, with respect to interests, and as ends or means, with respect to associations. We have here an implied simplicity that often accompanies seminal conceptions, but the development and application of this sociological trinity will be found to contain a measure of complexity appropriate to the variety of social phenomena.

The definition of "interest" is impeded by its close identification with what the psychologist calls "attitude." MacIver seems to "locate" interests in the conceptual "space" between "attitude" and

12 Ferdinand Toennies, *Community and Society*, trans. Charles P. Loomis (New York: Harper & Row, 1963); Emile Durkheim, *The Division of Labor in Society*, trans. George Simpson (New York: Free Press, 1947); Ludwig Gumplowicz, *The Outline of Sociology*, trans. F. W. Moore (Philadelphia, 1899); Karl Marx and Friedrich Engels, *The Communist Manifesto*, many editions.

13 MacIver, *Community*, pp. 101–102; *Society*, pp. 20–21, 252–267. See also Albion W. Small, *General Sociology* (Chicago: University of Chicago Press, 1905), Pts. 4 and 5, and Small's *The Meaning of Social Science* (Chicago: University of Chicago Press, 1910), pp. 145, 193–195, 203.

"social relation." Attitudes are said to refer to subjective reactions to objects and events in determinate situations, while interests correspond to the objects or ends to which the individuals adjust their behavior. Interests, therefore, are objectively verifiable motives for behavior. Since it is impossible to pursue any interest without some concomitant subjective reaction, these phenomena are basically correlative, but analytically distinct.[14] For the sociologist, attitudes—primarily analyzed by the psychologist—become relevant only when they enable the investigator to understand more clearly the relation between interests and behavior in specific social situations.

Interests, according to this approach, are ultimate facts (or inferences from behavior) that do not require further probing as to their source by the sociologist. In various discussions of interests, MacIver never refers to interests as inevitable, inherent, or as linked to "needs." The underlying assumptions seem to define interests as (a) mainly products of social experience and therefore acquired, (b) realizable only in some form of social organization, (c) infinitely diversified or diversifiable, and (d) variable in influence through time.[15] Thus, if interest is the principal basis of meaning for actors, the expression, implementation, and combination of interests offer significant clues to the nature and dynamics of social structure as translated into institutions and associations. MacIver therefore proceeds to classify interests in various sociologically relevant dimensions. But two typologies seem most useful.

Types of interests

The basic distinction between *like interests* and *common interests* [16] is often ignored by both laymen and social scientists. Like interests are those that are individually pursued—such as the continuing quest for higher status—without the development of social relations among the persons so engaged. Distributive phenomena, referred to previously, are obviously the fruit of like interests. On the other hand, common interests are pursued collectively for de-

---

[14] MacIver, *Society*, pp. 19–21.   [15] MacIver, *Community*, pp. 112–116.
[16] MacIver, *Society*, pp. 30–32.

sired results that cannot be individually apportioned, but instead become the property in some form of all cooperating persons. Without any doubt, common interests (and resultant collective phenomena) are inseparable from, and impossible without, organized social relations—in short, associations.

Within the realm of common interests, a further distinction is required to comprehend social complexity. Some interests are broad, inclusive, unspecialized; they unite persons into communal groups that encompass the performance of various types of activities—such as the family, youth groups, the community itself. These inclusive interests differ markedly from exclusive, specialized interests, which tend to divide a population physically and socially into separate and perhaps competing groups.[17] MacIver includes here such interests as the economic, the political, the scientific, the educational, the technological, the recreational, the sexual, the religious, and the artistic.

Institutional analysis

It is of course impossible to refer to human interests apart from the organizations and valuational systems that condition and express those interests. The valuational systems, which MacIver identifies as "modes or conditions of interpersonal relations," are likewise divisible into two important types—the *informal* and the *institutional*.[18] Among the former are the folkways and the mores, custom, ceremony, ritual, creed, fashion. Institutions are meaningfully constructed modes of control, formally established guides to social relations that embody one or more enduring interests. They constitute an important segment of what the anthropologist calls "culture."

However, MacIver specially emphasizes the empirical interrelations between such institutional sectors as the political and economic, the religious and political, etc. These "institutional complexes"[19] are considered as functional systems whose structure is not adequately described by a mere enumeration of the associations

17 *Ibid.*, pp. 27–29.   18 *Ibid.*, pp. 15–18, 144, 328–388.
19 *Ibid.*, pp. 268–272.

involved, since, according to MacIver, there are inevitable linkages between certain interests (e.g., political and economic). Furthermore, institutional complexes are said to provide higher orders of coordination and integration in social systems than can be contributed by any specified institution. In this conceptualization then, the meaningful aspects of behavior are discovered not only in the parts, but in their coherent interconnections. It should of course be recognized that institutional complexes sustain order and provide referential meaning by the functioning of determinate groupings and associations, even though the members of such groupings may not be fully aware of the ultimate effects of their respective operations.

Overriding these specific, empirical clusters of interrelated "conditions of conduct" are two broad reservoirs of human interests that correspond to the major categories of ends and means. Borrowing and elaborating on the seminal conceptions of Alfred Weber, MacIver distinguishes these two orders of interest and experience as the *cultural* and the *civilizational*.[20] In the cultural order are those interests (and their objectification) that pertain to ultimate ends and values, those interests that are pursued for their own sake. Religion, philosophy, and the arts, for example, possess this intrinsic significance for human beings. In this realm, values and practices are relatively immune to logic, reason, and verification; they seem and are arbitrary to those who do not believe. For these reasons, the cultural realm presents no pattern that can be evaluated against any scale of progress, improvement, or efficiency. Civilization, however, is "the vehicle of culture"; it comprehends all interests that produce the apparatus and mechanisms, instruments and techniques for achieving cultural ends. Technology, economic and political arrangements, and education are thus civilizational, since they are principally directed toward control of either the environment or of human beings in the service of non-material ends. Unlike culture, civilization can be rationally appraised according to the standards of efficiency and utility.

More recently, the concepts of culture and civilization have been partially renovated, but not substantially altered in MacIver's dis-

20 *Ibid.*, pp. 272–280; *Community*, p. 179; *The Modern State*, pp. 325–337.

cussion of *myths* and *techniques*.[21] Though these concepts were designed for analysis of the political institution, their wider applicability was also recognized by MacIver. However, myth (or culture) is now more clearly designated as both a component and a necessary support of all social relations, whatever the interest involved. The myth-complex is ". . . the secret of social unities and social continuities and its changes compose the inner history of every society." Techniques (or civilization) are treated once more as subservient to myth, but not inevitably so, since technique and myth continually interact in human situations. Consequently, MacIver here shifts the dynamics of social phenomena from the level of interest to that of the interplay between myth and technique, thereby avoiding the temptation to explain social developments by reference to psychological needs of human organisms. But we shall examine these concepts for their special significance in MacIver's analysis of social change.

Groups and associations

A fundamental premise of MacIver's articulated approach to society is the separable but coordinated status of the social (relational) and valuational (informal and institutional) aspects of social structure.[22] Just a few decades ago, many sociologists continually confused these obviously related components by extraordinarily inconsistent definitions of the concept of "institution" and by a concomitant reluctance to produce a clear-cut definition and classification of social groups—presumably a key conception of sociology.[23] Indeed, in the period from 1900 to 1930, only Toennies, Giddings, Cooley, Max Weber, and Wiese had given serious attention to a meaningful typology of groups,[24] resting their respective

[21] Robert M. MacIver, *The Web of Government* (New York: Macmillan, 1947), pp. 4–6.

[22] MacIver, *Society*, pp. 14–16, 143–144.

[23] See Florian Znaniecki, "Social Organization and Institutions," in Gurvitch and Moore, *op. cit.*, pp. 172–217; and Logan Wilson, "Sociology of Groups," in Gurvitch and Moore, *op. cit.*, pp. 139–171.

[24] Toennies, *op. cit.*, Pt. 5; Charles H. Cooley, *Social Organization* (New York: Charles Scribner's Sons, 1918), chs. 3–5; Max Weber, *The Theory of Social and*

contributions on the conception of the social group as a network of determinate social relations among social persons. MacIver, building on these developments, was probably the first American sociologist to submit a reasonably consistent, acceptable typology as the capstone to his architectonic trinity of sociological concepts—interests, institutions, and associations.

In this classification, persons in relationship are principally viewed through the prism of interests and consequently fall into three general categories.[25] First, there are *inclusive territorial unities*, in which social relations develop and mature about a multiplicity of interests that intertwine to form a social backdrop and context for the other types of groupings. These unities are *communal structures*, as exemplified in tribe, nation, village, city, and metropolitan region. Second, within the community are "interest-conscious unities without definite organization," which, strictly speaking, are not social groups but reservoirs for social groups. MacIver here includes (*a*) social classes and castes, which possess like or common interests as yet untranslated into more or less permanent structures of association, and (*b*) the crowd, which reflects emotionally charged but transient interests that provide a dramatic, elusive unity in the context of physical proximity. It is only in the third category—the *association*—that genuine social groups are found, i.e., what MacIver calls "interest-conscious unities with definite organization." Two familiar subtypes, drawn from Cooley, Toennies, and Weber, are the primary group and the large-scale association (or secondary group).

In all probability, one of the more significant conceptual contributions by MacIver is this typology and, in particular, his analysis of social class and caste groupings. Previously, with few exceptions, social class either was defined in strictly economic terms or was indiscriminately applied to any category of persons that seemed to suit the purposes of the social scientist (e.g., a banking "class," criminal "class," novel-reading "class," etc.).[26] MacIver,

---

Economic Organization (New York: Oxford University Press, 1947), pp. 136–139, 145–152; Franklin H. Giddings, ed., *Readings in Descriptive and Historical Sociology* (New York: Macmillan, 1906), pp. 11–13.

[25] MacIver, *Society*, pp. 144–268.   [26] *Ibid.*, pp. 166–167.

however, reclaimed "class" as a special sociological designation for a portion of the community characterized by similar or common complexes of interest—not necessarily expressed in definite associations—that serve as a ground for vertical social differentiation.

Two "principles" or factors, in MacIver's view, clarify the essential nature of class and class differences. Groupings of persons are clearly separable according to their respective objective characteristics—avowed interests, occupation, "life chances," market position, and role in overall community functioning.[27] But this objective "principle" is peculiarly overshadowed (not extinguished) by a subjective phenomenon—social status, a very difficult term to define because it is pervaded by the arbitrary, capricious stamp of the subjective realm. Perhaps status is best delimited as the relative position or recognition accorded individuals as measured against some referential scheme of evaluation. As MacIver wisely indicates, status is apparently linked with one or more objective factors, such as wealth, occupation, family name, but is fundamentally independent of any rational criterion. It is instead "an ideological creation," grounded in myth (in the sense previously discussed) and ultimately derived from the already accomplished facts of possession, power, privilege, and inheritance.[28] Consequently, stratification is to a great extent a derivative of the *institutional* aspect of social organization and, in particular, of the cultural component of human activity.

In his earlier writings, MacIver seemed to stress the objective character of class in terms of dominant interests pursued through associations. Indeed, he declared that class differences should be ultimately based on objective, functional differences ("intrinsic differences") rather than privilege and arbitrary status.[29] But there is something of a shift to the subjective principle in the definition of class as a separable part of the community distinguished "not by limitations arising out of language, locality, function, or specialization, but primarily by social status." [30] This "status-defined strati-

---

[27] *Ibid.*, pp. 167–171.   [28] MacIver, *The Web of Government*, pp. 114–116.
[29] MacIver, *Community*, pp. 110–111, 270–272.
[30] MacIver, *Society*, pp. 167, 173–176.

fication" therefore requires not only identifiable similarities among persons, but the recognition of these similarities and a consequent unity of feeling and sentiment—class consciousness. In all likelihood, MacIver developed this newer conception in opposition to the Marxian position (which he had basically accepted), with its double assumption that objective differences are automatically reflected in subjective differences (class consciousness) and that class consciousness inevitably leads to class conflict.

Perhaps MacIver substituted one extreme for another. There is some evidence that status no longer enjoys its former conceptual dominance in social class. In *The Web of Government*, for example, status joins "property" and "power"—two rather objective, functional criteria—in an interdependent trinity, which MacIver employs as a major tool in analyzing the "pyramid of power" in the community.[31] While the pyramid of power refers to graded divisions in the political sphere, it is clear that for MacIver government, political organization, and control are universal aspects of all human associations. Consequently, the pyramid of power corresponds to a determinate stratification system.

The real significance of this apparent dualism, it seems, lies in the necessary recognition of a continuum of social stratification. At one pole, dominated by status considerations and a clearly magical element, is the caste system.[32] Here the subjective principle is institutionalized to the point of rigidity. Peculiarly, a caste system seems to possess functional divisions, but these are truly consequences, not bases, of stratification. Where functional divisions occur, based on objectively differentiated "contributions" of groupings, an *open class system* (in MacIver's terms, the "democratic pyramid") comprises the opposite end of this continuum.[33] However, a purely objective standard of social differentiation is inconceivable; objective differences are in some respects always evaluated according to some arbitrary conception—the ubiquity of the mythical element in social phenomena. But myth itself is subject to change; develop-

[31] MacIver, *The Web of Government*, ch. 5.

[32] *Ibid.*, pp. 52, 100–101; *Society*, pp. 171–172; Robert M. MacIver, "The New Social Stratification," in Ruth N. Anshen, ed., *Our Emergent Civilization* (New York: Harper & Row, 1947), p. 108.

[33] MacIver, *The Web of Government*, pp. 103–107.

ments in technology, economy, politics, religion, etc., influence social evaluation just as social evaluation defines and sustains class and
caste divisions. By inference, therefore, MacIver finally arrives at a
composite conception of stratification, one we are again approaching after two decades of theoretically vagrant empirical research.

SOCIAL CHANGE AND CAUSATION

The various concepts and generalizations discussed above constitute an intellectual preparation for MacIver's analysis of social
change—perhaps the most significant application of his general approach to sociology. All too frequently, change has been approached as a conceptual afterthought, as a distinctively different
set of problems from the analysis of order, organization, and structure. But MacIver places social change and social kinetics at the
core of his system; these problems are inseparable from those of
structure because of the essential nature of social phenomena—the
reality of "society as process."

Social change, in MacIver's view, refers to a distinctive aspect of
those human phenomena that diverge from some expected or
typical process of social action.[34] Several crucial points are specially prominent in this synthetic definition.

First, the social dimension is analytically distinguishable from the
simultaneous operation of the cultural, technological, biological–
physical, and attitudinal dimensions of "change" phenomena. Social change therefore involves significant variations in social relationships only, which are not to be confused with related trends in
values, devices, demography, and psychological characteristics.[35]

Orderly, predictable development in social phenomena is,
strictly speaking, not "change." The student of social change is
primarily concerned with unanticipated "interruptions" in an ongoing social structure producing new or revised combinations of
social relations and groups. Therefore, phenomena such as the

[34] This definition has been synthesized from scattered discussions by MacIver.
See especially *Society*, pp. 395, 406; *Social Causation*, pp. 163, 176.
[35] MacIver, *Society*, pp. 466, 474, 478.

"family cycle," the "race relations cycle," etc., present few problems of analysis to the field of social change. Indeed, in this view, social change is inseparable from problems of social causation,[36] which are concerned with explaining processes of social deviation and their role in constructing new patterns of group organization.

Underlying this specifically sociological conception of social change is MacIver's often repeated insistence that social changes are inherently meaningful—both to the sociologist and to the human participants themselves. Consequently, MacIver persistently refers social change to processes of social action and social relationships, which are in his definition "responses" to conditions of human existence.[37]

With this conceptual foundation, MacIver's principal approach is to assess the interrelations among the various aspects or orders of variation in producing social changes. His strategy is quite simple and direct. Social change must be construed as a dependent variable (or variables), while culture (myth), civilization (technology), and attitudes are analyzed as relatively independent variables (with respect to social change) whose typical interconnections form the major problems of social change analyses. In this way, MacIver sharply excludes immanent or mystical explanations on the one hand and, on the other, a number of previously popular monistic determinisms that make sophisticated bias a poor substitute for understanding.

Surveying historical and contemporary phenomena of social change, MacIver asserts that in its immediate aspects social organization is primarily responsive to the "effective conjuncture" of cultural and technological variations.[38] In well-aimed criticism of the determinist theories of Marx, Veblen, and Ogburn,[39] he demonstrates that technical and economic changes are reciprocally related to changes in basic valuations; indeed, if technology can be said to determine cultural change in any verifiable sense, it is merely by

[36] This is the basic thesis of *Social Causation*, particularly on pp. 9, 63–65, 176. See also Znaniecki, *The Method of Sociology*, pp. 19, 293–297, and his *Cultural Sciences* (Urbana: University of Illinois Press, 1951), pp. 164, 229–231.

[37] MacIver, *Society*, pp. 395, 465, 477.

[38] MacIver, *The Web of Government*, p. 298.

[39] *Ibid.*, p. 294; *Society*, pp. 444–459, 469–473.

preparing the way for various alternatives in the direction of cultural change.[40] However, the temptations of a *cultural determinism*, occasionally evident in his writings of the thirties, are largely resisted by a situational–functional approach, whose ultimate development rests on a skillful application of Thomas and Znaniecki's famous concept—the "definition of the situation," to which we shall soon return.

Several problems immediately arise from this rather general analysis—problems MacIver clearly recognized and tried to solve by reference to additional factors. If social change derives from the confluence of cultural and technological developments, what explains (*a*) the development of each of these and (*b*) the nature of their joint operation in the process of change? Basically, techniques are largely responsive to the character of prevailing myth (culture), both in the kinds of techniques to which effort is devoted and in the uses for which techniques are applied. Likewise, with the exception of culture-contact processes, technical developments ultimately depend on the evaluated codification of past experience— the area of science.[41]

The cultural basis of technology, myth-determinism, has considerable foundations, as the sociology of science has increasingly demonstrated.[42] But the origins of myth, "the value-impregnated beliefs . . . that men live by or live for," present a more complex problem for MacIver, which he explores as an incidental task in his sociological analysis of government (*The Web of Government*, 1947). In this work, his most recent attempt at theoretical formulations, MacIver inevitably resorts to the analysis of interdependent factors. While myth (together with technology) accounts for changes in social relationships, myth itself possesses no appreciable role in social affairs without a specialized (but not always conscious) *myth of authority*, i.e., a guiding notion of hierarchical patterns in social relationships. What, however, determines the changing content of the authority-myth? MacIver assigns this

[40] MacIver, *Society*, pp. 465–466.

[41] MacIver, *The Web of Government*, p. 6.

[42] Bernard Barber, *Science and the Social Order* (New York: Free Press, 1952); Bernard Barber and Walter Hirsch, eds., *The Sociology of Science* (New York: Free Press, 1962).

function to the *situation and its changes*, a statement that obviously creates new problems.[43]

For what particular complex of factors is involved in the concept "situation"? By inference, since "situation" is never explicitly defined in MacIver's writings, the situation refers to the social-physical context of human behavior; it consists of "pressures," objects (human and non-human), and values. It is the "reality" to which adjustments are made or attempted by evaluation and action.[44] But how does the situation react on the myth-structure of a group or society? And what is the essential dynamics of situational change?

Perhaps the conceptual nature of the situation is inevitably vague until another conceptual component is introduced, simply because in human terms a situation has no organization, no meaning in itself; only through the intervention of human valuation can situational factors attain a recognizable unity. This process of apprehending and ordering or coordinating, which is inevitably a continuous aspect of society, constitutes a "definition of the situation," though MacIver calls it "dynamic assessment." [45] From the standpoint both of social-change analysis and the problem of social causation (in MacIver's view, these are inseparable phenomena) then, dynamic assessment assumes central significance. If social change is ultimately the product of myth and the situation, the two must be effectively linked through numerous instances of dynamic assessment, which converge sufficiently to create behavior directed toward altering the pre-existing pattern of social relationships. It may be questioned whether or not myth and the situation represent distinctive sets of conditions, since myth is not only a product of past situations, but a component of every current situation. In any case, the crucial connective function of dynamic assessment remains unchallenged.[46]

To avoid the obvious dangers of psychologism and biological determinism, MacIver is led to several partly developed explorations in the genesis of dynamic assessment. At first, he takes the uncom-

[43] MacIver, *The Web of Government*, p. 447.
[44] MacIver, *Society*, pp. 20–21; *Social Causation*, pp. 122–123, 374–377, 388–392.
[45] MacIver, *Social Causation*, pp. 298, 333, 372–377, 388–392.
[46] *Ibid.*, pp. 163, 388.

fortable position that dynamic assessment need not be examined on the subsocial level, that we can take for granted organic processes, physical environment, etc. "We are not asking what determines the focus [dynamic assessment] but what the focus determines." Yet this limitation is quickly and justifiably forgotten; dynamic assessment is interpreted as a function of personality organization, which in turn reflects value systems and the subtlety of social relationships.[47]

While this offers no fully developed theoretical explanation of dynamic assessment, it is likewise true that MacIver regards such phenomena at present as too complex for assured masterstrokes of generalization. Indeed, he calls for much more extensive investigation of dynamic assessment—too frequently ignored in studies of social change—unencumbered by blanket theories of premature certainty.[48]

Whatever the ultimate sources of dynamic assessment might be, MacIver tends to regard its operation as a precipitant of social change, as a determinant of deviation. However, deviation is initially an experimental variation from traditional social relationships. Genuine change requires coordination, direction, and legitimation of deviation. Consequently, MacIver rediscovers the important supplementary role of political organization in the change process. The system of political power (government) is considered the key component of the technological sphere (civilization), whose major function is to control the "effective conjuncture of techniques and myths."[49] This is not a political determinism to offset the attraction of an economic or technical determinism, but an attempt to view the functional interrelationships of all major dimensions in the social-change process.

Indeed, the "control" function of government seems to operate, according to MacIver, by determining the rate of change and the manner in which technological and cultural variations reverberate through component parts of the social structure.[50] Yet this is not an automatic process; political power "is called into operation" (presumably as a result of dynamic assessments by officials and/or

[47] MacIver, "Social Causation and Change," *op. cit.*, pp. 125–127.
[48] *Ibid.*, pp. 127–132.   [49] MacIver, *The Web of Government*, p. 298.
[50] *Ibid.*, pp. 39, 294–298; *The Modern State*, p. 47.

implicated members of the polity). Government itself is a product of "myth and the situation"; it is inherently responsive to changes in social structure, just as social structure ultimately records major trends in the growth or diminution of political power.[51] It seems to be implied that the respective roles of government and dynamic assessment do not maintain a constant ratio. Again by implication, there is a range of variation that can be incorporated into ongoing social organization without major changes in government. But beyond this as yet indeterminate range, the process of social change can proceed only with a concomitant reconstitution of the political order. Thus MacIver supplies no sociological nourishment for rigid conservatism and reaction or for exuberant, well-intentioned but untutored revolution.

This peculiarly complex combination of psychosocial factors (dynamic assessment) and a special form of technological determinism (governmental controls) is particularly significant for its ability to clarify the linkages between the various dimensions of social structure in the process of determinate social change. In accord with the pioneering insights of Max Weber and Cooley, MacIver has constructed a referential process of social change that underlies transformations in the institutional sphere (in religion, government, family, economics, etc.), in systems of social evaluation and attitudes, and in social stratification, all of which in turn "feed back" into the change process as subsequent components of assessment and control.[52] Thus, the essential unity of society is preserved without the necessity of totalitarian theory.

However, MacIver's mode of analyzing change is applicable to long-term trends and the knotty problems of "social evolution." Social evolution is a more or less regular development toward social differentiation, which is the product of continuous social change, derived from the processes discussed above.[53] The "schema of so-

51 MacIver, The Web of Government, pp. 143, 163, 289; The Modern State, p. 294.

52 MacIver, "The New Social Stratification," op. cit., p. 108; The Web of Government, pp. 98–99, 143, 447, 452. See also Cooley, op. cit., pp. 239–249; Hans H. Gerth and C. Wright Mills, trans. and eds., From Max Weber: Essays in Sociology (New York: Oxford University Press, 1946), chs. 7–9.

53 MacIver, Society, pp. 490–492.

cial evolution" begins with societies marked by *communal customs* and interlaced interests of an undifferentiated community (the kin group). Another major phase appears when technological developments—based on invention and diffusion—are rapid enough to enable persons to distinguish technique from myth and civilization from culture, and thus to engage in specialized activities, but still within the framework of a relatively undifferentiated social organization. Strictly speaking, this period of evolution— that of *differentiated communal institutions*—represents potential social change promoted by cultural and technical developments. In the third phase, *differentiated associations*, dynamic assessment of specialized activities ultimately dissolves traditionally inclusive relationships in favor of variably autonomous associations, thereby planting numerous nuclei of separate social-change processes and adding for the first time a third dimension—the *social order*.[54]

Human phenomena henceforth must be understood in terms of the dynamic interconnections among the three great orders, with dynamic assessment as the catalytic agent. With cultural trends as the proper sphere of the humanities, and with civilizational developments the concern of the natural scientists and technologists (political and economic), the social order and its transformations remain as the distinctive focus of the social sciences—notably, but not exclusively, sociology.[55]

SELECTED REFERENCES

Berger, Morroe, *et al.*, eds., *Freedom and Control in Modern Society* (Princeton: Van Nostrand, 1954).
MacIver, Robert M., *As a Tale That Is Told* (Chicago: University of Chicago Press, 1968).
Spitz, David, ed., *Politics and Society* (New York: Atherton, 1968).

54 *Ibid.*, pp. 482, 492–498.
55 This was the major contribution of Simmel, Max Weber, Alfred Weber, Leopold von Wiese, and Znaniecki. Of contemporary sociologists and sociology texts, few observe this delimitation seriously. See, however, Pitirim A. Sorokin, *Society, Culture, and Personality* (New York: Harper & Row, 1947); Talcott Parsons, *Essays in Sociological Theory* (New York: Free Press, 1954); Robert Bierstedt, *The Social Order* (New York: McGraw-Hill, 1957).

7

Pitirim Sorokin:
Integralist Sociology

One of the anomalies of modern sociology is the continued neglect of the essential contributions made by Pitirim Sorokin in his stormy career. In erudition as well as in basic viewpoint, Sorokin possessed the potentialities of a Max Weber when he was welcomed to American academic circles in the mid-twenties. Within a few years, many books and articles were to appear with his distinctive imprint and terminology, which were to culminate in the extremely controversial four-volume *Social and Cultural Dynamics*, published between 1937 and 1941. By 1930, Harvard University beckoned invitingly with a newly established Department of Sociology, which he was to direct until 1946.

It may be useful to distinguish four separate phases in Sorokin's career as a guide to the significance of limited portions of his work in sociology. During the first phase (1915–1921), Sorokin, a pupil of the gifted Russian legal philosopher Leo Petrajhitsky, was engaged in providing a conceptual identity for sociology. This was, of course, the approximate period in which similar efforts were being made by Simmel, Toennies, Weber, Giddings, MacIver,

Park, and Thomas and Znaniecki. The high point of this first phase was the publication in Russian of his *System of Sociology* (2 vols., 1921), which contains his basic formulations of the nature of sociocultural phenomena and of social causation. The second phase (1922–1935) was extraordinarily rich in empirical research, attempts at codification, and wide-ranging but responsible critiques of sociological writings. His most representative works were *Social Mobility* (1927), *Contemporary Sociological Theories* (1928), and a *Systematic Source Book in Rural Sociology* (3 vols., 1930–1932). During the third phase (1935–1941), Sorokin's personal philosophy and controversial spirit became increasingly evident— magnificently so in his *Social and Cultural Dynamics,* which demolished cyclical theories of change with impressive accumulations of tables and graphs, only to be replaced by Sorokin's etherealized version of Spenglerian and Toynbeean sociocultural cycles. Finally, the fourth period (since 1942) corresponds to the virtual repudiation of Sorokin by fellow American sociologists, a development for which mutual responsibility might well be assigned and in which both personal feelings and impersonal developments have played considerable parts. With negligible exceptions, Sorokin in this period forsook research for social criticism, apocalyptic philosophizing, propaganda, and (more recently) a quasi-evangelistic campaign for altruism and love. From a sociological standpoint, most of his publication in this period can be safely forgotten. However, one work, *Society, Culture, and Personality* (1947), effectively summarizes the best of the preceding phases and thereby validates Sorokin's claim to our continuing attention.

SOCIOLOGY AND SOCIOCULTURAL PHENOMENA

Future historians of American sociology may well disagree on the overall importance and role of Sorokin during a period of complex investigations. However, it seems likely that his most lasting contribution will be his analytical critique of fundamental methodology in sociology, a critique that is supplemented by forceful attempts to uncover the essential elements and objectives of a distinctive discipline. Diverging sharply from the "formal" school of Simmel and others,[1] Sorokin broadens the definition of sociology to encompass the study of "sociocultural phenomena," though acknowledging the analytical distinction of the social and the cultural.[2] This is of course the position of British social anthropologists—in particular, of Radcliffe-Brown—but it is disputed in principle while often accepted in practice by American sociologists. Sorokin builds a strong case for this conception by a masterful examination of the irreducible unit of human phenomena —*meaningful interaction*,[3] which is generally conceded to be the key sociological concept, with well-known terminological variations. For meaningful interaction inherently possesses three empirical components: (1) *human agents*, as subjects and objects of interaction; (2) *meanings and values*, which are exchanged and which constitute the distinctive ingredient in human phenomena; and (3) *material objects* ("vehicles"), which serve to objectify meanings in the process of interaction.[4] Consequently, human phenomena must be considered sociocultural phenomena; and sociology inevitably encompasses the study of cultural systems, social groups, and sociocultural factors in individual behavior. In short, sociology emerges as a quest for the conceptual trinity—society, culture, and personality.

In practice, Sorokin gives particular emphasis to society and culture, while personality remains a peripheral concern, to be called upon when needed. However, the conception and use of "culture" in Sorokin's sociology create certain difficulties that must be made explicit at this point. The cultural aspect is, on the one hand, very broadly defined as ". . . meanings, values, norms, *their interaction and relationship*, their integrated and unintegrated groups ('systems' and 'congeries') as they are objectified through overt actions and other vehicles in the empirical sociocultural universe." [5]

[1] Pitirim A. Sorokin, *Contemporary Sociological Theories* (New York: Harper & Row, 1928), ch. 9; Georg Simmel, *The Sociology of Georg Simmel*, trans. Kurt H. Wolff (New York: Free Press, 1950), pp. 21–23, 40–57.

[2] Pitirim A. Sorokin, *Society, Culture, and Personality* (New York: Harper & Row, 1947), pp. 63–64, 313.

[3] *Ibid.*, pp. 40–51.

[4] *Ibid.*, pp. 51–63; Pitirim A. Sorokin, *Sociocultural Causality, Space, and Time* (Durham, N.C.: Duke University Press, 1943), pp. 4–27.

[5] *Society, Culture, and Personality*, p. 313 (my italics).

Culture is further distinguished into three levels or parts: the *ideological*, consisting of norms and values; the *behavioral*, referring to actions by which meanings are objectified, conveyed, and accepted; and the *material*, the biophysical objects through which ideological culture is manifested.[6] Though matters of definition are always arbitrary, it is probably confusing to refer to "behavioral culture" as defined by Sorokin, for this aspect of human interaction might better be classified under social relationships and social interaction. More important, however, is the fact that Sorokin uses his culture concept to refer principally to "ideological culture."

This divergence of definition and usage is extremely important in another respect. Not only is there a tendency to mix social and cultural processes, but cultural facts seem to be analyzed by Sorokin in two separable ways. In his discussion of integrated groups, culture appears as an objective component in the form of "law-norms," [7] to which we shall later return. This approach corresponds to the functional anthropologist's view of culture. But Sorokin has more recently emphasized the three great cultural supersystems—the Ideational, the Idealistic, and the Sensate—not merely as descriptive summaries of cultural productions, but as evaluative tools.[8] As a result, personal philosophy and arbitrary judgments seep into his sociology with disturbing frequency. For example, sensate culture is often depicted as the villain of a gigantic human drama, while ideational and idealistic forms retain a special utopian glow. It may well be that Sorokin gives more than routine attention to the cultural component because this abets some inner compulsion to evaluate social phenomena—a possibility that is largely excluded by emphasis on the social dimension of human phenomena.

Since culture seems to be the most distinctive (though not the exclusive) aspect of meaningful interaction, the development of appropriate methods of describing culture and of discovering its interconnections with other aspects of social reality must be high on the agenda of sociology. While this problem was clearly recog-

[6] *Ibid.*, chs. 17, 18. See also John Gillin, *The Ways of Men* (New York: Appleton-Century-Crofts, 1948), pp. 180–184, 492–494.

[7] *Society, Culture, and Personality*, pp. 72–89.

[8] *Ibid.*, chs. 39–42; Pitirim A. Sorokin, *Social and Cultural Dynamics* (4 vols.; New York: American Book Co., 1937–1941), I, pp. 66–101.

nized by Max Weber, Cooley, Znaniecki, and MacIver, among others,[9] its solution has been subject to considerable criticism. Subjective bias and difficulty of verifying sociocultural generalizations have been the source of many legitimate criticisms of methodology. Yet Sorokin has contributed an extremely important analysis of these problems in the form of crucial distinctions in the nature of sociocultural data. If the resultant proposal for a methodologically versatile "integralist sociology" has not yet received much attention or approbation,[10] it nevertheless merits some review and perhaps some revision in our judgment.

For present purposes, Sorokin can be said to have reduced the multiplicity of social or quasi-social facts to three types or levels, each of which requires special methods of investigation.[11] Of least interest to the sociologist are data that exhibit accidental, "meaningless" connections derived from sheer concentration in a limited unit of space. The contents of a garbage can, the unique chaos of a woman's handbag, and traditional trait-lists in ethnography seem to be prevalent examples of this type of factual bundle, which Sorokin calls "congeries." It should be pointed out that congeries is a residual term, since further investigation may establish a more meaningful interdependence of individual facts. Thus, what is initially a bewildering mélange of incompatible articles in a woman's purse can be (perhaps) interpreted as the material reflection of an anxiety-ridden female perpetually prepared for numerous minor difficulties—shiny nose (powder); runny nose (face tissues); headache (aspirin); shortage of cash (checkbook); lapse of memory (address-book, shopping lists), etc.

A second level of concern stems from facts that are, in Sorokin's terminology, "causally or functionally integrated." Strictly speaking, "pure" causal or functional systems rest solely on physical and chemical interactions of component units. In such systems, specific

---

[9] See discussions of these authors in chs. 1–3, 6 of this volume.

[10] For examples of sharp criticism, see Robert Bierstedt, "The Logico-Meaningful Method of P. A. Sorokin," *American Sociological Review*, II (December, 1937), pp. 813–823; Hans Speier, "The Sociological Ideas of Pitirim Alexandrovitch Sorokin: 'Integralist Sociology,'" in Harry E. Barnes, ed., *An Introduction to the History of Sociology* (Chicago: University of Chicago Press, 1948), pp. 884–901.

[11] Sorokin, *Social and Cultural Dynamics* (Boston: Porter Sargent, 1957, one volume edition), pp. 4–9.

chains of events are correlated with and "explained" by precedent
events within a system. As Radcliffe-Brown has correctly indicated,[12] a causal connection (as distinct from a correlation) refers
to predictable and understandable variations expressed in terms of a
limited number of variables, while a functional connection requires an ideal knowledge of all variables and their interrelations in
a system. Obviously, then, "functional integration" presumes om-
niscience of systems; equally obviously, the so-called "functional
approach" must be somewhat "impure" and dependent on analogy.
And it likewise follows from the definition of social phenomena as
"meaningful interaction" that such phenomena cannot be approached in purely causal terms without a consequent lethal equation of social and non-social realms.

Sorokin (in company with others) sees no honest escape from
this "reductionist fallacy" without the conception of a third level
of factual integration—the logico-meaningful or meaningful-
causal.[13] The latter designation is more recent and probably a
more accurate and helpful summary of a distinctive sociological approach to human data. Basically, the meaningful–causal approach
tries to grasp the inherently mixed nature of social reality by including and giving special prominence to values and meanings, unlike the purely causal–functional approach, which can only produce statistical correlations. As in all methodological undertakings,
the meaningful–causal type contains an underlying set of theoretical premises, which Sorokin presents to justify this method. Of
course, implicitly or explicitly, theory in some form always precedes methodology;[14] otherwise methodology could not fail to be
blind, arbitrary, and scientifically sterile. Therefore, let us examine
the major theoretical arguments for considering social facts as
meaningful–causal systems.

In agreement with the well-known viewpoints of Znaniecki and
Thomas,[15] Sorokin adopts a genetic approach to social facts, in
which the nature of social facts becomes less significant than the

---

[12] A. R. Radcliffe-Brown, *A Natural Science of Society* (New York: Free
Press, 1957), pp. 40–41, 85–87.

[13] *Social and Cultural Dynamics*, 1957 ed., pp. 5–8.

[14] Cf. Florian Znaniecki, *The Method of Sociology* (New York: Rinehart,
1934), ch. 1.

[15] *Ibid.*, pp. 275–282.

processes of emergence and development of social facts. Several theoretical conclusions pertinent to our discussion consequently receive particular emphasis in Sorokin's scheme.

1. Sociocultural facts typically develop in three phases, or perhaps in three analytically separable aspects that are roughly sequential.
2. The first phase, Sorokin asserts, is mental conception, or the creation and fusion of meanings and values. This set of processes is characterized by the use of reason, logic, intuition, and sensory experience in varying proportions. In this phase, the concept of causality is only partially applicable. Sorokin seems to imply causal processes in discussions of "favorable heredity," physical needs, and perhaps in accidental cues, as these factors affect the conception of new meanings and ideas.[16]
3. Meanings are abortive social facts, however, and require effective objectification—the second phase—for survival. At this point, of course, material vehicles of meanings must be selected. Once again, strict notions of causality are found to be inapplicable by Sorokin, who instead emphasizes such factors as previous sets of meanings and the mental processes of abstraction and association in the objectification phase.[17]
4. Finally, social facts require socialization, the transmission of objectified meanings to other persons for their potential acceptance. Acceptance or socialization may be limited to the meaning itself (e.g., the idea of contraception), or to the use of the related material vehicle (e.g., driving an automobile without knowledge of the theory of internal combustion). But it is at the level of socialization that the causal aspect of sociocultural facts becomes most prominent. Only in this phase can we investigate the influence of meaningful action (accompanied and facilitated by material vehicles) on the behavior of others—a causal connection directed by motives and meanings that reflect both causal and symbolic antecedents. Therefore, experience dictates the conception of sociocultural facts as inherently meaningful–causal.

The implications of this conclusion are clear but difficult to translate into scientific practice. If it is acknowledged—as it must be—that social reality is integral (simultaneously composed of physical behavior, material objects, and meanings assigned to or re-

---

[16] *Society, Culture, and Personality*, pp. 537–554.   [17] *Ibid.*, pp. 555–562.

flected in the former), it is patently unwise to pursue each aspect of social reality separately by means of techniques uniquely appropriate to each (statistical correlation, causal analysis, reasoning, logic, *Verstehen*). Yet that course is one of the paradoxical conclusions set forth in the *Social and Cultural Dynamics*.[18] In later works, notably *Society, Culture, and Personality*, Sorokin assigns the highest significance to the meaning component,[19] thereby reversing his methodological position to a new determinism that is scientifically untenable unless proper modifications are introduced.

Let us see how Sorokin seeks to escape from the crucial methodological dilemma—the complex, unique nature of sociocultural facts as viewed with the discrete tools of scientific description and analysis. The first necessity lies in abandoning the fruitless labor of investigating congeries, which yield little knowledge of sociocultural phenomena, unless they can be validly related to meaningful-causal systems (an organized social group). But how does the sociologist reliably identify congeries? It is implied that, since congeries reflect chance or accidental juxtaposition of facts, the statistical method can clearly determine chance and non-chance correlations.[20] However, statistics cannot distinguish between causal–functional and meaningful–causal systems. Consequently, in Sorokin's view, genuine sociocultural systems must be analyzed in terms of the interrelation among agents, meanings, and material vehicles. This is both logical and admirable, but it is more aspiration than program. Sorokin makes the assumption that meanings are independent variables, with sufficient stability to permit proper investigation, and that vehicles and agents necessarily function as dependent variables in neat meaningful–causal chains. Under such an assumption, one need only identify cultural premises (meanings) by examining behavior or its fruits for evidence of consistency, identity, and contradiction, and then report the concomitant consequences on the behavioral and material levels.

The circularity of this approach is quite obvious, for the basic assumption inevitably determines the results. Yet Sorokin has contributed an instructive error, one that begins on solid ground but

---

[18] *Social and Cultural Dynamics*, I, pp. 48–53.
[19] *Society, Culture, and Personality*, ch. 18.   [20] *Ibid.*, pp. 332–334.

somehow strays toward unmarked quicksands. For Sorokin is quite right in focusing attention on the meaning component, but he is both logically and empirically wrong in supposing that the distinctive component of any system therefore determines the operation of that system. As approached by Sorokin, meanings are pure, timeless, unproblematic; but this descriptive, static view obscures other aspects of meanings—their emergent qualities and their objectification and institutionalization. If it is to any extent true that meanings influence behavior, it is likewise important to recognize that changes in meaning are not merely logical, but social in origin as well as in consequences.[21] Furthermore, the study of meanings by Sorokin blandly violates an integralist principle—and a psychological one as well. For in considering meanings in terms of logic and consistency alone, Sorokin has removed meanings from their proper context—the experience and attitudes of implicated actors —to the foreign realm of the logician–philosopher. A considerable body of research clearly demonstrates that persons selectively perceive and unpredictably modify meanings of all sorts,[22] thereby compelling sociologists to abjure preconceived descriptions of values for objective investigations of valuations, as reflected in speech, behavior, documents, projective tests, etc.

These fundamental criticisms do not detract from the essential value of the meaningful–causal approach, which Sorokin has ably characterized as a complex approach suited to the complexities of sociocultural phenomena. It is rather in the narrow application of this approach that serious problems arise, particularly the error of cultural determinism. Significantly, Sorokin does not completely rely on his meaningful–causal method in studying sociocultural change, to which we shall later devote considerable attention. As outlined and applied by Sorokin, the meaningful–causal method is capable only of describing highly integrated sociocultural systems and of placing them in appropriate ideal typical categories (e.g., Ideational, Idealistic, and Sensate). However, this general approach

[21] This is the major problem in the sociology of knowledge. See ch. 13 of this volume.

[22] See John T. Doby, *Introduction to Social Psychology* (New York: Appleton-Century-Crofts, 1966), chs. 5, 6.

does not require taxonomic absorption; the stress on social facts as systems with interdependent components (meanings, agents, vehicles) constitutes a holistic frame of reference and a prolegomenon to the functional orientation so popular in recent years. Indeed, in view of the above criticisms, the basic value of the meaningful–causal method can perhaps be salvaged by emphasizing and developing its implicit functionalism [23] in the direction of a cautious sociological functionalism applied to the twin problems of stability and change.

SOCIAL STRUCTURE

Unlike Simmel, who was intrigued by the subtle, semi-organized forms of human interaction,[24] Sorokin has chosen to emphasize the established systems of meaningful interaction, their genesis and underlying structure, as the legitimate province of sociological analysis. As Znaniecki has often declared, sociology is plagued by its failure to develop adequate conceptualization and classification of the distinctive products of human interactions—groups and institutions.[25] Consequently, the acknowledged taxonomic skill of Sorokin, wedded to a devastating critical faculty, is admirably suited to this task, the results of which warrant closer attention then they have previously received.

Taking meaningful interaction as his basic unit, Sorokin aims at achieving a classification that employs a number of basic variables in distinguishing the most prevalent types of sociocultural systems. Expressly excluded from consideration therefore are congeries, unorganized plurels, temporary interaction chains (publics, crowds, audiences), and social categories. The social group as a generic entity is a special, minimally organized, temporally stable system of interacting individuals, variations in which occur along three significant dimensions or interaction processes.[26] Of greatest impor-

---

[23] See the analyses of functionalism in Robert K. Merton, *Social Theory and Social Structure* (New York: Free Press, 1957 ed.), chs. 1, 12.

[24] See ch. 2, pp. 44–48.   [25] Znaniecki, *op. cit.*, pp. 120–129.

[26] *Society, Culture, and Personality*, pp. 147–158.

tance is the organized–unorganized–disorganized variable. This refers to the relative presence of clearcut "law-norms," which consist of standards by which rights, responsibilities, and privileges are allocated to interacting persons. The law-norms define, regulate, and coordinate the role-status structure of a group and, in Sorokin's view, are inseparable from the basic nature of social groups.[27] Unorganized groupings lack law-norms and therefore reflect temporary, non-cumulative forms of interaction. By implication, disorganized groups possess weakened or contradictory sets of law-norms.

A second dimension of human groups, somewhat independent of the first, takes account of the relative similarity in ends and interests (as expressed in behavior) of group members—solidary, antagonistic, and mixed forms of interaction.[28]

Finally, Sorokin distinguishes a synthetic variable, the interrelationship of meanings, agents, and material vehicles in given social groups—the integrated–unintegrated continuum.[29]

The classification of groups derived from these variables is exhaustive, continuing and modifying earlier typologies and yet unique in one important respect. Largely depending on the first and third dimensions, Sorokin categorizes organized groups in terms of the number of specific meanings and interests shared by their members. Groups organized around one set of meaningful interests are called *unibonded groups,* which correspond to some extent to the meaning assigned to "associations" and "secondary groups."[30] Race, sex, age, territorial proximity, occupation, religion, income, etc., may be the basis of such groups. On the other hand, groups that function by cumulating various types of activities and interests into a complex system of sociocultural interdependence constitute *multibonded groups,* such as families, tribes, castes, nations, and communities.[31]

An intriguing feature of this classification is the methodological and conceptual shift from emphasis on the quality of relationships to the number of meaning-sets shared by members of a group. Sociologists who have become accustomed to the dichotomy of pri-

---

[27] *Ibid.,* pp. 70–85, 91–92.   [28] *Ibid.,* chs. 5–7.   [29] *Ibid.,* pp. 313–316.
[30] *Ibid.,* pp. 171–178.   [31] *Ibid.,* ch. 13.

mary and secondary groups are understandably puzzled by this apparent neglect of established distinctions. Yet Sorokin has in effect compelled us to re-examine the utility of these well-worn concepts. Essentially, he points to the existence of varying types of primary and secondary groups, which can be ordered in terms of a more basic variable and a broader classificatory scheme. Consequently, he analyzes what he calls "structural varieties" of both unibonded and multibonded groups according to such important variables as size, duration, stratification, interaction type, centralization, and the interrelationships among agents, vehicles, and meanings. Particular attention is given to interaction types and the derivative classification of *familistic, contractual,* and *compulsory* systems.[32] The familistic type corresponds closely to the general conception of the primary group, while the contractual (or mixed) type may be considered a specially rewarding analysis of the secondary group as a composite form—not, as generally assumed, the polar antithesis of the primary group. Finally, the compulsory type, for which there has been no careful conceptualization, enables us to confront the unpleasant reality of groups and relationships perpetuated by coercion, both physical and psychological; this provides a backdrop for analysis of otherwise inexplicable behavior (e.g., such deviant acts as crimes, wars, revolutions, manias).[33]

Classifications, it should be remembered, usually reflect a basic viewpoint and, most significantly, an underlying set of theories concerning the units categorized. In Sorokin's case, this principle applies with special fitness, for he has worked out a high order of integration between classificatory schemes, description and analysis of group structure, and the nature of process and dynamics in social groups. The fundamental principles, already discussed, of emphasizing well-organized groups and considering groups as meaningful entities are conspicuous in both the unibonded–multibonded dichotomy and in the major types of interaction systems. But the clearest expression of Sorokin's viewpoint may be found in his analysis of group structure and dynamics.

Any social group is a minimally organized, durable system of interaction processes guided by a set of "core" norms–rules–

[32] *Ibid.,* pp. 99–110.   [33] *Ibid.,* p. 108.

meanings called the "law-norms." Thus the human group is for Sorokin principally a cultural product; indeed, variations in inter-action processes are explained by changes in the law-norms.[34] This anthropological view of group structure is undeniably the key to Sorokin's sociology, but it also brings to the surface important problems often ignored by sociologists in their multiform use of the group concept. Since group structure is, for Sorokin, concen-trated in the law-norms as the nucleus of a cell, their analysis be-comes the proper objective of sociology.

But it is perhaps useful to consider law-norms as a set of variables in a genetic sequence, as components of ongoing group processes, to which Sorokin devotes considerable attention. In substantial conformity with earlier "social process" theorists, Sorokin distin-guishes a series of "recurrent social processes" in human groups that can be reduced to the following approximate sequence: [35] (1) origin through initial contact and interaction, (2) basic or-ganization (differentiation and stratification), (3) continuity and maintenance of identity, (4) mobility and exchange of members, (5) fluctuations in social relationships, and (6) dissolution or resurrection. The law-norms, official and unofficial norms of con-duct that assign rights, duties, responsibilities, and statuses to inter-acting individuals, arise in phase 2 and achieve stability in phases 3 and 4. Whatever the origin of substantive law-norms, and Sorokin is significantly silent on this question, they are inseparable from the phenomena of organized groups. Indeed, law-norms constitute the bonds of organization, so that for Sorokin "organized group" and "institution" are synonymous terms.[36]

In effect, Sorokin has contributed another shift in analysis of groups and institutions. The importance currently assigned to such concepts as social relation, social role, and status is disturbing to Sorokin [37] because of (a) vagueness of definitions and (b) the failure to probe the underlying interrelations among these concepts in the study of genuine groups. The logic of Sorokin's analysis rests instead on the search for clarifying, codifying concepts—in short, the law-norms. Human phenomena initially confront the in-

[34] *Ibid.*, pp. 81–82. [35] *Ibid.*, Pt. 6, especially chs. 21–27, 34.
[36] *Ibid.*, pp. 88–91. [37] *Ibid.*, pp. 85–90.

vestigator as concrete interactions between persons. With repetition, the patterns of such interactions are conceptualized as *social relationships*, or products of interaction. But analysis and understanding merely begin at this point. Deeper investigation reveals for each person one or more sets of behavioral data (social roles) empirically related to characteristic behavioral patterns of other interacting persons, as well as related opportunities and responsibilities for initiating or coordinating interaction with others (social status). However, statuses, roles, and relations in organized groups possess unifying threads that cannot be ignored or taken for granted if the essential nature of human phenomena is recalled. These threads are the law-norms, which for Sorokin represent the ultimate empirically based objective of group-institution analysis.

This emphasis on the law-norms enables the sociologist to make a much-needed conceptual connection between institutions and the phenomena of stratification (particularly class and caste). In Sorokin's schema, both social differentiation and stratification of some kind are typical processes and structures of all organized groups.[38] We might assert, in more current terminology, that stratification is a functional necessity of organized groups or institutions. But the specific nature of concrete systems of stratification is recorded in the system of law-norms. Stratification is then a highly important institutionalized (legal or non-legal) system of interaction; indeed, institutions as human phenomena inherently possess a stratification dimension. Consequently, in a patently non-Marxian manner, Sorokin has placed stratification analysis in a central position and, by inference, virtually compels the sociologist to give special prominence to stratification aspects of all institutions and organized groups. This seems to be the major logical conclusion of Sorokin's approach to groups, a contribution that has not been generally acknowledged.

Modern sociologists are of course particularly interested in the more complex forms of stratification—class and caste. Sorokin, like Max Weber, many years ago distinguished three important dimensions that enable persons to habitually recognize social in-

[38] *Ibid.*, ch. 15; Pitirim A. Sorokin, *Social Mobility* (New York: Harper, 1927), pp. 12–17.

equalities.[39] But where Weber gave special attention to market position, social honor, and political power, Sorokin emphasizes wealth, type of occupation, and politico-legal status as *coalescing components* in the differentiation of social strata. Obviously then, social strata represent a very important variety of multibonded groups, the analysis of which cannot be reduced to any single dimension.[40]

Several problems concerning the definition and differentiation of social strata are of particular concern to Sorokin, as a direct result of his meaningful–causal orientation to social phenomena. There is first the matter of proper conceptualization of variant types of social strata—castes, estates or orders, and classes. Since these are multibonded groups, each type should be distinguishable in terms of the special character of its complex of interaction bonds. Once again, Sorokin's taxonomic proficiency yields a much-needed measure of conceptual order by creating an approximate, almost developmental, continuum of caste——>estate–order——>class.[41] The caste as a constructed type constitutes the highest form of stratum organization, characterized by the simultaneous operation of racial, kinship, occupational, linguistic, religious, and territorial bonds, which virtually eliminate vertical mobility. The estate, on the other hand, is a diluted caste; it reflects the same complex of bonds, with a clearly attenuated functioning of the kinship, racial, religious, and territorial bonds. Two significant consequences give uniqueness to the estate: (1) the opportunities for individual and group mobility are increased, principally by political and/or economic achievements; and (2) the pervasive solidary organization of the caste is replaced by the concentration of genuine social groups (as previously defined) in the upper segments of the social hierarchy. Social class systems are "chronological successors" of estates; essentially, classes develop with a concomitant reduction of interaction bonds to the distinctive trinity—wealth, occupation, and politico-legal status. In further contrast to the estate, the social class is, at all levels of a given hierarchy, partly organized and partly unorganized. Vertical mobility therefore becomes not only a distinct possi-

[39] *Society, Culture, and Personality*, pp. 271–275.   [40] *Ibid.*, chs. 13, 14.
[41] *Ibid.*, pp. 256–261, 271–274.

bility, but a realistic aspiration (or danger) for class members. However, as Sorokin rightly insists, opportunities for mobility are far from infinite, since classes are legally open but actually semi-closed groups.

From a meaningful–causal standpoint and in the light of current problems of class analysis, one aspect of this discussion merits special attention. Sorokin refuses to accept either of the scientifically sterile, yet somewhat popular, approaches to class description. The first focuses on objective similarities of status among persons and therefore defines "class" as a statistical aggregate or social category, thereby ignoring the problems of number, type, and direction of interaction among similarly "situated" persons.[42] In sharp contrast is the viewpoint, largely derived from the Marxian and "conflict" theorists, which regards social classes as consciously organized "corporate" groups in which status similarities generate widespread emotional identification and active allegiance to institutionalized forms of exclusion and conflict with other classes.[43] More realistically, Sorokin avoids this "objective–subjective" controversy by approaching social class as a dynamic "field" of interaction systems; at any point in time, a given stratum possesses specific foci of organization, as well as variably prominent "pockets" of little or no organization.[44] It is the task of the sociologist to construct an empirically faithful longitudinal account of trends in stratum organization, with appropriate concern for the factors that help to understand definable variations in class organization. At this point, of course, such phenomena as class-consciousness, "false consciousness," leadership, technological and social changes, demographic trends, and patterns of informal and formal association become especially relevant.

This flexible approach to stratification has therefore been especially fruitful for analysis of stratification dynamics, a field to which Sorokin has contributed several pioneer formulations in the course of his well-known monograph, *Social Mobility*. While these problems possessed a peculiar attraction for European sociologists, American sociologists were, before Sorokin's arrival in the United States, extremely vague about the essential nature of stratification

[42] *Ibid.*, pp. 261–262, 277–278. [43] *Ibid.*, pp. 268–270. [44] *Ibid.*, pp. 288–294.

and, in addition, seemed to be more devoted to philosophical or moralistic discussions of social inequalities. Sorokin, who has for a long time stressed the necessity of studying various aspects of sociocultural change, instead assembled a staggering mass of pertinent factual investigations from several nations that enabled him to construct and test many specific hypotheses concerning the "what," "how," and "why" of changes in stratification systems.

In retrospect, three major lines of investigation initiated or developed by Sorokin retain particular significance.

1. The well-known and much-used distinction between *horizontal* and *vertical* social mobility,[45] between a "substitution" and a "basic change" in social position, needs little discussion today. However, this distinction is related to the virtually disregarded admonition of Sorokin that some social strata cannot be properly included in a strict hierarchical order.[46] Indeed, some otherwise differentiated strata seem to share a roughly coordinate (horizontal) social position with other social strata (e.g., successful agricultural owner-operators and urban salaried professionals).

2. Until very recently, Sorokin was perhaps the only American sociologist to recognize the universal phenomenon of built-in social mechanisms that facilitate or impede the vertical social mobility of individuals and groups—the so-called "channels of mobility." [47] On the basis of carefully sifted empirical material, Sorokin once again substantiated a vital connection between institutions and stratification systems [48] by demonstrating the latent function of leading institutions as significant channels of mobility. The military services, civil government, education, religion, the family, and the occupational system consequently assume a new importance as socially distributive mechanisms in the continuous process of social mobility. Parenthetically, it is only in the last two decades or so that the school has been the subject of this type of analysis.[49]

3. In a sense, institutional selectivity may be considered a "factor" in social mobility. But Sorokin rightly approaches channels of mobility as intermediate variables rather than as explanatory–causal variables.

45 *Social Mobility*, ch. 7.   46 *Society, Culture, and Personality*, p. 264.
47 *Social Mobility*, chs. 8, 9.   48 *Ibid.*, chs. 17–19.
49 See, for example, A. B. Hollingshead, *Elmtown's Youth* (New York: Wiley, 1947); Aaron V. Cicourel and John I. Kitsuse, *The Educational Decision Makers* (Indianapolis: Bobbs-Merrill, 1963).

Following the classic analyses of Mosca and Pareto,[50] he attributes great importance to demographic factors—principally the differential birth and death rates of the various social strata—which produce personnel shortages (a social vacuum) in the higher strata. However, again in accord with the observations of Mosca and Pareto, Sorokin assigns particular prominence to the vicissitudes of sociocultural change, which provoke re-assessments of social worth and provide new opportunities for ascent or descent in the social scale.[51]

SOCIOCULTURAL CHANGE

From Comte to the present generation of sociological theorists, the construction of a theoretical system has been ultimately motivated by some personal interest in the character and direction of change in nations and civilizations. Sorokin is no exception to this trend; he has been primarily engaged in evaluating the significance of recurrent upheavals in Western civilization and, more pointedly, the maladjustments derived from specific social trends in modern societies. It is abundantly clear that Sorokin, like his famous sociological predecessors, is not a passive observer of change. He continually mixes analysis with judgments of value and desirability, description with admonitory prediction. But while Sorokin prefers an utopian sociocultural system pervaded by cooperation, altruism, humility, intuition, and spirituality, we can, whether we agree with him or not, search for those aspects of his approach to change that add more to understanding than to philosophy.

The initial approach to sociocultural change is consistent with Sorokin's structural analysis and basic methodological position, already discussed. Since the nature of human phenomena is triadic (consisting of agents, meanings, and material vehicles), analysis of change must be directed to all three levels and their interrelation-

[50] Gaetano Mosca, *The Ruling Class*, trans. Hannah D. Kahn (New York: McGraw-Hill, 1939); Vilfredo Pareto, *Mind and Society*, trans. Arthur Livingston (4 vols.; New York: Harcourt, Brace, 1935), ¶ 2546, 2548.

[51] *Society, Culture, and Personality*, p. 435; *Social Mobility*, chs. 14, 15. See also Alvin Boskoff, "Negro Class Structure and the Technicways," *Social Forces*, XXIX (December, 1950), 124–131.

ships. However, the meaning-component, the distinctive and there-fore strategic aspect of human behavior, requires the most intensive analysis both in establishing fruitful units of change and definable trends in change.

These propositions are, with proper cautions, theoretically ac-ceptable and likewise reflect a legitimate though tentative applica-tion of the meaningful–causal approach. Problems arise, however, in constructing and employing empirically faithful and widely ap-plicable units of change. Sorokin has worked with three types of unit analysis, which constitute progressive steps in the embodiment of the meaningful–causal method. On the lowest level of abstrac-tion, and most accessible to empirical investigation, are *systems of social relationships or organized groups,* which, it will be recalled, are classified into familistic, contractual, and compulsory types.[52] Secondly, Sorokin selects relatively self-contained *valuational sys-tems and their material reflection*—what we might call "institu-tional areas" [53] (art, science, government and law, etc.)—as more comprehensive units of sociocultural phenomena. But these levels of analysis, in Sorokin's view, furnish the mere beginnings of proper conceptualization since they do not reveal the important networks of meaning that distinguish human society. Conse-quently, the ultimate unit of sociocultural phenomena is the logically integrated nexus of values underlying specific institu-tional systems. This is variously called the supersystem, culture mentality, or integrated culture system,[54] and it is likewise classi-fied into three major types: Ideational, Idealistic, and Sensate. In practice, however, the supersystem becomes the referential unit, for Sorokin is primarily concerned with assessing groups and insti-tutional systems in terms of their "position" in the Ideational–Sen-sate continuum.

The supersystem concept is a peculiar mixture of admirable objectives and dubious applications, and therefore it requires some serious attempts at beneficent dissection. It should first be noted that the specific types of culture mentality are *constructed types,*

[52] *Society, Culture, and Personality,* pp. 99–107.
[53] *Social and Cultural Dynamics,* I and II.
[54] *Ibid.,* I; *Society, Culture, and Personality,* pp. 319–321, 589–592.

i.e., units of analysis that purposefully simplify and accentuate the significant variables in a given realm of data. But the very notion of supersystems, as developed by Sorokin, is also a constructed type, subject to the limitations and potentialities of this misunderstood method. Essentially, Sorokin has essayed a number of crucial, complex goals by means of this highly abstract conceptual organization.

First, the supersystem seeks to assimilate in one form the underlying similarity in basic premises of various empirically discrete sociocultural phenomena, to discover logical and valuational order in apparently autonomous spheres. The most significant criteria of similarity, according to Sorokin, concern typical attitudes toward reality—the nature of reality, the nature of human needs, the levels and extent of need satisfaction, and the means of satisfaction.[55] Consequently, the sociologist constructs an empirically relevant supersystem by assessing (qualitatively and quantitatively) a representative diversity of social phenomena in a given society or period in terms of these criteria. Ideally, this synthetic unit of analysis is suited to those rare interludes of human history in which *cultural integration* attains the wondrous levels of some preliterate societies. Realistically, however, most societies fail to achieve a structure congenial to a logician; congeries, mutually insulated inconsistencies, persistent subcultural autonomies, all of which Sorokin relegates to the historian,[56] are not merely deviations, but stubborn facts. Yet, in practice, Sorokin tends to emphasize numerically dominant cultural premises, without sufficient attention to his own evidence for competing cultural "themes."[57] This frequently spurious unity of his analytic unit therefore weakens any generalization about patterns of change composed of such units.

Second, the supersystem concept provides an empirically relevant standard by which to categorize and quantify material representations of culture mentality (e.g., art objects, books, legal codes, economic conditions such as production and systems of distribution). This is, of course, a special application of what has since

[55] *Social and Cultural Dynamics*, I, ch. 2.
[56] *Society, Culture, and Personality*, p. 638.
[57] *Social and Cultural Dynamics*, II, chs. 13, 14; III, *passim*.

been called "content analysis." [58] Though the quantification of qualitative data is inherently arbitrary and therefore often open to legitimate criticism, this type of "measurement" enables the sociologist to describe sociocultural fluctuations with verifiable empirical generalizations concerning direction, speed, and tempo. Sorokin himself seems to be justifiably uncomfortable with the statistical analysis of supersystems and their manifestations,[59] but he and his associates have at least demonstrated the possibilities of fruitfully combining the statistical (or causal–functional) and the meaningful–causal approaches. However, sociologists interpret these labors as an unwitting parody of modern "scientism." [60]

Third, Sorokin's use of supersystem analysis appears to be a herculean attempt to reformulate the basic methodology of sociological research. One of the perennially confounding difficulties in sociology, according to Sorokin, is the arbitrary selection of independent and dependent variables in research. Thus technology, religion, political organization, and ideology have each been regarded as "causal" variables related to the development of such phenomena as capitalism and its problems—and with obvious contradictory results.[61] To obviate the fruitless controversies engendered by these preconceived, fractionalized approaches, Sorokin suggests that developments in each cultural subsystem be considered as manifestations of the overall functioning of the supersystem.[62] In short, the cultural premises of the dominant supersystem are conceived as the only "proper" independent variables, while the various institutional systems are almost reduced to the status of dependent variables. This particular "solution" clearly raises the specter of cultural determinism and entirely ignores the logical and empirical problems of explaining fluctuations in the cultural prem-

[58] Bernard Berelson, *Content Analysis in Communication Research* (New York: Free Press, 1959).

[59] Pitirim A. Sorokin, *Fads and Foibles in Modern Sociology and Related Sciences* (Chicago: Henry Regnery Co., 1956), pp. 115–173.

[60] See the reviews of Robert E. Park, *American Journal of Sociology*, XLIII (March, 1938), pp. 824–832; Robert M. MacIver, *American Sociological Review*, VI (December, 1941), pp. 904–907; M. R. Rogers, John H. Randall, Jr., and Hans Speier, *ibid.*, II (December, 1937), pp. 917–929.

[61] *Contemporary Sociological Theories*, pp. 690–691; *Society, Culture, and Personality*, pp. 657–658.

[62] *Society, Culture, and Personality*, pp. 636–638.

ises, as we have already seen. But these important criticisms should not veil the recognition of another implication in this use of the supersystem: the necessity of analyzing both structure and dynamics in terms of functionally interrelated sets of variables, i.e., as systems.[63] This is often the underlying approach to supersystems, but Sorokin seems to leap unjustifiably from this conception to one in which the complex structure of the supersystem is fully represented by one component—the culture premise.

Perhaps one of the most enduring features of this orientation to change through identification of supersystems is its emphasis on specific changes, or clusters of changes, in the context of larger configurations of sociocultural phenomena. Indeed, Sorokin distinguishes two types of relationships between changes and established systems or supersystems. On the one hand are changes in the genetic development of a broad sociocultural system [64]—changes that merely add detail and complexity toward the development of a full-blown, distinctive system (e.g., the evolution of modern capitalism). Here the familiar processes of ideation, objectification, and socialization function in an experimentally tentative, cooperative fashion to produce sociocultural variations about a constantly developing set of sociocultural themes. These *changes by variation,* as Sorokin calls them, therefore constitute the history of a specific type of supersystem.

But Sorokin has been somewhat more attracted by the second type of change process—*change by substitution.*[65] In this case, the character of specific changes is sufficiently divergent from the pre-existing themes to cause either sociocultural disorganization—the dominance of congeries—fitfully countered by coercive coordination (cf. Toynbee), or the gradual or relatively rapid replacement of significantly different themes. The second contingency is, of course, the long-term process of creating newly dominant supersystems. "The supersystem is dead. Long live the supersystem."

To this emphasis on the supersystem unit and its dual processes of change by variation and substitution, Sorokin finally and most crucially applies his explanatory principles of sociocultural dynamics. Though it is never explicitly stated by Sorokin, his causal theo-

[63] *Ibid.*, chs. 43–46; *Social and Cultural Dynamics*, IV, Pt. I.
[64] *Society, Culture, and Personality*, pp. 643–654.   [65] *Ibid.*, pp. 655–657.

ries of change seem to be specifically adapted to the understanding of each major change process. Thus, change by variation receives a predominantly immanent explanation, which stresses the internally derived processes of change in a supersystem.[66] A basic order of phases in this process, which we have already noted in another context, is *conception* (invention and creation), *objectification* (use of material vehicles), and *socialization* (institutionalization). Sorokin, it must be noted, limits this generalization principally to organized sociocultural systems. If we focus our attention on the order of phases, we must inevitably recognize a direct challenge to the popular theory of *cultural lag,* to which Sorokin dedicates a powerful critique on methodological and empirical grounds.[67] Indeed, this critique should be required reading for students (young and old) who regard cultural lag as axiomatic.

The replacement of supersystems, which is taken to be "varyingly recurrent," likewise is explained by reference to the internal or immanent characteristics of sociocultural systems, though again external factors are largely conceived as "disturbers" of a self-determined course of development.[68] In all such processes—immanent and externalistic—sociocultural change of supersystems tends to conform to the principle of limits, which summarizes the inevitable restrictions on empirical variation derived from the close meaningful–causal integration of variables in genuine sociocultural systems.[69] Thus, Sorokin has constructed an impressively broad but disturbingly flexible orientation toward an "integral theory" of change, composed of the three principles of immanence, externality, and limits.

It might be plausibly assumed that these coordinated principles, which are accorded sweeping applicability by Sorokin, would necessarily erase the earlier distinction between change by variation and change by substitution. Each change process seems to bear the imprint of immanent and external factors, plus the related inhibitions embodied in the principle of limited possibilities. Sorokin himself does not, for example, pursue the logical possibility that each

[66] *Ibid.,* pp. 696–699; *Social and Cultural Dynamics,* IV. See also Pitirim A. Sorokin, *Sociological Theories of Today* (New York: Harper & Row, 1966), ch. 16.

[67] *Society, Culture, and Personality,* pp. 580–582, 663–673.

[68] *Social and Cultural Dynamics,* 1957 ed., ch. 38.   [69] *Ibid.,* ch. 39.

type of change process possesses a distinctive relationship of immanent and external factors (e. g., that immanence becomes a more significant determinant in change by substitution). By inference, however, change by variation appears to correspond to the early phases of supersystem formation, while the "mature" phases tend to evolve a dominance of changes by substitution, in accordance with the principle of limits. Consequently, these processes, though functioning simultaneously, possess typically different periods of dominance. If this inference is correct, the necessity of developing empirically relevant criteria for the differing phases of supersystems becomes especially urgent. At present, such criteria are mainly impressionistic.[70]

But the most important aspect of Sorokin's approach to sociocultural change—one that underlies and gives coherence to his analyses of supersystems, change processes, and the three principles of change—is his translation of the generic phenomena of change into structural–functional terms. This is, or should be, inordinately instructive, since critics of the structural–functional approach have repeatedly decried its presumed confinement to problems of structure and stability.[71]

There can be little doubt that, for Sorokin, the theory of immanence constitutes the core principle of sociocultural dynamics. However, this principle is derived from a series of interlocking conceptions of the nature of sociocultural phenomena as systems.[72]

1. From the very nature of social systems, analogous to biological systems, the component parts constitute an interrelated unity.
2. But sociocultural systems, as we have already seen, endure through meaningful–causal integration of persons, values, and material vehicles.
3. Furthermore, a sociocultural system is a going concern, constantly

[70] Sorokin deals with this problem only in terms of rhythms and time-sequences. See *Society, Culture, and Personality,* pp. 681–695.

[71] John Rex, *Key Problems of Sociological Theory* (London: Routledge & Kegan Paul, 1961), ch. 7; Wayne Hield, "The Study of Change in Social Science," *British Journal of Sociology,* V (March, 1954), pp. 1–10; Ralf Dahrendorf, "Out of Utopia: Toward a Reorientation of Sociological Analysis," *American Journal of Sociology,* LXIV (September, 1958), pp. 115–127.

[72] *Sociocultural Causality, Space, and Time,* pp. 25–27.

"working" or "in use," and therefore inevitably undergoing variations of a more or less cumulative nature.

4. These variations, which principally reflect the broad potentialities for change characteristic of specific types of systems, inevitably generate derivative or readjustive changes in other components of the system in the process of re-establishing equilibrium.

5. Every sociocultural system, because of its peculiar meaningful–causal unity, possesses inherent limits of development. When these limits are approached or exceeded, the operation of the system tends to produce counteractive variations that may radically alter the nature of component parts in maintaining the essentials of a system.

Keeping in mind Sorokin's supplementary use of the externalist principle, it is clear that sociocultural change of any significance is a natural, expectable property of human groups, that change is a functional necessity of society and its parts, just as physiological processes satisfy the system-needs of organisms and their parts. But since the supersystem is the focus of Sorokin's analysis of change, let us examine the application of this structural–functional orientation to changes by substitution, i.e., to shifts in dominant supersystems. In Sorokin's phrase, "the germ of its own decline" is contained in every supersystem.[73] For every supersystem can be devoted to only a fraction of "ultimate reality,"[74] which we might rephrase as the totality of systems available to actual or potential human experience. Indeed, the exigencies of organization and integration impose the necessity of selectively perceiving and conceiving the indefinable manifold called reality. At this point, Sorokin has made an imperceptible but necessary shift in his explanatory scheme. Not only must supersystems, as going concerns, evolve according to "inherent potentialities" (immanent destiny), but they must be periodically revised to survive in the context of wider, more inclusive systems or disintegrate. The pattern of changes in supersystems then may be completely understood in terms of functional analysis if it be granted that adjustive relations to other systems likewise constitute an important set of "immanent" needs.[75] Thus, the ultimate significance of Sorokin's "integ-

[73] *Society, Culture, and Personality*, p. 704.

[74] *Ibid.*, p. 705; *Social and Cultural Dynamics*, 1957 ed., pp. 679–683.

[75] *Society, Culture, and Personality*, pp. 698–699.

ralist" theory of change may well be the recognition that immanence and externalism are complementary, rather than opposing, orientations to empirical change.

The contrapuntal strengths and weaknesses of this comprehensive theory of change perhaps offer an appropriate occasion for closing remarks, particularly since this theory reflects corresponding contributions and limitations in Sorokin's entire system of sociology. Disposing of the apparent deficiencies first, an outstanding feature of Sorokin's approach is its emphasis on the later phases of highly integrated sociocultural phenomena. As reference points for analysis of intermediate phenomena of change, these supersystems are obviously helpful. But an overwhelming mass of social facts of some significance to sociologists does not seem to form a sufficiently tight unit of analysis. Moreover, the temporal gap between identifiably different supersystems, or periods of transition, is enormous, so the sociologist inevitably confronts various degrees of organization in social facts as a matter of routine, not as a residual problem.

Sorokin's undue focus on high orders of integration creates additional difficulties in understanding the processes of sociocultural change. There is first the one-sided emphasis on cultural premises as both logical and causal bonds of supersystem organization, with a resultant mysticism in the development of sociocultural variations. Sorokin tends to analyze and evaluate changes, therefore, as they seem to relate to the cultural premises alone, neglecting the social (relational) structure as a component of the process of variation. This narrowed theory of cultural immanence also leads to vague assertions about "inherent potentialities" of supersystems, which turn out to be either *a priori* judgments or, at best, *post hoc* statements of limited verifiability. The same problem of subjective evaluation likewise arises in unsubstantiated assertions about the "inadequacy" of supersystems and their dominant premises in their most highly developed stages.[76] "Inadequacy" is measured against the standard of "genuine reality," which we are told is simultaneously rational, supersensory, and empirical. It should be noted that

[76] *Ibid.,* pp. 705–706. Cf. Jacques Maquet, *The Sociology of Knowledge* (Boston: Beacon Press, 1951), p. 276 (note 35).

this standard is a logical, almost epistemological one—not a "practical" one. Paradoxically, the more highly organized the supersystem, the more "inadequate" it becomes, since its cultural premises retreat from reality in proportion as they develop logical cohesion. Genuine reality would then seem to require a plenitude of congeries and semi-autonomous subsystems, each set capturing a fragment of reality in its corpus of cultural premises. But is sociocultural change properly interpreted, as Sorokin implies, as a protracted "search" for existent reality? Or is change an interminable process of recreating, as well as adapting to, reality?

In spite of these criticisms, Sorokin's approach to sociocultural change remains as a classic transition between the broad theories of the nineteenth century and the highly specialized, empirical investigations of the last fifteen or twenty years.[77] Change as an intelligible process—accountable no longer in terms of geography, climate, race, "great men," or evolutionary necessity—is a major contribution of the meaningful–causal orientation. When combined with an analysis of change as a continuous process of determinate structural–functional systems, the resultant "integral theory" of change allows the dictates of broad theory to be translated into properly circumscribed empirical investigations. Finally, Sorokin reserves a respectable place in sociological theory for the study and understanding of tensions, maladjustments, and conflicts as normal components of social change, offering a much-needed emphasis on the ideological aspects of change.

SELECTED REFERENCES

Allen, Philip J., ed., *Pitirim A. Sorokin in Review* (Durham, N.C.: Duke University Press, 1963).

Cowell, F. R., *History, Civilization, and Culture: An Introduction to the Historical and Social Philosophy of Pitirim A. Sorokin* (Boston: Beacon Press, 1952).

Tiryakian, Edward A., ed., *Sociological Theory, Values, and Sociocultural Change* (New York: Free Press, 1963).

[77] Alvin Boskoff, "Recent Theories of Social Change," in Werner J. Cahnman and Alvin Boskoff, eds., *Sociology and History* (New York: Free Press, 1964), pp. 148–149.

8

Karl Mannheim: Theories
of Social Manipulation
in Transitional Society

In the recent history of sociological theorizing—as distinct from classifying and conceptualizing—few men have served as interpretive links between classic theorists and the significant pioneering theorizing of current working sociologists. Mannheim is one of this select few, though it is unfortunately true that much of his work has been ignored.[1] Yet Mannheim combines the essential contributions of such theorists as Marx, Simmel, Durkheim, and Weber with a modernized application of Machiavelli and Comte in an implicitly systematic manner that merits serious attention from students of contemporary society.

[1] Cf. Nicholas S. Timasheff, *Sociological Theory* (New York: Random House, 1957), pp. 274–277; Don Martindale, *The Nature and Types of Sociological Theory* (Boston: Houghton Mifflin, 1960), pp. 414–418; Lewis A. Coser and Bernard Rosenberg, eds., *Sociological Theory* (New York: Macmillan, 1957), pp. 560–562; Pitirim A. Sorokin, *Sociological Theories of Today* (New York: Harper & Row, 1966), pp. 152, 455, 597.

From Comte and the long tradition that sustains his fundamental role in sociological analysis, Mannheim has taken the notion of the interdependence of the intellectual–technical, the social–organizational, and the cultural facets of human society. Comte's "law of three stages" in intellectual development was supplemented by correlated sequences in dominant institutions and focal-group forms. Thus Mannheim was ultimately able—after theoretical flirtations with themes in Marx and the Kantian idealists—to replace dogmatic determinism with a fluid sociological explanatory scheme. In addition, from Machiavelli and his multiple interpreters, Mannheim derived a surprisingly modern emphasis on strategy and decision-making as universally applicable mechanisms of social organization and social change.

Mannheim's analyses were implicitly guided by his central quest for understanding social change, not so much as a product of antecedent principles (e.g., technological invention, migration, conquest, conflict, etc.), but as the catalyst in permitting men to select from the potentialities afforded by ongoing processes of change. His conceptual framework, in retrospect, thus ordered the phenomena of social interaction in a provisional sequence, the internal connections of which may be considered the fundamental theoretical problems of contemporary sociology. (See Figure 2.)

Somewhat in line with Weber, Mannheim was concerned with the operation of societies as organized applications of two not entirely opposed dimensions of human interaction—rationality and power. Rationality, in its major aspects, seems to refer to certain kinds of meanings that persons inject into, or acquire from, their social interactions. Power, on the other hand, summarizes the ways persons and groups convert meanings and resources into significant actions, programs, and predictable coordination of behavior. To Mannheim, rationality and power were highly generalized variables, inherently dynamic in nature. Consequently, analyses of society require the study of *transitional phases*, not as unique, accidental, or sensational, but as theoretically indispensable for an explanation of major social developments. In addition, and very closely related to the emphasis on transition, Mannheim gave con-

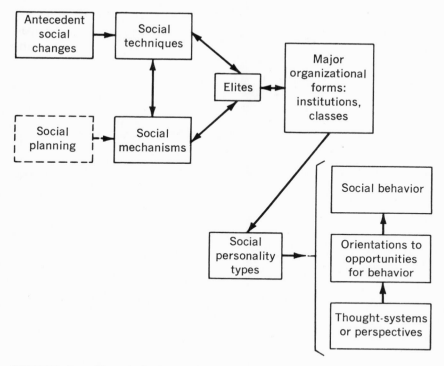

FIGURE 2.   Mannheim's basic conceptual scheme.

tinued prominence to the ways in which the concrete manifestations of rationality and power are translated into successive processes of perceiving, evaluating, and behaving by persons and social
categories.[2]

Logically, but not chronologically (Mannheim did not aspire to
systematic formulation), the first set of theoretical problems for
Mannheim was the social and psychological impact of social techniques. By "social technique," he meant to encompass all the methods through which there is a more or less intentional attempt to
influence (change, confirm) the content and organization of

[2] Karl Mannheim, *Man and Society in an Age of Reconstruction* (New York:
Harcourt, Brace & World, 1940), pp. 12–20.

human behavior.[3] Some examples are educational processes, propaganda, bureaucratic rules, the use of "white lies," competition, etc.

THEORY OF SOCIAL TECHNIQUES

One of the fundamental formulations in Mannheim's work is that the character of social techniques strongly conditions (or provides limitations on) the organizational structure of a social system.[4] As an important corollary, changes in accepted social techniques tend to be followed by innovations in social organization or frictions, lags, etc., which reflect the practical discrepancy between techniques and patterns of authority and coordination.[5] This is an important—if not a revolutionary—extension of Marx's and Veblen's technological determinism. For Mannheim concludes that the underlying theme of technological invention—organized application of rationality—can be found in non-economic pursuits, often with greater consequences for aspects of social organization than those derived from technological change.[6] Indeed, Mannheim hypothesizes that, as technology advances (thereby decreasing man's dependence on the physical environment), social techniques assume greater importance in the recognition and choice of alternatives in matters of patterned social interaction (power, social controls, opportunity for deviation).[7] In a sense then, progressive development of technology eventually reaches a point at which its former importance undergoes relative leveling off and decline. The old and wearisome debate about the alleged strength of "material" (technological) vs. "ideal" (normative and organizational) factors is thus transformed into a more realistic hypothesis about the changing relation between social and technological techniques.

[3] *Ibid.*, p. 247.
[4] *Ibid.*, p. 374.
[5] Karl Mannheim, *Freedom, Power, and Democratic Planning* (New York: Oxford University Press, 1950), p. 53. Cf. Ogburn's concept of cultural lag in William F. Ogburn, *Social Change* (New York: Viking Press, 1950; orig. ed., 1922), pp. 200–213.
[6] *Man and Society*, pp. 242–243.   [7] *Ibid.*, p. 374.

TECHNIQUES AND SOCIAL STRUCTURE

Mannheim was compelled by the logic of the previously discussed formulation to work out a sociologically useful classification of social techniques—first, to search for the social and cultural bases of each type and, second, to account for shifts in dominant forms of social techniques. Significantly, but perhaps not consciously, he experimented with a "qualitative" *rationality scale* in two related ways.

An important distinction among three kinds of techniques [8] underlies most of Mannheim's work in the latter part of his career. First and most "primitive" are techniques based on *chance discovery*, techniques that are accidentally created and hence require memory rather than understanding of the utility of the technique. For example, flattery may become an unwitting means of promoting congeniality in informal relations. But techniques based on *inventing* involve a more "rational" anticipation of a definite objective and an explicit search for a solution. The strategy of establishing monthly staff meetings for information and suggestions is clearly an application of this sort of social technique, though the effectiveness of this approach is not at issue. Third, Mannheim identified the ultimate in rationality of social techniques in the concept of *planning*. The characteristic features of planning are explicit concern for the interrelations of many subsystems and objectives and the attempt to achieve these objectives from central or key locations in the overall structure. Potentially, this level of technique is feasible in official governmental programs that integrate some set of desired developments with various fiscal policies and measures designed to encourage popular understanding of interrelated policies. On a more limited scale, the planning technique may be found in careful family budgeting, in the design of specific preparations for the expansion of business firms, in the attempted articulation of teaching, research, and community-service functions of a developing university.

[8] *Ibid.*, pp. 150–155.

Having conceptualized these three "stages" in dominance of social techniques, Mannheim assumed that each was prevalent in a congenial type of social structure. Discovery as technique is said to predominate in societies with mechanical solidarity (Durkheim) or "horde solidarity," while invention as a technique comes to be the modal form in societies marked by transition from mechanical solidarity into a phase of group and individual competition. However, as societies achieve greater internal specialization, the practical interdependence (organic solidarity) that is thereby produced is punctuated by growing frictions and frustrations if discovery and invention remain the focal social techniques. In such a social structure, "planning" techniques provide a "better fit" in accommodating multiple goals to one another. Mannheim recognized that there has been a notable tension between theory (expected relationships) and practice in complex societies.[9] But he tried to account for this discrepancy in another theoretical formulation (which is considered on page 175).

THE DYSFUNCTIONAL EFFECTS OF RATIONALITY

In a related manner, Mannheim approached types of social techniques as interacting factors in social structures, with particular concern for the organizational and behavioral effects of the simultaneous operation of different social techniques. At this point, he distinguishes between techniques that are rational in providing solutions to a given situation or specific objective and those that are rational in effectively organizing and coordinating adjustments to a set of interrelated situations. The first, called *substantial rationality*, seems to be characteristic of the inventing type, while the second, called *functional rationality*, well describes planning techniques. But Mannheim regards functional rationality not only as a predictable consequence of technological development, but also as a probable obstacle to substantial rationality. Other things being equal, the exercise of functional rationality (social techniques of planning) tends to transfer firsthand experience in responsibility and

[9] *Ibid.*, pp. 68–70, 150–152.

decision-making from a considerable portion of the population to a minority of persons in strategic positions.[10] Thus, not only does inventing become less significant over time, but its residual significance becomes increasingly narrowed by lack of training and experience in limited situations of rationality.

In effect, Mannheim seeks to explain the source of *anomie* and its derivatives not solely as a failure of normative guidelines or social controls, but as a structural effect of diminished opportunities to learn personally appropriate social techniques.[11] Normally, less rational social techniques (emotionality, impulsive actions) are quite common in all types of social structure. But the potential conflict between substantial and functional rationality (or between chance discovery and invention and planning) is implicitly forestalled by participation in "local" groups that drain off less rational actions before these can enter or affect the larger system.[12] (Essentially the same point has been made by Durkheim, Simmel, Lederer, and Nisbet.) The operation and significance of social techniques therefore require knowledge of other components of the structure of society.

TRENDS IN SOCIAL TECHNIQUES

A final theoretical issue concerns the patterns of change in social techniques and their consequences.[13] Mannheim contends that advances in technology have encouraged two important trends in social techniques—mass influence and growing interdependence among social techniques. In the first case, recognition of the problems derived from large numbers, plus the detection (or the assumption) of cultural and/or psychological similarities in a population, led to experimentation with more efficient forms of influence. Military organization—as Weber and others have indicated

[10] *Ibid.*, pp. 58–59.   [11] *Ibid.*, p. 62.

[12] See Robert A. Nisbet, *The Quest for Community* (New York: Oxford University Press, 1953); Emil Lederer, *The State of the Masses* (New York: W.W. Norton, 1940); Emile Durkheim, *The Division of Labor in Society*, trans. George Simpson (New York: Free Press, 1947), preface to 2d ed., pp. 26–29.

[13] *Man and Society*, pp. 252–265.

—is a particularly successful early illustration, though we may also mention political propaganda techniques, public education, and the octopal manifestations of advertising. On the other hand, as social techniques were transformed from a personal to a mass basis, the pre-existing segregation of influences could not long continue. The increasingly marked nucleation or clustering of social techniques is a practical necessity, given the need for effective influence. Consequently, other things being equal, strategic centralization of social techniques is hypothesized as a predictable, understandable effect of sociocultural complexity.

SOCIAL MECHANISMS AND CONTROL

Mannheim seemed to assume an implicit complementary relation between social techniques (mainly as positive influences) and social controls (supplementary techniques for limiting deviation from desired patterns in values and behavior). Indeed, he sometimes used these terms interchangeably, thus implying that the same mechanism (e. g., public education) possesses both "influence" and "control" aspects. However, social controls (or control aspects of social mechanisms) may be identified with the phenomena of power, which Mannheim simply defined as "every action which compels certain actions in others." [14] Implicit in power and control is the existence of conflict, i.e., resistance to the application of given social techniques. Consequently, social controls primarily encompass means by which social conflicts are limited, managed, or resolved by some group that can manipulate social techniques for that purpose. In short, Mannheim regards social techniques as means that generate active dissidence and therefore require some anticipatory or reactive control mechanisms.

The effectiveness of control therefore becomes a key theoretical problem for sociology. As the structure of society changes (specialization, technical capacity, formalization of rules and statuses), forms of social control likewise are altered, though in an experimental trial-and-error fashion. Mannheim notes a tendency toward

[14] *Ibid.*, pp. 167, 302.

indirect methods of social control as societies become more complex. Instead of coercion, direct threat, indoctrination, and personal surveillance, there is increasing evidence of subtle processes of structuring or containing the values and behavior of individuals. Some examples are legally sustained systems of competition ("market principles," "collective bargaining"), the mechanisms or channels of social mobility, the selective emphases of higher educational systems, psychotherapy, and governmental manipulation of fiscal and monetary devices. Likewise, he finds a clear pattern of shift from diffuse social controls to more centralized controls. If centralized but indirect social controls seem contradictory,[15] Mannheim is careful to point out that, though complex society requires some measure of centralized controls, the practical efficiency of their operation is enhanced by controls that produce not rigid conformity but a willing acceptance of minimally necessary attitudes and actions.

Essentially, Mannheim equates effectiveness of social control with degree of rationality in the exercise of power. The crucial paradox for Mannheim is that societies that possess the greatest structural capacity for rational power (i. e., complex, modern societies) simultaneously develop (or retain) subsystems that encourage irrationality and constricted use of material and social resources (through other social techniques). Ideally, social planning comprises a set of techniques and controls that maximize the rational application of power, although Mannheim recognizes the practical difficulties of inventing such a structure. Clearly then, another major theoretical problem intrudes at this point: what components of a developed social structure help to account for the application of social techniques and controls?

ELITES

The most important consideration in Mannheim's scheme, and one that serves as an attempted answer to the problem just discussed, is the dynamics of social elites. Unlike Pareto and Michels,

[15] *Ibid.*, pp. 311–327.

Mannheim did not define elites primarily as wielders of power, but rather as specialists in developing knowledge, values, and techniques and as interpreters or intermediaries between a population and specific problems of human organization.[16] By implication, Mannheim distinguishes between *elites,* whose role is that of creating and preserving cultural solutions, and *leadership,* which involves the sanctioned responsibility of applying these solutions in practical situations. Leaders are therefore dependent on the character of elite contributions in the various social spheres (government, economics, art, religion and morality, education).

It follows that the recruitment and composition of elites, as defined above, constitute key problems for the student of society. Mannheim hypothesizes that sociocultural change, in the form of technological developments and innovations in social techniques, profoundly affects the functioning of elites. Specifically, the role of elites depends upon (*a*) the number of competing elites, (*b*) the opportunity for independent thinking (cf. Toynbee's conception of "withdrawal and return"), and (*c*) the criteria actually involved in recruiting new members of elites.[17] For modern Western societies, Mannheim summarizes a major trend-line in the operation of elites as one of declining independence. Indeed, the former role-specialization of elite and non-elite, according to Mannheim, shows strong tendencies of disappearance by usurpation. In a highly condensed analysis of this process, Mannheim concluded that techniques of political democracy and mass communication had produced (*a*) proliferation and consequent diffuseness of impact in elites, (*b*) a growing vulnerability of elites to various distractions and to the blandishments of non-elites,[18] (*c*) an emphasis on non-rational criteria in selecting elites (e. g., family or lineage, and seniority), and (*d*) elites with "local" rather than "cosmopolitan" viewpoints.

The functions of elites then are theoretically linked with the state of social techniques. In societies of modest or relatively simple

16 *Ibid.,* pp. 82–84. See also Suzanne Keller, *Beyond the Ruling Class* (New York: Random House, 1963), ch. 4.

17 *Man and Society,* pp. 86–98.

18 William Kornhauser, *The Politics of Mass Society* (New York: Free Press, 1959).

techniques, elites serve as liaisons between social or cultural segments and the society as a whole. At this point, Mannheim's "sociology of knowledge" becomes significant, for its main function is
to analyze the conditions under which elites reflect (or overcome)
the peculiarities of specific "social positions" and also affect the
values and behavior patterns of their "clients."

In Mannheim's theoretical framework, the sociology of knowledge focuses on the pattern of communication between elites and
definable social categories whose experience requires interpretation.
Several premises underlie the body of theoretical propositions that
try to specify and explain variations in the functioning of elites.

1. Elites as specialists are in uniquely strategic positions to assess and
   reflect the experience of social categories.
2. The major theme in this assessment is the location of a dominant goal
   for subsequent organized action. Essentially, this takes one of three
   forms: (*a*) the wish to preserve the prevailing pattern of power,
   opportunities, etc. (*ideological perspectives*); (*b*) the desire to create
   a new structure (*utopian perspectives*); and (*c*) the attempt to resist
   effectively the competition of utopian thrusts (*counter-utopias*).
3. Elites are the sole source of creative ideas that organize and ra-
   tionalize these dominant goals.[19]
4. The contact between elites and relevant social categories does not
   seem to be treated explicitly. He seems to assume that elites correctly
   interpret the "will" of given categories and also successfully con-
   vince them that elite creations are specially fitted to the otherwise
   ineffable problems and desires of those categories. In short, for most
   historical periods, the elite appears to function as a kind of informal
   social technique.
5. Changes in the structure of experiences available to specific categories alter their perspective, and thus require relevant changes in
   the creations of their respective elites. This of course assumes either
   "internal" unaided perception of needs or acceptance from an elite
   that a portion of a population constitutes a meaningful category
   with an identity and that this category is best served by adopting
   for itself one of the three types of dominant objectives, for which
   the elite can provide detailed content and any needed justification
   for the choice.

[19] *Freedom, Power, and Democratic Planning*, pp. 191, 265.

In the relation between elites and social categories then, the major factor is the elite's perception of crucial attributes of given categories. These attributes, which assume the role of independent variables in his scheme, are class and power position, degree of social mobility, and social homogeneity–heterogeneity. The dependent variable is the basic structure of a derived perspective or value-system, which in turn is analyzed in terms of dominant time perspective, attitude toward change, degree of internal consistency, and level of abstraction.

SOCIOLOGY OF KNOWLEDGE

Using historical materials, Mannheim developed a set of theoretical conclusions that specify typical connections between perspectives or thought-styles and aspects of social position.

1. Groups or categories in process of upward social mobility (and their affiliated elites) tend to disavow traditional perspectives and to recognize the possibility of variant or conflicting values.
2. More specifically, upwardly mobile groups—or groups that anticipate social ascent—tend to develop utopian styles of thought, which are marked by considerable emphasis on intuition, specificity, and lack of systematic form.
3. Likewise, socially uprooted groups (adversely affected by social changes) and categories that possess relatively blurred identities tend to have disorganized or vague time-orientations, inconsistent ideas and valuations, and a rash of highly impressionistic notions.[20]
4. Mannheim also recognized the phenomenon of groups or categories without identities, which thereby implicitly encourage self-styled elites to offer themselves as "voices" of such categories. These elites, according to Mannheim, are opportunists who seek attachment to any stratum that is unorganized and therefore vulnerable to external influence. Since these categories have no clearly identifiable social position, the value system presented by potential elites tends to be vague—neither ideological nor utopian, but rather focused on the "representative" character of the elite.[21] Significantly, the social

[20] Karl Mannheim, *Ideology and Utopia* (New York: Harcourt, Brace & World, 1936; Harvest Books ed.), p. 142.
[21] *Ibid.*, p. 143.

category thus gains leaders, but not a meaningful set of values. (This may be interpreted, in Mannheim's terms, as a deviation from the normal function of elites.) It therefore follows that these categories remain essentially unorganized and without a referential social position. Such groups or categories are invitations to dictatorship; indeed, their lack of a definite value system may lend special attraction to the certainty of power in a totalitarian structure.

5. Groups or categories that have achieved mobility largely conceive of their world and their recent history as a mélange of isolated and unrelated events. But groups that become secure with an identity based on long-time similarity of experience, bolstered by channels of communication, tend to favor more systematic, though still highly specific, perspectives—which are predominantly ideological.

6. Categories that perceive themselves as exposed to threats from superordinate and subordinate categories seem to inspire perspectives that attempt to achieve synthesis or compromise of conflicting orientations. For Mannheim, the middle classes of Western society have been mainly concerned with "ideological" synthesis—i.e., with selecting from competing values only these that justify and conserve their achieved social position. Synthesis of a more utopian sort is theoretically possible only among categories or elites that possess no fixed or determinate position in society.[22] This raises the controversial problem of the "unattached intellectual," which on further analysis seems to rest not on isolation from a group or category, but on the feasibility of maintaining contact with and understanding of several strata.

7. Changes in the composition of groups, strata, or subpopulations affect the character of thought-styles in several ways. As groups or categories become more heterogeneous, their perspectives implicitly develop in the direction of greater abstraction, greater formalization, and conservatism (ideological orientation).[23] Indeed, Mannheim views this trend as a practical mechanism for organizing persons who are spatially dispersed and yet share superficial social similarities (such as income level).

Having treated the relation between social position and thought-style for specific types of categories, Mannheim was equally concerned with the overall pattern to which these segmented relations contributed. While categories and their elites may be analytically

---

[22] *Ibid.*, pp. 154–157.   [23] *Ibid.*, pp. 131, 248–249, 302.

isolated, in practice their interactions are inevitable consequences of developments in social techniques. In complex social systems, utopian values either recede toward ideological forms as social success is achieved, or competing utopias encourage compromises that erode the systematic features of previous outlooks.[24] The accompanying social homogenization further reduces perceived needs (*a*) for change, (*b*) for congenial thought-styles, and (*c*) for the operation of elites. Fundamentally then, the dissipation of utopian styles represents the revolutionary ascendance of technique over ideas, the replacement of elites, whose social justification is creation of values, by leaders, whose skill lies in manipulating techniques that tend to centralize power.

By implication, these social processes—if not effectively countered—create attitudes and behavior that have been labeled by others as "anomie," "alienation," "disillusionment," or "despair," all of which may be interpreted as intelligible responses to the absence of the social apparatus of utopian orientations.

SOCIAL STRATIFICATION

For Mannheim, the functioning of elites and social techniques is related to the *system of stratification* in historically variable ways. It is important to note that Mannheim (like Weber) regarded social strata as both antecedents and consequents of such social phenomena as power, influence, change, and specific cultural systems. But more specifically, how did he develop a generally applicable theory of stratification?

The elements of such a theory are far from being esoteric or dogmatic. First, specialization of function and its attendant distribution of prerogatives and opportunities create differential "social locations." These locations represent potentials for similar experiences among persons occupying a given position.[25] Mannheim most frequently discusses location in terms of strata (classes), but

---

24 *Ibid.*, pp. 250–252.

25 *Man and Society*, p. 43; Karl Mannheim, *Essays on the Sociology of Culture* (New York: Oxford University Press, 1956), pp. 106–108.

also gives prominence to such locations as generations and age-grades. Each location contains an objective component (opportunities) and a subjective one (awareness of and will to use these opportunities). A class is an emergent category of persons who individually act in similar fashion, in accordance with their opportunities, in a productive system. Class-consciousness is likewise an emergent but not inevitable or continuous phenomenon; it may be identified to the extent that members of a class act (e.g., vote, consume) individually or collectively in line with their perceived identity as a category and their difference from other social categories. The genesis of class-consciousness is located in periods of change or transition, when social categories find it necessary to assess their opportunities and limitations.[26] However, Mannheim provides rather vague and fragmentary clues to this process. The role of elites, for example, is not mentioned in this context, although this is an underlying theme in *Ideology and Utopia*.

Class-consciousness, however, is not the only form of "stratum" or "position" consciousness. Differentials in political strength, in social repute, in education and "taste" can generate grounds for evaluation of groups and categories. Parenthetically, Mannheim suggests that intellectuals as a category were the last to develop "group consciousness," which he explains as a result of the earlier insulated, "protected" position of intellectuals from "direct access to any vital and functioning segment of society."[27] Not until the diffusion of literacy and education and the rise of mass communication did the intellectual confront a decisive threat to his tolerated monopoly of "ideas." Since that time, somewhere in the nineteenth century, the "problem of the intelligentsia" has produced a disquieting identity marked by marginality and alleged cultural traits (such as non-responsibility, emphasis on privacy, and attraction for extremes).[28]

A second point of great importance is the dethronement of "class" (as well as class-consciousness and class antagonism) as the eternally dominant form of stratification (cf. Weber). Specialization in complex systems necessarily entails multiple locations (or

[26] *Essays on the Sociology of Culture*, pp. 96–100. [27] *Ibid.*, pp. 96–97, 101.
[28] *Ibid.*, pp. 111–170.

social habitats) for most persons—and consequently, competing, non-reinforcing, and even ambivalent values and motives. Mannheim does not deny the existence of cultural and attitudinal differences derived from distinguishable class positions. But he tries to account for deviations from the strict Marxian model of stratification and also for changes in the relative strength of different locations. Essentially, patterns of social mobility and the level of social technique seem to be core ingredients in his theory of stratification.

SOCIAL MOBILITY AND CLASS INTERACTION

"Class" as a form of stratification is marked by fluidities that stem from a formally "open" economic system, with its characteristic division of labor and skills and opportunities for change in position. The relations between classes or between social categories depend in part upon the dominant form of social mobility in a given period. For example, antagonisms or consciously organized opposition between classes are regarded as "marginal cases," as relatively infrequent, and as explainable by special rather than universal features of a stratification system. Mannheim's most general proposition at this point is that the basis for cooperation, supplementation, or competition between social categories is "future chances or past experiences." [29] Using clues from other discussions by Mannheim, we may interpret this phrase to mean the nature of achieved or potential mobility in available "channels."

One important aspect of mobility is the degree of movement from a given location. According to Mannheim, the ascent of individuals tends to produce links between positions and a reduced visibility of the system of positions and opportunities.[30] By inference, abrupt processes of mobility for large numbers may serve to emphasize the disparities between the non-mobile and the successfully mobile. Mannheim suggests that large-scale ascent encourages mobility orientations among the non-mobile as well. This thwarted portion of a stratum tends to become hostile either if alternative

[29] *Man and Society*, pp. 251–252, 342.
[30] *Essays on the Sociology of Culture*, pp. 143–147.

opportunities for mobility are unavailable or if an elite provides a crystallized "explanation" for frustration.

The emergence and growing influence of new roles or strata (reflecting social and cultural changes) likewise may deflect attention from "economic class" identification. In Mannheim's interpretation of medieval and modern Western historical periods, the rise of such categories as scholars, bureaucratic officials, jurists, and military experts tends to complicate the previously simple but transitional distinctions between economic skills. Mannheim in effect implies that "class" distinctions of a clear-cut character depend upon stability of skill patterns and dominance of a relatively autonomous market system.[31] Since both conditions cannot be satisfied in periods of substantial social and cultural change, it follows that class position is inevitably subject to competition with other types of social position (based on education, political influence, scientific knowledge, organizational skill, etc.).

Stratification is for Mannheim a structure of unequal opportunities that is sustained by relatively simple, relatively localized social techniques. With the development of widely applicable and monopolistic forms of influence, however, either the objective differences between categories are reduced or such differences lose their former significance for the persons involved. In other words, destratification follows the rationalization of social techniques. But as these techniques become centralized in a technically competent and single-minded minority—undeterred by practicable social controls on their functioning—a new stratification system emerges. The topmost stratum consists of those at the centers of communication–influence networks. Previously differentiated classes, categories, and social stations constitute a subordinate "mass." [32]

The third and final segment in Mannheim's analysis of stratification concerns the patterned effects of destratification and of a mass-central core system. Mannheim asserts that these processes, by removing meaningful differences, create anxieties, insecurities, and irrational expressions in behavior (violence, extremism in the political realm, and manias of various kinds). Subsequently, these indi-

[31] *Ibid.*, pp. 144–145; *Man and Society*, p. 47.
[32] Emil Lederer, *The State of the Masses* (New York: W. W. Norton, 1940).

vidual manifestations of social maladjustment may become organized and manipulated by leaders (not elites) who couple the desire
for unrestricted power with the apparatus to acquire and maintain
such power.[33]

SOCIAL CHANGE AND SOCIAL PLANNING

As an "engaged" theorist, Mannheim was interested in the extensions of theory required for realistically rational action. Consequently, much of his later work (1940–1947) represented an attempt to construct a theoretically sound guide to practical social
change in complex societies. The basic premise in his orientation to
social change, however, was a distinction between uncontrolled
processes of change and planned or directed change. In the first
type, innovations in technology create or expand economic specialization, which is reflected in class and power differences. Ultimately, these developments are followed by piecemeal innovations
in social techniques and methods of social control. Mannheim
concludes that, in processes of unregulated change, social techniques tend to become more effective than prevailing methods of
coordination and control. During the period of "lag" or "discrepancy" between techniques and controls, the phenomenon of "politics" is dominant in society.[34] By politics, Mannheim means non-
rational processes of competition between groups for positions of
decision-making (power). Politics, therefore, indicates transitions
in the attempt to accommodate techniques and controls. One possible (and frequent) consequence is centralization of power, the
eradication of the political element, and the subordination of techniques to controls—in short, totalitarian society.

On the other hand, this type of change process is only one possible implementation of the key theoretical problem of social change
—the mechanisms by which technological and technical innovations can be controlled without stifling further innovations, as these
are required in practical situations. At this point, Mannheim's the-

---

33 *Man and Society*, pp. 129–141.
34 *Ibid.*, pp. 360–363; *Freedom, Power, and Democratic Planning*, pp. 4–6.

ory of planning is specially relevant, both for its attempt at objective formulation and for the theoretical and practical difficulties it presents.

Planning may be regarded as a set of possible adjustments to perceived difficulties encountered in unregulated social and cultural changes. As Mannheim analyzes these difficulties, they are reducible to increasingly effective social techniques whose routine functioning tends to be accompanied by either fractionated controls or by centralized and immutable controls. Since Mannheim implicitly assumes that social techniques cannot be retracted (despite their latent consequences, they are too desirable), the only logical alternative is alteration in the area of social control and coordination.

Planning (or planned-change processes) rests on control mechanisms derived from a distinctive power structure. First, these controls are applied from locations in the social system that can be shown to permit prediction of the largest number of derivative consequences (the key positions) with the least mobilization of coercion. Consequently, neither an omnipotent state nor various types of decentralized power furnish bases for such a system of control. Second, key positions that function as foci of planning are marked by patterns of decision-making that attempt to accommodate the complementary and conflicting operations of subgroups in the system. Mannheim asserts thirdly that this type of decision-making presupposes persons with ability and dedication to a "planned-thinking" style, rather than to discrete invention or chance discovery modes.[35] But this in turn is found only in "socially unattached" elites or intellectuals.

Obviously, a theory of planned or regulated change requires in addition a theory of the mechanisms of transition from unregulated change processes to the hitherto unknown planning system(s). Mannheim was plagued by the ominous discrepancy between his sociological analysis of a desirable system and the available theoretical specification of valid linkage mechanisms. Unfortunately, he died before he could construct even a satisfactory tentative solution to these problems. But several clues may indicate the direction of his personal dialogue between theory and practice.

[35] *Man and Society*, pp. 43, 75, 195.

Intellectuals and decision-making

The recruitment of elites with planning thought-styles confronted him with more difficulties in the forties than his earlier writings foresaw. *Ideology and Utopia*, a product of the twenties, was somewhat optimistic about the possibility of a socially independent but societally responsible set of intellectuals. In the thirties, particularly in his essay "The Problem of the Intelligentsia: An Enquiry into its Past and Present Role," a brilliant sociological analysis of historical developments, Mannheim found that social origins and even some of the internal features of the intellectual's role (skepticism, aloofness, and introversion) were not consonant with the special role-requirements of elites in systems of regulated change.[36] However, he assumed that a latent function of higher education in democratic nations is the production of a small but significant number of "pioneer," planning-oriented intellectuals, who would necessarily face long delays in attaining the key positions required for adequate attempts at planned change.[37] Incidentally, Mannheim recognized the structural necessity for continuity in critical decision-making, though he offers no theory of the mechanism by which continuity is achieved in processes of deep-seated change. Presumably, co-optation of "new blood" by established elites is the most relevant process, but a genuine theory of co-optation is unknown in contemporary sociology.

Personality types and planning

Interaction between elites and other social groups and categories (rank-and-file, followers, masses, etc., are often inaccurate terms) in terms of mutual support and encouragement likewise presented serious problems for Mannheim's emerging theoretical structure. Because the controls in a planning structure depend primarily on timing and on predictable series of multiple consequences generated by key decisions, conflict and misunderstanding in various

---

[36] *Essays on the Sociology of Culture*, p. 159.
[37] *Man and Society*, pp. 195–198, 226–227.

forms among members of a social system clearly negate the purposes of a planning system. Therefore, Mannheim was concerned with the mechanisms best suited for creating social personalities that are congruent with the goals and techniques of societies engaged in directed social change, as well as with mechanisms for altering social structure (patterned opportunities and rewards, lines of authority, etc.). Again, Mannheim saw no practical alternative to formal education in subtly structuring personalities toward the cluster of attitudes and values required by a system of planning. These characteristics include sublimation of aggressive impulses, understanding of the practical needs of other social categories, adaptability to new situations.[38] By implication, the key process in the transition from unregulated (or partly regulated) to planned change is the determination of operational goals and their implementation for the major educational systems in modern society. Thus, the crucial arena is not the politics of government, but the politics of formal education.

The gnawing question that recurs through all of Mannheim's analysis and hopeful predictions on planned change is also a cardinal theoretical consideration in modern sociology and the social sciences in general: to what extent, and under what circumstances, can persons (and categories of persons) transcend the attitudinal and cultural cues of specific social positions? Mannheim's argument seems to suggest that position greatly conditions (or determines) behavior when positions are effectively isolated from one another —under conditions of limited communication and monopolistic socialization (education). With the development of technology and social techniques, segregation of positions becomes more difficult to sustain. Mannheim was well aware that these trends could result in either transcendance of position or destruction of prevailing positional differences—i.e., massification. It is reasonably clear that the latter consequence is more probable in late stages of unregulated change and under totalitarian power systems. The social bases of position transcendence remain to be identified. But Mannheim's formulations indicate that creativity in social-control mechanisms constitutes the only likely means by which sociocultural

[38] *Ibid.*, pp. 199–205, 223–228.

differences can be retained without at the same time producing destructive conflicts.

Mannheim is chiefly known for his analyses of social class and social mobility and their relation to meaningful perspectives, ideas, and philosophies—the province of the sociology of knowledge. Yet he has enriched the annals of sociological theory by creative work in at least five crucial areas:

1. The conceptual and theoretical prominence of *social techniques* in complex society has been effectively demonstrated by Mannheim in his *Man and Society in an Age of Reconstruction*. Furthermore, he has developed in a distinctively sociological manner the earlier interrelation between social techniques and systems of ideas—and the growing independence of these two sets of phenomena in recent decades. In this manner, Mannheim has refined and extended the long tradition of "lag theories," such as those of Marx, Vierkandt, Ogburn, Alfred Weber, Odum, Giddings, and Chapin.
2. Following Max Weber in part, Mannheim has clarified aspects of the complexity and dynamics of *social stratification*. In particular, he noted—and pursued the theoretical implications of—status inconsistencies and the behavioral consequences of subtly different kinds of mobility.
3. Again, in extension of valuable clues from Weber, Mannheim analyzed different levels and social contexts of *rationality* in social behavior. More important, he related types of rationality to problems of social control and social change.
4. We owe to Mannheim perhaps the most objective analysis of a highly controversial phenomenon—the *functioning of elites*. Mannheim quickly adopted a non-aristocratic and only partly Platonic approach to elites—unlike such predecessors or contemporaries as Comte, Pareto, Mosca, and Ortega. The implicit (and sometimes explicit) distinction between the elite role (intellectuals) and the leadership role—the one emphasizing goals and values, and the other emphasizing power and decision-making—is simple but indispensable. For the problem of recruitment to these roles and of the historical relation of these roles could now be a subject for responsible conceptualization and research, rather than speculation and assertion. Mannheim's analyses of trends in elite recruitment, for example, are

distinctly superior to Pareto's more popular (and often misinterpreted) theory of the "circulation of the elites." [39]

5. Finally, the perception of the distinction—only partially validated—between the explanation of *unregulated*-change processes and *planned*-change processes merits more serious consideration and critical renovation than it has received. In relatively complex systems, unregulated change ultimately results in protracted periods of anomie and violence, or in highly centralized power and authority systems. Planned change, on the other hand, involves both anticipation of derivative consequences and the opportunity of selecting both appropriate controls and effective social techniques to maximize (perhaps optimize) the production of desired changes. Mannheim in effect conceived of planning as the functional equivalent of utopian perspectives in processes of unregulated change. In this way, Mannheim suggested a sound theoretical base for self-corrective changes in complex societies.[40] However, scientific and political developments since his death indicate that the theoretical specifications of planned-change processes in one society must also give prominence to *intersocietal relations* as intervening—if not interfering—factors.

SELECTED REFERENCES

DeGré, Gerard L., *Society and Ideology* (New York: Columbia University Bookstore, 1943).

Maquet, Jacques, *The Sociology of Knowledge* (Boston: Beacon Press, 1951).

Merton, Robert K., *Social Theory and Social Structure* (New York: Free Press, rev. ed., 1957), chs. 12, 13.

Rempel, F. Warren, *The Role of Values in Karl Mannheim's Sociology of Knowledge* (The Hague: Mouton, 1965).

[39] Vilfredo Pareto, *Mind and Society*, trans. Arthur Livingston (4 vols.; New York: Harcourt, Brace, 1935), IV, ¶ 2484–2489, 2521–2548; Florian Znaniecki, *The Social Role of the Man of Knowledge* (New York: Columbia University Press, 1940), pp. 13–16.

[40] *Man and Society*, pp. 321–325.

9

Talcott Parsons:
The Quest for a
Dynamic Formalism

Most sociologists will agree that Talcott Parsons is the most controversial figure in modern American sociology. Indeed, the continuing stream of writings by Parsons and his followers is already supplemented by a formidable *corpus* of critiques, analyses, summaries, etc., which contribute heat, light, shadow, and substance to the Parsonian penumbra in sociological thought. Perhaps this situation can be clarified by suggesting that Parsons is one of the most probing critics of currents in sociology during the last two decades. In particular, he has directly or indirectly attacked empiricism, behaviorism, uncoordinated division of labor, conceptual confusion, and the hazy status of sociological subject matter.[1] His major objectives have therefore been (*a*) to define the basic nature and methodological approach of sociology; (*b*) to determine the re-

[1] Talcott Parsons, *The Structure of Social Action* (New York: McGraw-Hill, 1937), chs. 2, 3, 12 and pp. 728–731; Talcott Parsons, *Essays in Sociological Theory Pure and Applied* (New York: Free Press, 1949), pp. 23–28.

lations of sociology with psychology, economics, and anthropology in the realm of social science; and (*c*) to develop for sociology an interconnected set of "master" categories capable of application to all significant problems considered relevant for the maturation of sociology.

As in the previous chapters of this section, we are primarily concerned with what seem to be the valuable or potentially significant portions of Parsons' work. Consequently, we must omit a much-needed, detailed analysis of developments in his conceptual scheme and methodological position.[2] Furthermore, we shall not attempt to supply a comprehensive summary of those aspects of his work that are either of questionable value or open to serious criticism. These limitations should not be misconstrued as reflections of an uncritical acceptance. They have instead been consciously imposed in the focal quest for the *positive* contributions of Parsons' sociological career. One measure of Parsons' importance on the sociological scene is a substantial and growing body of criticism of his approach, conceptual scheme, implicit biases, literary style, and a presumed immodesty in failing to relate his work to earlier developments.[3] For perspective, this literature should certainly be consulted. But while many of these criticisms are correct, justifiable, and well-intentioned, it seems that they refer to essentially minor deficiencies and shortcomings that do not materially bear on the present discussion.

METHODOLOGICAL AND CONCEPTUAL CONTRIBUTIONS

The intimate and inevitable interdependence between theory and methodology is a cardinal principle in the writings of Parsons. Consequently, he has devoted considerable attention to fundamen-

[2] See the special issue of *Alpha Kappa Deltan* (Winter, 1959), particularly the papers by Martindale and Martel, pp. 38–46, 53–63; Max Black, ed., *The Social Theories of Talcott Parsons* (Englewood Cliffs: Prentice-Hall, 1961); Richard L. Simpson and Herman Turk, eds., *Institutions and Social Exchange: The Sociologies of Talcott Parsons and George C. Homans* (Indianapolis: Bobbs-Merrill, 1969).

[3] A bibliography of critical articles and book reviews may be found in the *Alpha Kappa Deltan, loc. cit.*

tal methodological issues—perhaps more than have any of the American theorists previously discussed (with the possible exception of Znaniecki). In fact, this engrossing methodological concern has prompted critics to evaluate his work as "eternal preparation" rather than sociological theory, as strategy rather than the tactical maneuvers connected with empirically relevant statements. Nevertheless, Parsons is primarily responsible for codifying a methodological approach that is rapidly becoming the common property of sociologists throughout the world—*structural-functionalism.*

This approach has been a progressive development in Parsons' works, a development that is not yet completed in some respects. It is interesting and perhaps crucial to note that Parsons first approached sociology as a residual field, since his first professional concerns were biology and economics. Biology's preoccupation with physico-chemical behavior was replaced by the emphasis on rational social behavior of classical economics, and this was followed by an emphasis on the problematic character of non-economic social behavior. Retrospectively, the strategy employed by Parsons in these transfers involved three interrelated decisions:

1. The adaptation of the "system" approach to sociological phenomena in the critical concept of the "social system."
2. The emphasis on "part" or "type" concepts [4] in analysis of social systems, with a resultant production of constructed types as the foundation of his evolving methodological position.
3. A dominant, though not exclusive, emphasis on *social action* in social systems, rather than on *social relations* or *cultural products.*

Structural-functionalism, as an organized inquiry into the "procedures by which . . . observation and verification . . . [are] carried out—including the formulation of propositions and the concepts involved in them, and the modes of drawing conclusions from them," [5] depends so heavily on these three features that the problems and potentialities connected with each should be briefly outlined. A full discussion would be desirable but does not seem appropriate here, and so it is not attempted.

4 Parsons, *The Structure of Social Action*, pp. 31–33.   5 *Ibid.*, pp. 24–25.

The social system as focus

Closely paralleling the basic approach of Znaniecki, Parsons regards social phenomena as most comprehensible in terms of relatively organized frameworks called "social systems." Perhaps the most significant characteristic of the social system as a methodological tool is its implicit status as a *constructed type*, a consciously sharpened and simplified picture of selected portions of human behavior. Social systems are relatively persistent constellations of relations between and among persons maintained as analytically and empirically distinct entities through continuous "balancing" of disruptive and constructive processes of interaction. This notion is closely allied to the conception of "open systems" in "steady states," which has for a long time been prominent in the theoretical biology of Ludwig von Bertalanffy.[6] Clearly, the social system rests basically on the concept of "equilibrium," which is a necessarily *dynamic structural* concept when applied to organic or social phenomena, since (as Bertalanffy indicates) "a true equilibrium is incapable of doing work"[7] (i.e., cannot function or survive, except as a fiction). Consequently, social systems are conceived as equilibria in process, the components and conditions of which can be discovered deductively and/or inductively.

For some years, Parsons seemed to identify system-equilibrium with integration. Integration ". . . is a mode of relation of the units of a system by virtue of which, on the one hand, they act so as collectively to avoid disrupting the system and making it impossible to maintain its stability and, on the other hand, to 'cooperate' to promote its functioning as a unity."[8] In this earlier formulation, furthermore, integration or equilibrium was conceived as a product of strongly held common values shared by members of a social system.[9] Without explicitly recognizing that this formulation is at

[6] Ludwig von Bertalanffy, *Problems of Life* (New York: Wiley, 1952), pp. 125–129.

[7] *Ibid.*, p. 132.   [8] Parsons, *Essays in Sociological Theory*, p. 183.

[9] Talcott Parsons, "The Place of Ultimate Values in Sociological Theory," *International Journal of Ethics*, XLV (April, 1935), pp. 282–316; Parsons, *The Structure of Social Action*, pp. 768–769.

185

best applicable only to "primary" systems and at all times disturbingly tautological, Parsons has recently re-appraised equilibrium as a complex resultant of pursuing and variably satisfying universal functional problems inherent in social systems. Thus, the dynamic properties of social systems are specifically emphasized, simultaneously supplying a methodological base for Parsons' focus on social action.

Essentially, this approach requires an exhaustive, generalized delineation of conditions, "needs," and "functions" that can be shown to be crucial for the operation of social systems, particularly in preserving their identity ("boundary-maintaining" problem). At this point, Parsons has developed two relevant classifications that should be distinguished. There is first a set of *functional prerequisites* of social systems,[10] the conditions necessary for the emergence and significant change of social systems (i.e., dynamic problems). Specifically, these conditions include satisfaction of biological and psychological needs of a sufficient portion of the membership, coordination of the activities of the members (order), and adequate motivation to perform essential roles in the system. Second, there is a series of *functional requisites* (or imperatives), which constitute the problems inherent in maintaining an already functioning social system. As summarized by Levy, these are: adequate physiological relation to the total environment, role differentiation and assignment, communication, shared cognitive orientation, shared and articulated set of goals, regulation of the choice of means for specific ends, regulation of affective expression, adequate socialization and motivation, effective control of disruptive (deviant) forms of behavior, and adequate institutionalization of values and practices.[11]

These criteria mix common sense, deduction, and observation and would seem to be particularly applicable to larger, more complex social systems. However, one may legitimately inquire if these inventories are sufficiently full. But even more disturbing is the understandable lack of success in defining (or supplying objective norms of) "adequacy" and "effectiveness." Presumably, this is a

[10] Parsons, *Essays in Sociological Theory*, p. 6; Marion J. Levy, *The Structure of Society* (Princeton: Princeton University Press, 1952), pp. 43–45, 71–72.
[11] Levy, *op. cit.*, pp. 62, 151.

procedure that can be followed in analyzing empirical types of social systems.

In any case, if the general approach is acceptable, a referential set of system needs is especially helpful—not merely as convenient summary of specific requisites, but as a means of linking critical needs with significant aspects of system structure. Parsons has recently suggested and initially used four generalized "problems" of social systems, which reflect the importance of the means–end dimension and the internal–external axis of social systems.[12] Table 3 graphically summarizes these problems, but their definition, significance, and interrelations should be understood in terms of their role in the structural–functional orientation.

	Instrumental (means)	Consummatory (ends)
External	Adaptive function	Goal-attainment function
Internal	Pattern-maintenance and tension-management functions	Integrative function

TABLE 3.

These functional imperatives simultaneously point to (*a*) the generalized conditions of "equilibrium," (*b*) the necessary specialization or differentiation of social systems, and (*c*) clues to the development and significance of substructures in the system. This scheme begins with the familiar premise that social systems must achieve order among their participants as well as adjustment to

[12] An earlier form may be found in Talcott Parsons *et al., Working Papers in the Theory of Action* (New York: Free Press, 1953), pp. 177–190. This has been considerably reworked and fully discussed in Talcott Parsons, "The Role of General Theory in Sociological Analysis," *Alpha Kappa Deltan*, XXIX (Winter, 1959), pp. 13–22.

conditions (physical and social) beyond their boundaries. It further recognizes that the phenomena of social systems tend to be focused on technical, instrumental aspects (means) or on achieving ultimate goals and satisfactions. For example, if we were to analyze the American university as a social system in this manner, the adaptive function (emphasis on means with respect to outside conditions) would be illustrated by the provision of heating or air-conditioning for classrooms and offices; the goal-attainment function (emphasis on achieving group ends with respect to external reality) might be pursued through research and services that enhance the prestige of the university; the pattern-maintenance and tension-management functions (which focus on developing proper motivation and acceptance of the normative structure of the system) would be performed by orientation sessions, allocation of rank and salary increases to the staff, and by machinery for handling grievances; and finally, the integrative function (stressing the emotionally satisfying nature of coordinated activities of all the members) would be served by the honorific use of the university name, by symbolic reference to "school colors," by rallies, convocations, and commencement exercises.

But Parsons further postulates a crucial component of his general methodological approach—that the necessity of satisfying these system needs entails a functionally appropriate differentiation of *structures* designed to secure specialized focus on each of the major imperatives. In earlier formulations, which primarily dealt with the society as the referential social system, Parsons distinguished three types of *institutional areas* ("invariant points of reference")[13]—the situational, the instrumental, and the integrative. Briefly, the situational type deals with problems of relating individuals and groups to common biological and physical circumstances (e.g., kinship, age and sex groups, the political community). The instrumental type deals with specialized technical problems in relation to either the social or physical environment—occupations, professions, property relations. Finally, integrative patterns are designed to coordinate situational and instrumental patterns—political organization, stratification, and religion are examples given by Par-

[13] Parsons, *Essays in Sociological Theory*, pp. 44-51.

sons. More recently, Parsons, Bales, and Shils have shifted their focus to less complex social systems ("small groups" experimentally designed) with resultant implications for the problem of role-differentiation. Essentially, their data suggest that these systems develop informal *instrumental–adaptive roles* (i.e., suggesting ideas and solutions) and *regulatory–"administrative"* roles (coordinating efforts of "idea" roles), and *positively integrating* roles (performed by those who are liked) and *negatively integrating* roles (performed by those who provoke hostility).[14]

The search for structural counterparts of specific system needs is part of a long sociological tradition, traceable at least to the work of Comte, Spencer, and Marx.[15] However, two dangers are inherent in this approach. There is the oft-noted "functionalist" temptation to interpret an existent structure as the "'best" or "only" solution of a given system need. This should be accompanied by the chastening search for *functional alternatives*—i.e., alternative solutions or structures that may satisfy the same system need. Furthermore, there is the "simplist" equation of one functional need with one structure, thereby failing to recognize that the same structure may be responsive (in varying degrees) to two or more system needs.[16]

Well aware of these methodological cautions, Parsons has suggested a simple but extremely promising typology of the structural components of society, which are functionally relevant and hierarchically ordered in terms of complexity and degree of responsibility.[17] The simplest unit or level of social organization is the *primary–technical* (e.g., the conjugal family, work groups),

---

[14] Parsons *et al.*, *Working Papers*, pp. 144–148.

[15] Auguste Comte, *The Positive Philosophy*, trans. and abr. Harriet Martineau (2 vols.; London: George Bell, 1896), II; Herbert Spencer, *Principles of Sociology* (New York: D. Appleton, 3d ed., 1898), I, pp. 439–447; II, pp. 24–34, 214–226, and chs. 17, 18; Karl Marx, *A Contribution to the Critique of Political Economy*, trans. N. I. Stone (New York: International Library, 1904), pp. 11–12; Karl Marx and Friedrich Engels, *The German Ideology* (New York: International Publishers, 1939), pp. 7–9, 18–20.

[16] Talcott Parsons, *The Social System* (New York: Free Press, 1951), pp. 167, 315. See also Robert K. Merton, *Social Theory and Social Structure* (New York: Free Press, revised and enlarged edition, 1957), pp. 33–36, 52–53.

[17] Parsons, "The Role of General Theory . . . ," *loc cit.*, pp. 17–21.

which performs all four functions but stresses the adaptive function. The *managerial structure*, as the name implies, coordinates the functions of subordinate primary units, thereby performing predominantly pattern–maintenance and integrative functions. Many administrative and supervisory units in bureaucratic organizations are examples of managerial groups. The *institutional structure* serves to coordinate and legitimize the operation of managerial systems and tends to focus on consummatory functions (both goal-attainment and integrative). Finally, the most complex level is the *societal*, which likewise stresses consummatory functions, but with a tendency to delegate integrative functions to significant institutional systems (religion, economic structures, and governmental systems) while reserving for itself the major responsibility for goal-attainment (i.e., foreign relations).

Social action, social system, and functionalism

Structural analysis of social systems and their components is an important methodological base for sociology. But it is inherently descriptive and "formal"; it tends to reify or hypostasize social phenomena and thereby disregards the teleological, active, dynamic aspects of human behavior. Parsons has been experimenting with a conceptual solution to this dilemma (which may be appropriately called "dynamic formalism"), the major ingredients of which are such key concepts as *social action, emergent properties, social function*, and *action processes*. Let us examine these concepts with a view to determining their articulation with, and strengthening of, the central notion of social systems.

In his initial approach to social systems, Parsons was principally concerned with structural components; yet two dynamic conceptions were belatedly and significantly added: [18] (1) "effort"—the active attempt to realize norms and values in specific situations—and (2) emergent properties of systems—by which is meant synthetic, analytical features derived from the interactive "contributions" of specific component parts. These conceptual "extras" were later recognized as the core elements in action systems and Parsons

[18] Parsons, *The Structure of Social Action*, pp. 396, 719.

has apparently developed his structural–functional approach from this base.

Essentially, "effort" has been embraced in the familiar concepts of social action and social process, which refer to units or series of normatively grounded and motivated behavior directed toward perceived and meaningful aspects of the environment. This renewed emphasis on action, rather than on structure, logically and empirically demanded a revised conception of social systems as "going concerns," characterized by orderly and meaningful constellations of social actions. But one conceptual link was still lacking—a means of relating overall system, component structures, and specific social actions. At this point, the necessary methodological "closure" was achieved by the much-used and variably defined concept of "function."

Perhaps the most useful approach to "function" is to regard it (together with common value systems) as an emergent property of social systems. Consequently, analysis of function must search for determinate processes through which the various components of a social system interact to produce identifiable consequences or relate the operation of specific components to the operation of a given social system. "Function" may be defined, therefore, as the relevance of specific patterned processes of social action to the satisfaction of system needs. A component possesses *positive functional* significance if it can be shown to contribute to the satisfaction of system needs and therefore to the maintenance of the system; it has *dysfunctional* aspects, on the other hand, if it can be shown to obstruct the satisfaction of system needs and thus constitutes a demonstrable tendency to disrupt the system.[19] It should be emphasized that analysis of function requires the antecedent identification—at least tentatively—of a relevant system. Otherwise, we have the ludicrous attempt to impute functional significance to items in congeries,[20] which Sorokin suggests is the cul-de-sac of sociological analysis in general.

[19] Parsons, *The Social System*, pp. 22, 29, 82, 188; *Essays*, pp. 6–7, 22–23, 276–277. Cf. Dorothy Emmet, *Function, Purpose and Powers* (London: Macmillan, 1958), chs. 3 and 4.

[20] See the critique of "misplaced functionalism" in Pitirim A. Sorokin, *Society, Culture, and Personality* (New York: Harper & Row, 1947), pp. 337–342, 638–644.

The application of this type of analysis has been marked by confrontation with salutary empirical obstacles, with a resultant modification that greatly strengthens this approach. There is first the distinction between *manifest* and *latent* functions (and dysfunctions),[21] which takes account of both the obvious, intended consequences and the underlying, unpremeditated consequences of system components. Second, there is the recognition of functional *equivalents* or *alternatives*, based on empirical evidence of the same system need satisfied through different (and presumably interchangeable) structures.[22] Finally, Parsons has distinguished a special level of functional significance in structures that "permit" the continuation of dysfunctional structures by providing a counterbalancing structure. This is called an *adaptive structure* [23] and may be illustrated by the functioning of political machines, which contribute solutions to problems of integration in the face of dysfunctional "structures," such as non-voting, emphasis on entertainment and pleasure, distrust of political personnel, etc.[24]

MAJOR THEORETICAL INSIGHTS

There can be no doubt that Parsons has been primarily a *methodologist* (concerned with the strategy of sociological analysis) and a *conceptualizer–taxonomist* (seeking to devise relevant definitions of variables and their organization into typologies). This emphasis derives from his dissatisfaction with the existent "embarrassment of riches" in sociological concepts and terms, and with the intensive "specialization without coordination" that still exists in contemporary sociology. But, despite the criticisms of Parsons' "abstractness," "high-level generality," and "empirical nonrelevance," he has often shifted his efforts to the theoretical level by formulating more or less empirically relevant statements on the relation of two or more important concepts (and variables). Since

21 Parsons, *The Social System*, pp. 30, 476–477; *Essays in Sociological Theory*, pp. 284–286, 301; Merton, *op. cit.*, pp. 51, 60–63.
22 Parsons, *The Social System*, pp. 167, 315.   23 *Ibid.*, pp. 168, 185–187.
24 Merton, *op. cit.*, pp. 72–82.

these forays into the theoretical realm are intermittent and admittedly non-systematic, it may be more accurate to refer to them as "theoretical insights."

Furthermore, it should be noted that these insights are conceived at different levels of generality. First, there are *empirical relations* imputed to specific social systems (e.g., the American middle-class kinship system).[25] Second, Parsons offers theoretical statements about *general institutional structure and dynamics* (e.g., the derivation of strain).[26] Finally, at a level almost indistinguishable from the methodological plane, he is concerned with statements of relations between concepts applicable to *all* social systems. Consequently, we shall try to select and codify from each of these levels those insights that seem to constitute current or potentially valuable additions to specific problem-areas of sociological theory.

Social organization and differentiation

Many of Parsons' formulations are concerned with generalized social systems and therefore largely contain methodological, axiomatic statements, which are valuable but not easily testable. However, his discussions of institutions (in general or specific terms), roles, and small groups are not only more substantive—theoretical in nature, but appear to be particularly focused on previously unexamined interstices of sociological theory. In all probability, the foundation of his social organization theory is a very recent, theoretically fertile classification of social organization levels, to which we have already referred, but which also establishes a newly clarified status for "institution."

It will be recalled that this typology distinguishes the primary level, the managerial level, the institutional level, and the societal level. However, phrased in hierarchical terms, this typology is accompanied by more or less explicit statements about the structure, development, and problems of societies and their constituent parts. First and foremost is the highly significant, empirically demonstrable proposition of a functionally necessary sequence in the genesis

[25] Parsons, *Essays in Sociological Theory*, chs. 10, 11.
[26] *Ibid.*, chs. 13, 14; Parsons, *The Social System*, pp. 206, 282, 331, 491.

and development of concrete societies and complex groups. Essentially, "new" systems begin with primary types of social organization. As primary units multiply and become more differentiated in purpose, managerial systems likewise develop to maximize efficient coordination. However, the necessity for coordinating managerial units evokes institutional organizations, which in turn acquire "organic solidarity" in some degree through the emergence of a societal system.[27] Thus, we have a simplified explanation of the unarrested, normal course of social complexity, as well as a firm foundation for the ubiquitous phenomena of *bureaucratization*.

Perhaps the most important aspect of this general theoretical orientation is a rejuvenated theory of institutions and their role in society. No longer is "institution" confused with "group," "collectivity," or "culture," [28] although it partakes of each of these. In Parsons' revised approach, the institutional level of social organization refers to those social groups that provide ultimate reference points for the values, behavior, and functions of subordinate managerial and primary groups within the same social segment (often known as the institutional area or realm). Institutional groups are guardians (not creators) of the most deeply cherished values, and therefore such groups operate by making basic decisions in terms of these values to guide, legitimize, and control the functions of subordinate groups. Consequently, as we have vaguely construed the term for many years, institutions constitute an obligatory (though not exclusive) focus for sociological analysis of human behavior. Institutional groups are likewise significant as "competitors" in the simultaneous process of societal dynamics, since the societal level is inherently incapable of formalization without the crucial "leap" of already functioning structures from the "institutional" to the "societal" plane. Empirically, this process may be described as composed of attempts by institutional groups to perform necessary services and exercise appropriate authority for which existent specialized value-systems are inadequate. Parsons regards this process as the realm of "power" phenomena, which are

27 Parsons, "The Role of General Theory," *op. cit.*, pp. 17–21.
28 Parsons, *The Social System*, pp. 39–40, 97–98.

significant as *bonds* between the institutional and societal organizational levels.[29] An important corollary, which has not yet been
elaborated, is that, since the locus of power is in institutional
groups, any power achieved or attempted by subordinate groups is
derivative from and dependent on dominant institutional organizations. To the extent that social change is responsive to the power
process, therefore, any significant innovation must in practice obtain the *imprimatur* of strategic institutional groups before it is
properly fitted into the sociocultural matrix.[30]

For Parsons, the prime theoretical problem in social organization
is the mechanics of persistence, the dynamics of structure. The
spurious solutions based on "culture," "common value integration," "common interests," "solidarity," "morale," etc., have been
essentially static in nature and psychologically mystifying. Consequently, Parsons has aimed at developing concepts that possess
simultaneous reference to cultural, psychological, and associational
aspects of social systems and that take account of all the significant
properties of social systems. These are the famous *pattern-
variables*,[31] which have recently been furloughed by Parsons, but
which are the basis for several important fragments of theory.
Very briefly, the pattern-variables consist of three complementary
groups of crucial system-variables (system-dimensions), each
phrased in dichotomous terms for simplicity, and each relating to
empirical orientations toward action within a system. In the first
group, the *diffuseness–specificity* and *neutrality–affectivity* variables refer to aspects of the *motivational* orientation of actors, i.e.,
attitudes toward socially significant objects. The second group,
comprising the *universalism–particularism* and the *quality–performance* variables, basically describes the *value-orientation* of
actors or the imputed relation of social objects to one another and

29 See the discussion pp. 202–206.

30 Alvin Boskoff, "Functional Analysis as a Source of a Theoretical Repertory
and Research Tasks in the Study of Social Change," in George K. Zollschan and
Walter Hirsch, eds., *Explorations in Social Change* (Boston: Houghton Mifflin,
1964), especially pp. 224–225, 231–234.

31 Parsons, *The Social System*, pp. 58–76, 101–112; Parsons *et al.*, *Working
Papers*, pp. 58–65.

to the existing motivational interests of actors. Finally, the *self–collectivity* variable concerns the *direction* of motivated action-chains—in terms of private or group interests.

From a theoretical standpoint, the descriptive function of the pattern-variables is a necessary first step toward discovering meaningful affinities between the dimensions, which are regarded by Parsons as "dilemmas of choice" for members of determinate social systems. With data of certain "small group" experiments as a provocative empirical referent, Parsons suggests that characteristic clusters of pattern-variables are intimately related to functionally distinctive phases of social systems.[32] (See Table 4.) These regularities appear to possess the status of *constructed types* and, as we

Adaptive – instrumental phase	Universalism – performance Specificity – neutrality
Expressive – instrumental phase	Performance – particularism Affectivity – specificity
Integrative – expressive phase	Particularism – quality Diffuseness – affectivity
Symbolic – expressive phase	Quality – universalism Neutrality – diffuseness

TABLE 4.

shall soon see, may be construed as referential hypotheses for discovering empirical variations (the principle of negative utility). However, one of the obvious corollaries of this statement of regularities is the proposition that social organization types inherently reflect a minimal linkage between types of motivation and types of valuational systems external to the actor. This is of course identical with the classic theory of "attitudes and values" in the much-cited methodological note of Thomas and Znaniecki.[33]

Since the pattern-variables in a given social system reflect the

[32] Parsons *et al.*, *Working Papers* pp. 179–180.
[33] W. I. Thomas and Florian Znaniecki, *The Polish Peasant in Europe and America* (5 vols.; Boston: Richard Badger, 1918), I, pp. 20–33, 38–44.

past conditions of learning, the social system may achieve an internal cultural consistency that is not well-adapted to immediate problems of its sociophysical environment. Indeed, Parsons concludes that the motivation of actors toward conformity varies with the type of pattern-variables to which they are exposed, a modification of the extreme "hostility" between individual and social system posited by Freud in his *Civilization and Its Discontents.* Thus far, an extensive analysis of the major empirical types of pattern-variables and their "pressures" on implicated actors has not been pursued; but Parsons has presented some convincing evidence that the *neutrality–achievement–universalism* cluster of variables "inevitably" generates strains, ambivalence, and conflict.[34] This position, it seems, underlies his structural–functional analyses of fascism, anti-Semitism, contemporary aggression, American youth culture, and the recent "religious revival" in the United States.[35]

Role differentiation

We have already noted Parsons' theoretical statements on the specialization or differentiation of groups within complex social systems. The recent but belated interest among sociologists in the *internal* structure of groups (illustrated by the development of sociometry, "group dynamics," and "small groups research"[36]) has also presented a challenge to the applicability of the Parsonian approach. Essentially, Parsons has conceived the internal structure of groups in functional and genetic terms, aided by experimental studies of student groupings and cross-cultural data on kinship groups. The development of group structure and functioning is accompanied by a process of specialization or qualitative differentia-

[34] Parsons, *The Social System*, pp. 206, 267–269.

[35] Parsons, *Essays*, chs. 9, 12; Talcott Parsons, "The Sociology of Modern Antisemitism," in Isacque Graeber and S. H. Britt, eds., *Jews in a Gentile World* (New York: Macmillan, 1942), pp. 101–122; Talcott Parsons, "Some Sociological Aspects of the Fascist Movements," *Social Forces*, XXI (December, 1942), pp. 138–147; Talcott Parsons, "The Pattern of Religious Organization in the United States," *Daedalus* LXXXVII (Summer, 1958), pp. 84–86.

[36] For a good summary, see Allan W. Eister, "Basic Continuities in the Study of Small Groups," in Howard Becker and Alvin Boskoff, eds., *Modern Sociological Theory* (New York: Holt, Rinehart & Winston, 1957), ch. 10.

tion of roles, which corresponds to the "functional history" of all groups. In the first stages of organization, social interaction produces two types of roles that relate to instrumental–adaptive problems [37]—roles emphasizing *solutions* of technical problems (practical ideas) and roles that involve *regulation* of interpersonal behavior in the application of technical solutions (administrative–managerial roles). According to Parsons, these roles in practice necessarily contribute pressures, strains, and consequent negative reactions among group members, who presumably are not properly socialized, since pattern-maintenance functions are not regularized in early stages of group formation.

To provide "equilibrium"—to counterbalance the potentially disruptive responses—two additional types of roles (or role fragments) likewise develop with respect to the integrative–expressive dimension of action. One type of these "derivative" roles is called the "scapegoat" or "displaced hostility focus"; in this case, the instrumental–adaptive specialist roles (either the "idea" or "managerial" role) are accorded non-rational hostility and distrust—or these reactions are directed toward scapegoats near the bottom of the emerging status hierarchy. At the same time, there develops a complementary role, which we might call "delegated charisma," in which positive attachment to persons near (but not at) the top of the instrumental–adaptive hierarchy is achieved. Perhaps the best illustration of these generalized roles is, as Parsons suggests, the changing structure of the American family.[38]

The nature of role differentiation likewise provides clues to some aspects of groups that are often thought to be explained solely by personality features of individual members. For example, the ubiquitous phenomena of intragroup factions and status-maneuverings might be considered a predictable consequence of the incompatibility between adaptive and integrative roles and the functionally understandable attempt to merge both roles in the same person. Parenthetically, we might redefine the quest for power and its consolidation as the enforced merger of the adaptive

---

[37] Parsons *et al.*, *Working Papers*, pp. 144–145.

[38] *Ibid.*, pp. 147–150; Talcott Parsons and Robert F. Bales, *Family, Socialization and Interaction Process* (New York: Free Press, 1955), pp. 22, 55, 103, 306.

and integrative roles in a determinate social system. But prolonged status struggles of this type severely impair the operation of both adaptive and integrative roles. Consequently, Parsons interprets this threat as the basis for widespread sociocultural phenomena, which he calls "coalitions." Thus, he is able to "explain" the incest taboo as a coalition between the technical-father role and the integrative–positive affective-mother role for insuring successful socialization of children. Similarly, Parsons suggests that various totemic and ritual "sacrifices" ultimately represent adaptive–integrative role coalitions or compromises that are significant for the stability of many groups.[39]

Stratification

With few exceptions, theories of stratification have been either disturbingly vague or notoriously polemical. Matters of definition and selection of appropriate indices (objective or subjective) have therefore seemed either premature or arbitrary and have engendered many fruitless controversies.[40] Though Parsons has devoted comparatively little attention to stratification, some of his recent formulations on related topics seem to provide a firm theoretical basis for stratification analysis. We may therefore point to an emerging structural–functional orientation to stratification.

Parsons constantly reminds us that stratification is an essential component of social systems, particularly of communities and societies, which derives from internal functional differentiation (as previously discussed) and crucial systems of evaluation.[41] Accord-

[39] Parsons *et al.*, *Working Papers*, p. 149.

[40] In particular, see the viewpoints of Oliver C. Cox, *Caste, Class, and Race* (New York: Doubleday, 1948); W. Lloyd Warner and Paul S. Lunt, *The Social Life of a Modern Community* (New Haven: Yale University Press, 1941); and Richard Centers, *The Psychology of Social Classes* (Princeton: Princeton University Press, 1949). For some critiques, see Llewellyn Gross, "The Use of Class Concepts in Sociological Research," *American Journal of Sociology*, LIV (March, 1949), pp. 409–421; Harold W. Pfautz, "The Current Literature on Social Stratification: Critique and Bibliography," *American Journal of Sociology*, LVII (January, 1953), pp. 391–418.

[41] Parsons, *Essays in Sociological Theory*, ch. 7. A more recent version is his "A Revised Analytical Approach to the Theory of Social Stratification," *Essays* (New York: Free Press, revised edition, 1954), ch. 19.

ing to this view, differentiation of roles in terms of adaptive, goal-attainment, pattern-maintenance, and integrative functions creates observable distinctions in the behavior and social relations of persons. In Parsons' own terms, this functional differentiation is accompanied by differences in *qualities, performances,* and *possessions* of actors in specific roles.[42] Since stratification systems reflect differential ranking of persons and roles, a basic ingredient is obviously found in the criteria of relative evaluation. Such critieria are difficult to trace to their ultimate origins but, in any case, they constitute non-rational, differential evaluations of the four functions. Perhaps the basic problem in evaluation, from the standpoint both of actors and of the social system, is the inevitable dilemma of emphasizing either adaptive or integrative functions. This is related to the "dilemma" in evaluation schemes of emphasizing qualities, performances, or possessions in ranking persons and roles. Apparently, an adaptive emphasis tends to be accompanied by an emphasis on performance variables (e.g., an open-class system in which position and mobility are dependent on "technical" achievements), while the integrative emphasis is allied with primary evaluation of qualities and, secondarily, of possessions (e.g., the feudal system of "estates" and "orders").

Stratification is, however, not a disembodied process of differential evaluation. Stratum differences are reflected in, and preserved by, some form of social organization. Theorists of stratification have sought to locate these organizations in "class" groups such as cliques, voluntary formal associations, power elites, etc.[43] It is not always clear in these instances whether such "class" groups are applications or extensions of already organized strata, or are the strata themselves. Parsons, it appears, provides a basis for distinguishing "organized" strata in his typology of functional levels of organization, which was discussed in another context on page 189. Generally, regardless of cross-cultural differences and variations in

[42] Parsons, "A Revised Analytical Approach," *op. cit.,* pp. 389–391.

[43] Warner and Lunt, *loc. cit.;* A. B. Hollingshead, *Elmtown's Youth* (New York: Wiley, 1949); Walter Goldschmidt, *As You Sow* (New York: Harcourt, Brace & World, 1947); C. P. Loomis *et al., Critique of Class as Related to Social Stratification* (Beacon, New York: Beacon House, 1948); C. Wright Mills, *The Power Elite* (New York: Oxford University Press, 1957).

stratum rigidity, the primary level of organization corresponds to the social position of lower classes. The managerial groups, as defined by Parsons, can be functionally equated with "middle" classes in the broadest sense. Finally, persons and groups operating at the institutional and societal levels clearly occupy the highest status positions.[44]

Though Parsons has not yet pursued the theoretical implications and potentials of such a scheme, several pertinent inferences in the form of hypotheses may be fruitfully derived. For example, the relative sharpness or looseness of stratum boundaries may be directly related to the development of clear-cut or vaguely defined differentiation among functional levels. Thus, in an open-class system such as ours, the difficulty of determining class position for certain groups (e.g., intellectuals and artists) may stem from an antecedent failure to identify their functional level (which may be explained on several grounds), as well as from the obvious problems connected with opportunities for rapid vertical mobility. In the same vein, the emergence of intermediate or middle classes may be principally connected with the multiplication and extension of managerial functions as *specialized* roles available to distinctive groupings.[45] Finally—for present purposes—it may be hypothesized that the pursuit of a career on a specific functional level (primary–technical, managerial, etc.) requires peculiar personal adjustments that are expressed in needs, ideologies, biases, aspirations, opportunities, and resultant facilities—in short, in functionally appropriate and distinctive cultural manifestations.[46]

However, stratification systems are in most instances not predominantly harmonious or rational. In recent years, Parsons has come to emphasize the role of power or unlegitimated control in the relations between strata. Power, or deviation from institutionalized patterns, is a consequence (or expression) of three accompani-

[44] Alvin Boskoff, "Stratification, Power, and Social Change," in Simpson and Turk, *op. cit.*

[45] Alvin Boskoff, "Status Phases, Social Mobility, and Differential Behavior" (unpublished paper read at the American Sociological Association, 1965), p. 15; Harold J. Laski, *The Rise of Liberalism* (New York: Harper, 1936).

[46] *Cf.* Karl Mannheim, *Ideology and Utopia* (New York: Harcourt, Brace, 1936).

ments of stratification: (1) the application of "dominant" values to behavior, despite the varying degrees of acceptance of such values; (2) opportunities for unsanctioned deviation from presumably common values; and (3) differential access to key possessions (land, money, machines, manpower), which allows certain strata to use the preceding forms of power with predictably high efficiency.[47] In short, power is here conceived as a practical source of competition with prevailing ranking systems, precisely because the phenomena of power tend to enhance specialized or fractionated goals rather than the ordered division of skills and responsibilities which characterize a stratification system.

It follows that stratification systems are inherently ambivalent, containing varying tendencies toward stability and change. Parsons assumes that the pace and character of larger social changes greatly determine the internal dynamics (stability and rationality vs. power and change) of stratification systems. In periods of rapid change (e.g., in shifts from folk-like to complex systems), value rankings tend to be ambiguous, while opportunities for access to possessions and conflicts of interest and interpretation rise appreciably. Under these conditions, stratification is quite fluid; but in addition, the relatively low consensus on key values is accompanied by considerable polarization of groups and social categories.[48] The ensuing conflicts may be interpreted as attempts either to *clarify* a pre-existing ranking system or to *introduce* a revised system. On the other hand, when social and cultural changes have become consolidated—and the pace of change is reduced or controlled—ranking systems tend to be sharper and yet more widely accepted, with greater concentration, but less frequent manifestation, of power.

Power and influence as social mechanisms

Social systems as differentiated entities (roles, ranks, functions, institutions) operate through the interplay of specialization and

[47] Parsons, *Essays in Sociological Theory* (rev. ed.), pp. 391–395.

[48] Talcott Parsons *et al.*, eds., *Theories of Society* (2 vols.; New York: Free Press, 1961), I, pp. 256–257, 263–264.

coordination. Structural theories in sociology largely deal with specialization and differentiation. Dynamic theories (which may or may not focus on significant changes in structure), on the other hand, inevitably seek to account for interconnections between subsystems. Parsons has begun to explore this ancient theoretical focus in a tentative fashion only in the last six or seven years. Consequently, statement of issues and conceptualization inevitably predominate over theoretical assertions. However, as I have tried to show elsewhere,[49] this "new" interest in Parsons' writings is intimately related to his analyses and theories of stratification and social change.

	Intentional	Situational
Positive sanction	Influence	Money
Negative sanction	Power A	Power B

TABLE 5.

Essentially, Parsons seems to locate the problem of dynamics in two related forms of coordination—the interaction of technical, managerial, and policy-making levels within a given functional realm; and the coordination or integration of social outputs from the four functional subsystems.[50] (The relation between these two forms is itself a crucial theoretical problem, but one that is not yet analyzed by Parsons.) In practice, there are three generalized means by which the end of coordination is pursued—*money*, *power*, and *influence*. Each means characteristically uses a different combination of sanction (positive or negative) and channel or approach to achieving control (indirect or situational and direct or aimed at individual intentions). (See Table 5.) [51]

[49] Boskoff, "Stratification, Power, and Social Change," *loc. cit.*
[50] *Ibid.*
[51] Talcott Parsons, "On the Concept of Influence," *Public Opinion Quarterly*, XXVII (Spring, 1963), pp. 37–62.

In contrast to earlier formulations, Parsons currently views power as the processes in which some role-occupant seeks to mobilize or integrate the operations of specific subsystems to achieve a goal or product identifiable with the larger system (organization, community, nation). Apparently, power provides coordination for unanticipated contingencies, while authority primarily deals with fixed and largely predictable situations. It is assumed, further, that power is "normally" exercised in conjunction with, or from a base of,[52] authority. Consequently, type B power, as indicated in the table, tends to be rare and short-lived, while type A power is considerably more widespread and a more effective tool.

Perhaps three major theoretical statements about power can be identified in Parsons' work:

1. Power (type A) as a social mechanism may be used either to promote continuity in existing organizations or to inspire alterations in subsystems and in their respective contributions to the larger system. Parsons, however, does not specify the conditions under which each application of power can be reliably predicted. However, it has been suggested that the more "radical" application of power (type A) is more likely to occur during early phases of stratification when cultural and social change is relatively rapid.[53]
2. Power phenomena may be regarded as social responses to variably serious "coordination crises." By implication, we may expect competition in using the techniques of power. Parsons theorizes that power (type A) necessitates minimal support or conformity to the "new" prescriptions on the part of specialized actors or organizations.[54] It follows that power (type A) is more likely to be effective among groups that either possess a credible base of authority or can "demonstrate" their superior interpretation of authoritative norms.
3. Power in practice tends to produce and/or interpret specific norms that guide or justify the demands of agents of power. These norms specify the time order of desired changes in subsystems (e. g., greater effort, higher quality, speedier "products"), and the range of adjust-

[52] Talcott Parsons, "On the Concept of Power," *Proceedings of the American Philosophical Society*, CVII (1963), pp. 232–262. Also in Reinhard Bendix and Seymour M. Lipset, eds., *Class, Power, and Status* (New York: Free Press, rev. ed., 1962).
[53] Parsons, *Theories of Society*, I, p. 257.
[54] Parsons, "On the Concept of Power," *op. cit.*, pp. 237–241, 250.

ments that may be imposed.[55] Indeed, the manipulation of norms that facilitate "boundary-interchange" (i. e., connect the material and behavioral products of specialized subsystems or functional areas) provides an important theoretical clue to understanding the phenomena of social change. (See discussion on pp. 206–210.)

Influence

Though Parsons had earlier conceptualized power in four forms (persuasion, inducement, activation of commitments, and deterrence), more recently he has "reduced" power to the latter two forms. In his revised statement, inducement is defined as a process of intended coordination that uses money as the most generally

	Intentional	Situational
Positive sanction	Persuasion	Inducement
Negative sanction	Activation of commitments	Deterrence

TABLE 6.

available and translatable medium.[56] (See Table 6.) The conditions of effective coordination through money have not been investigated (even in our presumably materialistic society), though a beginning was surely made by Simmel in his *Philosophy of Money*.[57] But influence as a medium (and persuasion as its major social goal) has received a lengthy analysis that requires critical attention.

Briefly, Parsons regards influence as a process characterized by presenting justifiable reasons for suggested changes in the behavior of persons in other roles or subsystems. Coordination is sought by

[55] Parsons, *Working Papers*, pp. 202–207.
[56] Parsons, "On the Concept of Influence," *op. cit.*, pp. 44–47.
[57] Georg Simmel, *Philosophie des Geldes* (Leipzig, 1900).

motivational changes under conditions of relative freedom and "rationality"—unlike the cases of inducement (no motivational change) or power (which is either non-rational or highly restrictive). But what accounts for *effective influence?* Parsons suggests that the intended changes are more probable when (*a*) relevant information is provided, (*b*) a justification for change is presented in meaningful terms, and (*c*) there is a high degree of solidarity and similarity between agents and objects of influence.[58] In short, influence (and persuasion) depends upon "primary-group" settings (or the counterfeiting of such settings, "pseudo-*Gemeinschaft*"). By implication, money is a very tenuous medium of producing coordination—as the extreme form, seen in blackmail, well illustrates—because it constitutes only a one-way "investment." However, power seems to be prevalent in complex, large-scale systems, where consensus is multiple and variable, and where the opportunity to produce new motivations is quite limited.

Social change: analysis of variations of social systems

One of the persistent criticisms of Parsons' approach is a presumed emphasis on system, equilibrium, and structure. Indeed, Parsons pessimistically concluded in 1951 that contemporary data and concepts were inadequate for a serious theoretical approach to social change, though the problem had often been recognized in his earlier writings as a crucial part of the sociological agenda.[59] Perhaps it is fair to conclude that the study of social change was for Parsons an ultimate problem, possibly a residual problem, which would require more detailed conceptualization and application of the structural–functional orientation before useful and properly interrelated formulations could be worked out. At present, by pursuing related methodological and theoretical concerns, Parsons has conceptually carved out the basic elements of social change theory, which need to be codified and, since Parsons has not yet done so, audaciously applied.

Inherent in the structural–functional conception of society is

---

[58] Parsons, "On the Concept of Influence," *op. cit.*, pp. 48–52.

[59] Parsons, *The Social System*, pp. 486, 494; *Essays in Sociological Theory*, pp. 11–12, 23, 278–282, 296–297, 312–318.

the *dynamic* quality of social systems, as expressed in such terms as "going concerns," "unstable equilibrium." Structural components (roles, groups) achieve, maintain, and vary their interrelations through symbols and norms expressed or created in social action processes. Consequently, society can be analyzed in terms of those social processes by which "structure" or "interrelationships" are developed. Following an important distinction made by Znaniecki and Sorokin, Parsons differentiates between processes *within* the system and processes *of* the system.[60] In the former case, social systems exhibit variations in structure due to *internal* differentiation and development. Thus, processes within a system produce structural variations on an evolving theme (or themes). Parenthetically, we might suggest that these processes constitute unwitting *rehearsals* for social change. However, in processes *of* a system, the variations are so significant that, following the previous analogy, essentially new themes and structures appear, which can be appropriately designated "social changes." Two fundamental problems of general theory therefore emerge at this point. (1) What factors account for changes *within* a system? (2) What is the relation between these processes and the factors or conditions that produce changes *of* a system?

Generally, Parsons has concentrated his analyses and conceptualizations on the first of the theoretical problems, since it logically precedes the second and since it provides a basis for isolating the components appropriate to the second theoretical problem.[61] The initial approach to process within a system was mainly centered on four conditions. First, Parsons noted an implicit *range of toleration* for actions with respect to institutionally defined roles and statuses in social systems. This permissible variation seemed to derive its specific qualities from personality differences and the peculiar features of concrete social situations. Second, inherent elements of *in-*

---

[60] Florian Znaniecki, *The Method of Sociology* (New York: Rinehart, 1934), pp. 12–19; Florian Znaniecki, *Cultural Sciences* (Urbana: University of Illinois Press, 1951), pp. 164, 229–231; Parsons, *The Social System*, p. 481.

[61] This emphasis should not be interpreted as reflecting a presumed attraction for analysis of structure, organization, and "statics," rather than change and "dynamics." Both problems share an intrinsic focus on processes of variation. See Alvin Boskoff, "Social Change: Major Problems in the Emergence of Theoretical and Research Foci," in Becker and Boskoff, *op. cit.*, pp. 261–263.

ternal conflict (both personal and cultural) characterize every social system, since a fully integrated, consistent, and satisfactory social organization is a utopian vision that has never materialized in the recorded segment of social reality. Third, Parsons gave some prominence to *strain*—the personally experienced disturbance of expectation systems—though the sources of strain were initially not clarified. Finally, intensified conflicts and strains were conceived as factors in weakened social controls (internal and external forms) and in the development of *motivation toward deviant behavior.*[62]

In a sense, these factors can be regarded as "potentialities" for internal system developments. A theory of process within a social system also requires a scheme for ordering and interpreting the consequences of potentialities with constant reference to the social system. Here, it seems, lies the major significance of Parsons' and Bales' analysis of *phase movements.*

Every social system, according to the phase movement theory, pursues the four functional problems as a succession of phases, in each of which special dominance is necessarily placed on one problem. This "normal" succession reflects a generalized reaction to experience in which *orientation, evaluation,* and *control* constitute a basic referential sequence.[63] Social structures can therefore be characterized by the peculiar importance attached to certain phases (e.g., the adaptive in American society, the integrative in traditional Chinese society). By implication then, process within a system entails the operation of the system (through its differentiated units) as it successively attempts to solve major functional problems. The phenomena of strain, internal conflict, and motivation toward deviance consequently indicate "dysfunctional" operation of the phase movement cycle, for which Parsons suggests three reasons.

1. Generally, the smooth operation of social systems is hampered by one-sided concentration of activity in any phase, thus creating "deficits" in attention to other important problems.[64] This is, of course, a special functional version of the "cultural lag" theory. In particular,

[62] Parsons, *The Social System*, pp. 206, 267–268, 321, 491; *Essays in Sociological Theory*, pp. 278, 312, 317.
[63] Parsons, *Working Papers*, pp. 140–141.   [64] *Ibid.*, p. 188.

Parsons points to the extraordinary salience (to the observer) of "functional lags" in a rapidly developing social system—where one would expect an accompanying acceleration of phase movements.

2. More specifically, Parsons tends to focus on the special stabilizing function of the pattern-maintenance, tension-management phase. This phase or aspect of system operation provides recuperative intervals between more "active" phases; it stabilizes important values against both vagrant and persistent pressures toward variation; and it creates and sustains motivational conformity with role expectations.[65] Therefore, insufficient or incompetent attention to this phase inevitably produces competing and disturbing processes within the system.

3. Phase movements are likewise subject to "exigencies of the situation" or the effects of conditions external to the social system.[66] These would include environmental facilities and resources, culture contacts, and military and economic pressures from other social systems.

The second theoretical problem has not yet been *directly* treated by Parsons, though scattered clues may be found in his more recent works. One early theoretical fragment suggests that processes within a system, including the dysfunctional tendencies previously discussed, do not result in processes *of* a system (social change) without the intervention of sources external to the system.[67] While the nature of these external pressures is not specified, their role in the process of change appears to be either weakening of existing motivations or providing alternative guides for already flagging motivations.

But more recent writings suggest new theoretical leads. For example, change *of* a system may now be interpreted as practically inseparable from the phenomena of power. By implication, the relative emphasis on the four functions depends on the judgments and behavior of persons in policy-making (institutional) roles—official or otherwise. Indeed, the major element of policy-making in relation to change consists of those actions that translate innovations from one functional area to another (what has been called

[65] Talcott Parsons, "Some Highlights of the General Theory of Action," in Roland Young, ed., *Approaches to the Study of Politics* (Evanston: Northwestern University Press, 1958), pp. 292–294.

[66] Parsons and Bales, *op. cit.*, pp. 300, 358.

[67] Parsons, *The Social System*, pp. 494–495.

"boundary interchange"). In retrospect, Parsons provided a currently useful link at this point (in his *Working Papers*) by developing the notion of *phase norms* and (my label for a further clue in Parsons' discussion) *transition norms*. The course of change, then, involves the application of power by interpreting and/or designing norms for evoking adaptations (quantitative or qualitative) in one or more related functional sectors (e.g., pattern-maintenance, following innovations in the adaptive sphere). It follows that the processes of social change—in terms of specific direction and relative speed—are largely determined or at least mediated by the dominant characteristics of those at the principal centers of power.[68] In addition, quite contrary to frequent criticisms, processes of change require attention to conflict—not only as a source of change, but as a consequence of boundary interchanges that inevitably entail opposition.

Another form of this approach is based on an *evolutionary framework*. Parsons relates social change to variations in the adaptive and organizational capacities of given societies, which are expressed in processes of *innovation* and *implementation*. In simpler societies, these capacities develop as consequences of a limited number of familiar specialized products (technology, kinship systems and incest taboos, language, and religion). However, opportunities for change are magnified by evolutionary developments in key social and cultural specializations—stratification on the basis of kinship and then responsibility and skill, bureaucratization, legal systems, money and market systems, and autonomous associations. Thus, cumulative forms of interdependent social and cultural differentiation increase structural autonomy, which in turn creates enhanced opportunities for consciously selected innovations. Inferentially, foci of autonomy are equivalent to centers of power; consequently, the greater the relative autonomy of subsystems, the greater the control (either positive or negative) of processes of change (a "cybernetic theory" of change).[69]

68 Boskoff, "Stratification, Power, and Social Change," *loc. cit.*
69 Talcott Parsons, "Evolutionary Universals in Society," *American Sociological Review*, XXIX (June, 1964), pp. 339–357; Talcott Parsons, *Societies: Evolutionary and Comparative Perspectives* (Englewood Cliffs: Prentice-Hall, 1966), pp. 11–14, 113–115.

Talcott Parsons: The Quest for a Dynamic Formalism

Over a period of thirty years of considerable publication, Parsons has shifted his conceptualization and general organization several times. And in the absence of an up-to-date, systematic overview by Parsons himself (or by anyone else), it has therefore been difficult to evaluate his writings with sufficient fidelity. However, I would suggest that two frameworks provide focal points for assessing developments in his work to date, as well as for anticipating emerging theoretical interests and issues. First, a detailed distinction of the four major functional components (adaptive, goal-attainment, pattern-maintenance, and integrative) provides a conceptual base for theories of social specialization, stratification, and social mobility, and for a "phase movement" approach to social change. More recently, Parsons' analysis of hierarchical levels of responsibility in social systems (primary–technical, managerial, institutional or policy-making) makes it possible to reconceptualize the phenomena of power and influence, not only as processes of organization, but as crucial components in the complex dynamics of social change.

SELECTED REFERENCES

Black, Max, ed., *The Social Theories of Talcott Parsons* (Englewood Cliffs: Prentice-Hall, 1961).

Boskoff, Alvin, "Functional Analysis as a Source of a Theoretical Repertory and Research Tasks in the Study of Social Change," in George K. Zollschan and Walter Hirsch, eds., *Explorations in Social Change* (Boston: Houghton Mifflin, 1964), ch. 8.

———, "Stratification, Power, and Social Change," in Richard L. Simpson and Herman Turk, eds., *Institutions and Social Exchange: The Sociologies of Talcott Parsons and George C. Homans* (Indianapolis: Bobbs-Merrill, 1969).

Loomis, Charles P., and Zona K. Loomis, *Modern Social Theories* (Princeton: Van Nostrand, 1961), ch. 6.

Parsons, Talcott, *Sociological Theory and Modern Society* (New York: Free Press, 1967).

PART II

*Major Theoretical
Problems:
Continuing Interaction
between Theory
and Research*

*Each theorist in the last seven chapters seems to have dual signifi-
cance: first as an individual attempting to cope with the currently
visible theoretical needs of sociology, by means of basic concepts,
selection of key problems, and some focus on empirical materials;
and second as an active participant in molding the contours of
sociological explanation. It is the latter aspect that concerns us
more directly in this volume. Consequently, it is desirable to take
stock of the collective contributions of these theorists in a tentative
fashion.*

*In retrospect, these theorists can be located in two rough cate-
gories. One category includes Thomas, Znaniecki, Mead, and Park,
and is distinguished by attempts to focus on nuclear theories—
primarily socialization and coordination, with some attention to
group formation and social change. As a consequence, none of
these men have developed theoretical systems of any great scope.*

*In the second category, I would place MacIver, Sorokin, Mann-
heim, and Parsons, all of whom have made decided attempts to
combine nuclear and general theoretical levels. MacIver and Soro-*

kin have given special prominence to social change issues, but seem to have regarded change as the source of interrelations among the other theoretical problems. The general theoretical level in Mac-Iver's work deals with the coordinate role of a central political structure and the ubiquitous importance of social perceptions and evaluations (dynamic assessment) in critical junctures of social interaction. The antagonistic nature of these general theories may disturb the logician, but they rest on reasonably solid ground and must be further treated by theorists. Sorokin's general theoretical position is simpler. Each major type of sociological phenomenon (stratification, group formation, etc.) reflects the coordinative role of law-norms. Therefore, by implication, variations in the content, strength, and applicability of law-norms constitute the necessary theoretical concerns of the modern sociologist.

Mannheim, too, viewed nuclear problems in relation to a more general theoretical position. But instead of focusing on nuclear problems as "contributors" to change, he seemed to approach such areas as adaptations or adjustments to preceding processes of change. His general theory asserts that the character of elites in complex society largely accounts for the subsequent course of social change and for patterns in group formation, socialization, and social stratification.

Finally, Parsons may be interpreted as demonstrating in the modern era the possibilities of deriving nuclear theories from his general theoretical framework. The basic principle of theory seems to be that within any social system, various types of social phenomena (nuclear problems) develop patterns in line with the practical difficulties of meeting the four crucial, simultaneous problems of social organization (i.e., adaptation, goal-attainment, pattern-maintenance, and integration). Therefore, particular social phenomena require explanation in terms of the major functional problem involved and the normal demands of minimally satisfying the three other functional imperatives with limited resources. Inferentially, the six nuclear theoretical problems are translated into specialized components of societal operation, no one of which can be isolated from the explanations that emerge in other nuclear fields.

Though each of the theorists has at some time been criticized or ignored, it is evident that their work represents a considerable intellectual achievement. Yet the beauty and satisfaction of written theories are inevitably short-lived unless they are continually confronted by relevant facts and more and more specific delineations of interlocking questions and correctable answers. To a large extent, the theories in Part I have directly or indirectly stimulated further theorizing and research. But the intricate interplay of numerous theories and even more numerous investigations in sociology during the past several decades cannot be adequately recorded in the limits of a single volume. More modestly, therefore, our objective in Part II is to illustrate in some detail the mutual enrichment of theory and research by focusing on five sets of theoretical problems. The following chapters will, I hope, indicate that while we "stand on the shoulders of giants," the future of sociology lies in encouraging new giants who can learn from, but not be limited by, their illustrious predecessors.

10

Theories of

Social Organization: Basic

Structures and Operation

With few exceptions, sociological theorists in the period 1890–1940 were more concerned with analyzing society (or given civilizations) than with the more localized subgroups that constitute the essential "working units" of societies.[1] Concepts and theories were devised to treat types of societies, or stages of society, and to delineate social processes of a societal nature. Even theorists of specific institutions and class systems dealt primarily with *social categories* and *cultural patterns*, rather than with sociologically distinctive organizations. However, Cooley, Weber, Durkheim, Simmel, Sorokin, and their disciples more or less unwittingly began to distinguish *types* or *levels of social organization* that have subsequently become specialized foci for study and theorizing.

[1] Cf. Logan Wilson, "Sociography of Groups," in Georges Gurvitch and Wilbert E. Moore, eds., *Twentieth Century Sociology* (New York: Philosophical Library, 1945), pp. 139–171.

Quite independently of one another, Cooley and Simmel directed the attention of sociologists to the highly significant but informally structured *small group* as an enduring entity and as a component in larger social systems. Cooley emphasized the socializing function of small groups, which he called "primary groups," and suggested their latent impact on formal institutional structures. In a unique and still inexhaustible set of formulations, Simmel legitimized the analysis of small groups by dissecting their basic structure and distinctive processes. For example, he provided unequaled analyses of dyadic and triadic varieties of small groups, specifying their operation through analyses of tact, power, secrecy, conflict, play forms, and morality. From such roots as these, the study of small, informal social systems—as separate but not highly specialized entities—has evolved in a somewhat uneven fashion. Variously known as "small group research," "group dynamics," "sociometric analysis," and "informal organization," this type of social unit has been extensively investigated since 1950.

A second type of social organization, the formal or *complex organization*, has likewise achieved identity and prominence among sociological theorists in recent decades. Originally, formal organizations were largely equated with official governmental structures and were the presumed specialty of the political scientist, the philosopher, and the journalistic essayist. But theorists such as Durkheim, Weber, Michels, Toennies, and MacIver foreshadowed the conception of a more generalized and yet distinctive kind of social system, one characterized by highly specific goals, high internal division of labor, and formalized sets of interactions and controls. Durkheim, for example, outlined a theory of "intermediary groups" that, he asserted, are practical alternatives to the domination either of primary groups (such as kinship and ethnic groups) or an omnipotent State.[2] Significantly, Durkheim's prime examples of the intermediary group are formal educational systems and occupational syndicates—in short, highly specialized and formalized complex organizations. Weber and Michels, on the other hand, tried to determine the operationally necessary characteristics of

[2] Emile Durkheim, *The Division of Labor in Society*, trans. George Simpson (New York: Free Press, 1947), pp. 17, 28.

219

formal organizations and to establish basic trends in the development of such systems (e.g., Weber's theory of rationalization and Michels' "iron law of oligarchy"). At the end of World War II, however, complex organizations were still viewed as "opposites" or "contrasts" to primary, informal groups. Yet a crucial theoretical problem was beginning to be recognized: what are the complementary relations between formal and informal structures, and between complex organizations and community and societal systems? Specifically, which structural features of complex organizations, as highly specialized systems, help to explain the *interdependence* between complex organizations and informal structures in modern societal systems?

Finally, most of the classic theorists had long since identified and variably analyzed society as a level of organization. Virtually all of their analyses on this level—from Comte to Parsons—treated society as an organization that served to interrelate the operation of distinctive institutional areas and their respective groups. Incidentally, theories about the societal level were predominantly analyses of sociocultural change and its presumed direction.

Recent developments in theory rest to a large degree on pursuing each of these organizational levels as a specialty, with secondary concern for interrelations between levels. In this chapter, therefore, we shall review the most significant innovations in the first two theoretical divisions as evidence of basic continuities in the enterprise of theory. In addition, attention will be given to a selected number of "applied areas" in which organizational theories have been explicitly or implicitly explored or tested.

INFORMAL GROUPS

Studies of "small groups"—most of which were contrived in experimental situations—have developed a veritable "population explosion." In the past decade or so, several attempts have been made to order and assess the results of such studies, with particular emphasis on the basic theoretical patterns that might be distilled from this vast supply.[3] This could not fail to be a continually frustrating and arduous undertaking, because these studies dealt with laboratory groups, relatively independent "natural" groups (the Corner Boys, for example), as well as clique-like formations within larger organizations, and because the investigators usually focused on limited aspects and time periods in the operation of such groups. Despite these difficulties, an emerging set of relevant theories can be identified or deduced. I shall try to discuss these theories in highly condensed form in terms of focal problems.

Formation

Since most small groups were "born" in a laboratory setting, the problem of initial formation seems childishly simple. But the physical location of x persons in a room is not itself the formation of a group. As Homans, Bales, Sherif, and others have interpreted it, the group as an entity is a product of interaction under certain conditions.[4] The conditions seem to be essentially either perceived pressure from a visible source (the experimenter, change in company policy, the sociophysical limitations of a neighborhood) or accidental contacts over some time span. But these provide *potentiality;* a group arises through interaction when (*a*) the persons involved agree on a common goal, task, or interest, and when (*b*) they come to accept one another in a minimal way as desirable objects of further interaction. In the latter case, as Blau has pointed out, acceptance is based on trust, which in turn is a consequence of exchange of satisfying cues and "services." Earlier theorists of pri-

[3] Michael S. Olmsted, *The Small Group* (New York: Random House, 1959); George C. Homans, *The Human Group* (New York: Harcourt, Brace & World, 1950); Terence Hopkins, *The Exercise of Influence in Small Groups* (Totowa, N.J.: Bedminster Press, 1964); Robert T. Golembiewski, *The Small Group* (Chicago: University of Chicago Press, 1962); Allan W. Eister, "Basic Continuities in the Study of Small Groups," in Howard Becker and Alvin Boskoff, eds., *Modern Sociological Theory* (New York: Holt, Rinehart & Winston, 1957), pp. 305–339.

[4] Homans, *op. cit.;* Robert F. Bales, *Interaction Process Analysis* (Reading, Mass.: Addison-Wesley, 1950); Muzafer Sherif, *Intergroup Conflict and Cooperation* (Norman: University of Oklahoma Press, 1961); Muzafer Sherif and Carolyn Sherif, *An Outline of Social Psychology* (New York: Harper & Row, 1956).

mary groups (Toennies, Cooley) assumed, or may be interpreted to assume, that common values create acceptance and cohesiveness. Homans has suggested that acceptance (sentiments of "liking") is directly related to "frequency of interaction"—though this is *not* independent of personal sentiments.[5] At this point, we must tentatively regard *a* and *b* as concomitant or complementary processes.

Differentiation

One of the most important but unheralded patterns in small, informal groups is internal differentiation. Toennies, Cooley, and others appeared to equate primary groups with diffuseness, social equality or communalism, and ineffable consensus. However, Simmel's discussions of triadic structure, of coalitions and strategies, of the essential phenomena of superordination–subordination furnished a very different analytic scheme for primary-like groups, particularly when these aspects are interpreted in connection with his famous analysis of the conditions and consequences of conflict and competition. Though Simmel did not always specify the type of group to which his remarks applied, his work reflected an awareness of complexity in presumably "simple" structures that was for a long time ignored.

Following the collaborative work of Parsons and Bales, however, a rather detailed theory of role-differentiation in small groups was supplied.[6] Since the small group faces the same practical problems as other groups and yet lacks the formalized mechanisms of complex groups, interaction processes experimentally (and necessarily) produce a set of informal roles. One subset, the *instrumental*, concerns skills and responsibilities in solving the problems or achieving the goals of the group—e.g., the supplier of ideas (Best Idea Man) and the guider of interaction. Another subset, the *in-*

[5] Homans, *op. cit.*, p. 112; Peter M. Blau, *Exchange and Power in Social Life* (New York: Wiley, 1964), p. 94; Theodore M. Newcomb, *The Acquaintance Process* (New York: Holt, Rinehart & Winston, 1961).

[6] Talcott Parsons *et al.*, *Working Papers in the Theory of Action* (New York: Free Press, 1953), pp. 143–150; Morris Freilich, "The Natural Triad in Kinship and Complex Systems," *American Sociological Review*, XXIX (August, 1964), pp. 529–540.

tegrative–expressive, arises from the necessity of harnessing the emotions of participants and of personalizing the flow of interaction. Typical varieties in this category are the sociometric star (Best-Liked), the Top Initiator (who is disliked but needed), and the scapegoat (who receives the brunt of negative action that cannot be directed toward the Top Initiator).

According to Parsons and Bales, groups without clear goals or tasks develop only positive integrative roles. As objectives become clarified and acquire importance, the Best-Liked or star either assumes an instrumental role (Ideas, Guidance), or other members come to perform these specialized functions. Normally, it is hypothesized, the Idea role constitutes a threat to the Best-Liked role and to most of the group, since the sociometric star thereby suffers a relative loss of esteem, and the remainder recognize their dependence on the avowedly "efficient" expert. Consequently, in groups that maintain their identity, one of two developments can be predicted. Either the Best-Liked and Idea roles are both assumed by one person, an undertaking difficult to sustain for any extended period, or the persons playing these roles form a tacit *coalition,* in which they mutually support each other (or fail to threaten one another) in their respective roles. Obviously, an informal coalition of this sort depends on highly developed motives for retaining the prestige of one's role. Also, the fact of a coalition probably does not guarantee "equal status" for the "high status" partner.[7] In informal groups, it may be predicted, the advantage may well lie with the Best-Liked role; consequently, the technical-idea role may be the greater source of strain unless the coalition is legitimated.

A complementary theory of differentiation may be called "exchange–dependence theory."[8] Briefly, it is assumed that members of groups tend to be initially different in experience, skills, ability, drive, discipline, persuasive powers, etc. Some persons, therefore, are willing and able to perform valued "services" (suggestions, de-

---

[7] Parsons, *op. cit.,* pp. 157–158.

[8] Blau, *op. cit.,* pp. 22, 43, 132, 193, 203; John Thibaut and Harold Kelley, *The Social Psychology of Groups* (New York: Wiley, 1959), pp. 127–136, 231–235; Richard M. Emerson, "Power-Dependence Relations," *American Sociological Review,* XXVII (February, 1962), pp. 31–41.

cisions, "inspiration," contacts with outsiders, etc.) for others, thereby establishing subtle claims of dependence and, following the implicit principle of minimization of costs, receiving special or higher status for their contribution (cf. Znaniecki's social circle theory). But status differentials in informal settings are marked by practical dilemmas whose resolution is crucial for group structure. In informal groups, special status (and its associated power attributes) tends to be weakened by "excessive use." Power (status reflected in effective action) generates both "service" and "dependence," both approval (for the service) and disapproval (for the visibility of dependence and the social distance that accompanies a power relationship). Consequently, those in favored positions tend to veil their status by minimizing sources of disapproval—by self-depreciation and "unexpected" modesty, by emphasizing the bothersome and tedious aspects of their roles, by experimenting with an optimal social distance (i.e., interactions mainly with equals, but strategic contacts with "dependents" in "non-service" situations).[9]

But these devices may create uncertainties among dependents, since ambiguities in the duties and privileges of high status persons prevent adequate prediction about the range and "fairness" of decisions by high status persons. Dependents, therefore, tend to desire norms and rules, which solidify and yet limit the behavior associated with higher statuses. The resultant security and legitimation of status, according to Blau, may erase (or lower the significance of) the practical dilemma of "informal" leaders.[10] Indeed, we may postulate that some formalization of differentiated roles is a practical necessity over time in informal groups.

[9] Blau, *op. cit.*, pp. 49, 132; Thibaut and Kelley, *op. cit.*, p. 233; Mancur Olson, *The Logic of Collective Action* (Cambridge: Harvard University Press, 1965), pp. 2–3.

[10] Blau, *op. cit.*, p. 325; Thibaut and Kelley, *op. cit.*, pp. 119–128; Jean Piaget, *Etudes sociologiques* (Geneva: Librairie Droz, 1965), p. 127; Henry W. Riecken and George C. Homans, "Psychological Aspects of Social Structure," in Gardner Lindzey, ed., *Handbook of Social Psychology* (Reading, Mass.: Addison-Wesley, 1954); J. Stacy Adams, "Inequity in Social Exchange," in Leonard Berkowitz, ed., *Advances in Experimental Social Psychology* (New York: Academic Press, 1965), II, pp. 283–290.

Coordination, conformity, and deviation

Differentiation in informal groups has likewise been used to explain their operation as reflected in selected products of interaction (productivity, cohesiveness, deviation). In groups with specific tasks, role and status differentiation (as indicated by patterns of communication and the analysis of behavior by "leaders") tends to facilitate problem-solving, if those with higher status do not *impose* their contributions on the group. Cohesiveness and generalized feelings of satisfaction with the group also seem to result from a differentiated structure that stimulates the phenomena of *distributive justice* (i.e., each person's abilities and responsibilities are matched with appropriate rewards).[11]

How, then, can deviation and conformity be explained in the absence of formal mechanisms of socialization and social control? First, the conditions that permit deviation have been identified theoretically (and to some extent empirically) as perceptions of injustice; ambiguity in goals and status, which develops *stress* (cf. Barnard's definition of tension: "attention of individuals is concentrated on uncertainties of their future personal status, as affected by current events or acts"); and ambiguity in power structure of the group. In short, the very nature of informal groups entails considerable opportunities for deviance.[12]

However, the response to these "opportunities" is the source of contradictory theoretical formulations.[13] Homans initially argued that conformity would be most evident among high status members, because their status depended on adherence to central norms.

[11] George C. Homans, *Social Behavior* (New York: Harcourt, Brace & World, 1961), pp. 350–354; Adams, *op. cit.;* Vernon L. Allen, "Situational Factors in Conformity," in Berkowitz, *op. cit.*, pp. 133–175.

[12] Robert L. Kahn *et al.*, *Organizational Stress* (New York: Wiley, 1964), p. 89; Chester I. Barnard, *Organization and Management* (Cambridge: Harvard University Press, 1948), p. 63; Robert K. Merton, "The Role-Set: Problems in Sociological Theory," *British Journal of Sociology*, VIII (1957), pp. 111–115.

[13] Cf. Homans, *The Human Group*, p. 141; Blau, *op. cit.*, pp. 296–297; Vernon L. Allen, *loc. cit.*, pp. 152–155.

Blau and others, on the other hand, expect nonconformity to be characteristic of both high status and low status group members—for different reasons. High status persons are said to deviate because of their relatively greater freedom, particularly when they are secure in their status, and because crisis conditions require deviation to preserve the group and to sustain their position. Low status members deviate because they have little to lose. More recently, Homans has revised his theoretical position to locate conformity in middle status persons,[14] who presumably have the greatest relative difficulty in deviating. Because of their intermediate status, disapproval of independent deviation by subordinates tends to "lower" status, while the same deviation involves a costly threat to higher status persons. In addition, as Blau has suggested, both higher and lower status members have less enduring attachment to the group —low status necessarily involving low levels of satisfaction and limited opportunities of enhancing status, and high status permitting access to other valued groups in the system. Consequently, middle status persons constitute a kind of core in such groups; they seem to retain adequate net levels of satisfaction and lack the external opportunities of high status members. Conformity, therefore, may be explained in terms of the practical attributes of relative position in a group.

Nevertheless, it is obvious that deviation beyond some acceptable set of limits is a special problem for informal groups, whatever the source of deviation. Control of deviation, essentially, is the use of mechanisms by which the cost of deviation is effectively made higher than the cost of conformity.[15] Theoretically, and in line with most relevant investigations, these mechanisms of control are inseparable from the duties and responsibilities of higher status positions. Indeed, failure to use these mechanisms when deviation approaches the borders of tolerance is a practical abdication of status. But note the additional consequence: processes aimed at insuring conformity by others in the group require visible evidence of conformity on the part of the controller—under the previously mentioned principle of distributive justice in informal groups. Yet

14 Homans, *Social Behavior*, pp. 346–355; Blau, *op. cit.*, p. 297.
15 Hopkins, *op. cit.*, p. 182; Homans, *The Human Group*, p. 366.

norms of performance are not equally valued. We would therefore expect controls by high status persons on matters involving only the most important norms. Indeed, the "influence fund" associated with high status would be quickly dissipated by concern for minor deviations. On less important norms, then, non-conformity or non-compliance would be more likely a responsibility of the peers of the deviant. But the lower the status of the deviant, the less likely peer control of deviance can be effectively applied, since the lower statuses have little to gain by conformity and little to lose from deviation.[16]

Perhaps we can find at this point the critical character of small, informal groups. To serve their members, role and status differentiation are indispensable. But to preserve the function and identity of the group without formalization, the span of differentiation must in practice be sufficiently limited to insure the commitment and conformity of those with lesser status. The greater the number of status gradations, the more likely control of deviation becomes a focal problem. As a consequence, the practical alternatives are either *disintegration* of the group or *formalization* of group structure.

Despite the vitality of small-group research, theoretical analysis has been comparatively slow and rather fractionated. Yet promising issues and variables have been newly identified (or effectively revived), and strands of theory seem at the point of readiness for satisfactory twining. Significantly, the past decade or two has shown that the behavioral processes and structure of small groups are far more complex and variable than had been supposed. We can no longer dismiss small groups in a phrase as "primitive," "stable," "communal," etc., or point to their immutable significance for human social systems. Instead, we may interpret the operation of informal systems—audaciously but still tentatively—in the following manner.

There seem to be three analytically distinct niches (in the ecological sense) for small, informal systems or groups.

[16] Hopkins, *op. cit.*, p. 108; Ezra Stotland, "Peer Groups and Reactions to Power Figures," in Dorwin Cartwright, ed., *Studies in Social Power* (Ann Arbor: University of Michigan Press, 1959), p. 55.

TYPES OF INFORMAL GROUPS

1. *Independence*

In this I mean to include informal systems that develop outside of existing organizations and whose existence does not depend on or appreciably affect such organizations. Examples include friendship networks, shipboard camaraderie, and neighborhood or block groups. The opportunity for this type is limited by the octopal coverage provided by formal organizations. In addition, the independent type tends to suffer from defections, or it evolves into formalized (but not necessarily fully legitimated) structures. Families, for example, possess internally derived formalization of duties and privileges in many cases, while many other family units—upon examination rather than conjecture or hope—are more accurately described as tenuous rather than informal, since a prevailing ambiguity or disinterest in goals and roles is merely a prelude to practical (if not legal) dissolution.

2. *Embedded*

This is probably the most frequently encountered type, one that develops within a complex organization as a consequence of inevitable gaps in the structure of such systems. Informal groups (cliques, peers, cells, "sets") derive from perceptions of common interests, grievances, as well as chance proximity. Significantly, they may either oppose or support the objectives of the larger organization (e.g., quota restrictions in work groups, factions in professional and sports organizations, the relay assembly workers and wire bank operators at Western Electric). In either case, the embedded type serves as a meaningful mechanism for the accommodation of its members to the formal organization. If the informal structure provides satisfactions that are unobtainable otherwise, it persists. But, unlike the independent type, it rarely develops a high degree of formalization. Clearly, formalization increases its *visibil-*

228

ity and perceived threat to the environing structure; therefore, maintaining the informal structure allows it to operate in a "zone of indifference" (Barnard). Indeed, the practical bar to formalization latently sustains the attractive aspects of informal groups (opportunities for participation, sociability, etc.).

3. *Ephemeral*

Finally, we may identify informal aspects of specific groups, or of the subtle interactions between members of different groups. Goffman has explored the latter set of phenomena as a separate area of sociological concern, with particular focus on the techniques by which persons try to manipulate impressions that are not clearly implied by their roles.[17] Since informal social behavior in these instances develops in the interstices of clear and well-ordered behavior patterns (either *within* groups or *between* group boundaries), such behavior does not eventuate in an identifiable, persistent group structure. For example, the members of a board that meets at monthly or quarterly intervals may interlard their formal deliberations with personal chit-chat and spontaneous exchange of remarks on extraneous matters. In this informal interaction, social background and the individual's position in board affairs are rarely detectable. Yet these informal exchanges do not often form the basis for informal subgroups, membership in which is empirically reflected in performance during formal organizational processes. Ephemeral informal "systems" may of course evolve into more permanent structures, but they may nevertheless be viewed as a distinctive subcategory of informal structures.

We may properly re-examine at this point an old theoretical issue about informal systems—their attraction and their affect on members. The ubiquitous nature of informal groups and quasi-groups has sometimes been interpreted as a mark both of indispensability and personal desirability. But, with the theoretical de-

[17] Erving Goffman, *The Presentation of Self in Everyday Life* (Garden City: Doubleday, 1959); Erving Goffman, *Encounters: Two Studies in the Sociology of Interaction* (Indianapolis: Bobbs-Merrill, 1961); Erving Goffman, *Behavior in Public Places* (New York: Free Press, 1963).

velopments previously discussed as fuel, we may well re-assess the operation of informal groups in terms of (*a*) variability of members' satisfactions and (*b*) self-recruitment.

Contrary to superficial, short-term analyses, participation in informal structures entails normal situations of power and status differentials, manipulation and dissimulation, and resultant stress, anxiety, dissatisfaction, and hostility. Other things being equal, these phenomena are more likely in groups with higher degrees of role and status differentiation. It has even been suggested that in informal structures of moderate size, participants do not act in accordance with common or group values, unless they are coerced or induced to do so by special devices.[18] In other words, "commitment" and emotional identification in small or informal groups are variables rather than givens. We would expect the "problem" aspect of informal interaction to be more prevalent in the independent and ephemeral varieties, since these tend to be either insufficiently structured or too highly structured for informal systems.

If we can reasonably assume that persons choose (consciously or unconsciously) whether or not to enter, remain, or withdraw from informal systems, then it is important to explain how recruitment of individuals operates—since all potential members do not become participants. From a motivational standpoint, several components may be hypothetically identified, but in different strengths in the variety of informal systems. The independent type, pursuing previous clues, tends to attract persons who are marginal to or emotionally detached from significant formal systems (occupations, religious organizations, kinship groups, etc.). But more specifically, it attracts persons with a considerable range of abilities (or disabilities) and expectations. The normal recruitment of both low-ego and highly confident persons (the former seeking support, and the latter seeming to search for alternative arenas of expression and opportunity) typically produces sharp status differentiation and the ambivalent attitudes associated with informal power relations. Yet there is a complementarity in motive and perceptions that helps to sustain this structure for months and years (cf. the Norton Boys

18 Olson, *op. cit.*, pp. 2–3.

studied by Whyte). By contrast, as Simmel so perceptively noted, intimate informal relations among equals are inherently vulnerable to explosive conflicts and bitter dissolution of pre-existing systems.

In the embedded type, there is perhaps greater likelihood of status similarity (or level of skill and responsibility), principally because proximity and interactional possibilities within the larger organization are major recruiting conditions. Admittedly, most of the relevant studies deal with informal structures of work groups and, to some extent, in correctional organizations.[19] Certainly, similar structures in educational, religious, scientific, and artistic organizations would provide needed comparative data. However, several provisional patterns may be posited for future modification and/or confirmation. In supportive informal structures, persons of above average ability and motivation tend to be core members, using "deviant" or innovative means to overcome the formal obstacles to organizational goals. Commitment to these goals is likely to be highest among persons who have little stake in the formal reward structure (promotion, etc.) and therefore are not concerned with the "risks" of deviation. By contrast, obstructive (or quasi-obstructive) informal structures are more likely to recruit persons with below average ability (compared to peers) or with perceived discrepancies between personal ability and recognition in the formal structure. Obstructive or non-supportive subgroups are therefore subject to internal problems. The *expressive* objectives of the average member practically contradict the *instrumental* or activist goals of the truly disgruntled or disaffected members. We would therefore expect this type of recruitment to produce a loosely structured, moderately large grouping of the expressively oriented or a small, "purified" cult of dissidents. As for the ephemeral type, the variety and frequency of such opportunities are as yet practical impediments to theorizing.

[19] J. L. Moreno, *Who Shall Survive?* (Beacon, N.Y.: Beacon House, 1953 ed.); Helen H. Jennings, *Leadership and Isolation* (London: Longmans, Green & Co., Ltd., 1943); Gresham M. Sykes, *The Society of Captives* (Princeton: Princeton University Press, 1958); Donald R. Cressey, ed., *The Prison* (New York: Holt, Rinehart & Winston, 1961); Donald Clemmer, *The Prison Community* (New York: Farrar, 1940).

To summarize, an explanation of informal (or less formal) structures now requires careful attention to the vicissitudes of recruitment, the different needs or services that are unique to each type, and the dilemmas and instabilities to which informal structures are specially exposed. The role of informal groups seems to be one of *interactional linkage* or liaison between more formalized or legitimated social systems. Consequently, we shall have to study the interactions of formal and informal groups—both direct and indirect—in more detail and with more attention to varieties in each category.

COMPLEX, INSTITUTIONALIZED GROUPS

Groups and social systems fundamentally differ from one another in terms of three dimensions—number of participants, number of roles and status levels, and degree of formalization of interaction patterns. Informal systems by definition are relatively low on these three dimensions, while genuine primary groups are composed of few participants, a limited number of roles and statuses, and a substantial formalization of interaction. In complex organizations, role and status specialization are extensive, size is relatively large, and institutionalization is comparatively advanced. Consequently, while theories of informal groups have emphasized the patterns that create adjustments to small numbers and relative absence of norms, and while theories of primary groups focus on responses conditioned by personal intimacy and deep-seated value consensus, theorists of complex organization have been faced with the problem of *ordering* the interrelations of these three dimensions and their effects on the operation of such systems. Most theorists, implicitly following the strategy of Max Weber, have tried to explain complex organizations by focusing on the presumed consequences of role and status differentiation.

Surprisingly enough, there has been virtually no theoretical interest in the genesis or sources of complex organization in recent years. Weber, of course, traced bureaucratic structures and their extension to societies (or stages of history) in which perceived needs for efficiency (rationality) in pursuit of power and/or profit prompted innovations in specialization and coordination. More recently, Parsons has followed MacIver in viewing the dissolution of "primitive fusion"—the evolving specialization of religious, economic, kinship, and political groups—as encouraging a growing complexity in pursuing highly specific objectives (production, distribution, salvation, recreation, protection, etc.). But these are general orientations rather than explanations of process. On the other hand, it is perhaps relevant to suggest that the genesis of one or more species of complex organization is a miniature form of social change, or "social movement." Furthermore, Znaniecki's theory of *social circles* (see pp. 76–78) is quite applicable to this problem. Briefly, complex organizations arise from the recognition of (and demand for) several kinds of skills, few of which can be adequately employed by the same or a limited number of individuals. A referential social circle (consumers or clients, peers in a trade or profession, or the source of financial support for a given enterprise) may be said to encourage or recruit specialized persons (in the university, corporation, government agency, professional sport, or laboratory) to contribute their respective skills in return for material and honorific rewards. Over time, established role and status categories become independent of the original specialists; the regularization (formalization) of qualifications and rewards makes possible orderly processes of recruitment and replacement.

Let us now focus on five areas of theoretical development during the past twenty years.

Recruitment and succession

Weber's theory clearly implied a rational process of uniform selection in complex, formal organizations. He assumed, in addition, that participants shared approximately similar conceptions of their function in the organization and similar identification with its stated objectives—allowing, of course, for obvious differences related to status or rank in the organization.[20] But recent theorists have questioned the validity of these assumptions. Following Merton's distinction between "locals" and "cosmopolitans," Marvick, Gouldner, Wilensky, Thompson, and others have noted wide variations in role conceptions and aspirations for given categories of positions.[21] Marvick, for example, discovered three types of "career perspective" among administrators in a state agency—the *specialist*, who emphasizes skills; the *institutionalist*, who is similar to Weber's conception of functionary, gearing his future to the organization; and the *hybrid*, who changes his role conception according to immediate opportunities. While a longitudinal study would be required, it may be hypothesized that changes in recruitment sources help to explain this diversity of role conceptions and levels of commitment. Two theoretical aspects may be suggested. First, as demand for a given skill increases, recruitment is likely to involve a wider range of qualifications for a given role, assuming that there are no special mechanisms for adjusting supply to demand. Second, recruitment as a continuous process coincides with historically (and sociologically) different phases of the organization. Typically, most of the early recruits would be specialists, while succeeding periods in organizational development would tend either to reward both skill and commitment or to convert some specialists into institutionalists as a consequence of seniority, promotion, and acquired power or influence. However, with the growing availability of competing organizations, the hybrid type probably receives considerable encouragement.

[20] Hans H. Gerth and C. Wright Mills, trans. and eds., *From Max Weber: Essays in Sociology* (New York: Oxford Univerity Press, 1946), pp. 196–204, 240–243.

[21] Dwaine Marvick, *Career Perspectives in a Bureaucratic Setting* (Ann Arbor: University of Michigan Press, 1954); Alvin W. Gouldner, *Patterns of Industrial Bureaucracy* (New York: Free Press, 1954); Roy G. Francis and Robert C. Stone, *Service and Procedure in Bureaucracy* (Minneapolis: University of Minnesota Press, 1956); Victor A. Thompson, *Modern Organization* (New York: Alfred A. Knopf, 1961), chs. 6–8; Harold Wilensky, *Intellectuals in Labor Unions* (New York: Free Press, 1956); Robert Presthus, *The Organizational Society* (New York: Alfred A. Knopf, 1962), chs. 6–8; Richard C. Hodgson, Daniel J. Levinson, and Abraham Zaleznik, *The Executive Role Constellation* (Boston: Harvard University Graduate School of Business Administration, 1965), chs. 4–6, 8.

Succession in complex organizations—the substitution of new men in higher levels of authority—presents a particularly difficult task for theorists. Pareto's "circulation of elites" hypothesis posited a regular alternation of leaders with contrasting qualities (the lions and the foxes). Weber suggested a highly probabilistic account of succession by reference to the inescapable problems of the "routinization of charisma"—the replacement of charismatic leaders by rational–legal or traditional types, followed by a resumption of the cycle.[22] However, these theories assume a simplified rationality and a smoother process of transition than experience permits. Despite the existence of rules and a graded system of authority, any change in top personnel evokes feelings of uncertainty among members. The basic reason for this is simply the mutability of organizational rules (or their interpretation and implementation) and the widespread recognition that authority entails a penumbra of power.

Surprisingly, organizational theorists tend to ignore the problem of succession, the recurrent "crises" of transferring authority.[23] It may be suggested, however, that the ingredients for theory are rather familiar and manageable. First, there is the issue of internal vs. external sources of a successor, which is related to past recruitment and its effects on the composition of organization and to internal opportunities to learn the special responsibilities of top positions. Second, the qualities perceived as crucial to high position, and the relative weight assigned to those qualities, constitute a major dimension. Third, the mechanism of selection—the individual or group responsible for seeking and designating a successor—is basic to the preceding relevant variables.

A theory (or theories) of succession should certainly demonstrate concern for significant differences in complex organization

[22] Vilfredo Pareto, *Mind and Society*, trans. Andrew Bongiorno and Arthur Livingston (4 vols.; New York: Harcourt, Brace, 1935), IV; Joseph Lopreato, *Vilfredo Pareto: Selections from His Treatise* (New York: Thomas Y. Crowell, 1965), pp. 109–116, 137–141; Max Weber, *The Theory of Social and Economic Organization*, trans. A. M. Henderson and Talcott Parsons (New York: Oxford University Press, 1947), pp. 358–373.

[23] An exception is Gouldner, *op. cit.*, Pt. 2.

(see pp. 245–247). But at this point, we may tentatively regard the process of succession as a reflection of the joint operation of two variables—adequacy of internal sources (in terms of perceived needs for qualities in new leaders) and the relative emphasis on administrative vs. policy-making (or creative) tasks. Table 7 summarizes the major combinations.

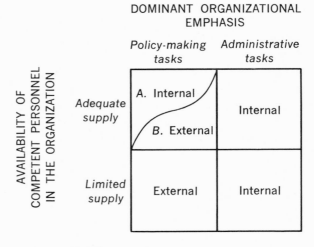

TABLE 7. Hypothetical sources of successors in organizations by internal supply and organizational emphasis.

We predict the most frequent selection of internal successors in complex organizations that possess adequate numbers of capable candidates and, with one exception, either administrative or policy-making tasks. The exception seems to be the case of organizations with factional conflicts that can be resolved only by the choice of an outsider. On the other hand, external sources of successors would appear to be more frequently used where emphasis on organizational performance (particularly in measurable terms, such as profits, growth, visible public image) is found. In practice, a performance or policy-making motif immediately confronts a situation of limited supply, since the opportunity to acquire such skills is not widely available.

236

Informal structures

Ever since the famous Western Electric studies,[24] the practical and theoretical significance of informal structures in formal systems has been a major rallying point from which to revise and renew the formulations of Weber on the one hand, and the prescriptions of Taylor and the human engineering model on the other hand. The first piece of theoretical heresy was the "discovery" that people in complex organizations are often culturally or psychologically "marginal" to the official purposes of the organization. As Selznick described the problem,[25] people tend to participate with values and attitudes that are non-rational, i. e., not clearly or consistently directed toward collective goals. Latent and manifest deviation, rather than commitment or meaningful conformity, is therefore normal.

This recognition is the empirical and logical basis for a medley of conceptual and theoretical developments that may be labeled simply "the analysis of informal adaptive structures." A fundamental proposition at this point is that, given the variability of members' commitments and the ambiguity or "stretch" in official rules, people necessarily create small, informal networks of interaction and dependence (cliques, or sociometric circles). These informal groups may reflect the gregarious attitudes of their members, but these patterns also help in clarifying goals and norms, and in reinforcing the motives individuals bring to informal associations. In short, informal groups are mechanisms that help bridge the inevitable gaps in formal structures and hence raise a number of problems for theory and practice.

First and most evident is the ubiquitous development of cliques,

[24] Fritz J. Roethlisberger and William J. Dickson, *Management and the Worker* (Cambridge: Harvard University Press, 1939); Henry A. Landsberger, *Hawthorne Revisited* (Ithaca: Cornell University Press, 1958); William J. Dickson and F. J. Roethlisberger, *Counseling in an Organization: A Sequel to the Hawthorne Researches* (Boston: Harvard University Graduate School of Business Administration, 1966).

[25] Philip Selznick, "Foundations of the Theory of Organization," *American Sociological Review*, XIII (1948), pp. 25-35.

personal interaction networks, or "sociometric" structures, which have been explained as a consequence of "opportunity" and motivational factors. Cliques, etc., tend to be formed by members who are commonly segregated (physically and functionally) from other segments of the organization. Since physical segregation is often a correlate of status and role segregation, these informal groups are usually composed of peers. The motives for participation in informal groups are somewhat varied and have more often been *identified* or *classified* than converted into theoretical statements.[26] These motives include: (*a*) the need for immediate sources of information about the organization or specific problems; (*b*) the desire for specific referential values; (*c*) the desire for recognition and status beyond the formal ranking of a position or role; (*d*) autonomy, or protection against authority; and (*e*) the attempt to affect the formal structure with some chance of success. From the case studies of cliques, however, we may tentatively conclude that the relative status of members is a major variable in the motivational complex of informal groups. Thus, an emphasis on autonomy and protection from authority would be more likely among lower status categories, while middle and upper status members would probably be more concerned with using informal groups to obtain desired positive changes in the functioning of the organization or of their particular segment.

A second aspect of informal structure is the "symbiotic" phenomenon of tacitly accepted deviation from formal rules on the part of subordinates. These "unwritten laws" (cf. Selznick) or "patterned evasions" (R. Williams) [27] possess very interesting qualities. Typically, they involve practices that are invisible or irrelevant to the operation of high status persons. The more complex the division of labor and delegation of authority, therefore, the greater the

[26] Philip Selznick, "An Approach to a Theory of Bureaucracy," *American Sociological Review*, VIII (1943), pp. 47–54; Barnard, *op. cit.*, p. 46; Peter M. Blau, *The Dynamics of Bureaucracy* (Chicago: University of Chicago Press, 1955), ch. 9; Abraham Zaleznik, C. R. Christensen, and F. J. Roethlisberger, *The Motivation, Productivity, and Satisfaction of Workers* (Boston: Harvard University Press, 1958), ch. 4.

[27] Selznick, "Foundations of the Theory of Organization," *op. cit.*; Robin M. Williams, *American Society* (New York: Alfred A. Knopf, 2d ed., 1960), ch. 10.

238

opportunity for such deviations. In addition, normally either the *extent* of the deviation or the *situation* of deviation is not sufficiently significant to warrant available social control mechanisms. Consequently, whether buttressed by the moral support of cliques or not, these deviant acts persist by default, serving either as inevitable barnacles on the organizational hull, or as unacknowledged complements to formal but limiting patterns. Informal bypassing of "channels," a marked slowdown in work fifteen to thirty minutes before official quitting time, and personal use of organizational facilities and supplies are a few examples of patterned evasions. "Knowing the ropes" in an organization (sociologically speaking) is a result of a careful but informal socialization process in which the individual learns the kinds of patterned evasion that are permitted. Yet, as Selznick has pointed out,[28] some evasions may be "absorbed" by agents of the formal structure as new rules, either because they are perceived as improvements or because they are considered the means of controlling the incidence of deviation.

Informal organization is exemplified, thirdly, in the obverse of the aspect just discussed. Barnard has perceptively noted (though Simmel must be credited with an earlier and somewhat neglected discovery of the same pattern) that within the formally prescribed (or permitted) range of decision-making and responsibility of a position, there is a tacitly unquestioned or unchallenged set of powers that subordinates "assign" to their superior. This so-called "zone of indifference" [29] is essentially an informal validation or supplementation of legitimate direction and control. Therefore, two theoretical points arise for our consideration. First, what explains the *emergence* of a zone of indifference? Subordinates, it is assumed, have a tendency to narrow the status gap by resisting superordinate demands as much as "the traffic will bear" and by segregating demands into "bargaining" and non-bargaining types. The latter are perceived as unworthy of argument and energy, while the former seem to have sufficient flexibility or symbolic impor-

---

[28] Philip Selznick, *Leadership in Administration* (New York: Harper & Row, 1957); Selznick, "An Approach to a Theory of Bureaucracy," *op. cit.*

[29] Chester I. Barnard, *The Functions of the Executive* (Cambridge: Harvard University Press, 1940), pp. 167–171.

tance to subordinates to warrant attempts to check the implementation of such demands. Consequently, to conserve efforts for more strategic and more hopeful types of contention, the zone of indifference is created by subtle consensus.

But what, secondly, is the *effect* of a zone of indifference on the formal role of the superior? In practice, the latent effect is to insure compliance on matters that are crucial to the superior, thus reducing the necessity of resorting to the encumbrances of authority and freeing the subordinate for devotion to other facets of his role. On the other hand, this also implicitly allows the superior to focus on attempted evasions from his subordinates.

A fourth "formally unaccountable" phenomenon is the elusive one of bargaining and "strategy," which in effect tests the effective range of (a) power of superiors and (b) the permissible deviation of subordinates.[30] Students of bureaucracy have noted that whenever given tasks or roles are vague or uncertain in some respects, the superior acquires or develops a range of discretion that threatens those in subordinate positions. The latter seek to limit or divert such discretionary possibilities by more or less subtle attempts to exchange "concessions" on a specific issue (e.g., coffee breaks or timing of vacations) or on a broad set of issues. Bargaining, gamesmanship, "political" maneuvering, veiled threats, use of other organizational channels, etc., thus are normal consequences of structural opportunities and resistant motivations.

Viewed from the superior's standpoint, bargaining processes are as unbearable as is discretion to subordinates. For bargaining accomplishes one of two things—either a legitimation of deviant values (if subordinates prevail) or an accentuated visibility of the superior's power (if he wins), which may enhance the original perception of threat. Therefore, according to March and Simon,[31] persons in higher status positions tend to redefine the situations in which bargaining arises as individual and idiosyncratic rather than as representative of "status" differences. Consequently, though the

[30] James G. March and Herbert A. Simon, *Organizations* (New York: Wiley, 1958), pp. 126–129; Michel Crozier, *The Bureaucratic Phenomenon* (Chicago: University of Chicago Press, 1964), p. 160.

[31] March and Simon, *op. cit.*, p. 131.

lineaments of formal organization do not prescribe such behavioral adjustments, superiors will usually reserve their authority and instead employ persuasion, cajolery, and appeal to facts. Indeed, sometimes these measures are prolonged beyond any reasonable hope of utility—a value-rational phenomenon of great prominence. In a sense, the refusal to bargain rests on implicit fictions, most basically the fiction that there is a common core of values or goals by which deviation or difference can be measured and exercised.

Bargaining and its correlates seem intimately related to another departure from classical organizational structure. Both Barnard and Dubin recognize the development of *organizational fictions*, which are defined as accepted but untrue or dubious beliefs about aspects of the organization.[32] The prestige of the organization, the importance of specific administrative roles, and the official response to creativity offer familiar opportunities for organizational myth-making as means of facilitating action over the rim of uncertainty and indecisiveness. In addition, fictions tend to converge at what March and Simon call "uncertainty absorption points"—areas of operation at which facts or information are restricted to a few persons and thus require inferences (and their application in action) that cannot be effectively checked by subordinates (and even by some peers). These fictions, ultimately based on informally structured ignorance, recall Simmel's classic analysis of secrecy in social relationships and of the implicit power that monopolistic access to information affords.[33]

To Barnard we owe the "discovery" of still another indicator of informal structuring. Unlike the stereotype of formal roles with highly predictable performance (allowing, of course, for personality differences), Barnard asserts that experienced occupants of superior roles in organizations necessarily approach policy issues in a tentative, non-logical, and unfolding manner. Following a major theme in Znaniecki's work (implicitly, of course), Barnard insists that such issues are rarely presented to the administrator in simple,

[32] Robert Dubin, ed., *Human Relations in Administration* (Englewood Cliffs: Prentice-Hall, 1951), pp. 432–437.

[33] Georg Simmel, *The Sociology of Georg Simmel*, trans. Kurt H. Wolff (New York: Free Press, 1950), pp. 334–336; March and Simon, *op. cit.*, pp. 164–166.

definite, or immutable terms. He must therefore act by (*a*) reserving decision, (*b*) responding to probable but yet unpredictable actions of others (especially those in other systems), and (*c*) changing his attitudes and behavior in accordance with cues from others.[34] Thus, there seems to be—to outsiders—a trail of individually meaningless and futile acts, which inspire criticism from the uninitiated, just as (by the same practical logic) we note the multiple and rapid gyrations of the Communist Party "line."

Finally, for our purposes, we may briefly note the widely recognized latent tendency toward converting specialized means into "competitors" with official objectives. The prevailing explanation of this phenomenon is that specialization of task and emphasis on successful performance according to definite criteria combine to motivate persons to inflate the significance of their roles, evaluating events, demands, opportunities primarily as these appear to affect specific roles rather than the organization as a whole.[35] Indeed, a practical dilemma of organization festers at this point: either the role specialist is permitted loose standards of evaluation and competence (in which case informal deviations from minimally acceptable role playing and role relationships are maximized) or definite standards of performance and focused commitment to role are stressed (thereby creating high probability of "unanticipated" displacement of official goals by specialized interests).

Technology and complex organization

In the past, theories of complex organization tended to ignore the *technological dimension* of social organization, perhaps because theorists were more familiar with governmental and political structures. The study of industrial and scientific organizations, on the other hand, has revived an old concern—often too exuberant, as in the case of Marx and Veblen—for the impact of technical knowledge and mechanical development on social relationships and power. Industrial sociologists in Britain and the United States have

[34] Barnard, *Organization and Management*, p. 75.

[35] Robert K. Merton, *Social Theory and Social Structure* (New York: Free Press, 1957), ch. 6; Selznick, "An Approach to a Theory of Bureaucracy," *op. cit.*, pp. 48–51.

accumulated evidence that strongly suggests that, in a given organization, technological changes require significant adaptations in the distribution of authority, and that different levels of technology in the same or closely comparable fields are associated with different organizational structures.[36] For example, Joan Woodward classified firms according to technological complexity (small batch and unit production, large batch and mass production, and continuous process or automated production). In general, the more complex the technology, (*a*) the greater the number of levels of authority, (*b*) the greater the span of control of the highest executives, and (*c*) the more relaxed the personal pressures and the existence of less personal conflicts. Also, some similarities in structure were found in the simplest and the most complex technologies. Both were more flexible in organization than was middle-range technology; both were marked by verbal rather than written communications; and both developed low ratios of supervisors to subordinates. Finally, both types had little functional specialization among top leaders (the old "staff-line" distinction).[37]

Inferentially, many of our studies of formal organizations deal with "low" or "medium" levels of technology, with products or services that are offered in "small to medium batches"—or with shifts from "unit production" to "mass production" (e.g., in colleges and universities, government agencies, and hospitals). An explanation of the processes of differentiation and coordination may therefore be quite different if such phenomena as power, authority, delegation, etc., are isolated from the practical opportunities and limitations that are directly or indirectly associated with the technological resources and objectives of the organization.

Organizational change

Formal organizations change over time, in structure or objectives, though earlier theorists were largely content to account for the interaction of components and the resistant system of success-

[36] Joan Woodward, *Management and Technology* (London: Her Majesty's Stationery Office, 1958); Frank Zacinski, "Adapting Organization to Technology," in Joseph A. Litterer, ed., *Organizations: Structure and Behavior* (New York: Wiley, 1963), pp. 322ff.
[37] Woodward, *op. cit.*, ch. 4.

ful coordination. By implication, formal organizations were viewed as multiple "Rocks of Gibraltar" in environing processes of demographic, economic, and political–legal developments. But a closer investigation of formal structures (by Whyte, Blau, Dubin, Merton, and others) indicated that structural change occurs with significant frequency and clarity to permit exploratory theorizing.

The most radical and yet simple foundation for such theorizing is the observation that complex organizations—particularly those with highly structured bureaucratic subsystems—normally experience conscious or latently developed shifts in organization. One theoretical view, represented by March and Simon, focuses on complex organizations with specific, *rational objectives* and explains organizational change as a consequence of discrepancies between objectives and achievements and of the example of achievements by competing organizations.[38] The major theoretical problem thus becomes one of discovering the conditions of innovation and social implementation. Innovation or creativity of a conscious sort has been tentatively traced to decentralized structures (peer groups, cliques, etc.), either as *initiators* of innovation or as *borrowers* of innovations from external sources. In either case, it has been suggested, the development, refinement, and application of substantive or significant procedural innovations depend on the creation of new subsystems (and thus greater specialization).[39]

Yet another type of change—in goals—may derive from organizational achievement itself. As several sociologists have indicated, organizations acquire a stake in persistence as a goal; hence, the loss of former objectives (either through aggrandizement by other organizations, or by efficient consummation of definite objectives) may often be followed by choice of new ones. Whether or not this *cultural* change necessitates *structural* or *organizational* changes remains an intriguing problem.

[38] March and Simon, *op. cit.*, pp. 175–182; James D. Thompson, *Organizations in Action* (New York: McGraw-Hill, 1967), chs. 6–8; Crozier, *op. cit.*, pp. 196–201; Sherman Krupp, *Pattern in Organizational Analysis* (New York: Holt, Rinehart & Winston, 1961), p. 174.

[39] March and Simon, *op. cit.*, p. 188; Crozier, *op. cit.*, pp. 195–313; Gary A. Steiner, ed., *The Creative Organization* (Chicago: University of Chicago Press, 1965), p. 37.

Another approach to organizational change focuses primarily on bureaucratic structures. According to Blau and Crozier, change in bureaucratic organizations is a practical necessity deriving from contacts with other organizations and/or the routine problems of daily operation. Blau hypothesized that subordinates can create informal changes in operation and influence if security of position and professional commitment to "service" are sufficiently strong. But Crozier concludes that resistance to change predominates until a crisis occurs—i. e., until a serious issue reaches a point at which no alternative to change remains.[40] Adjustment to a crisis typically involves innovations imposed from top positions—rather than from subordinates—which serve to remove the transitional "adjustments" of personal influence and deviation from existing rules. Consequently, bureaucratic changes of this type tend to cumulate toward centralization and impersonality, and hence, by implication, greater difficulty of encouraging innovation until other severe crises erupt.

Provisional typology of organizations

Part of the difficulty of understanding change in complex organizations lies in the variety of organizations encompassed by this label. Blau and Scott [41] have assumed that organizations differ most fundamentally in the distribution of positive effects (benefits) by the organization. Thus, they submit the following classification:

1. Mutual benefit type—members themselves are primary beneficiaries of the organization's operation (unions, clubs).
2. Business organizations—owners or directors receive most of the rewards (corporations).
3. Service organizations—a definite clientele is the major beneficiary.
4. Commonweal organizations—groups that serve the public at large (e. g., police, fire departments).

It is further assumed that the nature of the beneficiary determines—or significantly affects—the overall structural devel-

[40] Crozier, *op. cit.*, p. 196; Blau, *The Dynamics of Bureaucracy*, ch. 12.
[41] Peter M. Blau and W. Richard Scott, *Formal Organizations: A Comparative Approach* (San Francisco: Chandler, 1962), pp. 43–57.

opment of the organization, specifically, the system of power and authority and the participation of subordinates. Etzioni [42] has tried to simplify the conceptualization of these subsystems by suggesting typologies of organizational power and motivation of participants. (See Table 8.) In the former case, power is distinguished into three pure types—coercion (use or threat of force), normative (manipulation of symbolic rewards, such as status), and remuneration (manipulation of material rewards, such as money and possessions). These are hypothetically linked with three pure types of motivation—alienative (hostility to power), moral (devotion to the goals of the organization), and calculative (motives based on acquisition of material rewards).

DOMINANT MOTIVATIONAL TYPES

	Alienative	Calculative	Moral
Coercive	X		
Remunerative		X	
Normative			X

POWER TYPES

TABLE 8. Organization types by type of power and dominant motivation of participants.

Obviously, the confrontation of Blau and Scott's and Etzioni's classifications strains the contours of simplicity. However, we may suggest the following attempt at accommodation:

I. Mutual benefit:
   A. remunerative–calculative (many unions)
   B. normative–moral (sect or cult)
   C. normative–calculative

[42] Amitai Etzioni, *A Comparative Analysis of Complex Organizations* (New York: Free Press, 1961), pp. 5–17.

246

II. Business: remunerative–calculative
III. Service:
   A. normative–calculative (university faculty)
   B. normative–alienative
   C. normative–moral (social welfare staff)

What is the theoretical utility of this classification? By inference, each organization type possesses a structurally appropriate (or workable) control and motivation cluster (e.g., business type and a remunerative–calculative focus). Consequently, organizations that develop "inappropriate" control and motivation clusters can be expected to operate with persistent frictions. For example, Gouldner's study of a gypsum plant (business type) demonstrated the dysfunctional consequences of depending on coercive rather than remunerative power.[43]

In addition, the distribution of personal influence can be expected to vary by type of organization.[44] Business organizations typically develop concentration of personal influence in the top positions, while service and normative varieties of mutual benefit and commonweal organizations tend to diffuse significant personal influence through most levels of organization. Etzioni suggests a third influence structure (the so-called R type), in which personal influence is most powerful at intermediate levels. In the typology presented above, the R type seems to be found in organizations that are primarily normative but yet require some certainty of conformity (I C, II A, IV B). Again, it is assumed that there is an optimal "fit" between locus of personal influence and structural type. Consequently, the explanation of discrepancies between these two dimensions offers a significant but relatively unexplored problem for sociological theorists.

SELECTED REFERENCES

Blau, Peter M., *Exchange and Power in Social Life* (New York: Wiley, 1964).
Burns, Tom, "The Comparative Study of Organizations," in Victor H. Vroom,

[43] Gouldner, *op. cit.*, ch. 3, 5.   [44] Etzioni, *op. cit.*, pp. 207–228.

ed., *Methods of Organizational Research* (Pittsburgh: University of Pittsburgh Press, 1967), ch. 3.

Caplow, Theodore, *Principles of Organization* (New York: Harcourt, Brace & World, 1964).

Guest, Robert H., "Managerial Succession in Complex Organizations," *American Journal of Sociology*, LXVIII (July, 1962), pp. 47–54.

March, James G., ed., *Handbook of Organizations* (Chicago: Rand McNally, 1965).

March, James G., and Herbert A. Simon, *Organizations* (New York: Wiley, 1958).

Mills, Theodore M., *The Sociology of Small Groups* (Englewood Cliffs: Prentice-Hall, 1967).

11

Stratification
and Social Mobility

The problematic relation between theory and investigation in American sociology is perhaps most obvious in the field of stratification and social mobility. Despite the extreme importance of this area, a good deal of research has been (*a*) focused on a narrow range of substantive problems, (*b*) insensitive to certain theoretical clues, and (*c*) unproductive of needed theoretical refinements. This is a serious criticism, but our central purpose in this chapter is to indicate the way sociologists have implicitly borrowed from theorists and the way students of stratification may profit from several neglected theoretical clues.

EMERGENCE OF STRATIFICATION SYSTEMS

While the origins of particular or typical forms of stratification were a persistent source of concern to nineteenth-century sociologists, the last few decades have been marked by comparatively little interest in this fundamental problem. Certainly, research in this area is particularly difficult for sociologists, since it requires careful historical reconstruction based on limited documentary data. Then, too, the search for origins was dealt a devastating blow in the reaction to unbridled evolutionary theories. Consequently, students of stratification proceeded to explore the existence and functioning of contemporary class systems, with a primary emphasis on description and classification.

However, at least two lines of inquiry suggest that the problem of origins and development of social class systems retains some significance. Essentially, these developments have been dependent on Weber's analytical distinction of the economic, honorific, and political dimensions of stratification (see pp. 56–58).

Empirical bases

One such approach might be considered a by-product of relatively full-scale community studies. In the classic studies of Middletown and Yankee City, for example, some attention was given to the economic development of these communities, as well as to the emergent stratification systems to which industrial change might be linked.[1] Both Warner and the Lynds interpreted local stratification as a consequence of occupational and skill differences. Indeed, these analysts independently derived a six-class system that might be clarified by closer investigation of the process by which each stratum became identifiable. More recently, Hollingshead has described, with the aid of occupational and ethnic data, basic historical patterns in stratification in New Haven.[2]

Another facet of the community locus in studying early phases

[1] Robert S. Lynd and Helen M. Lynd, *Middletown in Transition* (New York: Harcourt, Brace & World, 1937, Harvest Books), ch. 12, especially pp. 458–461; W. Lloyd Warner and Paul S. Lunt, *The Social Life of a Modern Community* (New Haven: Yale University Press, 1941); W. Lloyd Warner and J. O. Low, *The Social System of the Modern Factory* (New Haven: Yale University Press, 1947).

[2] A. B. Hollingshead, "Trends in Social Stratification: A Case Study," *American Sociological Review*, XVII (December, 1952), pp. 679–686.

of stratification concerns the power or decision-making dimension.[3] In the Lynds' study of Middletown, economic advantage is translated into a differentiated power hierarchy (topped by the "X" family) that remained intact until the economic and political traumas of the depression provided a challenge (but a rather ineffectual one) to the prevailing structure. The same theoretical orientation was applied by Hunter in his study of informal leadership and economic position in Atlanta. In effect, Hunter described the apparent centralization of potential power in a grouping of about forty "dominants," who achieved their imputed political influence as a consequence of their crucial business and financial positions in the community. However, Dahl's study of New Haven seemed to demonstrate that differences in power potential are not equivalent to *exercise* of power. His analysis indicated both significant changes in political power not directly related to changes in class structure and, in recent years, the development of "diffuse" power, more significantly patterned around issues than around economic strata.

The rise of new nations has provided an interesting source of data on *restratification* or the emergence of genuine *class* differences. In most cases, stratification seems to develop from military and/or educational differences, rather than from the conventional economic bases, which are themselves largely due to differential contacts with more complex societies. One of the most intriguing case studies in this area is the rise of "strata" in the initially "classless" collective settlements (kibbutzim) of Israel.[4] Apparently, class differences develop as a result of *administrative–managerial* requirements. Higher status (honor) is attributed to persons capable of carrying out complex functions based on relatively scarce administrative skills. This is of course a partial confirmation of Par-

[3] Lynd and Lynd, *op. cit.*, ch. 3; Floyd Hunter, *Community Power Structure* (Chapel Hill: University of North Carolina Press, 1953; Anchor Books, 1963); Robert A. Dahl, *Who Governs?* (New Haven: Yale University Press, 1961).

[4] Eva Rosenfeld, "Social Stratification in a 'Classless' Society," *American Sociological Review*, XVI (December, 1951), pp. 766–774; Melford E. Spiro, *Kibbutz: Venture in Utopia* (Cambridge: Harvard University Press, 1956); Melford E. Spiro, *Children of the Kibbutz* (Cambridge: Harvard University Press, 1958).

sons' and Davis and Moore's "functional theory of stratification." [5] Yet the initial assignment of persons to responsible positions was based on the high esteem and personality qualities of these leaders. In any case, with continuing immigration, seniority or length of residence became an additional criterion, which served to reinforce social distinctions based on differential functions.

The contribution of the honorific dimension to an understanding of class origins has been quite limited. As Weber indicated many years ago, honorific differences tend to be derived from power and/or economic differences. Warner's initial focus on the prestige aspect of stratification was therefore criticized for the failure to explore the *sources* of such differentials.[6] Prestige seemed to be an independent variable for Warner in his earlier discussions of Yankee City. However, Warner's analysis of a major strike in Yankee City is accompanied by a significant shift in theory. Instead of explaining the existence of class divisions by differential prestige, Warner traced changes in prestige that could be attributed to changes in economic relations—such as greater division of labor and disappearance of older manual skills.[7]

Stratification derived from interaction

The second general approach to origins of stratification systems is considerably more abstract. But it is predominantly concerned with the power dimension of class.[8] This approach is derived from,

[5] Kingsley Davis and Wilbert E. Moore, "Some Principles of Stratification," *American Sociological Review*, X (April, 1945), pp. 242–249; Talcott Parsons, *Essays in Sociological Theory* (New York: Free Press, 1954 ed.), chs. 4, 19.

[6] Warner and Lunt, *op. cit.;* W. Lloyd Warner and Paul S. Lunt, *The Status System of a Modern Community* (New Haven: Yale University Press, 1947). See the following critiques: Harold W. Pfautz and Otis Dudley Duncan, "A Critical Evaluation of Warner's Work in Community Stratification," *American Sociological Review*, XV (April, 1950), pp. 205–215; C. Wright Mills, Review of *The Social Life of a Modern Community*, in *American Sociological Review*, VII (April, 1942), pp. 263–271; Oscar Handlin, Review of *The Social Life of a Modern Community* and *The Status System of a Modern Community*, in *New England Quarterly*, XV (September, 1942), pp. 554–557.

[7] Warner and Low, *The Social System of the Modern Factory*, pp. 160, 188.

[8] Oliver C. Cox, *Caste, Class, and Race* (Garden City: Doubleday, 1948); Ralf Dahrendorf, *Class and Class Conflict in Industrial Society* (Stanford: Stanford University Press, 1959).

252

or congruent with, theoretical clues available in the works of Marx, Cooley, Comte, Weber, and Simmel. Essentially, stratification is conceived as a process of interaction among persons who have achieved some critical difference in possessions or performance. According to Thibaut and Kelley,[9] such differences threaten future interaction with the unbridled exercise of advantage (naked power). Stratification emerges (from interaction) as an unplanned means of both acknowledging and using power differences. First, these differences are reflected in a value system accepted by most participants. The pressure of "superiority" prompts "lower status" persons to accept the higher position of the more powerful, thus sustaining a *status consensus*. This validation of the more powerful in effect creates a *class system* (as distinct from a power relationship) by regularizing and making more predictable the behavior of social subordinates and also by limiting the potential expression of power differences. This limitation acts as an added ground for status consensus. However, persons in higher status positions seek to prevent a permanent "freezing" of potential power, since lower status categories might successfully use their acquiescence to extract concessions that might critically reduce the original advantages of some skill, possession, etc. Consequently, class systems normally involve the creation and maintenance of social mechanisms by higher status categories—social distance and exclusiveness, prestigiously novel activities and possessions, public disclaimers of power intentions or activities, and special emphasis on the difficulties associated with higher status.

A more simplified form of this theory has been introduced by Dahrendorf through emphasizing the *conflict* phases of interclass interaction. Dahrendorf views classes as "conflict groups," which emerge from social systems marked by differential distribution of authority in complex organizations.[10] By contrast with Thibaut and Kelley, Dahrendorf seems to suggest that class is a late consequence of social and cultural organization. In the interactional

---

[9] John Thibaut and Harold Kelley, *The Social Psychology of Groups* (New York: Wiley, 1959), pp. 231–235. See also Richard Emerson, "Power-Dependence Relations," *American Sociological Review*, XXVII (February, 1962), pp. 31–40.

[10] Dahrendorf, *op. cit.*, pp. 76, 204ff.

approach, power differences are followed by class distinctions, which are expressed in authority structures and appropriate ideological systems. Nevertheless, the focus on intergroup power relations reinforces the theoretical heritage of Weber, Mosca, and Pareto, and also obliges the theorist of stratification to construct hypotheses on the changing patterns of interaction.

A somewhat different but not incongruent theory of stratification origins is an evolutionary theory, as formulated by the anthropologist Morton H. Fried.[11] Fried identifies four types of stratification in terms of the complexity of power and its dominant means of expression. In the simplest form—*egalitarian*—power is personal and erratic, limited by the wide distribution of valued skills in the community. A *rank system*, the second, more "evolved" type, occurs in societies that recognize differentially valued positions, but do not permit higher positions to be used for exploitation (economic or political). Instead, societal power potential is converted into authority that is lodged in familial or religious systems.

A third stage—called *stratified society* by Fried—occurs when persons and groups are able to remove kinship and religious restrictions and to develop differential "access" to strategic resources. At this point, power is unequally distributed in terms of some set of differentially evaluated positions. However, the legitimation of power differences does not derive from a single centralized source. When this centralization occurs, the most complex form of stratification is reached—*state society*. The distribution of power among classes comes to be the responsibility of a political institution, which employs legalized methods of insuring a prevailing pattern of differential opportunities. Among these methods are population control, fiscal policy, selective taxation, military conscription, and procedural law.

PATTERNS OF INTERACTION BETWEEN SOCIAL STRATA

During the thirties and forties, most stratification research was dedicated to the proposition that "classes exist," contrary to the

11 Morton H. Fried, "On the Evolution of Social Stratification and the State," in Stanley Diamond, ed., *Culture in History* (New York: Columbia University Press, 1960), pp. 713–731.

ideology of equality and the ubiquitous evidence of upward mobility. In this approach, it was often assumed that objective differences in status (as measured by occupation, income, education, possessions) could be used to predict observed or potential differences in behavior and attitudes. However, once this assumption was challenged (in line with theoretical insights of Marx, Weber, and MacIver), several specific theoretical issues necessarily emerged: (*a*) What types of perception of class identity and class difference may be found? (*b*) What factors account for the relative strength of these perceptions? (*c*) How are these class perceptions translated into interactions with other status categories? (*d*) In view of multiple status positions, what are the effects of inconsistent statuses on perception of class differences?

Class identification

Various attempts to obtain a simplified picture of class identification may be found in the forties and early fifties. A classic source is Warner's study of Yankee City, in which class "membership" was deduced from two kinds of data—patterns of association (visiting, membership in specific organizations) and the status placement of knowledgeable "judges" or "raters" in the community. In a national sample a decade later, Centers assumed that his respondents' self-placement in one of four "class" categories adequately reflected a class structure.[12] Indeed, self-placement was correlated with political opinions and voting, for which Centers developed his "interest-group" theory of social class. Briefly stated, this theory asserts that one's economic position implicitly develops appropriate attitudes and interests, which in turn, through interaction with like persons, creates a "class" identification.[13]

The problem with investigations of class identification or class consciousness is that they do not specify and examine differing forms and foci of class consciousness. As MacIver pointed out many years ago, members of a given stratum may emphasize the

[12] Richard Centers, *The Psychology of Social Classes* (Princeton: Princeton University Press, 1949), ch. 6.

[13] See Herman M. Case, "An Independent Test of the Interest-Group Theory of Social Class," *American Sociological Review*, XVII (December, 1952), pp. 751–755.

similarities of the members (*corporate class consciousness*) or the differences between strata (*competitive class feeling*).[14] However, this necessary distinction does not discriminate the varying motives involved and the objects of class identification.

Recently, Werner Landecker analytically reviewed the data on class consciousness and discovered six forms.[15] Very properly, class consciousness is recognized as emphasizing either *factual aspects* (differences in income) or *subjective judgments* about the desirability or injustice of such differences. This is an extremely important distinction, because it has often been assumed that class differences necessarily generate emotional or affective identification with some stratum. Either emphasis (cognitive or affective) may be directed toward either of three aspects of a given class system. First, one may locate oneself in a given stratum without reference to other portions of the system (*class status consciousness*). Second, one may be able to identify different classes (number and distinctive features of each). Landecker calls this "class structure consciousness." Finally, "class interest consciousness" involves a close connection (either cognitive or affective) between individual needs and problems and those of a given stratum. Table 9 summarizes Landecker's analysis.

This conceptual refinement in effect compels us to construct a new orienting proposition for studying the relations between classes. For any given time period and complex social system, the nature of interclass relations may be attributed to the prevailing forms of "class consciousness," which can be reliably identified with specific strata. The major theoretical concern, then, is to account for the emergence and continuation of dominant forms, and also for the non-appearance of alternative types of "class consciousness."

Since research on class consciousness has been largely devoted to establishing its presence or absence, the explanation of variations in the occurrence of the preceding forms is still unclear. One of the recurring findings, however, is considerable variation in degree of

14 Robert M. MacIver, *Society* (New York: Farrar and Rinehart, 1937), pp. 174–176.
15 Werner Landecker, "Class Crystallization and Class Consciousness," *American Sociological Review*, XXVIII (April, 1963), pp. 219–229.

TYPE OF PERCEPTUAL EMPHASIS

		Cognitive	Affective
"CLASS CONSCIOUSNESS" / TYPE OF	Class status	Self-placement by class	Solidarity with class
	Class structure	Discernment of different classes	Assertion of class barriers
	Class interests	Identification of personal interests with class interests	Hostility toward other classes

TABLE 9. Types of class consciousness
by type of perceptual emphasis
(as conceptualized by Landecker).

class consciousness among major strata.[16] Heightened identification and awareness seem to be a consequence of critical community issues, which crystallize potential differences into active "class interest consciousness." [17] Clearly, these are merely hypothetical formulations and require greater specification and incorporation in subsequent research designs.

Status consistency and class identification

Another promising approach to an understanding of class consciousness, as Landecker points out, is the phenomenon of status

[16] Stanley A. Hetzler, "An Investigation of the Distinctiveness of Social Classes," *American Sociological Review*, XVIII (October, 1953), pp. 493–497; Hubert M. Blalock, "Status Consciousness," *Social Forces*, XXXVII (March, 1959), pp. 243–248; Lionel S. Lewis, "Class and the Perception of Class," *ibid.*, XLII (March, 1964), pp. 336–340; John L. Haer, "A Comparative Study of the Classification Techniques of Warner and Centers," *American Sociological Review*, XX (December, 1955), pp. 689–692.

[17] Peter H. Rossi, "Community Decision-Making," *Administrative Science Quarterly*, I (March, 1957), pp. 415–443; James S. Coleman, *Community Conflict* (New York: Free Press, 1957), pp. 11–12.

consistency. Since persons in complex societies necessarily pursue numerous roles, often with differing degrees of skill, responsibility, and opportunity, there is always the empirical possibility of *inconsistent statuses* for given categories of persons. Likewise, as Marx was among the first to show, social and cultural changes may alter the connections between one's various statuses. Similarly, Weber's (and Sorokin's) distinction of economic, honorific, and political dimensions of stratification gives a conceptual and empirical introduction to problems of determining the nature and consequences of personal status consistency.

Some years passed before this major insight was transformed into theoretical and empirical terms. Benoit-Smullyan followed Weber's schema and posited the existence of different degrees of consistency or "status equilibrium." In a study of the 1940 presidential election, Lazarsfeld confronted a related phenomenon in voters who were subjected to "cross-pressures" (i.e., differential attitudes associated with conflicting ethnic, occupational, and religious affiliations).[18] Parenthetically, he found that cross-pressured persons delayed their final decisions and tended to react by losing interest in the campaign. More recently, Lenski has revived interest in the general problem by correlating degrees of status consistency (or status crystallization) with political ideology and behavior. In addition, he suggests that status inconsistency (or low status crystallization) is accompanied by problems in social interaction and by consequent motives for social withdrawal.[19] Finally, the status consistency phenomenon has been applied to an analysis of suicide, derived in part from Durkheim's pioneer study. Gibbs and Martin substitute status integration for status consistency and present con-

[18] Emile Benoit-Smullyan, "Status, Status Types, and Status Interrelations," *American Sociological Review*, IX (April, 1944), pp. 151–161; Paul F. Lazarsfeld, Bernard Berelson, and Hazel Gaudet, *The People's Choice* (New York: Columbia University Press, 1948), pp. 60–64.

[19] Gerhard Lenski, "Status Crystallization: A Non-Vertical Dimension of Social Status," *American Sociological Review*, XIX (August, 1954), pp. 405–413; Gerhard Lenski, "Social Participation and Status Crystallization," *ibid.*, XXI (August, 1956), pp. 458–464; Stuart Adams, "Status Congruency as a Variable in Small Group Performance," *Social Forces*, XXXII (October, 1953), pp. 16–22.

siderable evidence that suggests a negative relation between suicide rates and status consistency.[20]

Public and private reflections of class differences

According to Marx, class-interest consciousness (to use Landecker's term) is a predictable and inevitable consequence of objective status differences. Furthermore, this form of class consciousness was conceived to affect the nature of interaction between representatives of each stratum—particularly in the political realm. Unfortunately, Marxian theorists tended to restrict themselves to the societal or national level, thereby excluding a significant form of interclass interaction on the community level. The last few decades of community (particularly urban) research clearly indicate that prevailing theory has been oversimplified and unprepared for rather wide variations in class consciousness.

Studies of class interaction in communities of North America seem to yield two patterns. On the one hand, objective class differences are accompanied by emphasis on informal social exclusiveness or insulation. In short, most of the dominant institutional mechanisms (religious, recreational, family-residential) are congenial to interactions with those of similar status. Whether this is a matter of superordinate pressure or subordinate choice is not clear. But, on the other hand, the interaction of status categories on public matters or issues (through political means or the "community power structure") has been investigated with the mixture of results that normally precedes theoretical revisions. Some studies, based on imputed dominance of high-status persons, support a theory of conflicting interest groups and the effective victory of a solidified upper status group.[21] However, criticism of these studies emphasizes the subjective nature of the findings and the probability that

[20] Jack P. Gibbs and Walter T. Martin, *Status Integration and Suicide* (Eugene: University of Oregon Press, 1964). See also references in ch. 12 of this volume.

[21] Hunter, *op. cit.*; C. Wright Mills, *The Power Elite* (New York: Oxford University Press, 1956); William V. D'Antonio and William H. Form, *Influentials in Two Border Cities* (South Bend: University of Notre Dame Press, 1965).

potential rather than *actual* power was involved.[22] Several recent investigations have focused on specific community issues, with the finding that decision-making is rather diffuse and has its locus in status categories according to the nature of the issue. These results have been interpreted (*a*) as reflecting apathy, resignation, or anomie among presumably threatened "classes" and (*b*) as evidence of reluctance on the part of high status persons to expose themselves to wearisome and "unnecessary" participation in myriad activities that might interfere with attention to their genuine foci of responsibility.

Evidently, a theory of *muted* class consciousness (in all its forms) is very much needed, one that transcends the limited utility of the "false consciousness" tradition. The ingredients for such a theory are close at hand for the serious student—ethnic emphasis, widespread economic prosperity, status inconsistencies, mobility opportunities, and the apparently voluntary isolation of social class categories. Perhaps another theoretical clue may be taken from Marx. It may be that a given stratification system functions with minimal class consciousness, that the development and persistence of class-interest consciousness is a prelude (symptom) of a genuine *change* in the class structure.

BEHAVIORAL CONSEQUENCES OF CLASS

The overwhelming mass of research in stratification has been aimed at a single broad hypothesis: members of differing social strata behave in significantly different ways in various types of recurring situations. Using income, occupation, education (or some composite index of these), sociologists have identified class differences in leisure, friendships, voting, childrearing, political and economic attitudes, participation in voluntary associations, residential

22 Nelson W. Polsby, *Community Power and Political Theory* (New Haven: Yale University Press, 1963); Dahl, *op. cit.;* Edward Banfield, *Political Influence* (New York: Free Press, 1961); M. Kent Jennings, *Community Influentials* (New York: Free Press, 1964).

location, marriage choices, and class consciousness.[23] Some of these "class" differences undergo important alterations in time (e.g., childrearing, and political behavior), while others do not seem as sharp as prevailing theory requires (e.g., leisure, consumption patterns, home-ownership). In any case, the differences that have been found are often construed in a commonsense manner or are left uninterpreted. And rarely do the *similarities* between strata receive the attention they deserve.

The basic problem in this area is not simply one of explaining class differences, but rather of accounting for the special nature of those differences. In other words, what are the social and psychological mechanisms by which a given status (defined in terms of specific opportunities and limitations) is translated by its incumbents into behavior "appropriate" to that status? Obviously then, such objective indicators of status as occupation, education, and income possess limited *theoretical* utility since they merely reveal potentialities for behavior, not determinants of behavioral alternatives.

A fundamental premise in most "explanations" of class-linked behavior is a *meaningful consistency* between "position" and specific types of behavior, and also among these types of behavior, for any stratum in a given time period. Marx, for example, found "consistency" in the exploitative motive of the dominant class. Cooley and others have likewise found consistency in leading strata, though this is attributed to conceptions of responsibility, to the assurance that allegedly accompanies high status, and to the desire for distinctiveness. In any case, it is assumed or asserted that in any stratification system the higher strata set (or reflect) the prevailing criteria for behavior. If this has merit, what explains the development of *variations* in perceptions, values, etc., among other, subordinate status categories?

23 Bernard Barber, *Social Stratification* (New York: Harcourt, Brace & World, 1957), chs. 10–12; Joseph A. Kahl, *The American Class Structure* (New York: Holt, Rinehart & Winston, 1957), chs. 5, 6; Harold M. Hodges, *Social Stratification* (Cambridge: Schenkman, 1964), chs. 6–11; Leonard Reissman, *Class in American Society* (New York: Free Press, 1959), pp. 242–259; Thomas E. Lasswell, *Class and Stratum* (Boston: Houghton, Mifflin, 1965), chs. 11–14.

Logically, the first question for consideration—one that derives from the formulations of such diverse figures as Marx, Znaniecki, and Durkheim—is: how is a crucial social circle or reference group acquired by a specific status category? As Weber and others have pointed out, the upper strata *reduce* the possibility of their operation as reference groups by maximizing social distance. Consequently, separate and unique reference groups develop in line with the special characteristics of the population in each stratum— ethnic, occupational, religious. However, the structured opportunities for upward mobility may complicate the availability of "appropriate" reference groups and may produce a "false consciousness" that could not be explained by knowledge of an objectively defined stratum.

If class-linked behavior depends on the creation of special reference groups (which are consequences of the unavailability of a dominant reference group), a second theoretical problem concerns the *content* of values, norms, and typical attitudes associated with class-linked reference groups. What factors account for the explicit or implicit values and perspectives of a particular stratum and its reference group(s)? Though this is a classic question, one which is basic to the sociology of knowledge, careful theoretical attention to its solution is miniscule. But a major theoretical clue warrants considerable study—Weber's conception of *style of life*, which he analyzed as an extension of the status (honorific) dimension of stratification. In contemporary terms, style of life may be defined as a consistent set of values and aspirations by which members of a stratum (*a*) express their validated location in that stratum; (*b*) select, interpret, and use available material products; and (*c*) maintain their identity as a sociocultural entity.[24]

Style of life may be variably developed and thus more or less difficult to identify in given strata or reference groups. In general, stable upper strata possess the clearest and most consistent styles of life, because, it is hypothesized, the various dimensions of status are

[24] This approach is spelled out in Alvin Boskoff, "Status Phases, Social Mobility, and Differential Behavior" (paper delivered at meetings of the American Sociological Association, September, 1965); and Alvin Boskoff, "Simplist vs. Complex Theory in Stratification" (paper delivered at meetings of the Southern Sociological Society, April, 1967).

most crystallized or complementary in these categories. Since style of life depends upon consistency of experience, we would expect strata to develop relatively distinctive styles of life in line with their perceptions of experience. Therefore, we may identify several ideal typical varieties of perception (cf. "status consciousness").

1. *Expressive.* A style of life may be implicitly developed to extract the peculiar satisfactions or frustrations associated with a given stratum—e. g., the exurban life-style, the lower-class Italian families in Boston (as studied by Gans).[25]
2. *Defensive.* On the other hand, a style of life may emphasize exclusiveness or distinctiveness, as reflected in a search for new recreational activities, new or "odd" gadgets or speech patterns, secluded or inaccessible residential locations, etc.
3. *Propulsive.* We may also identify a style of life geared to the promotion of desired change for a stratum or for units of a stratum—as in the case of the easily caricatured, upwardly mobile "middle-class" families.

A major problem in analyzing American society is our inability to locate a style of life (as defined above) in persons characterized by inconsistent statuses or sudden shifts in position. Prediction of behavior under these circumstances is understandably marked by error. But instead of dismissing this problem, there is some value in locating it conceptually in the theoretical complex of social mobility (see pp. 264–269).

Let us return to the theoretical possibilities of style of life in relatively stable strata. Following Weber and Parsons, we may view a style of life as a more or less implicit means of adjusting to a special interpretation of social experience. From this standpoint, a particular style of life is a *functional consequence* of the complex opportunities and limitations associated with some stratum. Position does not necessarily "cause" style of life, but rather provides cues in specific recurring situations that tend to elicit an unplanned but "logico-meaningful" set of attitudes, values, and actions. The functional or adjustive value to the actors of a style of life may be inferred in part from the tenacity of such values and their relative immunity from external attempts at change.

25 Herbert J. Gans, *The Urban Villagers* (New York: Free Press, 1962).

To indicate the potential of this general approach, it may be useful to review three recent attempts to "explain" the behavior of lower-class persons in American urban areas. There is, first, Cohen's analysis of a delinquent subculture (style of life) among lower-class adolescents.[26] Very briefly, Cohen attributes the "irresponsible," destructive, antisocial, hedonistic nature of the boys to their rejection of unrealizable middle-class goals. Second, Porterfield's ecological study of suicide and homicide rates includes a very suggestive attempt to derive low suicide and high homicide rates among low-status persons from a set of distinctive features. Using census materials with some imagination, Porterfield found homicides to be most correlated with persons of recent rural residence, nonwhite status, low social well-being, and high concentration of churches and different congregations. These features were interpreted to form a "depressed folk" syndrome that either encourages or does not frown upon the expression of personal difficulties through violence to others.[27] Finally, and most recently, McKinley has tried with initial success to demonstrate that the peculiar frustrations associated with working conditions among lower-class (unskilled) males creates hostilities that affect family relations and the socialization of children.[28]

SOCIAL MOBILITY

In retrospect, the study of social mobility over the past thirty-five years has been based on two simple but important conceptual distinctions. First, Sorokin's identification of vertical and horizontal forms of mobility as co-existent processes is indubitably basic.[29] But in addition, sociologists have been compelled to disentangle the phenomena of *stratum mobility* (i.e., a change in position of a status category) from *personal* or *family mobility*.

[26] Albert K. Cohen, *Delinquent Boys* (New York: Free Press, 1954).

[27] Austin L. Porterfield, "Suicide and Crime in Folk and in Secular Society," *American Journal of Sociology*, LVII (January, 1952), pp. 331–338.

[28] Donald G. McKinley, *Social Class and Family Life* (New York: Free Press, 1964).

[29] Pitirim A. Sorokin, *Social Mobility* (New York: Harper, 1927).

However, the problems connected with understanding social mobility are intimately related to previously discussed theoretical issues in stratification research. Consequently, many of our earlier analyses in this chapter should be kept in mind.

Earlier studies of vertical mobility were exploratory and descriptive, seeking patterns and extent of mobility by focusing on the *occupational* dimension of status. It was assumed that measured occupational change provided a valid index of *social* mobility. Indeed, this assumption is still dominant, though methodological and theoretical criticisms are not absent. For example, at least three varieties of vertical mobility may be found in the sociological literature.

1. *Objective status change* refers to movement upward (or downward) along occupational, income, educational, or similar scales.[30]
2. *Attempted mobility or status imitation* concerns behavior of persons that can be interpreted as imitating values or activities of another stratum without prior or accompanying change in crucial objective statuses—e.g., affecting a "cultured" accent.
3. *Validated mobility*, which is certainly the core phenomenon in this problem area, is marked by either acceptance of persons who have achieved significant changes in one or more objective status dimensions or acquiescence concerning the altered social evaluation of a stratum—e.g., the professional military category.

It should be noted that only the latter two categories directly involve problems of theory and interpretation.

Obviously, the primary theoretical question in vertical social mobility is: what are the crucial social structures that facilitate or impede change in status for existing strata? Again, Sorokin is responsible for the widely used identification of major "channels of mobility" and for perceptive analysis of their role in processes of mobility.[31] These channels or mechanisms of mobility are mar-

[30] D. V. Glass, ed., *Social Mobility in Britain* (London: Routledge & Kegan Paul, 1954); Natalie Rogoff, *Recent Trends in Occupational Mobility* (New York: Free Press, 1953); Seymour M. Lipset and Reinhard Bendix, *Social Mobility in Industrial Society* (Berkeley: University of California Press, 1959); Neil J. Smelser and Seymour M. Lipset, eds., *Social Structure and Mobility in Economic Development* (Chicago: Aldine, 1966).
[31] Sorokin, *op. cit.*, chs. 8, 17–19.

riage, occupation, formal education, government office, the military, and religion. All involve institutionalized or legitimate means for social escalation; but clearly, each society at any given period of its development possesses only a few of these alternative channels. The key question then arises: what explains the *visibility* and *availability* of mobility channels for different categories of potentially mobile persons?

Though Thomas, Znaniecki, Cooley, MacIver, and G. H. Mead did not directly theorize about social mobility, the tradition they helped to create in social psychology has been a recurrent source of theoretical ideas. Essentially, one large segment of studies in social mobility has commonly pursued two premises. The first, drawn from the concepts of "definition of the situation," "dynamic assessment," "realistic attitudes," asserts that potentially mobile persons do not develop effective contact or use of mobility channels unless these are personally and realistically perceived as relevant to themselves. Most of these studies try to tap personal definitions of the accessibility of mobility channels by studying "aspirations." Secondly, it is generally hypothesized that these aspirations are conditioned by some "significant other" or reference group.

Since the dominant channels of mobility in the United States are the occupational and the educational, aspiration studies have focused on these and on a selected number of potential reference groups (family, peers, teachers).[32] In general, the importance of reference groups in perceptions of mobility opportunities has been confirmed. There is some evidence, however, that formal education is not as significant a channel as is generally believed.[33]

Unfortunately, little attention has been given to social mobility

[32] Joseph A. Kahl, "Educational and Occupational Aspirations of 'Common Man' Boys," *Harvard Educational Review*, XXIII (1953), pp. 186–203; Richard L. Simpson, "Parental Influence, Anticipatory Socialization, and Social Mobility," *American Sociological Review*, XXVII (August, 1962), pp. 517–522; David J. Bordua, "Educational Aspirations and Parental Stress on College," *Social Forces*, XXXVIII (March, 1960), pp. 262–269; Glen H. Elder, *Adolescent Achievement and Mobility Aspirations* (Chapel Hill: Institute for Research in Social Science, University of North Carolina, 1962).

[33] C. Arnold Anderson, "A Skeptical Note on Education and Mobility," *American Journal of Sociology*, LXVI (May, 1961), pp. 560–569.

as a *progression* of social processes, or as Cooley more generally characterized social behavior, as a "tentative process" in which any phase may be regarded as a set of adaptations to other phases.[34] How do persons "pursue" mobility through time? If class status is essentially identifiable by a cohesive style of life, what factors and processes explain the unlearning of one style of life and the acquisition of another?

Perhaps the phenomena of upward social mobility can be provisionally conceptualized in the following analytic phases:

1. Initial class status.
2. Influence of some "outside" reference group.
3. Aspiration for mobility.
4. Entrance into and progress through one or more mobility channels.
5. Status inconsistency—objective "success" in some mobility channels (income, marriage), while retaining former status attributes (e. g., accent, residential location, religious affiliation).
6. Reduction of previous "class" associations.
7. Heightened desire for converting objective ascent into social acceptance by superordinate stratum.
8. Identification and learning the appropriate "higher" style of life.
9. Conversion of practiced performance of this style of life into validated acceptance.

Phases 5 through 9 constitute the core of social mobility as an understandable "successful" or variably incomplete phenomenon in modern stratification systems. Though these are precisely the points at which theory is currently lacking, there are sufficient data to encourage creative theorizing. For example, young mobile persons seem to reduce their visiting activities, while visiting patterns also tend to increase over time. Other data suggest that mobile families (in selected suburbs) tend to develop new associational memberships in a variety of local voluntary associations.[35] While these

[34] Charles H. Cooley, *Social Process* (New York: Charles Scribner's Sons, 1918), pp. 3–8.

[35] Richard F. Curtis, "Occupational Mobility and Urban Social Life," *American Journal of Sociology*, LXV (November, 1959), pp. 296–298; Ruth H. Useem *et al.*, "The Function of Neighboring for the Middle-Class Male," *Human Organization*, XIX (Summer, 1960), pp. 68–76.

findings are merely suggestive, they pose one of the most significant problems in sociology: given a loosely structured community or society, what factors account for stability or change in social interaction patterns among persons with specific varieties of dominant motivations (e.g., mobility) or socially relevant goals?

Another interesting form of data concerns phase 8. In reporting on the activities of "high society," Lucy Kavaler provides much "inside" information on the mechanisms by which mobile families achieve entrance into the upper class. Essentially, this involves not only learning the appropriate style of life, but employing paid intermediary experts who constitute the only link to that style of life —and subsequently, to legitimated position.[36] Inferentially, then, the capstone of upward social mobility is an educational process that functions to reduce or eradicate the status inconsistencies of earlier phases. Furthermore, it may be worthwhile to analyze problem behavior in mobile persons as responses to difficulties in acquiring the social contacts and cultural skills that promote perceptions of status consistency in mobile persons and in their social circles.

Finally, the student of social mobility is increasingly concerned with determining and explaining the social consequences of given mobility patterns. Unfortunately, the classic theorists have contributed contradictory guidelines in this respect. Marx tended to view mobility as a consequence of change, but a consequence that requires the catalyst of force. Pareto's theory of the "circulation of elites" suggests a cyclical alternation of social mechanisms (negotiation and ruse vs. force and violence) that follow mobility into strategic positions in political and economic spheres. Sorokin and Parsons seem to interpret social mobility as an equilibrating process, rather than a source of further change. Cooley, Simmel, Park, and others, however, regard mobility as producing problems of marginality and personal adjustment.

Most of the investigations in this area have assumed that mobility —particularly, rapid mobility—creates identifiable personal problems that affect processes of social interaction. Thus, mobility has been related to delinquency, prejudice, mental disorders, social

[36] Lucy Kavaler, *The Private World of High Society* (New York: McKay, 1960).

isolation, and even to fertility.[37] Thus far, the results of such studies are by no means conclusive. Most significantly, it is often difficult to assign causal status to the mobility variable. On the other hand, if analysis and theory are shifted from the level of personal consequences (i.e., effects on behavior of individuals in informal settings) to that of social organization, certain theoretical questions can be explored.

For example, what is the relationship between the *location* and *span* of dominant mobility patterns and the phenomena of social change? A large concentration of mobility in adjacent strata, as opposed to extensive spans of mobility, may be followed by relatively few deep-seated changes in social structure (institutions, power structure). Perhaps the *amount* of mobility (in objective dimensions) is not as significant as the *span* of mobility. Most studies agree that the absolute amount of mobility has not diminished in the United States over the past sixty years, but it is likewise clear that mobility has become relatively more restricted to "movements" within the "middle class" range of the stratification scale. The fact that this period was also marked by very limited social changes (as distinct from numerous cultural changes) lends some credibility to this broad hypothetical formulation.

As Tumin has suggested, the *speed* of mobility is an important factor in the social products that mobility seems to inspire.[38] Rapid social mobility opportunities tend to outstrip invitations to legitimated entrance into higher statuses. This discrepancy, in Tumin's formulation, results in the formation by the "mobiles" of their own status-conferring organizations, as a counterpart to those from which "mobiles" have been excluded. Indeed, these new status organizations can be expected to produce additional elements of

37 Fred B. Silberstein and Melvin Seeman, "Social Mobility and Prejudice," *American Journal of Sociology*, LXV (November, 1959), pp. 258–264; Bruno Bettelheim and Morris Janowitz, *Dynamics of Prejudice: A Psychological and Sociological Study of Veterans* (New York: Harper & Row, 1950); A. B. Hollingshead and Fritz Redlich, *Social Class and Mental Illness* (New York: Wiley, 1958); H. Warren Dunham, *Community and Schizophrenia* (Detroit: Wayne State University Press, 1965); Charles F. Westoff *et al.*, *Family Growth in Metropolitan America* (Princeton: Princeton University Press, 1961).

38 Melvin M. Tumin, "Some Unapplauded Consequences of Social Mobility in a Mass Society," *Social Forces*, XXXVI (October, 1957), pp. 32–37.

MAJOR THEORETICAL PROBLEMS

stratification—usually of an ascriptive sort (in terms of ethnic background, religion)—which in turn sharpen vertical status distinctions within racial, ethnic, or religious categories.[39]

If sociologists are essentially interested in the dynamics and interrelations of institutional spheres (dominant goals, organizational mechanisms, patterns of authority and power), the relation between social mobility and institutional change merits continuing theoretical concern and investigation. What political changes, if any, may be interpreted as reflections of *achieved* mobility and of *retarded* mobility in different social categories? (This question has emerged in part in attempts to identify and explain voting shifts in presumably mobile suburban residents. The data are not yet adequate; indeed, there is considerable variety in these voting patterns, which probably derives from incomplete conceptualization and typologies.) Turning to the recently exalted formal educational structure, what changes in control, curriculum, and admissions can be attributed to upward mobility of the student population and faculty members in major types of schools and colleges? Finally, for present purposes, what economic consequences may be expected from programs (or inaction) that impede social mobility for specific population segments (e.g., unemployment, levels of bureaucratization, fiscal policy)?

The understanding of stratification and its social effects is one of the unique and crucial problems of a maturing sociology. However, the potential contribution to knowledge in this area is well beyond current achievement. Part of the difficulty may be attributed not to the absence of theory, but to the lack of *systematic, detailed theory* on the phenomena of stratification. Consequently, research has been descriptive and/or correlational in nature, with few cumulative consequences.

Earlier theorists depended on historical materials drawn from less complex societies than those of the contemporary Western world. As a result, their formulations tended to emphasize simplified aspects of stratification—explicit power differentials and con-

[39] E. Digby Baltzell, *The Protestant Establishment* (New York: Random House, 1964).

flict, objective indicators (such as occupation and wealth), and the mechanisms of social exclusion. On the other hand, theorists such as Marx, Cooley, Durkheim, and Weber (and more recent theorists, including Schumpeter and Parsons) have also examined three other facets of stratification that have tended to be either ignored or misunderstood.

First, the *functional* significance of stratification in general and of specific class systems might be considered a tentative approach toward discovering basic but not *definitive* explanations of class phenomena. In various forms, Comte, Cooley, Durkheim, Marx, Parsons, and others have suggested that, in a society marked by extensive specialization in social and cultural services, objective differences in role behavior come to receive a generally accepted ranking of worth, responsibility, and privilege. New roles, or changed evaluation of existing roles, therefore involve alterations in stratification systems. This phenomenon of differential evaluation of social categories is itself variable. For example, differential evaluation may be based on rational criteria or on imposed standards, and may vary from general implicit consensus to explicit dissension. It follows, therefore, that neither objective indicators of class nor the data of informal social interaction provide, by themselves, crucial indicators of the operation of class systems. In addition, the functional orientation to stratification requires concern for the mechanisms by which differential evaluation permits or compels interaction between strata (power, exploitation, mobility).

Second, as Marx, Schumpeter, and others have shown, at given time periods of change, there is an empirically necessary lag between traditional and revised ranking systems. Status inconsistency is not foreign to stratification, but is a symptom of *transition* in stratification systems. But status inconsistency is not equally distributed among strata. Therefore, major theoretical and research issues might focus on factors that account for (*a*) differential vulnerability to status inconsistency in some time period, (*b*) ideological and behavioral responses to status inconsistency over time, and (*c*) the consequences of *reduced* status inconsistency for specific strata.

Third, stratification is *analytically* distinguishable from other aspects of social organization; but, according to Cooley, Marx, MacIver, and others, it is intimately connected with several major institutions in the routine behavior of members of the various strata. Therefore, both "typical" and "deviant" behavior (and attitude) patterns of each stratum should be explicitly examined in two ways: (*a*) as direct or indirect *consequences* of a stratum's operation in relevant institutional spheres that can be shown to develop identifiable changes, stability, or extreme resistance to change; and (*b*) as direct or indirect *contributors* to the functioning of specific institutions or to the interaction between institutions.

For example, in relation to *a*, the political attitudes and voting patterns of different types of professionals might be examined as possible reflections of similarities and differences in the institutional setting of professionals (e.g., education, health, government, industry). Are changes in economic demand for specific skills reflected in changed or distinctive political behavior, consumption patterns, and attitudes toward education among these categories? On the other hand, pursuing the suggestion in *b*, sociologists could well be interested in discovering and explaining the impact of middle class and mixed suburban populations on alterations in religious beliefs and organization.

Implicit in all these clues and theoretical fragments is the necessity of viewing stratification, from the structural standpoint, as a complex system of processes and, from the standpoint of the individual, as a series of phases in each of which persons acquire special opportunities, limitations, and attitudinal foci. We may identify the following component processes that collectively give uniqueness to the stratification aspect of human experience.

1. *Role differentiation:* the process of changing the allocation of skills and techniques, and of developing new skills, among members of a delimited social system (society, region, community, complex organization).
2. *Differential evaluation:* the process of applying some standard of importance, worth, or responsibility (however rational or nonrational) to roles and persons, with a consequent scale of prestige.
3. *Role adjustment and performance:* the process of learning appropriate skills for a given position.

4. *Role exploitation:* the process of consciously transferring the fruits (material, psychic, symbolic) of one role (or cluster) to other role situations that are, in other respects, not yet differentially evaluated according to the former's scale of evaluation.

5. *Role–status segregation:* the process of limiting social interaction to persons of similar roles and evaluated positions.

6. *Role–status reservation:* the process of transmitting role–status advantages to selected successors on a non-competitive basis (normally, to children or relatives).

7. *Status conflict:* the process of interfering with the normal expectations (opportunities, etc.) of a specific status category, whatever the motives for such interference or whatever the ultimate source of the conflict might be.

8. *Status mobility:* the process by which individuals (or a specific stratum) are enabled to alter their crucial roles and/or social evaluation based on such roles.

Generally, the individual is aware of these processes as fragments that are intermittently important. As a participant in stratification, he typically "passes through" several successive phases of class membership. First, there are the "status-fit" stages, through which presumably all normal adults advance. Beginning with (*a*) status ascription, which is a consequence of family membership, the individual then learns (*b*) appropriate values and skills and (*c*) the distinction between his own status and that of persons at other status levels. As an adolescent, and frequently in early adult years, the individual may face problems of interpreting (*d*) inadequate or conflicting status cues (and also of accepting the demands or limitations of his ascribed status). "Status fit" occurs when the individual properly learns his responsibilities and the implicit social limitations, and he experiences a net of satisfactions and a proud identification with his stratum (professional, skilled workman, "solid middle class").

For many, the latter phases of status fit are either short-lived or undeveloped. When the individual (or a stratum) is unable or unwilling to retain his ascribed status (whatever the reasons), the potential for phases of "status mobility" rises. Here we may simply refer to the previous discussions of these phases on page 272. All phases, of course, involve two theoretical problems for the sociologist: what conditions account for "successful passage" through a specific phase; and how does experience in one phase facilitate or impede the operation of typical social processes in succeeding phases?

In behavioral terms, stratification refers to the differential attitudes and actions of identifiable subgroups (strata) in a population that can be attributed to demonstrably unequal opportunities (not personal abilities). However, the presence and impact of unequal opportunities may vary according to the phases of "class membership" in which a given population is distributed for any time period. Thus, for example, it seems premature to interpret differential patterns of voting, fertility, childrearing, or leisure as "class" differences unless it can be shown that these differentials refer to categories of persons (or family units) *in the same phase of "class membership."* Indeed, strata may only be tentatively distinguished from one another—using objective indicators of potential differences in opportunities—until comparisons of behavior are limited to persons in the same stage of class membership. On the other hand, the discovery of theoretically unexplainable *similarities* in behavior between members of "different strata" might be a consequence of the comparison of persons in *different phases* of class membership.

In short, a class system is the sociologist's (and the social participant's) summary of his attempt to predict and understand the behavior of persons from their social position (as structured opportunities) and their personal location in the sequence of processes associated with class membership. A stratification system is, from one standpoint, a latent mechanism for organizing complexity and population size. Its major features are hierarchy and ascriptive bases for evaluation. But these features are themselves variables; that is, we can identify different degrees of sharpness in vertical divisions and also varying strength of *ascription* and *achievement* in providing guides to behavior.

Stratification in modern society, apart from remnants of caste, is principally reflected in limited organizations by *bureaucracy*, and in the community by *class strata*. Presumably, all members of a community eventually occupy some temporary or relatively permanent social position. Increasingly, people in modern society participate in one or more crucial bureaucratic systems. In what ways does location in a key bureaucratic system *reflect* or *affect* relative location in community (or national) class systems?

Perhaps the phenomena of social mobility might be studied not only as movement in an *institutionalized setting* (e.g., the economic) or in *social reputation in a community*, but also as one kind of potential link between these two settings. Individuals who tend to be unwilling to use (or are discouraged from) mobility channels either cannot enter or have very limited access to bureaucratic organization (except as a client). The "typical" middle-class aspiration for mobility provides relatively high chances for bureaucratic recruitment and "promotion." At the upper status levels (where an aristocracy is relatively non-existent), the relation between community status and bureaucratic location is somewhat more complex. In general, movement into top layers of administrative, military, industrial, or commercial bureaucracies is prepared by the advantages of middle- or higher-class status. But the community status effects of high bureaucratic position seem to be quite varied.

Here an important distinction is necessary. Stratification in modern society exhibits both "public" and "private" aspects. The public aspect concerns differential behavior and differential evaluation that are readily available and routinely displayed. This is exemplified in the well-recognized *formal* aspects of bureaucratic systems. On the other hand, stratification involves differences in behavior that are of interest only to the members of a given stratum, or special activities are consciously withheld from the scrutiny of "outsiders." The private aspect tends to predominate in the community status system, solidified by what has been called a *style of life*. It may be suggested that the public aspect of stratification is more vulnerable to mobility processes. Indeed, the conversion of private to public forms of stratification (through advertising, public relations, education, and the mass media) intensifies aspirations for mobility, as well as the use of more effective mobility mechanisms.

Looked at as objectively as possible, stratification systems serve *both* to promote and sustain categorical social distinctions and to structure or control diminution or alteration of these distinctions. The major theoretical tradition in sociology has tended to emphasize the first aspect, while research has increasingly questioned the validity of this aspect, and has implicitly indicated the need for greater theoretical attention to the second aspect. This should not be misconstrued to be a denial of stratification, but rather a sensitivity to the unexplored complexities of stratification, as exhibited in the phenomena of social mobility. Certainly, sociologists cannot study social mobility without an underlying conception of systems of strata, since vertical mobility presupposes at least two meaningful and distinct locations in a rank order.

Consequently, to the behavioral differences that derive from structured inequalities of opportunity must be added the problems of behavioral differences due to mobility vs. immobility among members of an identifiable stratum. Specifically for any stratum, what conditions (*a*) account for perceptions of objectively unrealistic *opportunities* for mobility and of objectively unrealistic *limitations* on mobility and (*b*) account for the attitudinal and behavioral consequences of these types of perceptions when they eventuate in achieved mobility or frustrated mobility? Perhaps theoretical emphases of this type will enable us to understand the perplexing findings on attitudes toward fluoridation, on voting behavior and its variations, and on the complex processes of promoting or hindering social and cultural change. Perhaps, also, stratification and social mobility can furnish theoretical linkages to a much needed understanding of social change (discussed in Chapter 14).

SELECTED REFERENCES

Blau, Peter M., and Otis D. Duncan, *The American Occupational Structure* (New York: Wiley, 1968).

Gordon, Milton M., *Social Class in American Sociology* (Durham, N.C.: Duke University Press, 1958), ch. 6.

Lenski, Gerhard, *Power and Privilege* (New York: McGraw-Hill, 1966).

Lipset, Seymour M. and Reinhard Bendix, *Social Mobility in Industrial Society* (Berkeley: University of California Press, 1959).

Marshall, T. H., *Citizenship and Social Class and Other Essays* (Cambridge, Eng.: University Press, 1950).

Reissman, Leonard, *Class in American Society* (New York: Free Press, 1959).

Sorokin, Pitirim A., *Social Mobility* (New York: Harper, 1927).

———, *Society, Culture, and Personality* (New York: Harper & Row, 1947), chs. 15, 25, 26.

Warner, W. Lloyd, *et al.*, *Social Class in America* (New York: Harper Torchbooks, 1960).

12

Social Deviation
and Social Problems

A sociological approach to deviant behavior and socially disapproved social organization was for a long time hindered by psychobiological biases and by a moral–empirical concern for specific varieties of deviation (e.g., crime, suicide, psychosis, alcoholism, illegitimacy). However, the conceptual and theoretical foundations for understanding patterned deviance were initially constructed about seventy years ago, with intermittent modifications as suggested by the vast accumulation of relevant studies during the past twenty-five years.

The first and most necessary development, largely due to Durkheim and Thomas and Znaniecki, was the recognition that deviance derives from two different sources—the *biological* (as explained by brain injuries, neurological disorders, birth defects, etc.) and the *experiential* (derived from contacts and influences of the social environment). Not only did the second category come to be considered "normal" (i.e., expectable), but the sociological problem of deviance was reconceptualized as the study of phenomena of nonconformity to approved values, goals, and related behavior patterns.[1] Indeed, nonconformity was further specified—directly and indirectly—into four types—overconformity, unconformity (behavior traceable to failure to learn appropriate norms), disapproved innovative deviance, and approved deviance or creativity.[2]

PREPARATORY THEORIES OF DEVIATION

Let us briefly review the major components in an emerging theory of deviation up to approximately 1940. Perhaps the fundamental theoretical approach to deviation is that of Durkheim, who analyzed behavior as reflecting different degrees of control imposed by or accepted from significant groups and values. One type of deviation, which we would now call overconformity, derives from overpowering self-sacrificial dedication to a group or value system. While Durkheim discussed this type with respect to suicide (altruistic suicide),[3] it may be easily extended to extraordinary and therefore problematical adherence to any approved norm—e.g., scrupulous and embarrassing honesty, especially careful driving (which presents well-known obstacles to other drivers), the infuriating meticulousness of functionaries, the "holier than thou" attitude of the incontinently zealous religious adherent, and "superpatriotism." A second type involves a somewhat loosened control system, one that emphasizes individual responsibility in making decisions and therefore "permits" selfish, expedient courses of action (egoistic deviation).[4] Finally, Durkheim contributed his classic analysis of "anomic" deviation. This form derives from situations in which relevant norms are absent or unclear—primarily in periods of rapid social change. Durkheim, it will be recalled, concluded

[1] W. I. Thomas and Florian Znaniecki, *The Polish Peasant in Europe and America* (5 vols.; Boston: Richard Badger, 1918), III, pp. 52–57; Emile Durkheim, *The Rules of the Sociological Method*, trans. Sarah A. Solvay and John H. Mueller (New York: Free Press, 1950), ch. 3.

[2] Robert K. Merton, *Social Theory and Social Structure* (New York: Free Press, rev. ed., 1957), ch. 4, especially pp. 140–157.

[3] See ch. 2, pp. 34–35.

[4] See the attempt to "reduce" Durkheim's suicide types to the "egoistic" category by Barclay D. Johnson, "Durkheim's One Cause of Suicide," *American Sociological Review*, XXX (December, 1965), pp. 875–886.

that the development of specialization and correlated processes of social and cultural change produce greater probability of the second and third types of deviance. This, then, may be called a theory of *structural opportunities for deviation.*

In line with Durkheim's approach, several social-psychological theorists in the early twentieth century (Cooley, Baldwin, G. H. Mead, and Piaget) have suggested explanations of nonconformity through a focus on socialization and personality formation. Cooley, for example, regarded personality (and the approved patterns that essentially describe personality) as a continuous process of interpreting and being guided by the judgments of others in primary-group relationships. For Cooley, the deviant is marked by unlegitimated self-images, by self-feelings that for some reason are untested by "normal" limitation and control from others.[5] But what accounts for the incompatibility of the self-image and social judgments? While Cooley did not attempt to probe the causes of this discrepancy, several clues can be identified.

First, Cooley was aware of mistakes in evaluating or perceiving social cues. Second, the primary group was recognized as containing elements of disharmony and competitiveness;[6] by inference, then, primary-group experience may be inconsistent, overdemanding, or unrewarding—a view that is not incompatible with the primary-group tragedy *à la* Freud. Third, the normal mechanisms of the "looking-glass self" and primary-group influence do not operate effectively under conditions of social specialization and rapid increase in freedom. Cooley suggests that deviation necessarily follows expansion in the radius of freedom; because, for many, new freedom means vague norms, "moral strain," and little structured opportunity to manage the uncertainties of diminished controls.

Thomas and Znaniecki, together and individually, likewise tried to formulate explanatory schemes for problem behavior among both children and adults. Their famous pioneering work, *The Polish Peasant in Europe and America,* contained a tentative theory

[5] Charles H. Cooley, *Human Nature and the Social Order* (New York: Charles Scribner's Sons, 1902), pp. 258–260, 433.

[6] Charles H. Cooley, *Social Organization* (New York: Charles Scribner's Sons, 1909), p. 23.

that each man subsequently modified in significant ways. Essentially, this theory attributed deviation to the practical difficulties of translating basic and acquired needs into action in given social situations.[7] In *The Polish Peasant* and in *The Unadjusted Girl*, Thomas viewed deviant or problem behavior as a consequence of the absence of clear, meaningful moral rules, and the availability of some set of clear but "disapproved" rules that seem preferable to "mental uncertainty" among those who seek to express "needs" for new experience and for stability. Modern society creates (or effectively confirms) deviation because of its characteristically specialized (non-primary) groups, which are (in Thomas' view) insufficiently permanent and stable to develop and sustain organized sets of values and attitudes. Indeed, such experiences "force" many persons to become deviant in one of two directions: (*a*) overconformity, or the stubborn imitation of the old values of the "philistine"; or (*b*) the delight in highly contradictory values, or in values that directly challenge approved kinds of behavior (the Bohemian).

Significantly, Thomas and Znaniecki pointed out that, while deviation reflects difficulties in social organization (previously called social disorganization), these difficulties and concomitant deviations do not necessarily produce personal disorganization (or demoralization).[8] In other words, deviant behavior often occurs among otherwise "normal" persons. In fact, Znaniecki's analysis of *social circles* (see pp. 76–78) may be considered an extension and specification of this approach. It will be recalled that the components of a social system are, from the standpoint of a given actor, his role, his social circle, the social function of his role, the status assigned that role, and his social self or self-image. By inference then, deviation results when undue emphasis is given to any of these components. For example, overemphasis on the social circle is overconformity; overemphasis on self-image leads to aggressive, unscrupulous behavior; overemphasis on the role may express itself in ritualism and rigid immunity to other practical requirements.

Drawing on Durkheim, but certainly in accord with Znaniecki's scheme, Merton has conceptualized deviation as a variegated set of

[7] Thomas and Znaniecki, *op. cit.*, I, pp. 52–53.   [8] *Ibid.*, IV, pp. 2–3.

responses to a critical situation in complex society—an emphasis on achievement, "success," and attainment, but without the provision of adequate, legitimate means for reaching these goals. To Merton, this discrepancy—if perceived—requires individual resolution of the *temporary* anomie by which he is confronted. The alternative "deviant patterns" are overconformity (stubbornly holding to goals and to practically ineffective means), innovation (attempts to devise more effective means, approved or otherwise), ritualism (abdication of success as a goal and a narrowed concern with the means as significant in themselves), withdrawal or retreatism (disavowal of the worth of prevailing ends and means by constructing a private, isolated world), and rebellion (the substitution of new goals and means and the attempt to impose or "sell" these to other members of a given social system).[9]

The comprehensive nature of this attempt to order the empirical variety of deviant behavior has been recognized since its introduction in 1938. However, it is clear that Merton did not attempt to locate factors that would allow us to explain the selection of some deviant response by a specific social category. More recent studies and theories, as we shall see below, have intermittently taken up the theoretical challenge.

A final theoretical strand concerns role-conflict and marginality. Simmel was among the first to identify the problems faced by "the stranger," the person who as a consequence of mobility is "marginal" to past and present associations, who is largely freed from both sources of control and yet vulnerable to internal uncertainties and external stigma.[10] Park borrowed the concept of the stranger and applied it to the phenomena of migration and culture contact in complex society. Briefly, Park suggested that various kinds of deviant behavior (crime, delinquency, illegitimacy) reflected the experience of persons who, by migrating, had given up old values but had not adequately acquired the norms and skills of their new

[9] Merton, *op. cit.*, ch. 4; Robert Dubin, "Deviant Behavior and Social Structure," *American Sociological Review*, XXIV (April, 1959), pp. 147–164; Frank Harary, "Merton Revisited: A New Classification for Deviant Behavior," *ibid.*, XXXI (October, 1966), pp. 693–697.

[10] Georg Simmel, *The Sociology of Georg Simmel*, trans. Kurt H. Wolff (New York: Free Press, 1950), pp. 402–409.

setting. Thus, he and his students sought to explain deviation in "the zone of transition," in urban areas with diverse cultures and racial categories.[11] In *Culture Conflict and Crime*, Thorsten Sellin explained blue-collar crime as an understandable response to cultural conflicts faced by second generation immigrants. However, Parsons has generalized the problem of role conflict from the migration phenomenon (contacts between systems) to that of role-conflict inherent within complex, differentiated social systems. Deviation, according to Parsons, is generated by incompatible role demands, either through competition between roles for given persons or through divergent demands within the same role. In either case, deviant behavior is said to result from individually felt *strain* (disturbance or frustration of legitimate expectations) that develops from the practical necessity of satisfying incongruous social cues.[12]

FOCAL PROBLEMS IN SOCIAL DEVIATION

The phenomena of social deviation have been variously labeled (and pursued) as "social problems," "social pathology," and "social disorganization." Understandably, the practical and empirical aspects have received an overwhelming amount of attention. Yet the previously mentioned theorists contributed a theoretical base that focuses essentially on two problems:

1. What are the crucial structural (organizational, cultural) conditions that provide differential opportunities for deviant behavior in general, and/or specific types of deviance?
2. What social, cultural, and psychological conditions create and sustain motivations for deviation?

[11] Robert E. Park *et al.*, eds., *The City* (Chicago: University of Chicago Press, 1925), chs. 5, 6, 9; Everett V. Stonequist, *The Marginal Man* (New York: Charles Scribner's Sons, 1937); Pauline V. Young, *The Pilgrims of Russian-Town* (Chicago: University of Chicago Press, 1932); Frederic M. Thrasher, *The Gang* (Chicago: University of Chicago Press, 1927); Harvey Zorbaugh, *The Gold Coast and the Slum* (Chicago: University of Chicago Press, 1929).

[12] Talcott Parsons, *The Social System* (New York: Free Press, 1951), pp. 280–283.

With the advantage of hindsight, we can briefly note that a third theoretical problem was *not* clearly identified by this referential group of theorists. This problem concerns the way(s) in which chance or motivated deviance is reinforced or rewarded by patterned social contacts with other deviants and/or approved groups.

The major emphasis in research and theory has been on "problem" deviation—that is, deviant behavior that is widely disapproved and can be interpreted as interfering both with prevailing organizational patterns and welfare and with responsible processes of change. Thus, deviations intended to enrich or improve some social structure (creative innovations) are excluded from our discussion. But since a considerable variety of problem deviation still remains, some ordering of these phenomena is necessary to manage and evaluate the theoretical vitality of the past two or three decades. I would suggest a distinction between (*a*) deviant behavior that is available and can be learned by individuals or groups with little difficulty (such as many crimes, some vices, and alcoholism) and (*b*) deviant behavior that represents *individual response patterns* to perceived social pressures that cannot be managed by approved types of behavior (such as suicide, and most mental disorders or disturbances).

In the remainder of this chapter, theoretical developments in each of the three problem areas will be summarized in terms of (*a*) the kinds of deviance to be explained and (*b*) the conditions that underlie either the origins or the repetition of deviant behavior.

THEORIES OF STRUCTURAL OPPORTUNITY
AND SOCIAL PRESSURES

In the case of deviations classified as type *a* above, "opportunity" is probably more relevant than "pressure," since these kinds of behavior initially seem to involve some choice in the practice of deviant acts as provided by available models. On the other hand, type *b* deviation may be analyzed in its initial stages as resulting from "pressures" in the sense that the deviant is unable to follow normal patterns or finds no feasible alternative to deviance.

Ecological patterns

Ecologically oriented investigations and theories have been largely concerned with "opportunity" for deviance (e.g., personal and property crimes, vice), though the ecological method has also been applied to such phenomena as mental disorders and family problems. Ecological theory—as distinct from description and classification—generally attributes deviation either to concentration of deviant models in specific areas or neighborhoods or to socially patterned frustrations that lead to compensatory use of deviant models.[13] The difficulty in this kind of theory is its vagueness and its failure to account for non-deviant patterns in "vulnerable" areas.

Differential association

This classic theory, as developed by Sutherland, Cressey, Glaser, and others, seeks to specify conditions in which type *a* deviation occurs by treating deviance as a social learning problem. Essentially, Sutherland and his followers start from the empirical fact that most persons are exposed to normal and deviant models. Consequently, it is hypothesized that early patterns of deviance are acquired as a result of *preponderant* exposure to deviant models—either from acknowledged deviants or from implicit deviant clues furnished by otherwise normal actors.[14] Unfortunately, the theory of differential association fails to supply the conditions under which the distribution of deviant and normal influences operates and under which persons identify, interpret, and weigh the relative significance of competing models. However, Sutherland's analysis

[13] Robert E. L. Faris and H. Warren Dunham, *Mental Disorders in Urban Areas* (Chicago: University of Chicago Press, 1938); Bernard Lander, *Toward an Understanding of Juvenile Delinquency* (New York: Columbia University Press, 1954); Austin L. Porterfield, "Suicide and Crime in Folk and in Secular Society," *American Journal of Sociology*, LVII (January, 1952), pp. 331–338.

[14] Edwin A. Sutherland, *The Sutherland Papers*, Albert Cohen, Alfred Lindesmith, and Karl Schuessler, eds. (Bloomington: Indiana University Press, 1956). See also *Social Problems*, VIII (Summer, 1960), especially the papers by Cressey, Glaser, and Short.

of "white-collar crime" reveals that initially "honest" persons do learn deviant patterns from associates; [15] but this is explained by a theory of *social reinforcement* (which will be discussed later).

Status and deviation

Probably the most extensive and fruitful—though controversial —theory of opportunity-pressure is the *social class* and *subcultural theory* (in various forms). Significantly, this approach has been used to explain both type *a* and type *b* deviation, and so it merits particularly close attention. Theories of this type assert that specific social categories, by virtue of their relative status and internal characteristics, are implicitly or explicitly prevented from achieving either what is generally valued in society or even the special aims of the social category itself. Furthermore, each category develops a defensive or compensatory structure of deviance that is informally but effectively available to members of that category. In addition, if appropriate deviant models are not available or are unsuccessfully tried, then a second order of "pressures" toward deviance are said to occur (i.e., type *b*).

The dominant formulation of this approach has centered around the structural vulnerability of significant segments of lower-class urban families.[16] As Cohen, Merton, Miller, Cloward and Ohlin, and S. M. Miller have argued, the lower class has developed a cultural system that clearly offers delinquent values to juveniles and an accompanying pressure to enact these values through gang activities. True, Cohen theorizes that the delinquent subculture is a response to "frustrated" middle-class ideals, while Miller counters by asserting that lower-class culture is inherently and distinctively oriented to behavior disapproved by the larger community—e.g.,

15 Edwin A. Sutherland, *White Collar Crime* (Holt, Rinehart & Winston, 1949).

16 Albert K. Cohen, *Delinquent Boys* (New York: Free Press, 1955); Walter B. Miller, "Lower Class Culture as a Generating Milieu of Gang Delinquency," *Journal of Social Issues*, XIV (1958), pp. 5–19; S. M. Miller and Frank Riessman, "The Working-Class Subculture: A New View," *Social Problems*, IX (Summer, 1961), pp. 86–97; Richard A. Cloward and Lloyd E. Ohlin, *Delinquency and Opportunity* (New York: Free Press, 1960); Gilbert Geis, *Juvenile Gangs* (Washington: President's Committee on Juvenile Delinquency and Youth Crime, June, 1965).

getting into trouble, emphasizing physical strength, expediency and duplicity, aggressive independence. But the genesis of lower-class exposure to deviant models is here less important than the fact of exposure itself.

Two structural explanations of lower-class deviation are specially relevant and derive implicitly from Durkheim. One theory locates the opportunity as well as the pressure for deviance in the disorganized or ineffectively organized matriarchal lower-class family—such as is found among lower-class Negroes, unemployed or casually employed lower-class whites, and some categories of rural–urban migrants. Children under these circumstances, it is hypothesized, cannot be effectively socialized within the family (particularly in large families) and therefore gravitate to the only available functional alternative—the neighborhood gang. But as Cloward and Ohlin have pointed out,[17] gangs are differentiated in terms of subcategories of lower-class families: delinquent or stealing gangs, prestige or conflict gangs, social gangs, and retreatist (often narcotic) gangs.

The second explanation of lower-class deviation is the structural isolation of lower-class families from significant institutional structures of the community and society. This is largely a consequence of technological changes, the centralization of government and its bureaucratic extensions, and the increasing segregation of urban areas by status, education, and occupation.

As illustrations of the first structural explanation, let us briefly review the work of Reiss and of Hollingshead and his associates. In a perceptive analysis of delinquents, Reiss distinguished three psychosocial types.[18] The "relatively integrated delinquent" comes from a stable lower-class family that de-emphasizes formal education and encourages getting a regular job quite early. This sort of adolescent is usually oriented to available gangs in the area and thus engages in intermittent burglaries and car thefts. In this type, subtle economic pressures result in exposure of psychologi-

[17] Cloward and Ohlin, *op. cit.*, pp. 20–27, 174–182. See also Lewis Yablonsky, *The Violent Gang* (New York: Macmillan, 1962).

[18] Albert J. Reiss, "Social Correlates of Psychological Types of Delinquency," *American Sociological Review*, XVII (December, 1952), pp. 710–718.

cally healthy boys to deviant models. A second type, called "the defective superego delinquent," comes from a similar neighborhood, but from a disorganized family (divorce, separation, desertion, or death) that lacks conventional morals and, understandably, adequate methods of socialization and control of its children. Unloved and uncared for, this type exhibits psychopathic tendencies, is a relatively constant gang participant, and constitutes the greatest source of recidivism. But the lower class does not monopolize pressures for deviance, as Reiss' third type, "the weak ego delinquent," demonstrates. These youngsters come from geographically mobile middle-class families that are marked by parental hostility and conflict. The weak ego type is plagued by insecurity, low self-esteem, and internal conflicts; he therefore cannot abide peer groups or gangs, but becomes an aggressive lone offender—untutored in deviance and consequently easily apprehended.

Turning now to mental disorders, Hollingshead and others have shown that schizophrenia tends to be concentrated in lower-status families. Studies in New Haven, Chicago, and San Juan, Puerto Rico, support this with varying kinds of research designs.[19] An adequate explanation of schizophrenia is not yet available, but it has been suggested that (apart from the genetic and biochemical aspects) schizophrenics characteristically (a) develop a weak self-image, (b) find it difficult to communicate their self-criticism to significant others, and (c) consequently insulate themselves from persons. It seems likely that the position and associated limitations of lower-class persons not only creates a high probability of a, but the absence of approved, satisfying supports in lower-class settings intensifies b and c.

However, the second structural explanation helps in understanding the well-established connection between violent crime (homicide, assaults, etc.) and lower-class persons. Porterfield's studies

[19] Faris and Dunham, op. cit.; A. B. Hollingshead and Fritz Redlich, Social Class and Mental Illness (New York: Wiley, 1958); Lloyd H. Rogler and A. B. Hollingshead, Trapped: Families and Schizophrenia (New York: Wiley, 1965); John A. Clausen, "Mental Disorders," in Robert K. Merton and Robert A. Nisbet, eds., Contemporary Social Problems (New York: Harcourt, Brace & World, 1961), pp. 161–165. See also the recent evidence and theoretical formulation of H. Warren Dunham, Community and Schizophrenia (Detroit: Wayne State University Press, 1965).

seem to show that specific indicators and aspects of lower-class status are significantly related to high crime rates. These are high geographic mobility, low economic status, high density of small religious affiliations (mainly fundamentalistic), rural background, non-white. Together, these constitute "depressed folk" status, which graphically refers to a category that is marginal, bereft of economic and cultural opportunities, and in local competition with other marginals.[20] According to Porterfield, crime is an expressive reaction to an undesirable and unexplainable isolation—but a reaction made feasible by the opportunities afforded by dense population concentrations.

But we should not ignore the existence and explanation of deviation in *middle classes* in terms of characteristic pressures and opportunities. Empirically, middle-class persons are more likely to "select" suicide, "white collar crime," psychosomatic maladies, and mental disturbances that permit (but do not enhance) social participation. Theoretical clues to this patterning of deviation are few and more plausible than demonstrable at this point. Nonetheless, it has been suggested that middle-class status involves continuous pressure for achievement, an emphasis on personal skills and manipulation rather than on direct action or violence, a greater range of available facilities and experiences (as compared with lower classes), and a greater sensitivity to small or limited failures. Subtly "permitted" forms of deviation, therefore, would be expected to be generally non-violent, often turned inward, and reflective of discrepancies between high aspirations and actual achievement levels.

Thus, the middle-class delinquent, according to Reiss,[21] shows neurotic tendencies that reflect considerable introspection and inadequacy. Note that these youngsters shun organized gangs and their successful violence; instead, they engage in destruction of property (not personal assaults) and show great hostility to authority—in a sufficiently amateurish way to "invite" apprehension. Likewise, the middle-class adult criminal specializes in acts of misrepresentation, embezzlement, and the like.[22] Finally, as several writers have demonstrated, there is a consistent correlation be-

---

[20] Porterfield, *op. cit.* [21] Reiss, *op. cit.*, pp. 716–718.

[22] Sutherland, *White Collar Crime;* Donald R. Cressey, *Other People's Money* (New York: Free Press, 1953).

tween suicide rates and middle- and high-status categories. Henry and Short, following Durkheim, hypothesize that higher status categories are subject to fewer restraints or controls than those in subordinate statuses. Furthermore, higher status categories tend to share less responsibility with others; hence, if failure occurs, others cannot be blamed and the burden of guilt falls on the individual.[23]

Status inconsistency

In recent years, a crucial but implicit notion in Weber's approach to the complexities of stratification has been rediscovered and applied to political phenomena and deviant behavior. This notion, variously called status incompatibility, status disequilibrium, or status inconsistency, refers to practical and perceived discrepancies between a person's location in two simultaneous status scales (occupational, income, educational, ethnic, etc.). Essentially, status inconsistency confronts actors with competing demands, unclear social ties, and consequently personal disquietude. The resultant frustration, it is assumed, makes possible symptoms of stress (e.g., psychosomatic disorders, anxiety feelings, loss of sleep) and suicidal tendencies.[24] It is becoming clear that different types of status inconsistency are associated with different behavioral products. For example, Jackson finds physiological response to stress among those with high racial–ethnic status and low occupational or educational status. Recently, Gibbs and Martin explored the relation between suicide rates and various combinations of status inconsistencies. Discrimination of dominant patterns of inconsistency is not yet possible from their studies, though Breed has indirectly attempted to do so through the inconsistencies of occupational mobility.[25]

[23] Andrew F. Henry and James F. Short, Jr., *Suicide and Homicide* (New York: Free Press, 1954), pp. 56–58, 101–103.

[24] Elton F. Jackson, "Status Consistency and Symptoms of Stress," *American Sociological Review*, XXVII (August, 1962), pp. 469–480; Elton F. Jackson and Peter J. Burke, "Status and Symptoms of Stress: Addition and Interaction of Effects," *ibid.*, XXX (August, 1965), pp. 556–564.

[25] Jack P. Gibbs and Walter T. Martin, *Status Integration and Suicide* (Eugene: University of Oregon Press, 1964); Warren Breed, "Occupational Mobility and Suicide," *American Sociological Review*, XXVIII (April, 1963), pp. 179–188.

Occupational mobility: upward or downward?

A closely related attempt to discover differential pressures toward deviation emphasizes the significance of vertical occupational mobility.[26] It has been assumed, more or less explicitly, that mobility is accompanied by weakened social ties and uncertainties in role-playing. Downward mobility ("skidding") seems to be connected with suicide, though the significance of downward mobility varies by occupational level. For example, Breed found in a New Orleans sample that skidding was more prevalent in lower status suicide categories than in white-collar and professional cases of suicide.[27] On the other hand, several studies purport to establish a connection between upward mobility (social climbing) and psychosomatic disorders. Obversely, as Wilensky has intriguingly suggested, orderly work careers (defined as steady upward mobility) are reflected in a greater range of social and community involvements and perceived responsibilities than those with disorderly or inconsistent work histories.[28]

At present, we must await more adequate data on the relation between vertical mobility and deviation. The probable joint effects of mobility pattern and referential status position (e. g., upwardly mobile middle class and upwardly mobile lower class) require considerably more theoretical analysis on at least two points. First, which combinations of mobility and status provide the greatest opportunity or pressure toward deviation? And second, which of these is reliably connected with specific kinds of deviance (suicide, alcoholism, mental disorders, etc.)?

[26] See Robert J. Kleiner and Seymour Parker, "Goal-Striving, Social Status, and Mental Disorder: A Research Review," *American Sociological Review*, XXVIII (April, 1963), pp. 189–203; Lee N. Robins, *Deviant Children Grown Up* (Baltimore: Williams and Wilkins, 1963).

[27] Breed, *op. cit.*; Bruno Bettelheim and Morris Janowitz, *The Dynamics of Prejudice* (New York: Harper & Row, 1950).

[28] Hollingshead and Redlich, *op. cit.*; Harold L. Wilensky and Hugh Edwards, "The Skidder: Ideological Adjustments of Downward Mobile Workers," *American Sociological Review*, XXIV (April, 1959), pp. 215–231; Harold L. Wilensky, "Orderly Careers and Social Participation: The Impact of Work History on Social Integration in the Middle Mass," *ibid.*, XXVI (August, 1961), pp. 521–539.

The structural opportunities or pressures discussed above share two important features. First, these conditions reduce or remove the availability of meaningful, practicable, approved norms. But they permit rather than stimulate deviant behavior. Second, none of these conditions provides clear-cut *motivational clues* to participants as to how they should interpret and respond to such pressures or opportunities. Consequently, deviant behavior that is correlated with any of these factors may be accidental, exploratory, imitative, or intrinsically meaningful to the deviants. Responsible theories of deviation must therefore determine the presence and genesis of appropriate motivational patterns, as well as the ways in which (*a*) unmotivated deviance becomes motivated and (*b*) motivated deviance receives meaningful confirmation.

MOTIVATIONAL THEORIES

Motivations are notoriously difficult to study, but this does not prevent social scientists from hypothesizing specific motivations and their effective production of behavior—particularly deviant behavior. In general, two or three quite contradictory theories of deviant motivation have been pursued, though it is by no means clear that we must ultimately choose only one.

Estrangement or alienation

Essentially, this kind of theory derives from Marx, but has been broadened to include estrangement from any significant social group. In modern usage, alienation is presumed to be a result (or concomitant) of actual or perceived frustration. Individuals who become alienated respond to their frustration by interpreting other aspects of their experience as negative or below acceptable levels. And this interpretation provides the conscious or unconscious justification for personal or socially available deviant forms. Alienation theory, therefore, posits an intermediate process of *rejecting a known reference group*. This is, for example, the motivational key to Cohen's theory of lower-class delinquency, for which Landis and others have furnished some contributory evidence.[29]

However, the relevance of alienation to other types of deviation is more dubious. Sommer and Hall found less alienation, proportionately, among a sample of newly admitted mental patients than among long-term patients and an unselected population. Hollingshead's study of Puerto Rican families and mental illness similarly fails to support the theory of alienation. Indeed, several studies of alcoholism, drug addiction, and vice seem to suggest that alienation is a *consequence* of deviant behavior.[30]

Anomia

Ever since Durkheim's analysis of suicide and Merton's conceptualization of the disjunction of approved ends and legitimated means, anomic motivations have been freely used as explanatory devices for deviance. The anomic response (anomia in the individual, with anomie being the situation that prompts the response) is based on perceptions of incoherence and meaninglessness in significant aspects of social experience. From this perception arise feelings of impotence and fatalism, which presumably motivate erratic, drifting, and "care-less" behavior—some of which is necessarily deviant.[31] Suicidal intentions, mental disorders, alcoholism, and

[29] Cohen, *op. cit.*; Judson R. Landis and Frank R. Scarpitti, "Perceptions Regarding Value Orientation and Legitimate Opportunity: Delinquents and Non-Delinquents," *Social Forces*, XLIV (September, 1965), pp. 83–91; William F. Whyte, *Street Corner Society* (Chicago: University of Chicago Press, 1943).

[30] Robert Sommer and Robert Hall, "Alienation and Mental Illness," *American Sociological Review*, XXIII (August, 1958), pp. 418–420; Rogler and Hollingshead, *op. cit.*; Edwin M. Schnur, *Crimes Without Victims* (Englewood Cliffs: Prentice-Hall, 1965); Howard Becker, *Outsiders* (New York: Free Press, 1963).

Seeman made a worthy but somewhat unsuccessful attempt to specify five different meanings or aspects of alienation. In my opinion, only two of these (powerlessness and isolation) are relevant. Meaninglessness and normlessness both refer to *anomie*, which will be discussed shortly; while self-estrangement seems to be a very complex derivative condition whose motivational thrust remains unclear. Melvin Seeman, "On the Meaning of Alienation," *American Sociological Review*, XXIV (December, 1959), pp. 783–791.

[31] Marshall B. Clinard, ed., *Anomie and Deviant Behavior* (New York: Free Press, 1964); David Bordua, "Juvenile Delinquency and Anomie: An Attempt at Replication," *Social Problems*, VI (Winter, 1958–59), pp. 230–237.

drug addiction seem to provide substantial illustrations of such motivational patterns,[32] though it is not yet clear that anomia is a decisive preparatory phase of these forms of deviation.

Status concerns

The thwarted desire for status (i. e., appreciation of one's qualities by significant others) is a widespread theme in American society. Theoretically, persons in low-status positions, or in ambiguous status positions, would be specially sensitive to real or assumed deficiencies in their evaluation by others. Consequently, such persons would be expected to search for experiences that would enhance status. Most of the discussion of this point has dealt with delinquency and crime, particularly among low-status adolescents and lower-middle-class adults.[33] For example, gang delinquency (including offenses as serious as murder) has been shown to be a mechanism for acquiring and maintaining prestige or "rep." However, status anxiety seems to be connected only with relatively aggressive forms of deviance; it has not been identified with suicide, mental disorder, vice, alcoholism, or drug addiction. The status motive, parenthetically, is quite antagonistic to the anomic motive. The latter suggests negativistic or succumbing orientations, while status concern—somewhat similar to alienation—suggests a more positive, active attempt to overcome personal–social difficulties.

Self-concept

In the face of various deviant models (which are sufficiently widespread to be noted and to require some evaluation), the way

[32] Isidor Chein et al., The Road to H: Narcotics, Delinquency, and Social Policy (New York: Basic Books, 1964), pp. 27–28, 143–154; Edwin S. Shneidman and Norman L. Farberow, eds., Clues to Suicide (New York: Blakiston, 1957); Rogler and Hollingshead, op. cit.; Elwin H. Powell, "Occupational Status and Suicide: Toward a Redefinition of Anomie," American Sociological Review, XXIII (April, 1958), pp. 131–139.

[33] Harry M. Shulman, Juvenile Delinquency in American Society (New York: Harper & Row, 1961), chs. 8, 9, 18; James F. Short, Jr., and Fred L. Strodtbeck, Group Process and Gang Delinquency (Chicago: University of Chicago Press, 1965), pp. 179–180, 250–251.

the exposed "normal" responds to available deviance is a crucial theoretical problem. Reckless and his associates at Ohio State University attempt to answer this question by hypothesizing the "insulating effect" of a socially approved self-concept—one that is based on internalizing dominant middle-class morals and on the feeling that one's value is derived from conformity to these learned limitations. But how does a "favorable" self-concept operate? Reckless assumes and partly demonstrates that the normal self-concept motivates boys to isolate themselves from deviant friends and acquaintances.[34] By inference then, "correct socialization" supplies personal values and motives that cannot be satisfied by public deviation. In other words, if a person defines himself as normal (in the sense of identifying with legal and widely accepted moral norms), then his behavior tends to be normal. On the other hand, if he defines himself as deviant (troubled, or heading for trouble), then he is more likely to seek deviant paths.

Obviously, this kind of theoretical link is applicable only to deviation that is learned from definite sources and models (i.e., skilled crimes, most vices). It cannot be used in the case of personally devised (though socially conditioned) kinds of deviation (such as suicide, mental disorders, and possibly alcoholism).

Rationalization–neutralization theory

In recognition of the fact that much of the deviant's behavior is "normal," it has been suggested that deviants require "justification" of a special kind for their deviant acts. (Note that this does not deal with motivation for deviance, but with complex additions to the motivation for deviance.) The argument behind this suggestion needs specification, however. It is assumed that much deviance is really either an overabundance of, or inappropriate performance of, an otherwise acceptable (if not totally approved) behavior pat-

[34] Walter C. Reckless, Simon Dinitz, and Ellen Murray, "Self Concept as an Insulator Against Delinquency," *American Sociological Review*, XXI (December, 1956), pp. 744–745; Walter C. Reckless *et al.*, "The Self Component in Potential Delinquents and Potential Non-Delinquents," *ibid.*, XXII (October, 1957), pp. 566–570. See also Michael Schwartz and Sandra S. Tangri, "Note on Self-Concept as an Insulator Against Delinquency," *ibid.*, XXX (December, 1965), pp. 922–926.

tern. It is further assumed that the difference between normal and deviant behavior is magnified by custodians of the normal. Consequently, while the motivation for practicing deviation is similar to that of normals practicing normal behavior, deviants feel required to dissipate self-blame by justifying the recourse to deviant actions.[35]

Drift, exploration, curiosity, accident

Closely related to the foregoing theory is one that locates the source of deviation in unpredictable contacts between persons and structured deviant opportunities. Briefly, it is asserted that deviation is not motivated by needs for personal adjustment to perceived difficulties, but initially derives from chance encounters or "impulse" trial of deviance.[36] This has been applied to delinquency, alcoholism, and drug addiction. Under these circumstances, deviation is superficial and without much significance to the person, since it satisfies no insistent need.

In summary then, motivational theories of deviation fall into two types—those that view deviation as a response to socially located problems of personal adjustment and those that attribute initial deviation to "normal," unproblematic motives.

SOCIAL REINFORCEMENT

With the obvious exception of suicide, deviant behavior is truly social behavior—that is, it directly or indirectly affects other persons who in turn respond in patterned ways to the deviant. As

[35] Gresham M. Sykes and David Matza, "Techniques of Neutralization: A Theory of Delinquency," *American Sociological Review*, XXII (December, 1957), pp. 664–670; David Matza and Gresham M. Sykes, "Juvenile Delinquency and Subterranean Values," *ibid.*, XXVI (October, 1961), pp. 712–719.

[36] David Matza, *Delinquency and Drift* (New York: Wiley, 1964); Chein, *op. cit.*, pp. 12ff.; Howard S. Becker, "Marihuana Use and Social Control," in Arnold M. Rose, ed., *Human Behavior and Social Processes* (Boston: Houghton Mifflin, 1962), pp. 589–607; Thomas J. Scheff, *Being Mentally Ill* (Chicago: Aldine, 1966), pp. 34–54.

Znaniecki perceptively remarked on several occasions,[37] social action is based on tendencies (attitudes) that may undergo modification in the course of action and social response to action. In the case of deviants, the *repetition* of deviant acts is not automatic, but is itself a problem for analysis. It may not be legitimately assumed that deviance is intrinsically satisfying to the deviant. Indeed, we have considerable evidence of persons who are repelled by their deviance and of persons who ultimately discard deviant acts.

In some forms of deviation (delinquency, white collar crimes, prostitution), deviant behavior is encouraged and rewarded by significant individuals or groups (subcultures or contracultures).[38] Those who learn to depend on unapproved sources of approval because approved sources are unavailable or ineffective thereby acquire *new* or *magnified* motives for deviation. This confirms an important insight of Thomas and Znaniecki and others: social problems and deviant behavior reflect considerable organization rather than disorganization. Continued deviance, then, represents the effective functioning of "deviant" social controls.

A second type of social reinforcement emanates from orthodox, respectable channels. It has been asserted, with some evidence, that official labeling of persons as deviants isolates them from normal contacts and alters their self-image.[39] Deviant "behavior" is thus converted into a deviant "role." It has been further asserted that designating persons as specific types of deviants (drunks, juvenile delinquents, criminals, homosexuals) forces them into more frequent contacts with accomplished deviants. Thus, opportunities to learn deviant skills, motives, and justifications presumably multiply.

A third form of reinforcement is rather subtle. Perhaps we can call it the "gray belt of structured disinterest." The deviant who

[37] Florian Znaniecki, *Social Actions* (New York: Farrar and Rinehart, 1936), ch. 3; Florian Znaniecki, *Cultural Sciences* (Urbana: University of Illinois Press, 1952), ch. 7.

[38] Schwartz and Tangri, *op. cit.*, p. 926.

[39] Scheff, *op. cit.*; Schnur, *op. cit.*; Becker, *Outsiders*, pp. 9-14, 31-37; John I. Kitsuse, "Societal Reaction to Deviant Behavior," in Howard S. Becker, ed., *The Other Side* (New York: Free Press, 1964), pp. 87-102.

has not yet internalized or become totally involved in a deviant role "normally" experiments with approved practices or values—e.g., the criminal may try a legitimate job, the neurotic may attempt decisive actions, the promiscuous may temporarily develop a focal attachment. If these attempts fail to remove his underlying motive for repeated deviations, he comes to a critical point in the deviant process. Briefly, this involves the search for, or the effective availability of, approved alternatives to old "normal" models and deviant roles. When these alternatives are absent or limited (e.g., satisfying work or work associates, civic activities, etc.), we can expect resumption of the schizophrenic symptoms, chronic alcoholism, compulsive gambling, suicidal fantasies, "meaningless" depredations on strangers or public buildings, or whatever form the deviance takes.[40] In short, deviation may be implicitly confirmed by the parsimonious organization of the community, which "normally" caters to the extremes of acceptability and certified deviation, but tends to ignore the rarely articulate needs of the "transitional" or "marginal."

BASIC PROCESSES IN DEVIATION

Despite some inconsistencies, gaps in evidence, and the special characteristics of each type of deviant behavior, let us try to reconstruct the theoretical scaffold that shakes, but still stands, in the emerging explanation of "problem" deviation. Fundamentally, sociologists are developing a theoretical system that treats deviation as a set of processes that raise or lower the probabilities of *continued deviation* in a given population.

Exploratory deviance

The first link in the theoretical chain asserts the necessary causal significance of social experiences that provide either (*a*) clearly defined deviant models or (*b*) barriers to exposure or internalization of "approved" values and actions. Either *a* or *b* creates initial prob-

[40] Cloward and Ohlin, *op. cit.*, pp. 178–182; Chein, *op. cit.*, pp. 175, 192.

abilities of "trial" performance of deviant acts or of personal improvisations toward deviance (e.g., seclusion, unpredictable choice of accepted forms of behavior). At this point, it is premature to speak of "deviant motivations," since the evaluation of deviant acts by "deviants" themselves is not yet achieved.

Early feedback for deviance

Trial is followed by processes that determine the relative "isolation" of "potential deviants" from "normal" structures. In the absence of counteractive agencies, the probability of continued deviation increases. From scattered theoretical and empirical clues, the lack of counteractive controls may be viewed as (*a*) the absence of definite sanctions actually applied to specific deviant acts, (*b*) the ineffective or inconsistent application of such sanctions, or (*c*) the initial reinforcing effect of rewards from other deviants. An appropriate self-image (which clearly implies that normal models somehow were effectively learned, despite cultural and physical obstacles) operates as an "integrative" component, which tends to *reduce* the probability of repeated deviance by maintaining "normal" social contacts and minimizing deviant ones. Though the evidence is not yet definitive, it may well be that the social experiences that produce either a confident or a weak self-image ultimately determine the consequences of positive, negative, or non-existent sanctions.

Deviant motivation and reinforcement

From experiences in the latter phase, potential deviants acquire somewhat more explicit (and verbalized) motivations for deviant acts. But this is not yet the adoption of a deviant *role*. Internalization of a deviant role (consisting of deviant skills, recognized risks and appropriate methods of evasion, expected responses from other deviants, and predictable reactions from "normals") is a consequence of two interlocking experiences—learned gratifications from deviant acts themselves (the thrill of stealing and not being caught, the alleged euphoria of drugs, the presumed confidence that accompanies a few stiff drinks) and the implicitly "legitimating" effect of being labeled and treated as a specific type of deviant (either by official agents or by the network of informal, frequent associations).

Institutionalized deviance

The reciprocal effect of isolation from legitimate channels and motivation for continued deviance—the vicious circle of problem deviation—is a key theoretical point, one that is not limited to mental disorders or familiar forms of criminality, but perhaps is applicable to all forms of deviation. But the practical (and theoretically intriguing) consequence is that the deviant person (progressively insulated from most or all approved social groups) comes to achieve a *competitive form of integration.* At this point, persons playing deviant roles are satisfied by their isolation or, if the deviant role is not satisfying, it is perceived as more satisfying (or less punishing) than return to the doubly problematical normal social patterns. In short, when a deviant role is internalized, the deviant cannot or will not surrender his deviant advantages. His self-feelings are perceived to reach their highest level in the deviant role (deviant role addiction) and in contacts with relevant deviant circles.

Now it is certainly true that very substantial proportions of a population have practiced occasional or even repeated deviant acts, but yet lead relatively normal lives—and are defined as normal. How does this theoretical approach explain the phenomena of "part-time" or "discarded" deviation? It will be recalled that repeated, personally meaningful deviation is a probabilistic part of interaction processes. Some persons apparently learn deviant models inefficiently or develop inadequate and therefore unrewarding (and socially unrewarded) levels of skills at specific deviant forms. Others who experiment with deviation *before they are defined as deviants* find that deviation is morally offensive or demeaning, or that it simply does not provide satisfactions commensurate with the accompanying social risks. Still others apparently use deviation as *catharsis;* a few interludes of deviation (robbery, excessive liquor consumption) seem to dissipate growing tensions—if one is not caught or otherwise humiliated by others. Furthermore, in some cases, deviant acts (however satisfying) are found to interfere with or jeopardize other "normal" and highly valued social satisfactions (e.g., pride in one's work, devotion to family). In all these instances, some ties with approved channels are retained and the social isolation of a deviant role is thereby forestalled.

At this point, it might be well to consider a fairly recent problem in the theory of deviation: to what extent (and by what mechanisms) is there *succession* or *substitution* of deviant forms for given categories of deviants? This is based on the notion that continued deviant behavior represents conscious or unconscious attempts to obtain satisfactions (or reduced punishments) that are not possible by normal routes. However, salutary effects of any deviant form are themselves problematical: failure, disappointment, inadequate "deviant" skills may prove as threatening as normal, approved behavior patterns. Consequently, we may expect some evidence of additional experimentation with deviation on the part of "double failures" (i.e., in both normal roles and in some type of deviation). Cloward and Ohlin [41] present some evidence, for example, of teenage drug addicts who have turned to heroin after unrewarding attempts at gang delinquencies. Chein, on the other hand, found no such pattern in his study of teenage addicts in New York City.

It may be hypothesized, then, that in the pool of deviant behavior types, some forms are *functional alternatives* for one or more other forms. But the theoretical problem of deviant functional alternatives yields two distinct issues: (*a*) What characteristics of given deviation types help to account for their sequential practice by deviants? (*b*) Given this functional similarity, what processes explain the *prior* choice of one deviant form over its functional alternatives?

MAJOR DEVIANT FORMS

Fundamentally, the various forms of problem deviation are viewed as interrelated structures made possible (and perhaps im-

[41] Cloward and Ohlin, *op. cit.*, pp. 179–184. Cf. Chein, *op. cit.*, pp. 143–154, 186–192.

plicitly sustained) by a highly differentiated, changeful socio-cultural system. Durkheim, in effect, demonstrated the social production of deviation, but he was not primarily interested in the potentially meaningful relations between forms of deviance. From the preceding review of theorizing, however, it is possible to reconceptualize deviation in terms of three types.

Maladapted deviance

These persons are unable to acquire a deviant role, either from an available deviant model or through personal experimentation. Obviously, we are referring only to persons who perceive pressures and frustrations that cannot be handled through normal forms of adjustment (physical recreation, more focused work, more appropriate levels of aspiration). The prime example is suicide (completed and seriously attempted), which may be objectively defined as a deviant act "designed" to obviate the need for further deviation.

Insulated deviance

This type of deviant has developed a full-fledged and relatively self-contained deviant role, to which he is firmly wedded, if not addicted. Indeed, this form of deviation is extremely resistant to other, more "rational" forms of satisfaction. Furthermore, such deviance does not require the support of other deviants or deviant structures. It is, therefore, most removed from the "real world" of normalcy and from other deviant forms. Chronic alcoholism, most psychoses, and some drug addictions may be plausibly located in this category.

Deviant role in a congenial subculture

These deviants, unlike the preceding types, have acquired a specific pattern of deviant behavior whose practice is rewarded, or at least protected, by some independent but disapproved subsystem of the community or society—gang, vice ring, syndicate, "gay society," etc. Consequently, whatever the ultimate sources of deviant motivation, regular deviant behavior is constantly reinforced by segregated social contacts and membership. Some examples are gang delinquents, homosexuals, compulsive gamblers, prostitutes, some drug addicts, and "hate-mongers."

If we may assume that these types form a rough descending scale of seriousness (or of relative difficulty in resurrecting normal behavior patterns), then the two theoretical problems mentioned above (p. 283) can be translated into a single crucial question: what factors, pressures, experiences, etc., account for each of the following types of "deviant career"?

1. Settlement in a deviant subculture.
2. Initial subcultural deviance, followed by insulated deviance.
3. Settlement in insulated deviance.
4. Initial insulated deviance, followed by suicide.
5. "Short-circuiting" of deviance to suicide.
6. While other "career combinations" are logically possible, they are either improbable or, at this point, theoretically meaningless.

Major theoretical clues to this problem seem to center on two sets of factors—(*a*) the relative amount of perceived "pressure," frustration, inconsistency, as interpreted by some category of deviants, and (*b*) the perceived availability and utility of normal and deviant alternatives. In very broad and tentative terms, but in line with the emerging tradition of deviation theory, we may hypothesize that the greater the perceived pressure, the more likely the immersion in the suicidal form. (See Table 10.)

Similarly, we may hypothesize that the greater the perceived availability and utility of normal roles or specific deviant roles, the greater the adoption of deviant subcultural roles as compared with insulated deviance. On the other hand, we must recognize that perceived availability is colored by past ingrained attitudes toward components of deviant roles (physical aggressiveness, for example). Consequently, availability must be further subdivided into deviant roles for which previous socialization provides *no* bars, as opposed

PERCEIVED PRESSURE

TABLE 10. Hypothetical distribution of suicide rates by level of perceived pressure.

AVAILABILITY OF NORMAL ROLES

TABLE 11. Hypothetical distribution of deviant roles by differences in availability of normal roles and socialization types.

to those for which meaningful moral prohibitions present decisive obstacles to acceptance by the potential deviant. (See Table 11.)

There is little logical or empirical basis for considering "deviant careers" as reversible, i.e., moving from deviance in a subculture to insulated deviance. In the other, more meaningful direction, movement from one level to the next may be provisionally "explained" by the same two factors (*a* and *b*), with a needed modification of *a*—or supplying a third factor, if necessary. Let us interpret failure at level 2 as "added pressure" or significant increments to original frustration. Then, we may hypothesize that "movement" from level to level is directly related to added pressures and inversely related to the availability of functional alternatives at the same level. (See Table 12.)

	General satisfaction	Frustration, but alternatives available	Frustration, no functional alternatives
Movement in deviant sequence			X
Persistence of deviant type	X		

TABLE 12. Hypothetical distribution of deviant careers by success or failure in deviant roles and presence of alternatives.

Sociological theories of problem deviation exemplify the classic theoretical emphases on social structure and the interdependence of formal and informal subsystems. From such theorists as Marx, Durkheim, Sorokin, MacIver, and Parsons, we have derived the basic notion of "normal" social constraints and the social mechanisms by which persons develop and sustain minimum conformity. But the theoretical necessity of considering differential response to social constraints—as proposed by Durkheim, Thomas, and Znaniecki—provided the crucial underpinning of deviation theory. From this base, it has been possible to analyze the production of *exploratory* and *organized* deviant structures, as well as the complex social components of motivation that help to explain the mobility and stability of sets of persons in deviant systems. The old complaint—that the study of social problems and social disorganization is chaotic—is no longer justified. While there are certainly some dubious points in the applicability of this approach to all kinds of problem deviation, the pioneer formulations, as specified by the vigorous theorizing of the last twenty years or so, constitute a theoretical core that has withstood criticism and the hygienic test of multifarious data.

SELECTED REFERENCES

Clinard, Marshall B., ed., *Anomie and Deviant Behavior* (New York: Free Press, 1964).

Cloward, Richard A., and Lloyd E. Ohlin, *Delinquency and Opportunity* (New York: Free Press, 1960).

Cohen, Albert K., *Deviance and Control* (Englewood Cliffs: Prentice-Hall, 1966).

Henry, Andrew F., and James F. Short, Jr., *Suicide and Homicide* (New York: Free Press, 1954).

LaPiere, Richard T., *A Theory of Social Control* (New York: McGraw-Hill, 1954).

13

Sociology
of Knowledge, Opinion,
and Mass Communication

Within the boundaries of American sociology, it is difficult to find a problem area viewed with more ambivalence than is directed toward the sociology of knowledge. For some, it seems to be an exotic preciosity reserved for the "upper reaches" of sociology, an intellectual plaything for the philosophically inclined in the fraternity of sociologists. To others, the sociology of knowledge implies an alien orientation peripheral to the accepted pattern of investigation and characterized by lack of precision and inevitable bias. In contrast, there is an incipient bloc among American sociologists who approach this new specialism as a logical and necessary application of a basic sociological viewpoint—i.e., the study of concrete social and cultural phenomena in the context of definable social environments. But so powerful is the first attitude that neither the aims nor the researches of the sociology of knowledge have attracted more than intermittent interest on the part of most practitioners of sociology. In fact, few works in general sociology and virtually no introductory textbooks ever refer to the distinctive problems that constitute the domain of the sociology of knowledge.

There is, nevertheless, a significant body of theoretical and empirical work in the sociology of knowledge that must be recognized as a promising introduction to a potentially expanding sociological area. Hence the compound title of this chapter. Moreover, despite the misapprehension of critics, the literature is not a repetitious pile of sociological embroidery; it is rather the reflection of self-critical sociologists whose forays in the sociology of knowledge have produced a radical awakening in methodological sophistication and conceptual clarification.

WHAT IS THE SOCIOLOGY OF KNOWLEDGE?

As several sympathetic observers and practitioners have noted, the problems pursued by sociologists of knowledge have been so extensive, and the definitions of "knowledge" so heterogeneous, that their focus is not easily appreciated. Merton has even distinguished a "European" and an "American" version, which appear to have quite different but complementary emphases in selection of research problems and empirical data. It might well be asserted, too, that the label "sociology of knowledge" is more confusing than instructive. Yet we might best describe this area in terms of two components—(1) a *core* of basic questions, problems, and objectives (the major orientation of the sociology of knowledge); and (2) a quite fluid *periphery* of specific theoretical problems, techniques, and marginal studies that may be interpreted as clarifications and extensions of the core. And to the extent that these parts can be realistically distinguished, they tend to correspond, respectively, to the "European" and "American" versions of the sociology of knowledge.

Essentially, the sociology of knowledge rests on a limited number of premises and observations:

1. Complex societies are composed of empirically different roles and statuses that are filled by definable sets of persons.
2. Each role or status (or social position) entails a set of experiences, opportunities, limitations, etc., that are more or less accurately perceived by its incumbents.
3. Over time, many social positions develop interrelated cues, norms, attitudes by which members learn to perceive in a selective fashion the social behavior of persons in other roles and statuses.
4. Consequently, the same events or social processes tend to be perceived and evaluated in notably divergent ways by persons in different social positions.

The sociology of knowledge, therefore, is primarily applicable to social systems of minimal internal differentiation. A mass society, in which most participants share the same position, the same experiences, and the same conceptual equipment for social perception and evaluation, is plainly inappropriate for this theoretical orientation. In addition, the sociology of knowledge assumes a basic incompatibility of differing positions and their respective social perceptions. Consequently, social categories can be expected to engage in "ideological" disputes (conflicts) and in attempts to influence changes in the perceptions and behavior of other social positions.

THE CORE

The basic theoretical problem in the sociology of knowledge is: how do the objective positional features (opportunities, limitations, skills, etc.) of a social category help to account for its distinctive, patterned orientations toward events outside its normal role responsibilities? For example, are there discernible differences in political choices between occupations that can be attributed to implicit biases in each occupational setting? To what extent are *recency* of mobility and *amount* of mobility helpful in understanding differences in prejudice and discrimination against a minority group? Or, working from the standpoint of *exploring* sources of cultural products, what are the primary positional sources of support for the "radical right," for anti-fluoridation attitudes, for SNCC, as against the NAACP or the SCLC?

The core is composed of a limited set of methodological and theoretical problems.[1]

Identification of some organized system of thought

The first task of the sociologist of knowledge is to construct from the verbal and social behavior of relevant individuals and groups the underlying premises, values, objectives, interests, and meanings that give coherence to the specific behavior patterns of that group or category. A particularly perplexing problem, however, relates to the delimitation of "thought" appropriate to the sociologist of knowledge. Both "thought" and "knowledge" are admittedly broad categories, whose study in one or more respects legitimately belongs to philosophy, law, art, etc. But there is evidence of a specialized concern that stresses the analysis of the *perception and significance of facts* for individuals and groups. In other words, the sociology of knowledge selects as its "dependent variable" notions of "truth," things as they are or appear to be to given persons—not primarily notions of what ought to be (imperatives), or the emotional reactions to reality. Essentially, then, the sociology of knowledge deals with group or categorical interpretations of reality—or more popularly, with *ideologies*.

Identification of appropriate groups

The most elementary knowledge of human beings indicates that all socialized persons acquire ideologies as the price of socialized existence. But most people lack the time or the inclination to develop some organized pattern that integrates a number of seemingly diverse or discrete attitudes and ideas about contemporary events. Consequently, the sociology of knowledge has largely analyzed the ideologies of "professional" purveyors of knowledge—intellectuals

[1] Robert K. Merton, *Social Theory and Social Structure* (New York: Free Press, rev. ed., 1957), pp. 460–484.

and articulate elites.[2] Since these individuals and groups are like-wise important in the creation and development of ideologies, focus on their activities thereby contributes a certain economy to ideological analysis.

The problem of imputation

The mere identification of some relatively integrated ideology is an important but quite preliminary achievement. If, as is often the case, an ideology is analyzed from the expressions and behavior of articulate individuals, it is obviously necessary to discover the *range of influence* enjoyed by such a constellation of central ideas. Clearly, the sociological significance of ideologies rests ultimately on their diffusion, acceptance, and practice by definable groups— processes that are of tremendous theoretical import since they aid in illuminating the career of ideologies. But when an ideology is thus located as a "property" of some grouping or category, in what sense may this ascription be justified as shedding light either on the ideology or the grouping? Here we face the critical problem of *imputation*—the necessity of demonstrating that the connection is neither fortuitous nor arbitrary, but rather represents some genuine relation between the nature of the group and the character or content of the ideology. As a consequence, the sociologist of knowledge must satisfactorily meet two conditions: (*a*) he must explain *differential* acceptance of an ideology, i.e., why some groups and not others think primarily in terms of a given perspective; and (*b*) he must also account for shared acceptance by groups that apparently possess significant differences in their respective social characteristics.

Analysis of the "social position" of designated groupings

Perhaps the most fundamental premise in the sociology of knowledge is its distinctive answer to the problems of imputation.

[2] Karl Mannheim, *Ideology and Utopia* (New York: Harcourt, Brace, 1936, Harvest Books); Gerard L. DeGré, *Society and Ideology* (New York: Columbia University Bookstore, 1943); Werner Stark, *The Sociology of Knowledge* (London: Routledge & Kegan Paul, 1958).

Sociologists of knowledge assume a *causal* connection between an ideology and specific aspects of the group to which it is ascribed; and both collection of data and mode of analysis are employed to demonstrate as plausibly as possible that a particular ideology derives from the peculiar experiences and problems of that group. This search for sociological sources of ideology demands a detailed analysis of the "social position" of a group, its functions and status with respect to other groups and to the overall social structure. In practice, such an analysis has focused on a few presumably relevant aspects, namely those that help to uncover critical differences between groups, such as social class position, generational differences, differentials in power and influence, differential pressures on given social roles, rural–urban differences, and specific occupational differences.[3]

The connective process between social position and ideology

An early tendency seemed to imply a more or less mechanical, deterministic connection between social position and a "resultant" thought-system. In fact, a semi-mystical element in such an approach undoubtedly antagonized other sociologists, who have been suspicious of sweeping analyses for which the underlying facts are grudgingly set forth not as "proof" but as illustration. Therefore, this deficiency has been raised to the level of explicit concern. Generally, one (or both) of two "solutions" recurs in the literature. (*a*) In accord with developments in social psychology, sociologists increasingly admit the significance of active individuals and their *selective* interpretation of objective conditions. (*b*) The alternative method of connecting group positions with ideological systems is considerably more indirect, inferential, and subject to error. It consists of carefully contrived evaluations of the *manifest and latent functions* subserved by particular ideologies in the operation of identifiable groups. In effect, a high degree of correspondence is

[3] Mannheim, *op. cit.*, chs. 2, 4; Karl Mannheim, *Man and Society in an Age of Reconstruction* (New York: Harcourt, Brace, 1940), pp. 98–106, 342–344; P. A. Sorokin and Carle C. Zimmerman, *Principles of Rural-Urban Sociology* (New York: Holt, 1929), Pt. 4; Robert Blauner, *Alienation and Freedom* (Chicago: University of Chicago Press, 1964).

sought between the problems peculiar to the social position of a group and the direction of practical solutions implicit in the ideology created or accepted by that group. Thus, if a group is demonstrably losing a great measure of its former power and influence, and clearly resents the social consequences of its declining social prestige, that group's creation or acceptance of an ideology that, in practice, tends to restore superior status may be considered a substantiation of the connective process and a justification of the accuracy of imputation.

The problem of "false consciousness"

Implicit in the preceding statement of problems is the notion of *rationality* in social behavior, an assumption that is frequently contradicted by undeniable facts. It is often thought that individuals are constantly aware of their interest and are capable of selecting expedient means for realizing their objectives. If this faculty is denied to some persons, it must certainly be evident in the behavior of elites and "intellectuals." But every age yields one or more examples of groups with thought-systems that fail to reflect their social position and even operate to the detriment of their supporters. Here lie the critical phenomena of "false consciousness," which Marx and Engels recognized so well and named so provocatively. The explanation of false consciousness (ideologies inappropriate to the social position of specific groups) offers the severest challenge to sociologists of knowledge, for it seems to undermine the most basic idea of this specialty. As we shall see later (pp. 331–333), some recent developments seem to promise substantial solutions to this problem.

CONTRASTING ORIENTATIONS: SOROKIN AND MANNHEIM

These core problems are largely an importation into American sociology of a continental sociological tradition, traceable most signally to the writings of Marx and Engels. Perhaps two men can be credited with its introduction to American sociology—Sorokin and Mannheim.

As we have seen in Chapter 7, Sorokin analyzed total societies (not delimited groups) in terms of characteristically dominant cultural themes or premises that embody perspectives about the nature of reality, how reality may be apprehended, etc. Thus he distinguished the ideational, idealistic, and sensate ideal types. Furthermore, in his *Social and Cultural Dynamics,* Sorokin tried to demonstrate that fluctuation in the emphases of art, architecture, religion, political organization, etc., have been logically related to changes in basic cultural premises. But instead of regarding these sources as groups and group processes, which is the realm of sociological study, Sorokin has taken the "idealist" position by assigning to *underlying ideas* the status of "independent variables." While this is in general agreement with the European origins of the sociology of knowledge, it disregards two very perplexing but significant questions. How do these cultural premises arise and change? And why do such changes develop? The answers require an extended holiday from philosophical analyses and some sort of empirical investigation of the units of society—i.e., of social groups and categories.

Mannheim's studies in the sociology of knowledge introduced an emphasis on empirical investigation, though his techniques were not well developed according to more recent standards. But Mannheim's concern for analysis of limited groupings was guided by a conceptual and theoretical orientation that markedly differs from Sorokin's approach. For Mannheim, thought-systems reflect the peculiar perspectives of specific groups (classes, sects, generations), which in turn are derived from group interests and purposes, from the will to change or maintain the social position of a group, and from the underlying social structure of the group. Following this putative connection between the nature of a group and the system of central ideas imputed to it, Mannheim distinguished two ideal types of thought-system—ideologies and utopias.[4]

The former refer to habits of thinking (and their behavioral products) that, prodded by the desire to maintain a given social po-

[4] Mannheim, *Ideology and Utopia,* ch. 4.

314

sition and to repel potentially disruptive changes, tend to interpret reality in accord with those desires. Utopias, on the other hand, involve ideational systems that envisage some active attempt to effect desirable alterations in a group's social position. These thought-systems consequently interpret reality in such a way as to minimize those objective aspects that conflict with group desires. At another point, however, Mannheim employs a pragmatic criterion for distinguishing ideologies and utopias: the extent of their realization in a proximate future. Thus, if they fail, thought-systems are merely ideologies, "distorted representations of a social order." Should they succeed, they are classified as utopias, "realistic distortions." Apparently then, Mannheim has extended the concept of "false consciousness" in such a way as to include all perspectivist systems, recognizing that false consciousness does not necessarily prevent their successful implementation. Only the "unattached intellectual," it seems, is capable of thought-systems that take account of the more representative aspects of reality. Since this variety of intellectual constitutes an ideal type as well, false consciousness is perhaps attenuated rather than obliterated.

Unlike his predecessors in the sociology of knowledge, Mannheim contributed a brief but important analysis of the method that properly defines the perspective of any individual or group. In common with such men as Weber, Simmel, Scheler, Sorokin, Cooley, and Znaniecki, he stressed the importance of *Verstehen*, or sympathetic introspection, in explaining the reactions of groups to their milieus. This requires not only identification of relevant ideas, but the discovery of their meaning for the groups concerned. The way is left invitingly open for quantitative analysis, but only as an auxiliary tool. The heart of the investigation is a careful qualitative content analysis on the following issues: (*a*) What practical and theoretical concepts are used by a group, and what meaning do they possess for the members? (*b*) What is the central attitude that gives coherence to particularized concepts used by the group? (*c*) Which potentially relevant concepts are absent or are soft-pedaled? (*d*) What ideas are taken for granted and remain unstated, perhaps as unwitting, unchallenged assumptions? (e) How vague or specific are the most frequently used concepts and how is this related to the objectives of the group? (*f*) What concepts are designed to compete with rival thought-systems—the counter-concept? (*g*) What changes occur in the conceptual repertory of a group in relation to significant social and cultural changes in their environment? [5]

SELECTED STUDIES ON THEORETICAL ISSUES

During the past twenty-five years or so, a number of studies have employed the orientation of the sociology of knowledge—often without using the term. These investigations have focused on social classes, professions, scientific bodies, political parties, the military, labor and managerial groups, and racial or nationality minorities. Of particular interest, since they strike so close to home, are analyses of the perspectives of American sociologists. Kurt Wolff, for example, has contributed a tentative analysis that perhaps organizes suspicions rather than demonstrable facts. Without presenting any evidence of a quantitative sort, he seems to identify among American sociologists of the thirties and forties a certain acquiescence toward the *status quo,* which appears in the fields of race relations, social pathology, and cultural sociology. In addition, he notes a possible relation between this attitude and the selection of research problems, specifically pointing to the relative absence of studies on power in American society and to a disinterest in problems of "spiritual man" and "spiritual suffering." [6]

With considerably more focus, Mills prepared an ideological analysis of a number of popular textbooks in social disorganization, social problems, and social pathology.[7] A number of recurrent, interrelated themes were found that apparently underlie the choice of problems and the way in which they have been defined. Most apparent was an implicit normative orientation to social problems,

[5] *Ibid.,* pp. 306–309.
[6] Kurt H. Wolff, "Toward A Sociocultural Interpretation of American Sociology," *American Sociological Review,* XI (October, 1946), pp. 545–553.
[7] C. Wright Mills, "The Professional Ideology of Social Pathologists," *American Journal of Sociology,* XLIX (September, 1943), pp. 165–180.

in which the criteria of judgment seemed to derive from emphasis on primary groups, community welfare, and rural mores. As these texts viewed social change, it appeared as a bothersome intrusion on existing social affairs; adjustment to such change, however, was consistently approached in terms of the present social order, so that failure to achieve such adjustment was not deemed exploratory or "pioneering" but "pathological." Indeed, the extremely popular concept of "cultural lag" was, according to Mills, employed primarily as a label for such failure to restore an already defined social equilibrium. Mills has also provided some material on the social background of social pathologists, which must, however, be considered an introduction to the problem of imputation.

When the research focus shifts from ideological analysis to questions of imputation, a considerable gain in potential explanation may be noted. A particularly intriguing case in point is the analysis of the groups in Germany that either accepted or rejected Nazi ideology before World War II. Heberle, a son-in-law of Toennies, concentrated his investigations on the province of Schleswig-Holstein, for which he prepared two complementary analyses—(1) the voting distribution in specific elections for three subregions and (2) a series of economic, demographic, and social studies of these three areas.[8]

The western *coastal marshes* were characterized by fertile soil, specialized agricultural production for export markets (dairy products), large farming units with relatively few hired hands, and a highly stratified social structure. Since dairy farming does not impose heavy regular work on farm owners, they also dabbled in commercial enterprises, law practice, and political life in moderate-sized villages and towns. On the eastern coast, a *hill zone* was composed of large estates, tenant farmers, and a series of interspersed communities of small farmer-owners. In this area, soils suitable for grain production were the basis of comparatively prosperous communities, which also manifested a high degree of religious interest. By contrast, the middle zone—the *sandy Geest*—was a relatively

[8] Rudolph Heberle, *From Democracy to Nazism* (Baton Rouge: Louisiana State University Press, 1945).

poor area of peasant freeholders in dairying and poultry enterprises. The Geest was dotted with small peasant villages in which, traditionally, social pressures were well organized.

In correlating voting results with these socio-geographic divisions, Heberle discovered rather clear patterns. The conservative parties (the so-called "middle" parties) derived their support from the landowners, the prosperous farmers, and the bourgeoisie—in other words, the areas of the coastal marshes. Leftist parties (the Social Democrats and later the Communists) drew most successfully from the landless agricultural workers and urban laborers of the hill and marsh areas. The rural and urban middle classes of the hill and Geest sections, however, became warm adherents of the Nazi party. In fact, the smaller the village, the larger the voting majority for the Nazis. As Heberle sifted his data, the acceptance of Nazism seemed to be related to two aspects of social position. The rural middle classes, particularly in the smaller villages, were unable to maintain a cherished community solidarity in the face of war and severe depression. Their naive political experience impelled adherence to the party that promised both economic renewal and return to village solidarity. Furthermore, in communities that lacked political leadership (e.g., the Geest and parts of the hill zone) and "party tradition," the new parties entered the political vacuum with increasing success.

A similar study by Loomis and Beegle [9] for selected rural areas of northern and southern Germany bolsters the validity of Heberle's results by statistical correlations between voting distributions and a number of relevant indices. By correlating the Nazi vote for specific areas and election years with such variables as socio-economic class, size of farm, religious affiliation, proportion of non-voters, etc., they were able to substantiate the imputation of Nazism to definable groups. As a result, the bulk of Nazi adherents in the areas studied can be identified by the following characteristics: (a) they comprise elements of the rural middle class most subject to economic insecurity and anxiety accompanying loss of social solidarity; (b) groups with limited experience and obliga-

[9] Charles P. Loomis and J. Allan Beegle, "The Spread of German Nazism in Rural Areas," *American Sociological Review*, XI (December, 1946), pp. 724–734.

tions as active members of large-scale political or religious organizations were specially prone to Nazism; and (c) somewhat less clearly, groups with folk-like traditions, with longings for the good old days before the depression, seem to have flocked to the Nazi banner.

Studies of middle classes and their perspectives were much in fashion in the late thirties and forties, but their interest for us is their more or less conscious use of the orientation of the sociology of knowledge. In general, these studies tended to focus on tensions deriving from the "exposed" social position of middle-status categories. More important, and incidentally more difficult to analyze, is the appearance in such groupings of confused perspectives—reflecting perhaps gross instabilities in status and growing incongruence between older thought-systems (liberalism, progress, etc.) and the continuing reconstruction of modern political and economic systems.[10] Mills' study of "middle classes in middle-sized cities" during World War II confirms the psychologically uncomfortable position of middle classes and, in addition, through intensive interviews, locates strands of a middle-class perspective with great clarity. Small businessmen, for example, maintained an ideational identification with big-business decisions, plus their acceptance of a general notion of "business enterprise." This was clearly demonstrated in resentful attitudes toward labor; but at the same time, small businessmen reflected the difficult position of small enterprise in their ambivalence toward the government—impatience with regulations and restrictions, yet "pleas for economic aid and political comfort."[11]

White-collar workers, whom Mills found to be relatively leaderless and unorganized, as well as quite heterogeneous in terms of social origins and income, occupied a somewhat unique position in the American middle classes. Clerks, salespeople, foremen, and salaried professionals were, as a group, more exposed to the realities of social and economic power than the small businessmen (who

[10] Gerard L. DeGré, "Ideology and Class Consciousness in the Middle Class," *Social Forces*, XXIX (December, 1950), pp. 173–179.

[11] C. Wright Mills, "The Middle Classes in Middle-Sized Cities," *American Sociological Review*, XI (October, 1946), pp. 520–529.

had the partial solace of business and trade organizations). Furthermore, the white-collar grouping was assigned roles and statuses that, in terms of skills, income, property, and power, are subject to uncomfortably accurate identification (by others) with laboring groups. The perspective of white-collar people reflected a search for a cheap but unique distinction from "wage workers." Mills discovered four meaningful themes in this perspective: (1) the conception of white-collar occupations as "educational" experiences in which people learn about human nature; (2) a feeling of reflected prestige, either from the customer or the product sold to the customer; (3) a sense of personalized power in influencing the customer's appearance or home; and (4) the notion of *service* rendered as an apparent psychological substitute for limited salaries.[12]

Critics of the sociology of knowledge tended to assess analyses such as these as factually illustrated intuitions, as prepared juxtapositions of dubiously related conditions. It is certainly true that many attempts at linking group perspectives with social backgrounds rely unduly on assertion, and often neglect consideration of crucial gaps in data. These are not inherent properties of the sociology of knowledge, but defects in research design. In line with this general criticism, it has been suggested that a rough approximation to the experimental approach might be salutary, particularly if one could analyze the perspectives of "control" and "experimental" groups.

The author therefore selected a group that could be shown to have undergone a significant alteration in perspective over a definite period, with a complementary concern for changes in social position that could be related to revised thought-systems. A particularly dramatic instance was found in the experience of the American farmer as reflected in the emergence and dominance of the Farm Bloc and representative farm organizations during the period between world wars.[13] As a matter of fact, a rather sharp shift in both ideology and social position could be traced from approxi-

12 C. Wright Mills, *White Collar* (New York: Oxford University Press, 1951; Galaxy Books, 1956), pp. 172–178.
13 Alvin Boskoff, "Agrarian Ideology and the Farm Bloc," unpublished Master's Thesis in Sociology, Columbia University, 1948.

mately the Civil War, so that the preceding century (the Agrarian Century) could be viewed as a *control period* or base point, from which situational changes and ideological manifestations might be "measured." An intensive historical review clearly demonstrated the political and economic dominance of rural America, with, however, some instances in which nascent industrialism and commercial enterprise presented grave but manageable challenges to agricultural security. Corresponding to this situation was an agrarian temper marked by optimism, a belief in progress, the pressure for geographic expansionism, and a de-emphasis on centralized government.

But the Civil War and its aftermath reduced the American farmer to an uncomfortable dependency. Free virgin lands, the pride and sanctuary of an expanding agriculture, were becoming scarce in the seventies; the railroads and the corporations were gaining strength in the arena of economic decision; the growing mechanization of agriculture, a wartime expedient, heightened rural debts; the increase in land values prompted increasing crop specialization, disturbing the relative self-sufficiency of farm units; and perhaps for the first time since the republic was formed, the party system was found to be controlled by merchants, bankers, and manufacturers. From the chagrin and disappointment born in the Reconstruction period there grew a defensive orientation among farmers that emphasized the notion of an agricultural-industrial balance, a self-conscious comparison of rural and urban fortunes that was to blossom into the ideology of "parity" following World War I. Agrarian thought consequently seemed to be, in Mannheim's terms, neither an ideology nor a utopia; but, with its emphasis on a receding past, it might be called a *retrospective ideology*.

However, it was discovered that the social position of farmers was far from uniform, that such variables as crop, size of farm, income, and identification with non-agricultural groups (e.g., big business and labor unions) tended to create differential social positions within agriculture and crystallized an ideological Agricultural Schism. This split appeared between the smaller, family-sized farmers producing wheat and range livestock, and the larger, big-business oriented farmers in corn, hogs, cotton, and dairy products. The Farmers Union representing the first and the Farm Bureau the latter agricultural faction were then studied for possible significant differences in origins, policies, and underlying objectives. Apparently, as the second group came to stand out more sharply from the traditional core of agriculture, it developed ideas more and more akin to those of the industrial world. The result was a genuine divergence in outlook between the Farmers Union and the Farm Bureau on such major questions as farm production policies, farm income and prices, agricultural welfare, relations with the rest of American society, and international policies.

THEORIES OF IDEOLOGICAL TRANSMISSION

The traditional core, as exemplified in the studies described above, suffered from two serious deficiencies that impeded the potential development of this theoretical node in sociology. First, as a consequence of concern with historical phenomena (recorded in documents, literary productions, voting tabulations, etc.), it was possible to construct only a qualitative correlation between a social category and some definable "product" (perspective, ideology, etc.). Second, and closely related, the broad theoretical orientation of the pioneer theorists did not receive adequate translation into more specific theoretical concerns—primarily for determining the "mechanics," the intermediary processes, of these correlations. In short, to return to the simple fourfold table on page 4, the core perspective was unsuited for explaining either the predicted patterns in cells 1 and 4 or the deviations from predicted patterns in cells 2 and 3.

But let us re-examine the implicit points in analysis that derive from the core perspective. Essentially, these studies posit the role of an elite or leadership category, which creates or sifts perceptions that are "appropriate" to a social position. However, the practice of an idea-system by non-elites in a given social position indicates processes of *successful transmission* from elites to members of that category. Few if any studies in the sociology of knowledge accept the premise of spontaneous generation of perspectives among social categories. In addition, it has been assumed that the targets of such elites are immune to other—perhaps competing—ideas and perspectives. The fundamental problem, therefore, may be expressed in two related parts: (1) What are the social conditions that sustain insulation from incongruent perspectives? (2) Given conditions of adequate exposure to conflicting perspectives, what factors account for either successful or inefficient propagation of specific values in specific time periods?

Answers to these questions have been implicitly available in two forms—(1) the seminal theories and related investigations of a few sociological theorists and (2) a mass of studies since World War II, which were designed for quite different objectives. With respect to the first source, a substantial basis for pursuing such questions has long been available in American sociology and social psychology—particularly in the works of Mead, Baldwin, Cooley, Park, Thomas, and Znaniecki. It is interesting to note, too, that Arthur Child, a philosopher who had been extremely interested in the methodology of the sociology of knowledge, saw immense explanatory possibilities in the social psychology of attitude formation.[14] But perhaps Mills, Znaniecki, and Merton provided the major links with our modern approach.

Seeking a concept of the individual mind that "incorporates social processes as intrinsic to mental operations," Mills applied Mead's analysis of the "self" and the "generalized other" to the problem of connective mechanisms.[15] In essence, the experience of socialized individuals (in this case, intellectuals and molders of thought) is regarded as a subtle interplay or "conversation" between the individual and significant actors. The latter, in effect, function as an "internalized audience" composed not of persons, but of their attitudes on some issue of mutual interest. Thus the self

[14] Arthur Child, "The Existential Determination of Thought," *Ethics*, LII (January, 1942), pp. 153–185; Child, "The Problem of Imputation in the Sociology of Knowledge," *ibid.*, LI (January, 1941), pp. 200–219; Child, "The Theoretical Possibility of the Sociology of Knowledge," *ibid.*, LI (July, 1941), pp. 392–418.

[15] C. Wright Mills, "Language, Logic, and Culture," *American Sociological Review*, IV (October, 1939), pp. 670–680; Mills, "Methodological Consequences of the Sociology of Knowledge," *American Journal of Sociology*, XLVI (November, 1940), pp. 316–330; Mills, "Situated Actions and Vocabularies of Motive," *American Sociological Review*, V (December, 1940), pp. 904–913. These also can be found in *Power, Politics and People: The Collected Essays of C. Wright Mills*, Irving L. Horowitz, ed. (New York: Oxford University Press, 1963).

develops orientations in thought and behavior that arise from interaction mediated by meanings and from a language that is their vehicle. Since many persons may be exposed to similar contacts and attitudes, a series of parallel perspectives among individuals may be found to arise in a substantially credible manner.

Znaniecki, it will be recalled from Chapter 3, developed a conceptual scheme that specified the elements of this process even more clearly. Basic to his approach is the recognition of the individual as a series of distinctive role patterns, each of which is performed with reference to a *social circle*, which evaluates both the role and the performer by assigning a definite social status more or less appropriate to the function fulfilled by the role. In this way, thought-systems or perspectives may of course be viewed as resultants of social interaction; yet this scheme presents complexities that help clarify the nature of connective mechanisms. Implicit in this analysis are the needs or interests of the social circle as interpreted by key members—which constitute some initial perspective. A social role relevant to this circle, however, is ordinarily affected by, but not necessarily determined by, the needs of the circle. In addition, each role possesses a certain acceptable latitude that in practice may reflect, extend, or even distort the perspective of the circle. Similarly, the personal characteristics of the actor may assert themselves in differential emphasis on role, status, or circle, thus further complicating the nature of the connective process. Finally, the intrusion and competition of other social circles must be regarded as a potential factor in the derivation of perspectives.

Since Znaniecki's formulation, ideological analysis and imputation have assumed a more empirical character by focusing on the publics or social circles relevant to given perspectives. Most often, this involves investigation of the interplay between specific social circles and the social role of some intellectual category. One of the earliest, careful works of this type (which barely antedated Znaniecki's version) is Merton's search for the origins of the modern acclaim of scientific procedure in the physical sciences.[16] Fol-

[16] Robert K. Merton, "Science, Technology and Society in Seventeenth Century England," *Osiris*, IV, Pt. 2 (1938), pp. 360–597. Also available with the same title (New York: Howard Fertig, 1967).

lowing the implications of Weber's correlation between aspects of Protestantism and the basic spirit of modern capitalism, Merton traced the development of the Protestant Ethic in England toward the formation of specific "scientific" groups, most notably the Royal Society. The implicit utilitarianism, rationalism, and empiricism of Protestantism were the foundations of such derived social circles; and from these orientations grew the approved research patterns in various branches of physics in the seventeenth century. As Merton tabulated the types of research, he found an unusual emphasis on utility—in the economically crucial areas of transport and navigation—which was in response to the wider commercial publics of Protestant England.

A few years later, Mills applied the same orientation to an understanding of the great pragmatic philosophers—Peirce, James, and Dewey.[17] Starting with a lengthy analysis of the professionalization of American academic life, Mills demonstrated the emergence of "scientific" publics in higher education, with their emphasis on training, skepticism, empirical research, and demonstration. Peirce's pragmatism, minutely analyzed with respect to leading concepts, is interpreted as a reflection of Peirce's exclusion from the circle of academic philosophy and his devotion to a select circle of scientists and the scientifically inclined—the Hyperion Club. Dewey's pragmatism, which was less abstruse and more concerned with educational and social problems, on the other hand, is for Mills a running conversation with a philosophically "starved" teachers' public, whose members operate in a changing educational situation (i.e., mass education) that stresses practicality and are, in most cases, ascending the class scale, and reflect a continuous emphasis on "success." Pragmatism, by inference, is construed as a thought-system created by "attached" intellectuals for American publics directly concerned with demonstrable, practical interests.

In the same manner, the peculiar perspective of the intellectual as bureaucrat has been greatly clarified by reference to the interac-

17 C. Wright Mills, "A Sociological Account of Pragmatism," unpublished dissertation in Sociology, University of Wisconsin, 1942. Now available as *Sociology and Pragmatism: The Higher Learning in America* (New York: Paine-Whitman, 1964; Galaxy Books, 1966).

tion between the social role of the intellectual and the social circle of public administrators at the federal level.[18] Focusing on intellectuals in the social-science field, Merton notes some difficulties in their role in government—a certain indeterminacy in their findings, removal from the protective aura and prestige of a professional society or university, the annoying belief on the part of their superiors that they too qualify as experts in human affairs. For the intellectuals who aspire to be more than social technicians, these difficulties are magnified by the demands of the larger bureaucratic structure. Essentially, these require that (a) the intellectual accommodate himself to the policies of bureaucratic leaders; (b) specific factual information rather than policy suggestions be presented; (c) in general, his entrance into the decision-making process be late and consequently shorn of discretionary powers; and (d) under the "pressure for action," "practical" compromises with intellectual principles became routine and even justifiable. The inevitable result is either flight from bureaucracy or the development of an implicit partisan thought-structure alien to the free, nonresponsible perspectives of the "unattached" intellectual.

THEORETICAL CONTRIBUTIONS OF INFLUENCE RESEARCH

Perhaps these interpretations of the core were inherently limited in their ability to revitalize the basic thrust of the sociology of knowledge without aid from other sources. Implicitly however, the core concerns of the "traditional" sociology of knowledge have been extended, specified, and to some extent redirected by the enormous body of investigations and partial crystallizations in the areas of mass communications, social influence and propaganda, advertising and "motivational research," and voting behavior.[19] By focusing on publics, audiences, constituencies—rather than on

18 Merton, *Social Theory and Social Structure*, ch. 7.
19 See for example such collections as Bernard Berelson and Morris Janowitz, eds., *Reader in Public Opinion and Communication* (New York: Free Press, 1966); Daniel Katz *et al.*, eds., *Public Opinion and Propaganda* (New York: Holt, Rinehart & Winston, 1954); Reo M. Christensen and Robert O. McWilliams, eds., *Voice of the People* (New York: McGraw-Hill, 1962).

elites or intellectuals alone—these fields have furnished unanticipated supplements to the core, both in data and in formulation of
important substantive problems.

Perhaps the most obvious and yet insufficiently noted "discovery" in studies of influential communication is a general lack of
harmony or logic in the values, attitudes, and judgments of social
categories (in terms of occupation, religious affiliation, etc.).[20]
This should not be surprising, since many people are normally exposed to a variety of influences and most people are simply not
trained in (or do not show any serious interest in) developing congruent sets of ideas and values from their experiences. Several theoretical solutions to this ideological potpourri may be suggested.
First, following clues from Mannheim, modern society has tended
to "produce" relatively ineffectual elites, who cannot inspire sustained confidence in their publics. Second, it has been repeatedly
asserted (without much serious contradiction) that Americans are
largely uncongenial to organized, doctrinaire appeals of an abstract
sort (cf. *The End of Ideology*).[21] Third, the lack of consistent
ideological viewpoints may be explainable by the routine phenomenon of segregating or insulating accepted ideas from one another.
In short, persons tend to avoid the necessity of critical evaluation
by the expedients of relatively indiscriminate acceptance and of
ignoring the logical and/or practical discrepancies between and
among goals, values, and opinions.

Studies in mass communication and influence processes have
been most significant, for present purposes, in specifying key
aspects of the communication processes linking elites and definable
social categories.

Characteristics of the "target" social categories

The basic generalization, to which most studies contribute, is an
implicit resistance or an independence of publics—in contrast to

[20] V. O. Key, *Public Opinion and American Democracy* (New York: Alfred
A. Knopf, 1961), ch. 3.
[21] Daniel Bell, *The End of Ideology* (New York: Free Press, 1960); Daniel
Boorstin, *The Genius of American Politics* (Chicago: University of Chicago Press,
1953).

the prevailing image of "mass man" and "brainwashing." But this generalization requires concern for the factors that explain both resistance and acquiescence or acceptance. Apparently, the crucial variable is *degree of interest* in the problem or situation to which an ideology refers (e.g., interest in government, or the formal educational system, or minority rights).[22] Interest level seems to find expression in three types of selectivity—*selective exposure* (availing oneself of sources only if these fall within the range of interest), *selective perception* (attention to those aspects of communication that are congruent with one's pre-existing views), and *selective retention* (longer recall, and therefore greater opportunity for impact on the receiver, of portions of communication that are congenial to members of a public).

The implications of these patterns for the sociology of knowledge are in part corroboratory, in part disquieting. They suggest, on the one hand, that elites can successfully transmit an ideological position if their audience is already aware of and minimally concerned about a "public" issue or if the elite acts to generate awareness and concern in preparation for an attempt to influence values and attitudes. But, on the other hand, it is quite clear that persuasive communication by elites is primarily successful as a *reinforcement* of pre-existing values—rather than as a means of *conversion*.[23] Obviously, then, the sociology of knowledge must seek to explain how—independent of a communicating elite—a given value perspective arises in a specific category or public.

A tentative theoretical solution to this problem—at least in part —is that definite value perspectives (as distinct from either vagrant and unsure fragments of opinions or fitful awareness of relevant issues) minimally require high and sustained interest and communication *within* a public.[24] The generation of interest, however, seems to be dependent upon amount of formal education and the perceived problematic consequences of social experiences that characterize some significant social category. In the latter case, implicit

[22] Joseph T. Klapper, *The Effects of Mass Communication* (New York: Free Press, 1960), pp. 72–97.

[23] *Ibid.*, pp. 15–19.   [24] Key, *op. cit.*, chs. 4, 9, 11.

values are found to be either threatened or inapplicable; in short, interest is aroused by crisis—which now shifts our theoretical concern from the characteristics of social categories to aspects of "issues."

Crucial aspects of the "content" of influence: issues and media

Much of the research in social influence has been focused on limited or fractionated attitudes and on relatively short time periods; hence, much of the findings are peripheral to the core interest of the sociology of knowledge. However, the principal findings appear to support two theoretically relevant conclusions. First, with respect to issues, the effectiveness of communications seems to be greater in cases of *new issues*, presumably in part because the message suffers from no preconceived attitudes or values in the target public. It seems likely, in addition, that when new issues are also perceived as *crises*, the level of interest rises and serves as a supplement to the monopolistic advantage of the message.[25] However, successful retention (internalization) of a perspective in this situation depends on the actuality or perception of a continued crisis.

Second, concerning the role of the various media of communication, the evidence is rather consistent in demonstrating the limited power of all mass media as promoters of new or altered values and attitudes among readers, viewers, or listeners.[26] Apparently, mass media are primarily effective either in confirming existing attitudes, or in imparting information.

Purveyors of influence: elites, peers, and personal influence

The independent thinker, the person who makes up his own mind, has been found to be a mythical creature. More accurately, values and perspectives among adults are largely and most effectively disseminated by personal, informal interaction. Normally, strategic persons act as links between *sources of values* (e.g., intellectual elites, specific media of communication) and meaningful seg-

[25] Klapper, *op. cit.*, pp. 111–115. [26] Klapper, *op. cit.*, pp. 129–132.

ments of a community or society.[27] This "gatekeeper" function may be observed in the active persuasions of visible "opinion leaders" or in the subtle operation of guidelines derived from so-called "reference" groups or individuals.

In the case of influence by personal contacts, the characteristics of influentials seem reasonably clear. Such persons tend to be peers or of slightly higher status than their followers.[28] Furthermore, influentials may be differentiated in terms of their locus of interest and primary sources of information and values. *Local influentials* are primarily oriented to their community; therein lies their upbringing, their store of information and anecdotes, and their future. They rely on participation in organizations of a personal, sociable character, ignoring or only slightly using externally based mass media. Locals, therefore, have continued appeal to non-mobile persons with locally circumscribed interests. It has been suggested that locals are effective over a comparatively wide range of issues and it may be presumed that locals employ their powers to confirm and sanctify existing values.[29]

By contrast, *cosmopolitan leaders* are usually migrants from other communities and retain significant contacts with extra-community affairs—especially through reliance on regional and national mass media. Indeed, their influence is expressed in their ability to *interpret* the content of mass media to their followers. Cosmopolitans seek and maintain affiliation with organizations that reward skills and knowledge rather than personal manipulation and "politics." Consequently, cosmopolitans tend to be socially mobile and of somewhat higher status (in education and occupation) than their followers, who prefer to heed the persuasions of those with greater access to superior sources of information. Since influence

[27] Elihu Katz and Paul F. Lazarsfeld, *Personal Influence* (New York: Free Press, 1955), Pt. 2; Bernard Berelson *et al.*, *Voting* (Chicago: University of Chicago Press, 1954).

[28] Katz and Lazarsfeld, *op. cit.*, chs. 10, 11, 13; Everett Rogers, *Diffusion of Innovations* (New York: Free Press, 1962), ch. 8; James S. Coleman, *Medical Innovation* (Indianapolis: Bobbs-Merrill, 1966).

[29] Merton, *Social Theory and Social Structure*, ch. 10; Alvin W. Gouldner, "Cosmopolitans and Locals: Toward an Analysis of Latent Social Roles," *Administrative Science Quarterly*, II (December, 1957; March, 1958), pp. 281-306, 444-480.

thus rests on knowledge, the existing specialization of information and knowledge also limits the effectiveness of given cosmopolitans to fairly narrow spheres (e.g., education, health, artistic productions). But the cosmopolitan typically aims at a modestly defined set of prescriptions, as compared with the locals, because he seeks to promote the acceptance of *change* (in values and action) in line with specific "achievements" developed in other, more "advanced" (or enlightened) social settings.

REFERENCE GROUP ORIENTATION

The subtle transmission of viewpoints and perspectives through the operation of reference groups or individuals is one of the most significant (though theoretically obvious) patterns that have emerged from a generation of attitude and opinion research. Essentially, the model of early socialization, as constructed by Mead and his followers, contains the theoretical seed of reference-group analysis. Mead, it will be recalled, posited the conception of a generalized other, whose values are used as a guide to behavior as a consequence of interaction with specific persons. However, Mead likewise noted the existence of multiple generalized others, and the phenomenon of shift from one to alternative forms. In this way, as social experience expands, a person may (and does) develop sufficient identity to select a non-obligatory source of values. And so the notion of reference group entered a long-term period of conceptual incubation.

Briefly, the theory of reference group influence asserts that certain values, attitudes, and behavior of given persons are derived from groups to which one does not belong, or from persons with whom one is not in regular, direct interaction.[30] But if values and perspectives are frequently adopted from non-membership groups and contexts (though membership groups likewise serve as refer-

[30] Merton, *Social Theory and Social Structure*, chs. 8, 9; Muzafer Sherif, *An Outline of Social Psychology* (New York: Harper & Row, 1948), ch. 6; Muzafer Sherif and Carolyn W. Sherif, *Reference Groups* (New York: Harper & Row, 1964); Muzafer Sherif and Carolyn W. Sherif, *Groups in Harmony and Tension* (New York: Harper & Row, 1953), ch. 7.

ence groups in many instances), the *determinants* of the reference-group phenomenon become a crucial item for sociological theory.

Since persons must first alter their perception of their membership groups and subsequently shift their source of values from membership to non-membership groups, it has been suggested that perceived limitations in group experience and/or changes in individual aspirations account for the selection of new reference groups.[31] At present, however, specification of the variable involved in these processes is quite fragmentary. A major theoretical clue, certainly, is upward mobility aspirations, which, thwarted or delayed by the structured opportunities of the membership group, encourage persons (consciously or unconsciously) to seek social substitutes for support and prestige.

In addition, Merton has properly reminded us that many persons in complex societies function in *role-sets* [32]—that is, clusters of different role obligations that validate a given social status (e. g., businessman, student, housewife). As a consequence, there is the practical problem of relating to persons of different statuses, values, and perspectives. Inconsistency, instability, and some anxiety are therefore predictable consequences of role-sets. It follows, then, that some actors in given role-sets attempt to make adjustments to incompatible elements in several ways (which we shall omit in this discussion). One of these mechanisms of adjustment, according to Merton, is reduced role performance in one or more segments of a role-set and disaffection with the persons and/or goals of that segment. Patently then, such persons are open to the attractions of individuals and groups that appear to confer either compensation for perceived deprivations in the role-set or the promise of a new and more rewarding role-set.[33]

In terms of the orientation of the sociology of knowledge, these processes also shift channels of communication and influence away from former referents. But disaffection does not insure more than self-defining availability to new reference groups, since the latter

[31] Merton, *Social Theory and Social Structure*, pp. 301–326.

[32] *Ibid.*, pp. 369–380.

[33] Raoul R. Andersen, "An Analytic Approach to the Study of Cross-Pressures in Selected Sociological Fields," unpublished Master's Thesis in Sociology, Emory University, 1964.

are normally unaware of their new or potential adherents. At this point, the crucial theoretical problem thus becomes: what factors account for the phenomenon of unwitting influence?

With some freedom of interpretation, Merton's tentative analysis of significant "structural" elements in reference-group behavior may be briefly suggested here. By implication, persons who select reference groups do so informally and without the reference group's knowledge. Consequently, there is attempted imitation of referent values, style, etc., without the aid of the referent. It follows that imitation depends on (*a*) the relative *visibility*, (*b*) the *clarity* and *specificity*, and (*c*) the *imputed authority* of the reference model.[34] We would expect some variability in these respects among reference groups, and likewise variability in the perceptions of a given social category in choosing reference groups. Thus it may be concluded that those conditions that encourage alternative reference groups for some population segment also increase the probability of differing (if not discordant) perspectives in that segment.

The classical statement of the sociology of knowledge asserted a more or less determinate relation (*a*) between some indicator of social position—class, religion, etc.—and a distinctive value cluster and (*b*) between the perspective of focal persons or elites and the attitudes of "dependent" social circles or categories. In the last few decades, with little explicit concern for amending this theory, sociological theorists have furnished a number of relevant problems and tentative answers, which indicate future possibilities for the sociology of knowledge.

1. While there are obvious "strains toward consistency" in personal organization, it is important to recognize that the development and maintenance of a cohesive set of values and attitudes occur with some variability in modern society.
2. A relatively coherent perspective is a product of social interaction and diffusion of ideas under conditions of competition and selective perception.

34 Merton, *Social Theory and Social Structure*, pp. 338, 352.

333

3. The role of elites or leaders in the diffusion of perspectives is more complex than was formerly asserted. Specifically, elites seem to function as initial disseminators, while peers or "secondary elites" often operate as crucial intermediaries in the adoption of values in a social category.

4. Social position—as exemplified in occupational and economic status, socially relevant age and sex distinctions, access to power and authority, and the like—seems to be a *necessary but not sufficient* factor in receptivity to specific perspectives. For one thing, a given "position" usually involves several different kinds of demands and opportunities for occupants of that position. The key problem thus becomes one of determining how members of a position focus on specific components of their role-set. In addition, the implicit assumption that all or most positions contain similar communication structures, levels of social sophistication, and acquired awareness of common needs is no longer tenable (if it ever was). The phenomenon of "false consciousness"—as delineated by Marx—seems to be endemic in complex societies. It is, then, the responsibility of sociological theorists to specify the conditions of selective interpretation of one's position, as foreshadowed by the emerging framework of reference group behavior.

5. Recent studies in communication and influence processes have more or less accidentally undermined the traditional presumption of *continuity* in viewpoint or perspective.[35] Even successful diffusion of values and attitudes must brave the ravages of time—as manifested in diminished recall, variations in earlier levels of interest, and the competition of other activities. Consequently, the sociology of knowledge must consider the social sources of *reinforcement* of value systems, of positive feedbacks in the circumscribed communication that is posited in the generation and nurturing of perspectives.

6. Finally, as a logical and empirical extension of earlier theoretical statements, the sociology of knowledge must recognize *changes* in perspectives for a given social category, stratum, or public.[36] As Mannheim demonstrated in several essays, "position" is relative; the opportunities and limitations provided by a "status location" contribute to the development of perspectives in line with perceptions and attitudes toward other social segments and crucial events and

[35] Elihu Katz, Martin L. Levin, and Herbert Hamilton, "Traditions of Research on the Diffusion of Innovations," *American Sociological Review*, XXVIII (April, 1963), pp. 237–252.

[36] Mannheim, *Ideology and Utopia*, pp. 131–154; Harold J. Laski, *The Rise of Liberalism* (New York: Harper, 1936).

334

patterns that upset the pre-existing structure of opportunities. Mobility aspirations, perceptions of opportunity or blockage of opportunity, and the political and economic consequences of wars offer only a few theoretical clues to this problem. This requires not only a renewed use of valid historical materials by sociologists, but also more emphasis on sociological investigations that will enable our successors to account for ideological transformations responsibly.

With these additions and partial clarifications, the area of the sociology of knowledge seems to possess a more secure, multifaceted base than was evident before World War II. Indeed, its conceptual framework and set of theoretical problems may be said to provide major clues to the explanation of many specific patterns that concern the sociologist. The following are only a few examples:

1. The formation and change in political orientation of different social categories, as expressed in voting and verbalized attitudes.[37]
2. Differentiation and change in life-styles in urban areas and regions, as manifested in family consumption patterns, childrearing, and associational patterns.[38]
3. Direction, intensity, and behavioral consequences of personal and/or family aspirations.
4. Alienation as a syndrome reflecting perceived "positional" deficiencies.
5. Anti-fluoridation attitudes in otherwise inexplicable social strata or categories.[39]
6. Prejudice and discrimination against specific minority populations.

[37] Lester W. Milbrath, *Political Participation* (Chicago: Rand McNally, 1965); Angus Campbell *et al.*, *The American Voter* (New York: Wiley, 1960); Raymond E. Wolfinger, ed., *Readings in American Political Behavior* (Englewood Cliffs: Prentice-Hall, 1966); Philip E. Converse, "The Nature of Belief Systems in Mass Publics," in David E. Apter, ed., *Ideology and Discontent* (New York: Free Press, 1964), pp. 206–261.

[38] For example: Daniel R. Miller and Guy E. Swanson, *The Changing American Parent* (New York: Wiley, 1958); Lee Rainwater *et al.*, *Workingman's Wife* (New York: Macfadden Books, 1962); Alvin Boskoff, "Social and Cultural Patterns in a Suburban Area: Their Significance for Urban Change in the South," *Journal of Social Issues*, XXII (January, 1966), pp. 85–100.

[39] Benjamin D. Paul *et al.*, eds., "Trigger for Community Conflict: The Case of Fluoridation," *Journal of Social Issues*, XVII (1961); Maurice Pinard, "Structural Attachments and Political Support in Urban Politics: The Case of Fluoridation Referendums," *American Journal of Sociology*, LXVIII (March, 1963), pp. 513–526.

7. Differences in linguistic skills among children and adults, as demonstrated by the work of Bernstein and others,[40] which appear to correspond to class-related family differences.

8. Variable success in "modernization" or "social development" of underdeveloped (now called "developing") nations, which may be conceived as a consequence of the relative adequacy of disseminating appropriate attitudes and values to different status levels in those nations.[41]

As the sociology of knowledge has developed, through criticism and clarification of theoretical issues, it is now more evident than a generation ago that this specialty in effect combines and is nurtured by three nuclear problems. First, there is the dynamics of *social differentiation*, which deals with the production of specialized skills, opportunities, and judgments. Second, we may note the phenomena of *control and coordination* (attempted and achieved) as exercised by elites, opinion leaders, reference individuals, etc. Finally, a necessary component is the analysis of *socialization processes*, by which influence and control are communicated to relevant social categories. Further progress in the sociology of knowledge, therefore, requires more explicit integration of these nuclear areas and also the search for more varied linkages between social experience and patterned orientations to "social reality."

SELECTED REFERENCES

Hyman, Herbert H., ed., *Readings in Reference Group Theory and Research* (New York: Free Press, 1968).

[40] Basil Bernstein, "Some Sociological Determinants of Perception," *British Journal of Sociology*, IX (June, 1958), pp. 159–174; Bernstein, "Language and Social Class," *ibid.*, XI (September, 1960), pp. 271–276.

[41] Daniel Lerner, *The Passing of Traditional Society* (New York: Free Press, 1958); Lucian W. Pye, *Politics, Personality, and Nation-Building* (New Haven: Yale University Press, 1962); S. N. Eisenstadt, *Modernization: Protest and Change* (Englewood Cliffs: Prentice-Hall, 1966); David E. Apter, *The Politics of Modernization* (Chicago: University of Chicago Press, 1965); Daniel Lerner and Wilbur Schramm, eds., *Communication and Change in the Developing Countries* (Honolulu: East-West Center Press, 1967).

Klapper, Joseph T., *The Effects of Mass Communication* (New York: Free Press, 1960).

Mannheim, Karl, *Ideology and Utopia* (New York: Harcourt, Brace, 1936).

Maquet, Jacques, *The Sociology of Knowledge* (Boston: Beacon Press, 1951).

Merton, Robert K., *Social Theory and Social Structure* (New York: Free Press, rev. ed., 1957), Pt. III.

Stark, Werner, *The Sociology of Knowledge* (London: Routledge & Kegan Paul, 1958).

14

Social Change

In the history of sociological theory, few problems have been so passionately pursued and so rich in empirical illustrations as that of social change. But two features seem to predominate in this perennially intriguing quest. On the one hand, most discussions of social change have been descriptive and classificatory, with a predominant emphasis on capturing the *direction* of change through the use of dichotomous or trichotomous types. Toennies, Simmel, Spencer, Comte, Ross, Park, Becker, Sorokin, Redfield, and others, provide well-known examples of this tendency. On the other hand, sociological explanations of social change have normally employed rather broad (and often somewhat vague) formulations that in effect interpreted change as an essentially simple, unitary phenomenon.

During the late twenties and thirties, sociologists unofficially reacted to the prevailing approaches to social change by devaluing or ignoring it as an area of primary concern. In the forties and early fifties, a period of incipient re-evaluation intervened, led by such men as Becker, Mannheim, MacIver, Odum, and Ogburn.[1] At

[1] See earlier summaries of these trends in Alvin Boskoff, "Social Change: Major Problems in the Emergence of Theoretical and Research Foci," in Howard Becker and Alvin Boskoff, eds., *Modern Sociological Theory* (New York: Holt, Rinehart

the same time, the analysis of acculturation, colonial administration, social planning, technological experiments, and then the rise of new nations, furnished a compelling "practical" base for a revivified interest in the processes and effects of change. Of course, it is painfully true that the mushrooming necessity for understanding and explaining change (and lack of change) was not greeted with immediate or effective attempts at theories of change. Some insisted that the crucial researches had not been accomplished; others viewed change as inexplicable; and still others advanced the enervating opinion that change must await the fuller understanding of organization and stability. To the confident and assertive "classic" theories of change, therefore, were opposed the diffident formulations of "modern" sociologists, who sought their destinies in the study of crime, courtship, community structure, class and caste, and "collective behavior."

However, several premonitory clues from distinctly reputable sources may be seen, in retrospect, as theoretical lifelines in a choppy sociological sea. Essentially, these served to define social change more clearly and also to reformulate social change as a set of interrelated problems.

Perhaps the most basic notion was a conceptualization of social change as a *cumulative network of significant variations* from a referential social structure. Equally important, as an antidote to narrowly deterministic and classical evolutionary theories, sociological theorists from Marx to MacIver came to regard these variations as possibilities, as reflecting social processes in which critical decisions about permitting or accepting new forms intervened as successive "locations" in the overall process.[2]

Marx had, in effect, distinguished several phases of change—*innovation* (which he narrowly defined as technological), application of innovations to existing social structures, conflicts between new and old roles, derivative effects of such conflicts on other cultural areas, and resolution of social and cultural discrepancies

& Winston, 1957), pp. 260–302; Alvin Boskoff, "Recent Theories of Social Change," in Werner J. Cahnman and Alvin Boskoff, eds., *Sociology and History* (New York: Free Press, 1964), pp. 140–157.

[2] Boskoff, "Social Change," pp. 265–270.

339

(through violent, or at least, "power" mechanisms). Weber broadened this analysis by pointing to the significance of religious, legal, and military innovations, as well as the crucial process of attributing legitimacy (cf. Durkheim's moral obligation) to innovative persons and roles. Thomas and Znaniecki, and MacIver reemphasized the importance of individual and collective evaluations of innovations (definition of the situation, dynamic assessment). Sorokin reversed the prevailing concentration on external innovations by hypothesizing normal "immanent" processes of innovation characteristic of rather integrated sociocultural systems. Finally, theorists such as Mannheim, Parsons, and Park gave needed attention to the tensions, strains, and conflicts that engender deviation or innovation and provide motivations for accepting available innovations.

By 1950, therefore, theories of social change pointed in a more or less definite fashion to several generic issues. (1) What are the structural and personal sources of deviance that achieves public attention? (2) What processes encourage or impede the trial and diffusion of innovation? (3) What mechanisms account for the more significant social and cultural reverberations (derivative effects) of initial innovations?

FACTORS IN INNOVATION

In the past, theorists of social change were relatively vague about the nature of innovation as a phase of change. They tended to view innovation as a product of elites, creative minorities (Toynbee), or charismatic leaders. More recently, theories of innovation have either focused on the pyschosocial characteristics of innovators, or on structural factors that are presumed to encourage organized deviation and positive innovation.

Sociologists have understandably been hesitant in focusing on the first of these two themes. Instead, social psychologists, economists, and some cultural anthropologists have explored the motivational bases of social and cultural innovations. Barnett, summarizing data from preliterate cultures, finds innovators (and early advocates) to be marginal, maladjusted, or frustrated.[3] Another anthropologist, Richard Adams, suggests that Barnett's thesis applies to relatively disorganized societies. In stable societies, innovations are more likely to derive from persons of high status, who innovate to "conserve" rather than "change" a given organization.[4] Other theorists—notably Hagen and McClelland, as well as Schumpeter—attempt to explain *economic innovation* (and early advocacy) as a consequence of the striving of persons with recently lowered status and high levels of need for achievement (occupational aspiration and success) among persons who have been implicitly socialized in this manner by parents.[5] More generally, Erasmus attributes economic innovation and the desire for "progress" to a differentially acquired desire for social recognition.[6]

Structural theories seek to explain motivations for innovation by reference to critical aspects of the organization and functioning of groups, communities, or societies. A very generalized and neglected theory is Bateson's formulation of *schismogenesis* in role systems.[7] Briefly, this theory asserts that persons in role relationships with one another develop implicitly *innovative role components* as a consequence of following out the practical implications of each role in the relation. Schismogenesis, therefore, is a normal process in social systems that involves predictable pressures toward restructuring of roles in one of two ways—*symmetrical* (i. e., redefining one's role in line with the features of a reciprocal role; for example, the typical student role may become redefined to focus upon the professional interests of the teacher) and *complementary* (i.e., re-

[3] H. G. Barnett, *Innovation* (New York: McGraw-Hill, 1953), pp. 131, 319.

[4] Richard N. Adams, "Personnel in Culture Change: A Test of a Hypothesis," *Social Forces*, XXX (December, 1951), pp. 185–189; Snell Putney and Gladys Putney, "Radical Innovation and Prestige," *American Sociological Review*, XXVII (August, 1962), pp. 548–551.

[5] Everett E. Hagen, *On the Theory of Social Change* (Homewood, Illinois: Dorsey Press, 1962); David McClelland, *The Achieving Society* (Princeton: Van Nostrand, 1961).

[6] Charles J. Erasmus, *Man Takes Control* (Minneapolis: University of Minnesota Press, 1961), pp. 309–312.

[7] Gregory Bateson, *Naven* (Cambridge: Cambridge University Press, 1936), pp. 184–194; Gregory Bateson, "Bali: The Value System of a Steady State," in Meyer Fortes, ed., *Social Structure* (Oxford: Oxford University Press, 1949), pp. 35–53.

defining one's role through emphasizing components that are opposed to dominant features of a reciprocal role; for example, an administrator might develop a rigid emphasis on the regulatory aspects of his role that in practice serve as impediments, not necessarily intentional, to the technical operation of a subordinate worker).

In Bateson's analysis, schismogenesis is inherent in role systems *per se*, unless the larger system contains latent controls. Rigid hierarchical systems (e.g., a caste system), socialization that emphasizes avoidance of competitive interaction, the intervention of a powerful and legitimate third party (e.g., government) are probably typical structural barriers to schismogenesis. In short, the greater the structural "looseness," the more *opportunity* for role innovations and cumulative reactions to such innovations.

Bateson's theory is basic to the more familiar structural theories of conflict, strain, and tension as sources of innovative possibilities. Some theorists view conflict as an ineluctable component of complex social systems and further assume that differential opportunity to achieve commonly valued objectives heightens conflict to the point where innovative resolutions of some kind are created.[8] Theorists of the *origins of revolutions* obviously find this approach congenial, but it is by no means necessary to equate conflict with violence in understanding social change.[9] Unfortunately, the *mechanisms* by which conflicts produce innovations have not been detailed, with the possible exception of the theory of schismogenesis.

Another structural explanation of innovation merits some attention. As discussed by Williams, Florence Kluckhohn, Mannheim,

[8] Lewis A. Coser, "Social Conflict and the Theory of Social Change," *British Journal of Sociology*, VIII (September, 1957), pp. 197–207; George K. Zollschan and Robert Perrucci, "Social Stability and Social Process," in George K. Zollschan and Walter Hirsch, eds., *Explorations in Social Change* (Boston: Houghton Mifflin, 1964), p. 121; George K. Zollschan and Philip Gibeau, "Concerning Alienation: A System of Categories for the Exploration of Rational and Irrational Behavior," *ibid.*, pp. 158–167; Neil J. Smelser, *Theory of Collective Behavior* (London: Routledge & Kegan Paul, 1962).

[9] Lyford P. Edwards, *The Natural History of Revolutions* (Chicago: University of Chicago Press, 1927); Crane Brinton, *The Anatomy of Revolution* (New York: W. W. Norton, 1938); James C. Davies, "Toward a Theory of Revolution," *American Sociological Review*, XXVII (February, 1962), pp. 5–19.

and others,[10] many social systems contain permissively variant practices or subdominant patterns that are for some time privately or quietly practiced by small circles of adherents. These "patterned evasions" and related "cultural fictions" constitute a reservoir of potential innovations; at appropriate periods of discontent, one or more of these sequestered alternatives may be translated into public proposals for change.

Finally, several "built-in" sources of highly probable innovations have been identified by such functional theorists as Durkheim and Parsons. Durkheim, it will be recalled, gave special emphasis to the role of internal differentiation or social division of labor in explaining broad patterns of change—from mechanical to organic solidarity.[11] But he also formulated a more specific theoretical complex that is relevant at this point. Societies characterized by social complexity (presumably, some minimal degree of complexity is necessary, but Durkheim does not discuss this) are concomitantly marked by significant degrees of individuality, emphasis on generalization and rationalization, personal mobility, and diminishing influence of traditional values. Thus, inferentially, Durkheim has identified the necessary social conditions (not technological or psychological) that can be interpreted as components of "innovation potential." More recently, Parsons and others have provisionally "located" higher probabilities of innovation in the adaptive and goal-attainment structures, since the pressure for achievement and the feasibility of "measuring" achievements or deficiencies are greater than for pattern-maintenance and integrative subsystems.[12]

While there is a tendency for theorists to search for temporally

[10] Robin M. Williams, *American Society* (New York: Alfred A. Knopf, 1960; 2d ed.), ch. 10; Florence R. Kluckhohn, "Dominant and Substitute Profiles of Cultural Orientations: Their Significance for the Analysis of Social Stratification," *Social Forces*, XXVIII (May, 1950), pp. 376–393; Karl Mannheim, *Freedom, Power, and Democratic Planning* (New York: Oxford University Press, 1950), pp. 191–195; Alvin Boskoff, "Structure, Function, and Folk Society," *American Sociological Review*, XIV (December, 1949), p. 757.

[11] Emile Durkheim, *The Division of Labor in Society* (New York: Free Press, 1947), pp. 283–303.

[12] Talcott Parsons, *Structure and Process in Modern Societies* (New York: Free Press, 1960), chs. 2, 3; Alvin Boskoff, "Functional Analysis as a Source of a Theoretical Repertory and Research Tasks in the Study of Social Change," in Zollschan and Hirsch, *op. cit.*, pp. 226–230; Melville J. Herskovits, *Man and His Works* (New York: Alfred A. Knopf, 1948), ch. 32.

limited and highly specific sources of innovation, a processual approach to change should caution us about undue dependence on the more visibly dramatic phases of innovation. As Mannheim has perceptively remarked,[13] we "must not overlook the fact that entirely new principles of construction can be found even in trivial microscopic processes . . . . Thus major principles are not infrequently concealed behind the mask of petty details . . . . The sudden emergence of surprising new situations is very often nothing but such previously suppressed and obscured factors coming to the fore." Consequently, we must remain intelligently dissatisfied with theories that seek to provide an organized explanation of internal sources of significant innovation. However, the increasing evidence of imposed, planned, or external sources of innovation— drawn from practical attempts at industrialization, modernization, "development," and even sociopolitical revolution—presents us with obvious theoretical solutions in many instances. Thereafter, the crucial question becomes: what factors account for the reception and diffusion of important innovations?

THEORIES OF INTERMEDIATE PROCESSES IN SOCIAL CHANGE: TRIAL, EVALUATION, AND DIFFUSION

Earlier theorists of social change, limited by historical sources and the paucity of ongoing change processes, largely neglected analysis of diffusion as a process.[14] In addition, it is now apparent —on hindsight—that "innovations" may include a range of meaningful items, each of which involves somewhat different contributions to a potential course of social change. For example, if we study innovations as variations in *social roles*, there are several distinguishable forms of innovation.

[13] Karl Mannheim, *Man and Society in an Age of Reconstruction* (New York: Harcourt, Brace, 1940), pp. 12, 189.
[14] Roland B. Dixon, *The Building of Cultures* (New York: Charles Scribner's Sons, 1928); Robert Lowie, *The History of Ethnological Theory* (New York: Rinehart, 1937), chs. 10, 11; John Gillin, "Acquired Drives in Culture Contact," *American Anthropologist*, XLIV (October–December, 1942), pp. 545-554.

1. Innovations that provide substitutes for a role component, without changing the overall functioning of the role—e.g., the use of hybrid corn, new drugs for medical purposes.
2. Innovations that alter the operation of an existing role by providing (*a*) new goals or values, (*b*) altered opportunities for interaction, power, or control, or (*c*) new techniques or skills.
3. Innovations that can be applied only by creating new roles—e.g., banking and credit, computer programmers, case work, psychotherapy, the artist-in-residence.

In addition, innovations and their diffusion may be distinguished on the basis of differential degrees of pressure to adopt a given innovation. Certainly, it is theoretically indispensable to recognize variations among three kinds of settings—(*a*) *coercive diffusion,* such as accompanies military conquest or a police state; (*b*) *indirect control,* which determines reception of an innovation by manipulating other desired opportunities (e.g., occupational future); and (*c*) *relatively voluntary diffusion,* based on processes of persuasion and circumscribed influence (such as advertising).

Until recently, the major theoretical issue in diffusion has been the relative importance of *prestige* (in the diffusing agent) and marginality or discontent (in some category of potential adopters). Generally, theorists such as Linton and Veblen and the classical diffusionists analyzed coercive situations and hence gave prominence to imitation of superior agents of diffusion of matters of technique.[15] However, some anthropological theorists—Gillin, Herskovits, and Devereux—in effect applied the concept of *dynamic assessment* in accounting for resistance (or variable response) to diffusion. Gillin, for example, in several articles and his *The Ways of Men,* strongly emphasized the importance of subprocesses in diffusion—adequate presentation, motivational change by providing rewards, evaluation of innovation, and selective performance (form meaning).[16] Thus, simplified patterns of motiva-

[15] Ralph Linton, ed., *Acculturation in Seven American Indian Tribes* (New York: Appleton-Century-Crofts, 1940); Robert Lowie, *The History of Ethnological Theory* (New York: Rinehart, 1937), chs. 10, 11; Thorstein Veblen, *The Theory of the Leisure Class* (New York: Modern Library, 1934).

[16] Melville J. Herskovits, *Acculturation: The Study of Culture Contact* (New York: Augustin, 1938); John Gillin, *The Ways of Men* (New York: Appleton-

tion in diffusion (desire to imitate, concern with prestige, or working off social frustrations) do not adequately grasp the variations in adoption.

But there was an implicit and unwarranted "equalitarian" bias in theories of diffusion: it was assumed that given innovations must achieve wide acceptance to eventuate in significant change. However, it is becoming clear that innovations of categories 2 and 3 (see p. 345) require adoption and propagation only within a strategic minority. Why? Because there is a stratification of interest and relevance among innovations in a differentiated system. The future extension of an innovation may well be a consequence of social change, rather than a precondition of such change.

Thus, the theoretical problem of diffusion must be reformulated: what conditions help to explain adoption of an innovation among some relevant circles of recipients, so that necessary readjustments (in behavior and social organization) are made by adopters, and by groups and categories affected by the functioning of adopters? In short, a theory of diffusion that is a component of a theory of social change must be concerned not only with the superficial aspects of acceptance (how many, why accepted, etc.), but with the adaptations that are inseparable from the diffusion process.

There is a great deal of evidence (which serves as a prod to theory) that the practice of innovation normally includes *supplementary* practices that facilitate its use. Odum had earlier conceptualized these supplementary practices as *technicways* and developed important theories on two aspects of the technicways. On the one hand, he pointed to the social "awkwardness" of innovation, no matter how intriguing or desirable or how effectively imposed by some superior source. Consequently, Odum suggested that technicways are empirically necessary to permit trial or adoption, so as to integrate the innovation into ongoing cultural and organizational patterns among adopters.[17] By inference, innovations among early

Century-Crofts, 1948), pp. 543–550, 555–557; George Devereux and Edwin M. Loeb, "Antagonistic Acculturation," *American Sociological Review*, VIII (April, 1943), pp. 133–147.

[17] Howard W. Odum, *Understanding Society* (New York: Macmillan, 1947), ch. 20; Howard W. Odum, "Notes on the Technicways in Contemporary Society," *American Sociological Review*, II (June, 1937), pp. 336–346.

adopters generate additional, adaptive innovations (technicways). Subsequently—and this is the second prong in the theory of technicways—the relative success or failure of diffusion depends upon the provision of acceptable technicways along with the innovation itself. It follows that valuational innovations (moralities, ultimate goals, philosophies, etc.) diffuse with difficulty because they are usually bereft of practical technicways. Indeed, the role of the charismatic leader is essentially one of acting as a functional alternative to technicways in the propagation of new ideas or goals.

Successful diffusion, then, can be explained as a process in which agents of diffusion link the innovation to the dominant features of the social setting in which adopters function. Studies of diffusion of *technical innovations* (in one society)—such as hybrid corn, drugs, fluoridation—can be interpreted as indicating the social characteristics of adopter categories that are most relevant to positive evaluation of the innovators, but *cannot* be interpreted in terms of the associated technicways.[18] By contrast, studies of diffusion of technical innovations *across cultural boundaries* illustrate the difficulty of disseminating "naked" innovations without attention to practical technicways.[19]

DERIVATIVE EFFECTS: SOCIOLOGICAL LINKAGES IN THE PRODUCTION OF STRUCTURAL CHANGE

With the apparent exception of planned programs of social change, most attempts at creating and disseminating innovations have rather limited aims and limited vision concerning the byproducts of successful adoption. Even planners are often unable to anticipate important consequences of their proposals. But both

[18] Everett M. Rogers, *Diffusion of Innovations* (New York: Free Press, 1962); Elihu Katz, Martin L. Levin, and Herbert Hamilton, "Traditions of Research on the Diffusion of Innovation," *American Sociological Review*, XXVIII (April, 1963), pp. 237–252; James S. Coleman, *Medical Innovation* (Indianapolis: Bobbs-Merrill, 1966).

[19] S. Herbert Frankel, *The Economic Impact on Under-Developed Societies* (Cambridge: Harvard University Press, 1953); Edward H. Spicer, ed., *Human Problems in Technological Change* (New York: Russell Sage Foundation, 1952); Benjamin Paul, ed., *Health, Culture, and Community* (New York: Russell Sage Foundation, 1955).

theory and a staggering mass of empirical studies (historical, anthropological, and social-psychological) indicate that innovation and diffusion are but necessary (not sufficient) preludes to the core processes of social change. For convenience, we may call these *derivative consequences or effects*.[20] More specifically, we can identify the core processes as creation of exploratory technicways, emergence (or re-emergence) of various forms of related conflict, development and/or manipulation of adaptive mechanisms by strategic elites, and alterations in other subsystems (status and power systems and functional or institutionalized sectors, such as religion, education, kinship).

At this point, these processes seem to form an approximate progression through time. Consequently, it is possible to speak of qualitative (and perhaps quantitative) phases in the achievement of social change. Yet this analytic scheme is sufficiently flexible to allow for more complicated sequences of such phases. For example, some of these phases may co-exist or overlap in time; and it is clearly possible that some phases (e.g., conflict, adaptive mechanisms) may occur at two or more different points in a given social-change sequence. These, of course, are matters that require careful comparative study, guided by the concepts and theoretical problems to which we may now turn.

Exploratory technicways

Virtually every theorist concerned with social change as process(es)—from Marx to the present—has noted the initial practical difficulties of implementing an accepted (though not necessarily legitimated) innovation. In view of the weblike nature of skills, values, and interaction patterns in a social system, a substantial innovation in a role—or the creation of new roles—implicitly or explicitly generates needs for relatively immediate additions or substitutions in routine behavior and social relations. These technicways seem to be informal and easily learned practices that facilitate the

[20] William F. Ogburn, *Social Change* (New York: Viking Press, 1950; orig. ed., 1922), pp. 344–345; William F. Ogburn, *The Social Effects of Aviation* (Boston: Houghton Mifflin, 1946).

348

continued use of a desired (or imposed) innovation.[21] Thus, an innovation in record-keeping in a state employment agency quickly resulted in unplanned changes in the interaction patterns of interviewers in relations with applicants. Or, during the early years of its acceptance, TV was accompanied by rearrangements of leisure time, adjustments in eating habits, and by appreciably lessened patronage of movie theaters.[22] But the fundamental notions in these and other illustrations are (*a*) structural inevitability of inconvenience, tension, and temporary incompatibility perceived by recipients and (*b*) the universal search for means of conserving desired innovations and of reducing the costs of conforming to imposed innovations. In addition, as suggested by Myrdal in a sweeping and somewhat incautious fashion, these innovative responses to innovation constitute a cumulative thrust that implicitly but effectively points subsequent innovations and adaptations in a single, coherent direction. According to Myrdal, the effective character of early alterations in a community or society does not evoke countervailing or successfully resistant patterns. However, this is still a debatable formulation, even if one is not wedded to the sharply defined animus of the dialectical approach.[23]

The testing-ground of conflict

The classic and still vigorous interpretation of subsequent developments in social-change processes is that of Karl Marx, who postulated an inherent perception of discrepancy between technical innovations and established patterns of power, authority, and control—as well as organized attempts to remove such discrepancies through violence. With somewhat more objective goals, other theorists have likewise accorded great theoretical significance to

[21] Odum, *Understanding Society*, ch. 20.

[22] Peter M. Blau, *Dynamics of Bureaucracy* (Chicago: University of Chicago Press, 1955), pp. 33–44; Peter M. Blau, *Bureaucracy in Modern Society* (New York: Random House, 1956), pp. 50–52, 91–96; Leo Bogart, *The Age of Television* (New York: Ungar, 1956).

[23] Gunnar Myrdal, *Rich Lands and Poor* (New York: Harper & Row, 1957), pp. 16–21, 88; K. William Kapp, *Toward a Science of Man in Society* (The Hague: Nijhoff, 1961), pp. 187–189.

conflict, but with certain modifications suggested by empirical studies. Odum, building upon the formulations of Toennies, Sumner, and Giddings, analyzes change as mediated by practical opposition between *technicways* (and the social categories that employ them) and the *folkways, mores, and institutionalized forms* to which other social categories adhere. For Odum, such conflict is unavoidable, but it involves friction between roles, between large categories, rather than between status levels.[24] Godfrey Wilson likewise regards the social-class struggle as a special case of a more general phenomenon. He finds intrapersonal conflict to be crucial in acculturation situations. That is, the same people come to accept innovations and technicways without rejecting previous role definitions.[25] And we must surely remember that Max Weber attributed to periods of significant innovation not conflict between classes, but conflicts between *status categories* and *economic categories* (classes).[26]

If conflict of some sort is a normal accompaniment—or consequent—of early phases of social change, in what specific forms does conflict occur? What conditions account for varying severity and ramification of conflicts within a system? And what factors condition the resolution of conflict in the direction of (*a*) further change, (*b*) regression to pre-innovative stages, or (*c*) maintenance of an accommodative limbo? Conflict theorists such as Dahrendorf, Lynd, Mills, Lockwood, and Rex [27] tend to ignore

24 Odum, *Understanding Society*, chs. 12, 20. See also Katharine Jocher *et al.*, eds., *Folk, Region, and Society: Selected Papers of Howard W. Odum* (Chapel Hill: University of North Carolina Press, 1964); Alvin Boskoff, "Structure, Function, and Folk Society," *American Sociological Review*, XIV (December, 1949), pp. 749–758.

25 Godfrey Wilson and Monica Wilson, *The Analysis of Social Change* (Cambridge: Cambridge University Press, 1945), pp. 125–127.

26 Hans H. Gerth and C. Wright Mills, trans. and eds., *From Max Weber: Essays in Sociology* (New York: Oxford University Press, 1946), pp. 185–194.

27 Ralf Dahrendorf, *Class and Class Conflict in Industrial Society* (Stanford: Stanford University Press, 1959); C. Wright Mills, *The Power Elite* (New York: Oxford University Press, 1956); Robert S. Lynd, "Power in American Society as Resource and Problem," in Arthur Kornhauser, ed., *Problems of Power in American Democracy* (Detroit: Wayne State University Press, 1957), pp. 1–45; John Rex, *Key Problems of Sociological Theory* (London: Routledge & Kegan Paul, 1961), ch. 7; David Lockwood, "Social Integration and System Integration," in Zollschan and Hirsch, *op. cit.*, pp. 244–257.

these problems, though their general theoretical position would probably be bolstered by attention to *theoretical specifications*. On the other hand, in recent years, several promising analyses have been available for evaluation and use.

Without doubt, Simmel's scattered insights on the operation of social conflict constitute the major source of subsequent theorizing, though Simmel was not concerned with conflict as a response to innovation. Nevertheless, his writings established two fertile theoretical points.[28] (1) The forms and immediate consequences of conflict can be understood in terms of the *kinds* of social system in which they occur—e.g., intimate groups as compared with bureaucratic organizations; and (2) conflict serves to create and/or sustain integrative mechanisms by clarifying and presenting in a public fashion issues to which decisions must be addressed.

Thus, in the face of innovations, relatively simple or folk-like systems tend to develop sharp, dramatic, and even disintegrating kinds of opposition, with a "pervasive factionalism" that cuts across many facets of life among informally opposed subcategories.[29] In such situations, the consequences of conflict tend to halt or delay further, predictable phases of social change. On the other hand, complex organizations (such highly differentiated systems as corporations, urban political entities, and national societies) respond to conflicts derived from change in a typically different fashion. Drawing on theoretical clues from Mannheim, the Wilsons, March and Simon, and Boulding,[30] we can hypothesize that

[28] Georg Simmel, *Conflict and the Web of Group-Affiliations,* trans. Kurt H. Wolff and Reinhard Bendix (New York: Free Press, 1955), ch. 3.

[29] Bernard Siegel and Alan R. Beals, "Pervasive Factionalism," *American Anthropologist,* LXII (June, 1960), pp. 394–417; Alan R. Beals and Bernard J. Siegel, *Divisiveness and Social Conflict* (Stanford: Stanford University Press, 1966), chs. 4, 5, 8; Wilson and Wilson, *op. cit.,* pp. 127–134; P. Mayer, *Townsmen or Tribesmen* (Capetown: Oxford University Press, 1961), chs. 5–7; Ralph W. Nicholas, "Factions: A Comparative Analysis," in *Political Systems and the Distribution of Power* (New York: Praeger, 1965; for the Association of Social Anthropologists), pp. 21–60.

[30] James G. March and Herbert A. Simon, *Organizations* (New York: Wiley, 1958), pp. 129–131; Kenneth Boulding, "A Pure Theory of Conflict Applied to Organizations," in Robert L. Kahn and Elise Boulding, eds., *Power and Conflict in Organizations* (New York: Basic Books, 1964), ch. 12. See also Victor A. Thompson, *Modern Organization* (New York: Alfred A. Knopf, 1961).

(*a*) conflicts develop in relatively non-cumulative ways, so that the sources of difference remain only partly crystallized; (*b*) such conflicts may continue without threat to the integrity of the system and without interfering with the general course of social change; (*c*) in the case of bureaucratic organizations, the authority structure responds to conflict by defining it as reducible to differences between persons (rather than between roles or groups) and hence as amenable to persuasion and techniques of problem-solving.

Strategic elites and adaptive mechanisms

Both the "Great Man" theory and the theory of vaguely potent "social forces" have proved to be impressionistic substitutes for careful analysis of empirical decision-making processes at crucial points of the change process. By contrast, there have long been available theories of the significant functioning of strategic positions or roles—such as is found in the works of Marx, Pareto, Mosca, Lasswell, and Toynbee.[31] In essence, two problems can be identified in such theories: (*a*) What factors account for the way in which elites (or strategic role incumbents) respond to the phenomena of internal conflicts? (*b*) What new or revised social mechanisms are employed to implement this response?

Organizational theory posits a relatively rational and decisive approach to change-induced conflicts by leadership positions,[32] but the autonomous position of such organizations *permits* (but does not insure) the development of such a pattern. On the other hand, in more diffuse and less protected social systems (modern urban communities, new nations, societies in acculturation), the patterned responses to early stages of change are a variable composite of decisiveness, trial and error, and sheer confusion. This situation has been widely discussed and even has been labeled in

[31] Vilfredo Pareto, *Mind and Society*, trans. Andrew Bongiorno and Arthur Livingston (4 vols.; New York: Harcourt, Brace, 1935), IV; Arnold J. Toynbee, *A Study of History*, abr. D. C. Somervell (New York: Oxford University Press, 1947), pp. 230–240, 307–336; Harold D. Lasswell and Abraham Kaplan, *Power and Society* (New Haven: Yale University Press, 1950), chs. 4, 5.

[32] March and Simon, *op. cit.*, pp. 189–196; James D. Thompson, *Organizations in Action* (New York: McGraw-Hill, 1967), chs. 2, 9.

rather dramatic ways (Time of Troubles, "failure of nerve," etc.). Following some clues from Mannheim, Odum, and the Wilsons, I tried to account for the characteristics of this "transitional phase" as a consequence of the social and ideological attributes of strategic elites.[33] Elites characterized by retrospective utopianism (a desire to recapture an outmodeled past) and/or an inflexible ethnocentrism and parochialism, it is hypothesized, tend to exhibit behavior that represents "postponement of social decision" or "social indecision." Briefly, this behavior confronts the phenomena of innovation and its attendant technicways and conflicts in these ways:

1. Inability or unwillingness to perceive the crucial, central difficulty; instead, emphasis, resources, and personnel are expended on superficial and tangential issues.
2. Where essentially adequate diagnoses of difficulties *are* made, solutions tend to be impulsive, largely irrelevant, or halfhearted.
3. The attempt to handle practical problems of innovation and conflict by measures that "reduce scale" (i.e., by lessening the number and/or intensity of interactions between and among groups).

Mannheim's theory of the dynamics of elites [34] is particularly appropriate for an understanding of variations in social indecision. In complex systems undergoing further complexities, there is an initial tendency to select elites with decisive, "creative" qualities, because the selective process is largely in the hands of persons and groups actively interested in certain innovations. But, Mannheim theorizes, to the extent that diffusion of interest extends to irresponsible categories, there develops a "negative democratization" that complicates the selection of elites. Under these circumstances, elites (*a*) become more numerous and internally competitive (resulting in extraordinary emphasis on power maintenance); (*b*) are increasingly recruited on the basis of *ascribed* qualities (family, honorific status); (*c*) more often represent "local" (rather than cosmopolitan), regional, or "nativistic" viewpoints; and (*d*) tend to become "accessible" to the understandably narrowed percep-

[33] Alvin Boskoff, "Social Indecision: A Dysfunctional Focus of Transitional Society," *Social Forces*, XXXVII (May, 1959), pp. 307–311.
[34] See ch. 13 of this volume and Mannheim, *Man and Society*, pp. 79–96.

tions and values of their constituents.[35] In short, following Mannheim, social indecision in transitional phases of social change is a consequence of the pre-existence or development of weak or diffuse leadership structures. Consequently, it is extremely important to explore those factors that sustain strategic elites and explain their adoption of facilitating or restrictive responses to the probable course of change.

Unfortunately, a theory of the operation of elites as "intermediaries" in social change is not yet in our grasp. MacIver certainly provides a base in his contention that the political system and its key roles (i.e., the government of a nation, but by inference, the legitimate political structure in any social system) serve to direct (or delay) the further diffusion and implementation of accepted or partly institutionalized innovations. Specifically, political elites control the relative speed of these processes, the costs and benefits that derive from innovation, as well as the resolution of serious difficulties between contending groups.[36] But MacIver does not probe into the factors that condition either a positive or a negative orientation in the political elite. Mannheim, of course, regards the dynamics of elite recruitment as an explanatory tool. It may also be suggested that differences in the interrelations between elites and their subordinates or clientele affect the response of elites to the flow of innovations. For example, positive action by the elite is more likely (a) when opportunities for two-way communication are well structured; (b) when normal mechanisms of control are relatively indirect, reflecting the secure, legitimate position of the elite; and (c) when crisis and emphasis on achievement are most visible.[37]

Concomitant with the operation of political elites—but not necessarily as consequences of elite functioning—there seem to be various sociocultural products that help to sustain the overall change process. Unlike the exploratory technicways, which are practical and immediate implementations of specific innovations,

[35] William Kornhauser, *The Politics of Mass Society* (New York: Free Press, 1959).
[36] Lucian W. Pye, *Politics, Personality, and Nation-Building* (New Haven: Yale University Press, 1962), p. 80.
[37] Boskoff, "Functional Analysis," in Zollschan and Hirsch, *op. cit.*, pp. 231–234.

354

the patterns referred to at this point serve to coordinate or correlate various technicways and some well-established patterns. Following Parsons, let us call these *adaptive structures*,[38] "modes of adaptation to the exigencies of institutionalizing the value patterns in question . . . in the light of the strains to which the population in question are subjected. . . ." It is very likely that a theory (or theories) concerning the genesis and operation of adaptive structures will furnish an important link in the evolving complex of formulations that is required for an explanatory system of social change. However, very little explicit attention to this problem has been allocated by theorists of change. I shall therefore try to indicate some promising conceptual and theoretical clues.

If we remember that early phases of change are marked by new specialties (skills, controls, etc.), it is clear that the essential practical (and therefore theoretical) problem is one of understanding how specialties can be acquired with the least cost or threat to the system and its major components. One device or adaptive structure is *ritual*,[39] which we normally associate with tradition and ossified patterns of behavior. But as should be evident with a little reflection, ritual in the broadest sense has a history; and it is by now abundantly clear that patterns alter in meaning and consequences over long periods of time. According to Max Gluckman, a most perceptive social anthropologist, ritual frequently "freezes" or "contains" internal tendencies toward conflict, revolt, or rebellion. Participation in ritual, Gluckman suggests, provides opportunities to "act out" conflicts in a way that implicitly emphasizes the underlying cohesion within which the conflicts arise.

In his famous but largely unread *Principles of Sociology*, Herbert Spencer likewise pointed to the presumed origins of ritual (he called ritual "ceremonial observances or institutions") as a means of accommodating conflicts, though he assumed (*a*) that such conflicts usually involved social unequals and (*b*) that fear of the stronger was the dominant theme. Nevertheless, the theory of the

[38] Talcott Parsons, *The Social System* (New York: Free Press, 1951), pp. 168–169.

[39] Max Gluckman, *Custom and Conflict in Africa* (New York: Free Press, 1955), pp. 110–135; Max Gluckman, ed., *Essays on the Ritual of Social Relations* (Manchester: Manchester University Press, 1962), pp. 34–45.

adaptive function of ritual in periods of stress or crisis merits consideration along the lines sketched by Gluckman. With the license of interpretation and some extrapolation, Gluckman may be revised for our purposes in the following tentative way.

During the early practice of innovation and associated technicways in a society or social system, the lines of authority, cooperation, and interdependence between roles become blurred and the expectations of persons become uncertain. If in addition, innovations place persons in overlapping or contradictory roles, the practical necessity of adaptive devices is even greater. Ritual, defined as symbolic observances that are faithfully practiced by some category of persons, thus develops as a means of separating and yet ordering in an arbitrary but workable manner the skills and responsibilities of the old and the new. Gluckman's theory, however, contains a vital assumption—that the persons in conflict retain an underlying acceptance of the environing sociocultural system (the identity of a basic heritage, allegiance to a charter, constitution, or value system).[40] Given the validity of this assumption, ritual evolves in an experimental way, emphasizing unity, continuity, and yet an isolated opportunity for stylized freedom or license.

The study of ritual and its vicissitudes therefore provides clues to the relative development of social change. If in a given process of change, people take a "ritualistic" attitude toward ritual or convert ritual occasions into frequent criticism of innovations, this may be interpreted as a sign of diminished adaptation and a bar to further developments in social change. Indeed, the character of ritual suggests that its adaptative contributions in the process of change are limited; ritual in this context represents adaptation by *isolation* from pressing issues, while change processes require in practice continued adjustments and decisions through non-ritual participation.

A functional alternative to ritual is known among organizational theorists as "organizational fictions." Dubin defines organizational fictions as guides for behavior that fill structural gaps in social systems that derive from changes in experience.[41] In practice, organi-

[40] Cf. Simmel, *Conflict*, pp. 76–78.

[41] Robert Dubin, *Human Relations in Administration* (Englewood Cliffs: Prentice-Hall, 1951), p. 341; Victor Thompson, *op. cit.*, p. 92.

zational fictions constitute unchallenged (but objectively false or misleading) notions about the real locus of control, the worth of specific subsystems, the effectiveness of cooperation between subsystems, etc. This type of adaptive structure appears to provide momentum for piercing potential obstacles in organizational development and change. March and Simon refer to approximately the same kind of adaptive mechanism when they discuss "uncertainty absorption points"—that is, those positions in the organizational structure that assume the power to create binding (but not specifically assigned) interpretations of ambiguous facts or experiences for the organization as a whole.[42] Born out of practical necessity, fictions and uncertainty absorption points in a real sense respond to innovation and its attendant conflicts with stabilizing adjustments that are themselves latent components of change—however conservative or cautious they might at first appear.

A widespread, theoretically important adaptive mechanism is initially simple—segregating the innovation from interference by means of a relatively autonomous unit, bureau, department, or division.[43] For example, many New Deal attempts at innovation involved the creation of new agencies (NRA, NLRB, AAA, SEC, PWA, WPA, FSA). Similarly, industrial firms that expand their operations into new product areas often establish separate divisions for that purpose. New programs in teaching and research at universities likewise tend to be placed in new institutes, centers, divisions. In short, autonomous new units reflect conscious attempts to foster innovation and its consequences on the part of strategic elites, who thereby hope to prevent competition, corrosive jealousy, and premature evaluation. One aspect of this mechanism has long been recognized as crucial in complex systems—*secrecy*, or the organized withholding of information from potential competitors or intruders.[44] Ideally, secrecy sustains the identity and the

[42] March and Simon, *op. cit.*, pp. 189–192; Chester A. Barnard, *The Functions of the Executive* (Cambridge: Harvard University Press, 1938), pp. 169–171.

[43] March and Simon, *op. cit.*, pp. 187–188.

[44] Georg Simmel, *The Sociology of Georg Simmel*, trans. Kurt H. Wolff (New York: Free Press, 1950), pp. 330–344; Wilbert E. Moore and Melvin M. Tumin, "Some Social Functions of Ignorance," *American Sociological Review*, XIV (December, 1949), pp. 787–795; Louis Schneider, "The Role of the Category of Ignorance in Sociological Theory: An Exploratory Statement," *ibid.*, XXVII (August, 1962), pp. 492–508.

morale of crucial adopters of innovations while it protects the autonomous unit from those wedded to traditional forms.

On the other hand, insulation has its practical limitations. It is a truism that the major tensions and difficulties of change are spawned and exacerbated by non-rational fears and misunderstanding of the present and future import of given innovations. Every innovation was first greeted with passionate criticism of its impracticality, danger, or immorality; and yet every established pattern contains innovations that eventually achieved acceptance. Consequently, insulation may also stimulate—or aggravate—negative judgments among other units in the social system. In addition, isolated manipulators of innovative chains require interchange and responsible criticism, since the effects of autonomy can well be self-confirmation and the reinforcement of incommunicable sets of new patterns. Finally, specialization by insulation may also lead to reciprocal ignorance; that is, the failure of the autonomous unit to recognize those problems, alterations, and derivative consequences in other parts of the system, which must be considered to sustain the progressive functioning of that unit. In short, this kind of adaptive mechanism requires in addition the operation of a strategic elite that can coordinate the contributions of the autonomous unit with the functioning of other subsystems. If not, the adaptive device creates further conflicts and generates the practical need for other adaptive structures. Social indecision is thus a perennial possibility as the change process evolves.

Unplanned and/or unforeseen structural effects in other subsystems

At this point, the diffusion of innovations is replaced by the problem of the reverberation or successive effects of initial alterations through the interdependent components of social systems. Most theories of the structural consequences of innovation, however, deal with three interrelated questions.

1. Which subsystems can be expected to change, in structure and/or functioning?

2. What is the sequence of structural effects? [45] If alternative sequences occur, what conditions account for each type of sequence?
3. To what extent are these derivative effects compatible or incompatible with one another, thus avoiding or creating new problems of adaptation and adjustment? What factors are most directly related to compatibility–incompatibility and management or alteration of a given pattern of effects?

Until quite recently, the most generally accepted theory on these points was largely derived from Marx and his un-Marxian followers in sociology and anthropology. Essentially, this theory has been applied to simple societies in acculturation or to moderately complex systems in transitional phases of change—not to highly complex, bureaucratized and centrally planned (or controlled) social systems. The major components of this theory may be summarized for convenience in this way.[46]

1. Derivative effects are necessarily unevenly distributed in time among component patterns or institutions.
2. Material and technological subsystems are more quickly and more markedly affected by the approved implementation of earlier innovations.
3. Eventually, change occurs or is imposed on all institutional areas, stratification systems, and power.
4. The unevenness (lag) in derivative effects produces or intensifies periods of conflicts and social problems.
5. Such unevenness is a necessary consequence of either the weakening of a previously rigid control system or the persistence of unarticulated, autonomous sub-units in a society.

Marx, Veblen, Sumner, Ogburn, Park, and others assumed that primary innovations (those that initiate change processes) always

[45] Bert F. Hoselitz, "Levels of Economic Performance and Bureaucratic Structures," in Joseph LaPalombara, ed., *Bureaucracy and Political Development* (Princeton: Princeton University Press, 1963), p. 188; Talcott Parsons *et al.,* *Working Papers in the Theory of Action* (New York: Free Press, 1953), pp. 187–190.

[46] F. Stuart Chapin, *Cultural Change* (New York: Century, Inc., 1928); Ogburn, *Social Change;* Charles A. Ellwood, *Cultural Evolution* (New York: Century, Inc., 1927); Morris Ginsberg, *Evolution and Progress* (London: Heinemann, 1961), ch. 4; N. L. Sims, *The Problem of Social Change* (New York: Thomas Y. Crowell, 1939).

(or very often) occur in the realm of technique or material means. Consequently, derivative effects would necessarily develop in the spheres of guiding valuations, controls, and status. Thus, Marx posited a technological determination of property systems, law, political organization, religious systems, and family structure. But the plausibility of this approach has been challenged or modified by such theorists as Weber, MacIver, Sorokin, LaPiere, and Moore.[47] According to the latter set of views, the simplified regularity of technological determinism ignores four important aspects of social dynamics and change.

1. Both primary and subsequent technical innovations—and their reception—depend upon prior development of congenial value systems. In fact, traditional value systems (and associated groups) can effectively impede technical innovation—as in India and China.

2. Changes in value systems (ethics, morals, philosophies, ideologies) do occur, with consequences for technology, political organization, and other subsystems. Weber's comparative analyses of the relation between religion and economic systems, and between legal and economic systems, illustrate these processes of change in classic fashion.

3. As Herskovits has suggested,[48] social systems at given periods differ markedly in terms of dominant concerns (cultural focus). Whatever the dominant focus might be, Herskovits theorizes, innovations tend to originate in the focal area (religion, economics, the military), followed by derivative changes in one or more closely related subsystems.

4. Types of social systems provide clues to the possibility of alternative sequences of derivative effects. According to Odum, simpler societies subject to external sources of change tend to show more rapid change in technical spheres (e.g., production, military tactics) than in basic value systems (such as religion or world view). Cultural lag, then, is specific to early stages of societal complexity. On the other

47 Max Weber, *The Protestant Ethic and the Spirit of Capitalism*, trans. Talcott Parsons (London: Allen & Unwin, 1930); P. A. Sorokin, *Society, Culture, and Personality* (New York: Harper & Row, 1947), pp. 668–673; Robert M. MacIver, *Society* (New York: Farrar and Rinehart, 1937), ch. 24; Richard T. LaPiere and Chang Wang, "The Incidence and Sequence of Social Change," *American Journal of Sociology*, XXXVII (November, 1931), pp. 399–409; Richard T. LaPiere, *Social Change* (New York: McGraw-Hill, 1965), chs. 8, 9; Wilbert E. Moore, *Social Change* (Englewood Cliffs: Prentice-Hall, 1963), pp. 85–88.
48 Herskovits, *Man and His Works*, ch. 32.

hand, relatively complex systems (with past social changes cumulatively recorded in their present structure) tend to conceive ambitious and complex aspirations or goals, which in practice inspire appropriate revisions and extensions of technical and organizational capacities. Odum recognized that the "fit" between goals and technology (and organization) is variably imperfect ("achievement lag").[49]

As matters now stand, the cardinal question in the issue of derivative effects is not their *range* or *variety*, but the necessary *time order* of their occurrence. Likewise, more attention is being given to the phenomenon of institutional areas and role systems that do not seem to develop derivative alterations in structure—and yet function in complementary fashion with environing change processes. For example, Goode has analyzed Far Eastern and African societies for the effects of technological and political change on family and kinship structure.[50] He concludes that thus far change in family structure has been rather limited and represents accentuation of gradual developments that preceded political and technological innovations. However, Goode presents no theory to account for this set of findings, nor does he suggest that the probability of derivative changes in family structure will increase with time.

Similarly, Parsons' theory of necessary changes in family type as a consequence of industrialization and concomitant emphasis on occupational and social mobility has been challenged by Litwak.[51] Using survey data that was obtained in Buffalo from a sample of middle-class wives, he found little evidence of alteration in aspects of family organization in families that had achieved geographic and occupational mobility. Litwak concluded that basic structural fea-

[49] Jocher, *op. cit.*; Erasmus, *op. cit.*, p. 312; Marshall Sahlins and Elman R. Service, *Evolution and Culture* (Ann Arbor: University of Michigan Press, 1960), p. 118.

[50] William J. Goode, *World Revolution and Family Patterns* (New York: Free Press, 1963), pp. 367–369.

[51] Talcott Parsons, *Essays in Sociological Theory* (New York: Free Press, rev. ed., 1954), ch. 9; Eugene Litwak, "Occupational Mobility and Extended Family Cohesion," *American Sociological Review*, XXV (February, 1960), pp. 9–21; Eugene Litwak, "Geographic Mobility and Extended Family Cohesion," *ibid.*, XXV (June, 1960), pp. 385–394.

tures of a modified extended family system support, and perhaps encourage, the adoption of new opportunities. Apparently then, new or revised functions can be acquired by subsystems without substantial alteration in structure. Certainly, this is also a "derivative effect," one that compels sociological theorists to analyze the conditions under which *functional* changes can develop without prior or subsequent structural changes in a given subsystem.

Currently, perhaps only two theorists appear to hazard general statements about time order in change processes. Parsons (and his associates) has constructed a theory of *phase movements* drawn from analysis of laboratory groups that has principally been applied to the development of a differentiated group structure. Briefly, a cyclical progression is asserted: adaptive roles receive initial emphasis, followed by emphasis on goal-attainment roles, pattern-maintenance roles, and then integrative roles. The basic rationale is the assumption that, both under normal operation and under the impact of significant innovations, practical problems are encountered in this time order. In addition, it is assumed that special focus on one functional problem (or adaptations made in one institutional sphere) necessarily creates in one or more other institutional areas "deficits" or difficulties, which eventually are treated by derivative changes in the institutional areas. Thus, by inference, any system in process of change—whatever the content of initial innovations—normally exhibits alterations in technical systems and distributive systems; then in systems of authority, power, and critical decision-making; successively in systems of socialization; and finally in structures that serve as custodians of fundamental and binding values.[52] Indeed, the failure of systems to enact this order of derivative effects suggests a fruitful way of conceptualizing "lags" or arrested processes of social change.

Hoselitz accepts Parsons' conceptual apparatus relating to change, but hypothesizes a very different time order for societies in "secular evolution"—i.e., societies that have achieved a high degree

[52] Parsons, *Working Papers*, pp. 180–188; Alvin Boskoff, "Stratification, Power, and Social Change," in Richard L. Simpson and Herman Turk, eds., *Institutions and Social Exchange: The Sociologies of Talcott Parsons and George C. Homans* (Indianapolis: Bobbs-Merrill, 1969).

of complexity and ability to promote controlled change.[53] Because of their developed structure, Hoselitz speculates, these societies tend to develop variations in the integrative subsystem (basic goals, values, or interpretation of these), after which changes in the political structure are appropriately devised. Subsequently, congenial technical and/or scientific innovations are created or encouraged, thus in effect implementing original processes of change through reverberations of increasing concreteness.

The sequence of derivative effects remains a thorny theoretical problem—perhaps because the empirical basis for its solution is simply not available. But an understanding of the consequences of a set of such secondary innovations and adjustments poses still another intriguing problem for the sociologist. From a theoretical standpoint, the way or ways in which members of a social system respond to the challenge of specific changes and permissible alternatives (some of which may be contradictory) in several spheres of social participation require rather complex formulations. A strong theoretical tradition in sociology regards multiple and rapid changes as a necessary source of social and personal disorganization. But more recent analyses, stemming from the important concept of *scale*, temper this apocalyptic approach in the search for the conditions of *differential consequences* of change processes.

Scale refers to the relative complexity of a social system, as indicated by the number of persons in direct or indirect interaction and the degree of specialization in the performance of valued roles. As used by Mannheim, Wilson, and others, processes of social evolution and development normally *increase* the scale of a society. But the major consequences (or concomitants) of increase in scale are (*a*) greater autonomy of some subsystems and (*b*) decrease in the speed and significance of changes from other subsystems. Consequently, social-change processes in systems characterized by "high" scale (advanced civilizations?) produce diversity without necessarily creating direct and irreconcilable conflicts—as compared to small scale systems, in which the flow of innovation and derivative effects tends to create conflicts that cannot be isolated

[53] Hoselitz, *op. cit.*; Lucian W. Pye, *Aspects of Political Development* (Boston: Little, Brown, 1966), p. 66.

from one another.[54] By inference then, the ability to absorb or digest the sequence of innovations and adjustments that constitutes an extensive process of social change is dependent upon the prior organizational flexibility of a society.

It is impossible to avoid the conclusion that "organizational capability" and flexibility are ultimately phenomena of decision-making in strategically placed roles. In small scale systems, both the opportunity and the experience of making adjustive responses to the processes of change are generally not available to the leadership roles. By contrast, in large scale systems, strategic elites—given the structural opportunities for such decisions—do react to processes of change. This decisive response may be conscious and planned, as in the case of the elites in the Meiji Restoration in Japan or the New Deal in the United States; or response may be fitful, vacillating, inconsistent, as illustrated in Athens of the fourth century BC and the Roman Empire in the second through four centuries AD.[55] It is likewise an inescapable conclusion that analyses and explanations of change as a whole, or of specific phases of change, can no longer rely upon "master processes" —such as rationalization, progress, simplicity-to-complexity, secularization, etc.[56] Instead, just as "man makes himself" (V. Gordon Childe), social-change processes are probabilistic resultants of facilitative or obstructive decisions, the consequences of which are

[54] Wilson and Wilson, *op. cit.*, pp. 108, 134; Karl Mannheim, *Freedom, Power, and Democratic Planning* (New York: Oxford University Press, 1950), pp. 4–5.

[55] On Japan, see Albert M. Craig, *Chosu in the Meiji Restoration* (Cambridge: Harvard University Press, 1961); John Whitney Hall, *Government and Local Power in Japan, 500 to 1700* (Princeton: Princeton University Press, 1966); Bernard Silberman, *Ministers of Modernization* (Tucson: University of Arizona Press, 1964); Bernard Silberman and H. D. Harootunian, eds., *Modern Japanese Leadership* (Tucson: University of Arizona Press, 1966), especially pp. 233–288, 371–410; Johannes Hirschmeier, *The Origins of Entrepreneurship in Meiji Japan* (Cambridge: Harvard University Press, 1964). On the New Deal, see Bernard Sternsher, *Rexford Tugwell and the New Deal* (New Brunswick: Rutgers University Press, 1964); Samuel I. Rosenman, *Working with Roosevelt* (New York: Harper, 1952). On classical instances, see Alvin Boskoff, "Social Indecision in Two Classical Societies," in Cahnman and Boskoff, *op. cit.*, pp. 246–257.

[56] Talcott Parsons *et al.*, eds., *Theories of Society* (2 vols.; New York: Free Press, 1961), II, Pt. 5; Boskoff, "Social Change," in Becker and Boskoff, *op. cit.*; Sorokin, *Society, Culture, and Personality*, pp. 657–674; Pitirim A. Sorokin, *Sociological Theories of Today* (New York: Harper & Row, 1966), pp. 586–609.

narrowed probabilities of planned and unplanned social and cultural adjustments.

In retrospect, the most important lesson we have learned (or are in process of learning) is that the most efficient way of understanding social change is to view change as a set of analytically separable processes or problems. Each of these requires its own concepts and theoretical formulations. But theories applicable to any one phase of change do not *determine* theoretical solutions to succeeding phases; they merely allow some confluence of newly implemented decisions and immediately available possibilities for action and interpretation. In addition, we can no longer theorize about change in social systems generally, but rather about change processes in different types of social systems—small scale vs. large scale systems, highly centralized vs. more diffuse systems, systems with considerable autonomy vs. highly dependent systems. In this way, theories of social change may well lose their traditional character of polemical competitiveness and assume their rightful place as responsible—as well as significant and interesting—formulations in sociology.

SELECTED REFERENCES

Boskoff, Alvin, "Stratification, Power, and Social Change," in Richard L. Simpson and Herman Turk, eds., *Institutions and Social Exchange: The Sociologies of Talcott Parsons and George C. Homans* (Indianapolis: Bobbs-Merrill, 1969).

Cahnman, Werner J., and Alvin Boskoff, eds., *Sociology and History* (New York: Free Press, 1964), Pt. I.

Moore, Wilbert E., *Social Change* (Englewood Cliffs: Prentice-Hall, 1963).

Rogers, Everett M., *Diffusion of Innovations* (New York: Free Press, 1962).

Smelser, Neil J., *Theory of Collective Behavior* (New York: Free Press, 1963).

Sorokin, Pitirim A., *Society, Culture, and Personality* (New York: Harper & Row, 1947), chs. 43, 46, 47.

Wilson, Godfrey, and Monica Wilson, *The Analysis of Social Change* (Cambridge: Cambridge University Press, 1945).

Zollschan, George K., and Walter Hirsch, eds., *Explorations in Social Change* (Boston: Houghton Mifflin, 1964).

Index

366

Date Due

MAR 17 '71					
NOV 23 '77					
DEC 11 '84					